OUR TROTH

3rd Edition

OUR TROTH

3rd Edition

edited by Ben Waggoner

with contributions from members of The Troth
and other Heathens

Volume One:
Heathen History

The Troth
2020

Published by The Troth
325 Chestnut Street, Suite 800
Philadelphia, PA 19106
http://www.thetroth.org/

ISBN-13: 978-1-941136-34-8 (hardcover)
978-1-941136-35-5 (paperback)
978-1-941136-33-1 (PDF)
978-1-941136-36-2 (EPUB)
978-1-941136-37-9 (MOBI)

Library of Congress Control Number: 2020932882

Troth logo designed by Kveldúlfr Gundarsson; drawn by 13 Labs, Chicago, Illinois
Typeset in Junicode 12/10

Cover design: Ben Waggoner

First Edition published 1993
Second Edition published 2006

In memory of
Dianne Luark Ross,
Rod Landreth,
Wayne Morris,
Gamlinginn,
Jane Ruck,
and all our departed Troth leaders,
kin of blood and spirit.

May they ever live in memory,
and may they ever inspire us to new deeds,
guarding and guiding our steps.

Contents

Introduction

In June 1993, while a graduate student at Cambridge University, Kveldúlfr Gundarsson placed an announcement in the Troth's journal, *Idunna*:

What is *Our Troth*? It is the weave of the wisdom of our elder kin and the treasures they have left us, wrought with our own true hearts and the fresh-springing might of the gods and goddesses in this new day. No single man or woman can tell all of it alone: it must be shaped from the words of all the folk who hear the call and know that they ken something of the soul and the deeds of the North, whether that lore is gained from books, from the whispering of the runes and the mighty ones, or simply from the clear understanding of a true heart. Thus I call upon all the folk of the Troth to take part in this work, lifting up the swan-feather quill and writing what you know of the ways of our forebears and their rebirth, so that when the book of our history and holy ones, our rites and works is brought forth at last, it may truly be named—*Our Troth*.

Six months later, the 711-page book was at the print shop, and heroic efforts by the printers William West and Joel Radcliffe saw it into print. Kveldúlfr drew on his own knowledge of the Heathen past and present, enriching it with contributions from forty of the most active and knowledgeable Heathen writers at that time. It was dedicated to Dianne Ross, the first editor of the Troth's journal *Idunna,* whose tireless labor from 1989 to 1991 as the Troth's publisher and secretary kept the infant organization alive. Kveldúlfr's words of dedication to Dianne should be remembered long:

No one gave more or worked harder; others held true, but she kept the Troth alive till our spring.

Unfortunately, once the original edition was sold out, the Troth did not have the resources to print and warehouse more copies. For some years, the book was completely unavailable, until most of the text was made available on the Troth's website in 2000.

Ten years after the first edition of *Our Troth*, both Heathen understanding and academic scholarship had evolved. Furthermore, desktop publishing software have evolved to the point that *Our Troth* could now be formatted without the use of scissors and gluesticks, and print-on-demand publishing meant that it could be kept in print indefinitely. In 2002, Kveldúlfr made some additions for a new edition and passed them to the Troth's Shope (publications director) Diana Paxson, who edited the book for publication. She and over twenty Heathen writers joined to contribute additional edits and copious new material, including illustrations for the first time. The second edition had to be divided into two volumes: *History and Lore* (2006), and *Living the Troth* (2007).

Now another fourteen years have passed. Both Heathen understanding and academic scholarship have continued to evolve. Kveldúlfr has gone on to other endeavors, but other hands have taken up the banner he once held. The time is ripe for a new vision for *Our Troth*.

This first volume of the third *Our Troth* began as an update of the original historical chapters. The update turned into a complete rewrite nearly from the ground up, and it came to include topics that were overlooked in earlier editions, as well as new scholarship published in the twenty-six years since the first edition came out. As a result, the chapters have been greatly expanded, especially those dealing with recent history. Although some of the details gathered here may not seem important, the decision to include them was not made gratuitously. There is a great deal of historical background to our faith, as we practice it today, that many Heathens are unaware of. Much of the early history of Heathenry as an organized religion is poorly documented and in danger of being lost. We as Heathens need to understand our own *ørlǫg*—the deeds that have been laid down in the past that still shape our present. The goal of this volume is to enable us to do that better.

Rich archives of photos and illustrations, now in the public domain or generously made available under Creative Commons licenses, have allowed us to illustrate this book far more richly than before. And improvements in the e-book production process have enabled us to offer this book for the first time in several electronic formats, as well as print.

The second volume of the new *Our Troth* will cover gods, goddesses, and other beings and powers. The third volume will cover ethics, daily life, rituals, and holidays.

The Troth is proud of, and humbled by, the labor, passion, and generosity that went into the first and second editions of *Our Troth*. We are even prouder of the third edition of *Our Troth*. We are glad to offer our best work to the Gods and Goddesses who inspire us, to our forebears who still guide us, and to all readers who may be drawn to know more of the old and new ways of worship and living.

More people than I can name have contributed to this book: their opinions on the matters discussed here, or their questions that inspired the writing, have ultimately made this book better. But I would especially like to thank those who wrote for this book, and those who have checked it for accuracy. Luke Babb, Thomas DeMayo, and Meghan D'Amore all deserve large horns of mead for proofreading and commenting on the entire manuscript, and Lyonel Perabo caught some embarrassing typos at the last minute. Diana Paxson's contributions to the second edition provided a firm foundation for this edition to build on. Others have critiqued individual chapters at different stages of development; they are listed at the end of each chapter. Some contributors are no longer affiliated with the Troth, and some no longer have their words represented in the current edition. Yet their influence remains woven into its wyrd.

I thank the institutions that have made images of artifacts and artworks available for reproduction in this volume: the National Museum of Denmark; the Swedish Historical Museum; the Kunsthistorisk Museum at the University of Oslo; the Cleveland Museum of Art; the Walters Art Museum in Baltimore, Maryland; the Bundesarchiv (German Federal Archives); the Staats- und Universitätsbibliothek, Hamburg; the Kunglinga Biblioteket, Stockholm; and the National Library of Australia. The creators of several massively useful online resources also deserve much thanks: Sean Crist (Germanic Lexicon Project); Jon Julius Sandal, Carsten Lyngdrup Madsen, Jesper Lauridsen, and their volunteer scanners and editors (Heimskringla); Sveinbjörn Þórðarson and his volunteers (Icelandic Saga Database); and all those who contributed images to Wikimedia Commons.

I would like to add my personal thanks to the indefatigable Inter-Library Loan librarians at the University of Central Arkansas, Tim Purkiss, Amanda Bryant, and Karen Pruneda, and their staff, who over the past decade have tracked down a seemingly endless number of books and papers for me, some of them so obscure as to seem downright whimsical. Karen Pruneda has my special thanks for continuing to supply sources while the library was shut down during the coronavirus pandemic. The fellowship of many members of the Troth, and the support of its leadership, have been my strength and support for years, and the wise counsel of Kathy Walters proved indispensable during the editing process. I also thank Rick Riedlinger, whose generous gift of books made the research far easier and more thorough than it would have been otherwise; and the memory of Jerik Dænarson, without whom none of this might ever have happened. Finally, as ever, I thank Lauren Crow Thacker and the folk of Black Bear Kindred, for their unwavering fellowship; and my wife and son, who have indulged my walking around with one book or another in my head for many years, and who love me anyway.

—Ben Waggoner
June 2020

List of Abbreviations

BCE: Before Common Era (equivalent to BC, but no religious connotation)
CE: Common Era (equivalent to AD, but no religious connotation)
ÍF: *Íslensk Fornrit*, the standard edition of Icelandic sagas
OE: Old English
OHG: Old High German
ON: Old Norse
PIE: Proto-Indo-European
S/H/M: Refers to different manuscripts of *Landnámabók*, known as *Sturlubók*, *Hauksbók*, and *Melabók*.
*: marks a word or root that is not directly known from texts or speakers, but has been reconstructed by linguists

Very brief notes on pronunciation: In Old Norse and Icelandic, the letter Þ, þ ("thorn") represents an unvoiced *th* sound (as in *thick and thin*), and the letter Ð, ð ("eth") represents a voiced *th* sound with the vocal cords vibrating (as in *this and that*). In Old English, the two are nearly interchangeable, and either may be voiced or unvoiced depending on position in a word.

Accents on Old Norse–Icelandic vowels do not represent stress, but vowel quality. Vowels with accents are usually long (for example, *u* and *ú* represent short and long vowels similar to those in English *dud* and *dude*). In modern Icelandic, the exceptions are *á*, which is pronounced like English *ow* (so *Ásatrú* sounds like "ow-sa-true") and *é*, which is pronounced with a glide, like "yeh". In Old English, vowel length is usually represented by macrons (short bars over letters), although some texts use accent marks or don't mark vowel length at all.

The normalized Old Norse letter Ǫ, ǫ, called "tailed o" or "o with ogonek," is close to the *o* in formal British *not*. The letters Ø, ø, Œ, œ, and Ö, ö represent a lip-rounded vowel as in French *bleu* or German *schön*. In Old Norse and Old English, Æ, æ (called "ash") represented the sound of *a* in English *hat*, but in modern Icelandic it sounds like English *eye*. A hip young Reykjavíker might greet you with *Hæ!* and bid you farewell with *Bæ!*, which sound exactly like English *Hi!* and *Bye!*

A full pronunciation guide will appear in Volume 3.

Neolithic dolmen (*dysse*) at Skalstrup, Roskilde, Denmark. Watercolor by J. Kornerup, 1864. National Museum of Denmark, CC BY-SA 2.0.

CHAPTER ONE

The Stone Age

40,000–1800 BCE

The cultures and religious traditions of the people who historically spoke Germanic languages didn't just appear overnight. They are the products of a long and complex history of many different human populations and cultures, fusing, splitting, and influencing each other. The religious traditions that we are trying to revitalize cannot be discussed in isolation from the history of the humans that developed them, and that history is interwoven with the rest of humanity. As we seek to reconstruct our religion, we need to understand its deepest foundations. How can understanding these connections help us to practice our religion today?

Rock art at Alta, Norway.
Image by Bair175, Wikimedia
Commons, CC BY-SA 3.0.

Ages of Mankind

In 1819, the Danish scholar Christian Jürgensen Thomasen was sorting the collection of artifacts that would later grow into the National Museum of Denmark. He noted which types of artifacts were found together, and in what order they appeared through time. This led him to propose a three-part division of prehistory, based on what the primary material for tools had been: the Stone Age, the Bronze Age, and the Iron Age (Fagan, "Three-Age System," pp. 712-713).

The underlying reason for this division is the technology required to make use of each material. Stone is available in most parts of the world, and suitable stone can be made directly into tools. Thus, stone tools have been made for over two million years, longer than modern *Homo sapiens* has existed. Copper can be found in a few places as nearly pure nuggets and veins, but most copper is found in ores, and working out how to smelt copper

1

took time. Alloying copper with arsenic or tin gives bronze, which is easy to work, but harder and tougher than copper. But this discovery took more time, especially since copper and tin are rarely found in the same ore deposits and had to be brought together by long-distance trade. Iron is far more abundant than copper or tin, but iron smelting requires specially designed kilns that can reach higher temperatures. Usable iron is also tricky to make, because its carbon content must be carefully controlled: too much and the iron is brittle, too little and it bends. Working out how to smelt usable iron took centuries more, before iron could replace bronze as the material of choice for tools and weapons.

With refinements, Thomasen's ages are still used to refer to the prehistory of Europe and Asia. But their calendar dates vary from place to place: there was no single date when everyone simultaneously ditched stone tools and started smelting bronze. The Bronze Age in the Near East began about 3300 BCE; the Bronze Age in Scandinavia began about 1700 BCE. Iron was first smelted in the Near East around 2500 BCE, but it took over a thousand years before iron replaced bronze as the metal of choice: hence the Iron Age is said to begin around 1200 BCE in the Near East—but 500 BCE in Scandinavia. Nor does the scheme work well with cultures outside of Eurasia: African and Native American cultures are studied using different time frames. Nonetheless, the three ages are still useful in understanding Eurasian prehistory.

Some Heathens may wonder why we should care about Stone Age prehistory. In the absence of writing, we can never fully know the spiritual beliefs of the Stone Age Europeans. Yet it is almost certain that some spiritual and other cultural practices from the Stone Age survived into much later times. Furthermore, Heathenry is a past-focused tradition with a strong tradition of honoring the dead. It is good for us to know at least a little about the earliest roots of the religious traditions that would develop in northern Europe.

The First Europeans

The primate genus *Homo* appeared in Africa over two million years ago, but soon dispersed to Europe and Asia. These migrants included the ancestors of European hominids that are now generally classified as distinct species from our own, the best known being *Homo neanderthalensis* (250,000-30,000 years before present). However, our own species, *Homo sapiens*, evolved from *Homo* populations that stayed in Africa; the oldest known has been dated to 315,000 years ago (Hublin et al., "New Fossils from Jebel Irhoud"). *Homo sapiens* populations dispersed out of Africa several times, but the most important for us took place about 70,000 years ago, when a group crossed the Red Sea and spread from the Near East into Eurasia. These migrants interbred with the Neanderthals, while those that moved eastward through Asia also interbred with a population known as the Denisovans. A non-sub-Saharan may have as much as 2.1% of his or her DNA derived from Neanderthal ancestors (Sánchez-Quinto and Lalueza-Fox, "Almost 20 Years of Neanderthal Palaeogenetics"). By roughly 45,000 years ago, modern *Homo sapiens* had entered the Balkans; by 40,000 years ago they had spread as far as France, Spain, southern Germany, and southern England. Further migration was blocked by expansion of the ice sheets that covered northern Europe, which were at their maximum extent between 26,500 and 19,5000 years ago.

The migrants into Europe were indeed fully human; their brains and bodies were not significantly different from ours. They brought with them abilities and skills that their African ancestors had developed: they made stone and bone tools, clothing, jewelry, and art. Although they left no writing, the complexity of their culture means that they must have had language as complex as any modern language. This culture is now called the Aurignacian culture; it was replaced by the Gravettian culture about 33,000 years ago. People of both cultures depended primarily on hunting large game animals in cold climates. They made use of caves and rock shelters, although they didn't necessarily live in them; the Dolní Věstonice site in what is now the Czech Republic preserves traces of outdoor huts from 26,000 years ago. They made finely crafted

Painting of an extinct European rhinoceros from Chauvet, France. Photo by Inocybe, Wikimedia Commons. Public Domain.

tools from flint, bone, and antler. We know less about what they made out of perishable materials, but fragments of dried clay from Dolní Věston-ice showed imprints of cords, basketry, netting, and remarkably fine cloth (Adovasio et al., *The Invisible Sex*, pp. 181-183). Ochre (red or yellow iron minerals) is common at Aurignacian and Gravettian sites, as well as contemporary sites as far away as Africa and Australia. Powdered ochre was often used to coat buried bodies. Mixed with fat, it became paint; the oldest of the famous cave paintings from southern France and Spain, at sites such as Chauvet, belong to the Aurignacian culture (Sadier et al., "Further Constraints," pp. 8002-8006).

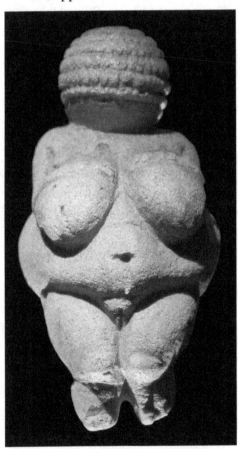

The "Venus of Willendorf" figurine, about 30,000 years old. Willendorf, Austria. Photo by Matthias Kabel, Wikimedia Commons, CC BY 2.5.

Early Europeans made beads, bracelets, and pendants from bones, ivory, animal teeth, and snail shells. They also made portable carvings and figurines. Their most famous works, the "Venus figurines," depict stylized female figures with exaggerated breasts and genitals, molded in clay or carved in stone or ivory; they include the famous "Venus of Willendorf" from the Danube Valley of Austria (24,000–26,000 years old). At Dolní Věstonice, ivory carvings included one figure that is essentially a stick with a large pair of breasts; another is a pair of breasts with almost no trace of the rest of the body. These have been interpreted as representing "the idea of nourishment;" whatever they mean, they show a highly developed capacity for abstraction. The Dolní Věstonice people also made miniatures of baked clay, including beautifully modelled animals and a "Venus" figure, between 28,000 and 23,000 years ago (Sandars, *Prehistoric Art in Europe*, pp. 43-48).

Caves in what is now southern Germany, along tributaries of the Danube River in the Swabian Jura mountains, give us another glimpse of Aurignacian culture. The caves at Hohle Fels have yielded the oldest known "Venus figurine," dated to 35,000-40,000 years old. This "Venus" had a loop for suspension

Carving of a wild horse from Vogelherd Cave. Museum der Universität Tübingen. Mogadir, Wikimedia Commons, CC BY-SA 3.0.

in place of a head, and was probably worn as a pendant (Conard, "A Female Figurine," pp. 248-252). Hohle Fels and other caves in the region have also yielded bone and ivory flutes, some of the oldest known musical instruments (Conard et al., "New Flutes," pp. 737-740). Finely carved and polished ivory miniatures of animals are also known from this area, including an ivory bird from Hohle Fels, and a horse and cave lions from nearby Vogelherd Cave (Sandars, *Prehistoric Art in Europe*, pp. 41-42) The nearby cave at Hohlenstein-Stadel contained a small ivory statue of a human figure with a lion's head, the *Löwenmensch* or "lion-man," one of the oldest known pieces of figurative art. A similar lion-man was later found at Hohle Fels (Dowson and Porr, "Special Objects—Special Creatures"). The people also painted stones, bones, and possibly the cave walls with ochre designs (Velliky et al., "Ochre and Pigment Use").

The Ice Begins to Melt

The climate began warming 19,500 years ago, and the ice sheets began to retreat, although the

The "Löwenmensch" from Hohlenstein-Stadel. Dagman Hollman, Wikimedia Commons, CC BY-SA 4.0.

process was not uniform; several cooler periods, known as *Dryas* periods, alternated with warmer *interstadials*. This climate instability seem to have led to the death of some of the early European human lineages (Posth et al., "Pleistocene Mitochondrial Genomes"). The time between 19,500 years ago and the introduction of agriculture is known as the Mesolithic. As the ice retreated, the large animals that were adapted to tundra-like vegetation shifted northwards. Some people migrated to follow them, creating a new culture known as the Magdalenian. Most of the famous cave art sites in southern France and northern Spain, such as Lascaux, Trois-Frères, Altamira, and others, date to the Magdalenian period. There is controversy over where, when, and how many times dogs were domesticated, but we can say with certainty that human populations in Europe had domesticated dogs at some time between 18,000 and 10,000 years ago. Domestication may have happened several times independently (Horard-Herbin et al., "Domestication and Uses of the Dog," pp. 23-24).

By about 15,500 years ago, humans were living in present-day northern Germany and the Netherlands and seasonally migrating into southern Scandinavia. A series of archaeological cultures succeeded each other, each one showing different preferences in tool materials and styles. These peoples survived by hunting reindeer: hunting weapons and kill sites are found along reindeer migration routes at points where the animals would have been vulnerable, such as narrow valleys or lake crossings. Traces of temporary huts or tent sites have been found, but these people made no permanent dwellings (Price, *Ancient Scandinavia*, p. 41-52).

The climate finally stabilized and the glaciers retreated for the last time around 11,700 years ago. By this time, some of the large animals depicted so beautifully in art had died out, whether because of human hunting, inability to adapt to climate change, or possibly a combination of factors. The Eurasian lions that had inspired the *Löwenmensch* carvings died out about 13,000 years ago, as did the Eurasian wooly rhinoceros, steppe bison, giant deer, cave bear, mammoth, and other animals. Other animals, notably reindeer, migrated northwards to survive. In the wake of the retreating ice sheets, birch was the first tree to colonize the land, followed by aspen, rowan, and hawthorn—all of which have long been recognized as powerful in folk magic, as well as for practical uses (Watts, *Dictionary of Plant Lore*). Hazelnuts were an important food source that were probably gathered and stored for the winter; hazelnut shells have been found in great numbers at Stone Age sites, and humans may have been responsible for introducing the hazel tree into northern Europe after the glacial retreat (Eriksen, "Resource Exploitation," p. 122). The people who remained in what is now northern Germany adopted new hunting techniques to take bear, wolf, lynx, wolverine, elk,[1] bison, wild horses, hare, and beaver in the expanding woodlands. Those near the coasts made use of the sea's bounty, taking whales, seals, and walrus in addition to many species of fish and shellfish.

Spirituality of the Earliest People of Europe

In cultures around the world, certain spiritual practitioners will, at need, enter altered states of consciousness, using drugs, pain, drumming, singing, and/or dancing as aids. The practitioner's visions and experiences while in this state are interpreted as taking place in another world inhabited by beings of its own. While in this other world, specialists can act to affect the human world. They may bring about healing, success in an endeavor, knowledge of the future, changes in the weather, or other benefits. This ability is often called *shamanism*, and the specialists that practice it called *shamans*, from a word in the Tungusic languages of Siberia. Broadly similar practices have been recorded around the world, in which a practitioner enters trance, travels to another world, interacts with beings that live there, and brings benefits in the mundane world (see Eliade, *Shamanism*, especially pp. 3-8).

But shamanism is not an "–ism": it is not a single, unified "religion" with a common doctrine. Even within Siberia, the details of how shamanism was worked, who did it, and what it meant varied considerably among tribes. Shamanic practice was not the only focus of Siberian indigenous religions, and shamans were never the only magico-religious practitioners in a tribe; several types of practitioner could have "shamanistic" functions, working alongside other ritual specialists who did not practice "shamanism" (Kehoe, *Shamans and Religion*, pp. 52-55; Hutton, *Shamans*, pp. 47-57). Writers such as Mircea Eliade have sometimes papered over this diversity (Hutton, pp. 120-127). Some anthropologists prefer to use the term "sha-

---

1. The animal called "elk" in northern Europe (German *Elch*; Danish *elg*; Swedish *älg*; Old English *eolc, eolh*; Proto-Germanic **elhaz, *algiz*) is the same biological species as the North American moose (*Alces alces*). In North America the name "elk" has been reapplied to a North American deer species also known as the wapiti (*Cervus canadiensis*).

man" only for practitioners among the Siberian peoples, noting that other peoples have their own names and roles for their spiritual practitioners, who don't necessarily do what Siberian shamans do (Kehoe, p. 102). They note that many common elements of "shamanism" can be found independently of shamanistic traditions. Others have pointed out that defining "shamanism" as a single phenomenon goes back to 18th century racist ideas of "primitive peoples" as Others, radically different from "civilized" Westerners (Kehoe, pp. 81-102). This book will use culture-specific terms for spiritual practitioners whenever possible, such as Sámi *noaidevuohtta* practiced by a *noaide*, or Norse *seiðr* practiced by a *seiðmaðr* or *seiðkona*. However, we have no way of knowing what Stone Age people called their spiritual practices, and many details of what they did are forever unrecoverable. Since there does not seem to be any better word, for the purposes of this book we will use "shamanistic practice" in the most general sense of "ritual evocation of altered states of consciousness by specialists in these techniques, perceived as travel or communication with beings in an Otherworld, with the goal of affecting events in the mundane world."

With that disclaimer in mind: Much of the art of the Stone Age may reflect altered states of consciousness. Parallel lines, dots, curves, and swirls are common in Stone Age art, and in later rock art around the world. Such patterns are universally seen in altered states, arising from the ways in which the visual nervous system is wired. As a person enters a deeper altered state, the geometrical figures grow more complex and begin to integrate themselves into the shapes of living beings and objects (Lewis-Williams and Dowson, "Signs of All Times"; Lewis-Williams, *The Mind in the Cave*, pp. 126-130; although see Kehoe, *Shamans and Religion*, pp. 71-80, for a critique). Historically documented shamanistic practitioners often see mental images "projected" around them; Stone Age artists may have been trying to "fix" these images when they painted them on walls or sculpted them in three dimensions. Sometimes they inserted bones, teeth, or other objects into cracks in the cave walls. These walls may have been seen as "membranes" between the known world and the spirit world, and it's possible that the shamanistic practitioners were returning these objects to the spirit world through the "membrane" (Lewis-Williams, *The Mind in the Cave*, pp. 180-227). Shamans often perceive their transition into the unseen world as shapeshifting into an animal's form, and human-animal hybrid figures are fairly common in artwork that reflects shamanistic practice—which may include the *Löwenmensch* of Vogelherd and some of the cave pictures of southern France. The lack of well-made feet on many carvings may reflect another aspect of shamanic trance states: the feeling of floating (Dowson and Porr, "Special Objects—Special Creatures"). Finally, a common feature of shamanistic trance is the experience of traveling to a variable number of vertically arranged worlds, above and below the world of everyday experience. These may be connected by a great central tree or pole, or else the shaman may feel himself flying, swimming, or passing through tunnels to reach them. This may also be reflected in rock art (Lewis-Williams, *The Mind in the Cave*, pp. 144-148; Hutton, *Shamans*, pp. 60-61).

While we will never know the details, it is at least likely that the earliest Europeans knew various shamanistic practices, although different groups would have had different understandings of their meaning and purpose. We may guess that they had ways of working with the many spirits that populated the landscape and animated the animals and plants on which they depended for survival. They may also have believed in life beyond death, judging by their burial customs: the dead were placed in poses (often turned on their sides, but occasionally in a seated position), covered with red ochre, and buried with tools, adornments such as shells and teeth, and other

Drawing of "Le Sorcier," a cave painting from Lascaux, France, possibly representing a shamanistic practitioner shifting into animal form. Image courtesy of Wellcome Images, Wikimedia Commons. CC BY 4.0.

goods. Cremation was also sometimes carried out. Complex burials, such as the "nests" of severed human heads covered in ochre, found near the entrances to caves at Hohlenstein and Grosse Ofnet in Germany, also hint at complex beliefs and rituals (Grünberg, "Mesolithic Burials," pp. 13-21).

The "Venus figurines" in the early Stone Age may express some sort of spirituality as well, but exactly what it is has been intensely debated. They might be amulets to ensure easy pregnancy, childbirth, and nursing; symbols of marital alliances between tribal groups; images of goddesses or female ancestors; sexual aids for men; or quite possibly something else. Some of them show detailed carving of woven caps, bands, aprons, and skirts; these might be ceremonial or high-status dress (Adovasio et al., *The Invisible Sex*, 186-192). These figures may not have meant the same thing everywhere, but may have carried different meanings in different regions and times (Dobres, "Venus Figurines," pp. 740-741).

The Scandinavian Story

At the height of the last glacial period, Scandinavia was completely covered by an ice sheet up to 3000 meters thick. As the glaciers melted, the sea level rose, and a huge depression gouged out by the moving ice sheets, now known as the Baltic Sea, began to fill with melted water. The southern Baltic was a freshwater lake until 11,620 years ago, when it broke through to the ocean across what is now south Sweden (Stroeven et al., "Deglaciation of Fennoscandia," pp. 101-108). At the same time, as the Scandinavian landmass was freed from the pressure of the mile-thick ice, most of it slowly began to rise, an ongoing process known as *glacial rebound*.

The interplay between rapidly rising seas and slowly rising land repeatedly altered northern European geography. Until about 6500 BCE, lower sea levels allowed for a sizable land mass in the North Sea (now called *Doggerland*) forming a bridge between Britain and present-day Netherlands and Denmark. Doggerland was populated and seems to have been a rich hunting ground, since stone and antler weapons and tools are occasionally brought up by fishing trawlers today. Between 7200 and 6000 BCE, there was a land bridge between Denmark and southern Sweden, and the Baltic Sea was again a freshwater lake, draining into the North Sea by rivers that flowed west from what is now Lake Vänern. Rising sea levels have since divided Denmark from Sweden and Britain from France, and flooded Doggerland. On the other hand, steady glacial rebound has caused most of the Scandinavian coastline to retreat; archaeological sites that were originally on the coast are now several miles inland (Eriksen, "Resource Exploitation," p. 107-109).

Southern Denmark and northern Germany, however, have been slowly sinking, and several important archaeological sites are now underwater (Price, *Ancient Scandinavia*, p. 66).

Humans may have established a presence in Scandinavia as much as 15,000 years ago, when foragers made forays into ice-free Denmark and southern Sweden, leaving behind tools and campsites. As the ice retreated, forests began to grow on what had been tundra. The reindeer moved northwards, and human hunters followed them. People spread into Scandinavia in two directions: one group migrated from the south as the glaciers retreated, and a second group followed the Atlantic coastline, which was free of ice. Analysis of ancient DNA reveals that the first group, migrating from the south, had dark skin and blue eyes, while the second coastal group had lighter skin but dark eyes. The resulting mixed people, the Scandinavian Hunter-Gatherers (SHG), adapted to colder and darker climates, evolving lighter skin and better metabolism in cold weather (Günther et al., "Population Genomics"). These two people may possibly be identified in the archaeological record as the Hensbacka/Fosna cultures, which closely resemble the north German foragers and probably migrated from the south, and the Komsa culture, which colonized the ice-free coast of Norway. The Komsa people probably used boats to travel along the Norwegian coast (Price, *Ancient Scandinavia*, p. 58). Then, as now, Norway was literally the "North Way," the best corridor for north-south travel.

As the glaciers melted, the birches that had colonized the newly exposed land were replaced by stands of hazel and pine, and eventually to forests of oak, linden, ash, and elm. Aurochs, wild swine, and red deer and roe deer expanded into Scandinavia with the new forest habitats, while creatures such as giant deer and wild horses declined. New cultures appeared in various parts of Scandinavia, adapting to the changed environments; reindeer hunting persisted in the north, while new means of finding food developed in the south. Early Scandinavians made stone axes and projectile points, bone fish hooks on twisted fiber lines, and, after 4800 BCE, pottery vessels. They fished and hunted with the help of dogs which resembled the modern Norwegian elkhound: a medium-sized wolf-like dog with thick fur and a curly tail (Burenhult, *Arkeologi i Sverige* I, p. 68). On the coasts, people used boats—the oldest known is a dugout canoe from Holland, dated to 8000 BCE, and dugout canoes were in use in Scandinavia by at least 6000

Stone Age carvings on a bone. Ryemarksgård, Denmark.
National Museum of Denmark, CC BY-SA 2.0.

BCE. The people on the coast caught fish with hooks and traps, hunted sea birds and marine mammals, and ate shellfish. They piled up the empty shells in huge mounds known as *middens*—the midden at Bjørnsholm in Jutland is 250 meters long (820 feet) and 50 meters (164 feet) wide, and may have taken nearly a thousand years to accumulate (Cunliffe, *Europe Between the Oceans*, pp. 72-76). Scandinavian foragers probably followed a seasonal round of activities, moving out to hunting camps and stations in the summer, and joining in larger encampments in the winter.

By about 6000 BCE, Scandinavian people were beginning to settle in more permanent sites, living in small clans or family groups. If the behavior of modern foraging societies is any guide, then the men probably carried out long-range hunts for large animals, while the women, having small children to care for, might have hunted smaller animals near the settlement, gathered edible plants (and shellfish in coastal areas), and so forth. Skeletal injuries from blows show that their society was not especially peaceful, although we cannot tell whether violence was due to arguments within groups, fights between groups, or both. The two most dangerous periods were early childhood, and young adulthood, when men risked dying in hunting and/or fighting and women risked death in childbirth. Roughly 40% of males born could expect to reach middle age, a figure that did not significantly change until after the Viking Age. Mesolithic women had about the same chances of reaching middle age, but Neolithic women were less likely to survive; only about 20% reached middle age, possibly because larger families, correlated with the adoption of agriculture, increased the risk of death in childbirth (Boldsen and Paine, "The Evolution of Human Longevity").

Stone Age Spirituality

We have two main sources for knowledge of the spiritual life of the Stone Age people of northern Europe: graves and artworks. By the later Stone Age, burials included a range of grave goods, and cemeteries grew. The dead were often sprinkled with red ochre; burial of the whole body is most common, but cremation was also sometimes done, and in some instances bodies were dismembered, either soon after death or years later. The oldest dated burials in Scandinavia, at Kams on the island of Gotland, date to about 6000 BCE (Larsson, "The Mesolithic of Southern Scandinavia").

One of the oldest surviving graves on the mainland, at Bäckaskog in Skåne, Sweden, has been dated to around 5000 BCE, and contains a person buried in a seated position. Because the grave contained a bone spearhead edged with flint microblades, as well as a chisel, the person was assumed to be male—until careful examination of the pelvis revealed scars from multiple pregnancies. The hastily renamed "Bäckaskog Woman" had borne 10-12 children in her lifetime of some forty-seven years (Gejvall, "The Fisherman from Barum," pp. 286-289). At about the same time, people were living in huts with sunken floors at Nivå, on north-western Sjælland in Denmark;

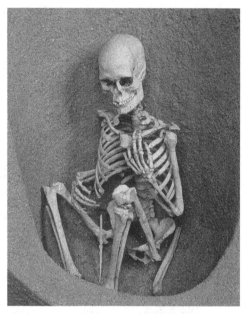

Bäckaskog Woman displayed in burial position, seated upright. Swedish Historical Museum skeletal collection 222358, CC BY 2.5.

they buried their dead right beside these huts. These huts contained ritually deposited objects alongside debris from everyday life, such as refuse from hunting, fishing, and toolmaking. For example, in one hut, human bones had been deliberately deposited in the center, along with deer antlers and a stone phallus. (Price, *Ancient Scandinavia*, pp. 71-73).

While the spear and chisel buried with Bäckaskog Woman might suggest that her roles and duties within society were not especially different from the men's, Mesolithic grave goods usually reflect gender and status differentiation (Meiklejohn et al., "Anthropology and Archaeology of Mesolithic Gender"). At the cemetery at Vedbæk-Bogebakken in Denmark, dated to about 5000 BCE, most women were buried with jewelry, while men (even male infants) were buried with flint blades. In a mass grave at Stroby Egede in Denmark, the females were placed on the south side and the males were placed on the north side (Price, *Ancient Scandinavia*, pp. 93-94). The Skateholm site at the southernmost tip of the Swedish mainland contains 87 documented graves; one of them held the remains of a woman buried in an unusual seated posture on a bed of antlers, wearing a feather cape and a belt made of over a hundred animal teeth. She has been nicknamed "the Shaman;" while the name is speculation, she certainly seems to have had a prominent social role (Romey, "This 7000-Year-Old Woman"). At Dejro in Sweden, human skeletal remains were found in a canoe buried underwater (perhaps the oldest "ship-funeral"?) People were often buried with animals or parts of animals; at Vedbæk-Bogebakken, a small child was buried lying on the wing of a swan, and adults were buried with deer antlers placed under the head (Jochim, "The Mesolithic," pp. 138-141). At Skateholm, eleven dogs were buried with red ochre and grave goods, exactly like the human burials—suggesting that the dogs had the same spiritual status as humans (Herva and Lahelma, *Northern Archaeology and Cosmology*, p. 72) Several burials at Skateholm, and at the later Ajvide site on Gotland, had had bones deliberately removed, possibly by outside groups that moved in, years after the earlier inhabitants had buried their dead (Fahlander, "Messing with the Dead," pp. 24-30). And at Kanaljorden in middle Sweden, the remains of at least eleven humans, along with complete carcasses of wild boars and body parts of other animals, were deposited in a lake between 6000 and 5600 BCE. The heads or skulls of at least two humans had been displayed on long wooden stakes in the middle of the lake (Price, pp. 87-88).

The best-known rock art of Scandinavia dates to the Bronze Age and will be discussed in that chapter, but Stone Age people also made abundant rock art. Some sites were used for thousands of years, suggesting that they were "places of power" in the landscape: for example, the carvings at Alta in northern Norway span almost 4000 years, from 4200 to 500 BCE,

Rock art at Alta, Norway, 4000-5000 BCE.
Photo by Hans A. Rosbach, Wikimedia Commons. CC BY-SA 3.0.

and the rock art at Nämforsen in northern Sweden spans approximately the same time frame (Sjöstrand, "Product or Production," pp. 252-254). A rough generalization is that Stone Age rock art is likelier to depict wild animals and hunting, while Bronze Age rock art more often depicts humans engaging in warfare and ceremony alongside abstract symbols such as the sun-wheel. The oldest rock art, made by the Komsa people at Dyreberget, Norway, is a carved panel of elk, reindeer, bear, and whales. Similar art from somewhat later, about 5000 BCE, at Vingen near Bergen, is dominated by roe deer but also includes elk, reindeer, and other animals, together with human figures (Price, *Ancient Scandinavia*, pp. 53, 83-84). Rock paintings are also known from this time: those from Fångsjön in Jämtland, Sweden, depict elk, while one from Medbo shows elk, deer, birds, and fish (Burenhult, *Arkeologi i Sverige* I, pp. 88-89). Rock paintings of human and animal figures have been found in hard-to-reach caves on the coast of Norway as well, harking back to the cave paintings of southern France, which were also done deep inside caves and were not on "public view" (Lødøen and Mandt, *The Rock Art of Norway*, pp. 84-97). These paintings are all done in deep red, probably with ochre.

It's often assumed that rock carvings of animals represent "hunting magic," and that the carved images represent what the carvers wanted to kill and eat. In some cases this is probably true; some rock art is found along animal migration routes, at sites where ambushes or traps could be set (Mikkelsen, "Religion and Ecology," pp. 127-136). However, this does not necessarily apply to all carvings. Animals in rock art may represent transformed shamans or their spirit guides, or may have mythological or metaphorical meanings that are not obvious to outsiders (Lewis-Williams, *The Mind in the Cave*, pp. 174-176; Sjöstrand, "Product or Production," pp. 263-266).

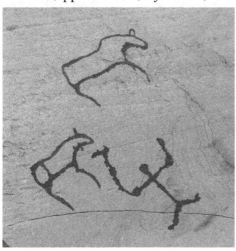

Man holding an elk-headed staff. Alta, Norway, 4000-5000 BCE. Photo by Hans A. Rosbach, Wikimedia Commons. CC BY-SA 3.0.

Ceremonial elk-headed staff or axe head, from Alunda, Uppland, Sweden. Swedish Historical Museum 123172, CC BY 2.5.

To give one example, the Evenk people of Siberia had a myth of an elk stealing the sun, plunging the world into darkness until a hero shot the elk. This was the origin of day and night and of the seasons. We can't know if the Neolithic Scandinavians had a similar myth, but the point remains: a carving of someone shooting an elk does not necessarily mean "I have killed an elk" or "I want to kill an elk" (Hultkrantz, "Rock Drawings as Evidence of Religion," pp. 59-61).

Rock art from several Mesolithic and Neolithic sites, notably Alta in Norway and Nämforsen in Sweden, depict human figures carrying staffs topped with elk heads. Several of these staffs have been found at sites all around the eastern Baltic; some have stone heads with a socket for a shaft, such as the head from Alunda in Sweden, while others were made in one piece. These resemble the animal-headed staffs used in re-

16

cent times by Siberian shamans to travel to other worlds, and sometimes to fight beings in those worlds (Herva and Lahelma, *Northern Archaeology and Cosmology*, pp. 75-80). Rock paintings and carvings from Scandinavia also depict boats with high prows topped with elk heads. Sometimes these boats are shown being carried by human figures; they may represent light, portable boats made from skins stretched on a wooden or bone frame, similar to Inuit *umiaks*. Such light boats would have been suitable for long-distance travel, fishing, and hunting seals and whales (Paulsson et al, "Elk Heads at Sea," pp. 412-417). The elk heads may signal a spiritual meaning as well, similar to the elk-headed staffs. In fact, some of the boats are carrying elk-headed staffs and/or people wielding them, suggesting that the boats might be traveling to a shamanistic otherworld (Herva and Lahelma, p. 77-80).

Rock art at Alta, Norway, 4000-5000 BCE, showing hunters in boats, one with an elk-headed prow. Photo by Hans A. Rosbach, Wikimedia Commons. CC BY-SA 3.0.

The First Farmers

Agriculture—both cultivating crops and keeping herds of animals—entered Europe around 8000 BCE, moving north and west from the Fertile Crescent (present-day Iraq and southeastern Turkey). The earliest agriculturalists developed from foraging cultures that had been in the Near East since the early dispersals out of Africa (Lazaridis et al., "Genomic Insights," pp. 419-425). Evidently, large numbers of people migrated into Europe from the southeast, bringing crops and animals with them; roughly 20% of modern European human genetic lineages can be traced to these Near Eastern farmers. However, crops and herds were soon adopted and spread by European native populations (Richards, "The Neolithic Invasion of Europe"). Agriculture reached most of central and western Europe before 5000 BCE (Diamond, *Guns, Germs, and Steel*, p. 109). The peoples of the northern coastal zones took longer to adopt agriculture, possibly because they preferred to exploit the abundant marine resources in their areas, and also because clearing thick Northern forests took considerable time and effort. Denmark and southern Norway and Sweden didn't adopt agriculture until around 4000 BCE, although once they did, they did so very rapidly (Price, *Ancient Scandinavia*, pp. 106-112). In fact, the people of Sweden and northern Denmark seem to have abandoned agriculture and domestic animals around 3400 BCE, creating a distinctive foraging culture known as the Pitted Ware Culture. These people didn't adopt agriculture again until around 2300 BCE (Diamond, p. 109; Price, pp. 170-175), while some peoples of the Baltic Sea coastal region didn't adopt agriculture until well into the Bronze Age or even later (Richards, p. 143).

Funnel beaker, late Stone Age (ca. 3200 BCE). Skarpsalling, Denmark. National Museum of Denmark, CC BY-SA 2.0.

In northern Europe, the arrival of agriculture is correlated with the appearance of a new culture, known as the Funnel Beaker or *Trichterbecher* (TRB) Culture for the predominant shape of its ceramics. Farther south, agriculture is associated with a different style of pottery called Linear Pottery or *Linearbandkeramik* (LBK), which is later replaced by the TRB style. We know that these early farmers used simple plows and hoes to break the ground. They grew wheat, flax and lentils, and raised cattle, sheep, pigs and goats. Agriculturalists continued to hunt game and gather wild plants as needed, and in some areas they coexisted and traded with foragers for centuries. "Ötzi the Iceman," the mummified body of a 45-year-old man found in 1991 on the Austrian-Italian border, belongs to this time period; he's been dated to 3300-3200 BCE (Milisauskas and Kruk, "Middle Neolithic," pp. 193-246). Neolithic trade routes covered long distances: sites in Denmark have yielded axes made of stone quarried near present-day Prague, copper artifacts from the Tyrolean Alps of what is now Austria, and jadeite axes quarried in the Italian Alps and finished in Brittany. The people of Denmark probably traded amber for these precious objects, and they also traded high-quality flint, which they quarried from chalk beds in Skåne and Jutland (Price, *Ancient Scandinavia*, pp. 114, 121-125, 137-138).

Agriculture transformed both the natural environment and social organization. People moved into the uplands, clearing the forest: Neolithic polished flint axes have been shown to be quite effective at cutting down trees (Price, *Ancient Scandinavia*, pp. 104-105). Population density increased, since cultivation can support more people than hunting and gathering on the same amount of land. So did social inequality: the adoption of agriculture

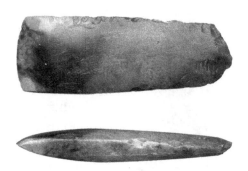

Polished flint axe from Hallegård, Denmark. Funnel Beaker culture. National Museum of Denmark, CC BY-SA 2.0.

means that (in good years) there was a surplus of food, which could be traded. By the Late Neolithic we see the development of better transportation, including road networks, watercraft, and draft animals. This allowed some people to trade, taking economic risk but accumulating wealth. Local elites began to adopt different lifestyles from the rest of their people (Bogucki, "How Wealth Happened," pp. 108-114). Hostility among groups may have increased as well: fortified enclosures, made up of concentric ditches and mounds, were constructed in Europe at this time (Milisauskas and Kruk, "Middle Neolithic," p. 232-236). In Denmark, 17% of all male skeletal remains from the Neolithic show signs of violent death, often by blows to the left side of the head (where a right-handed enemy would strike). Evidently those stone axes could cut down more than just trees (Price, p. 156).

At about 3200 BCE in continental northern Europe, and about 2800 BCE in Scandinavia, the culture shifted again. People were buried individually, in pits underneath low mounds, with ceramic vessels, amber jewelry, and (in male burials) weapons, notably stone axes. The name for this culture is the Corded Ware cultural complex, because their pots were decorated by pressing cords into the wet clay before firing. The Scandinavian expressions of the Corded Ware culture are known as the Single Grave Culture and the Battle-Axe Culture. These people were probably speakers of Indo-European languages, and are discussed more thoroughly in the next chapter.

Soon after, yet another migration or cultural diffusion, this time probably from the west, introduced what is known as the Bell Beaker culture into northern Europe. It's not clear how much of the shift to Bell Beaker cultural practices results from migration of people, and how much from local people adopting goods, ideas, and practices (Cunliffe, *Europe Between the Oceans*, pp. 203-208). Bell Beaker sites across Europe tend to show uniformity in some aspects but not others; people drank from similar vessels, but built different styles of house, for example. Chemical and genetic analyses of human bones associated with Bell Beaker culture show that many of the people were not buried in the places where they grew up; in particular, many women seem to have traveled some distance between where they were born and where they were buried (Knipper et al., "Female Exogamy," pp. 10084-10087). Bell Beaker culture may have been spread by women who moved to their husbands' residences, bringing ideas and technology with them. Whatever the case, the Bell Beaker people made increasing use of metals. In Denmark, they are noted for mining high-quality flint and making beautifully crafted flint daggers, too thin to be practical weapons and so probably made for ritual, symbolism, or display. As increasing trade brought more and more bronze into southern Scandinavia, the Stone Age ended.

Flint dagger, late Stone Age, Krabbesholm, Denmark. National Museum of Denmark, CC BY-SA 2.0.

Neolithic Religion

The religion of Europe in the Neolithic has sometimes been depicted as the worship of a single Great Goddess, going hand in hand with a peaceful, matriarchal, agrarian society. Both the religion and the way of life were allegedly destroyed by the invasion of the patriarchal, warlike Indo-Europeans. Many archaeologists and mythographers now think that this matrifocal utopia never existed. While there is no reason why goddesses could not have been worshipped in the Stone Age as they certainly were in later periods, and no reason to assume that women could not have been honored and empowered in Stone Age societies, a diversity of beliefs throughout Neolithic Europe is far more likely than a single continent-spanning cult of one Great Goddess. This controversy is discussed further in the next chapter. (See Eller, *The Myth of Matriarchal Prehistory*, and Motz, *The Faces of the Goddess*, for critiques.)

The change from a foraging lifestyle to an agricultural lifestyle was probably marked by a significant alteration in religious perceptions. The type of spirituality loosely defined as "shamanism" is widespread among foragers, who need to remain on good terms with the spirits of the animals they hunt, and who can and do move when the animals do. By and large, foragers do not re-engineer their own environments on a massive scale. On the other hand, an agricultural community creates its own "built environment" of homes and fields, and it must actively work to maintain it. Seasonal cycles become extremely important: the seasons determine what people must do and when they must do it. Barring some catastrophe, the endless cycle of the seasons establishes a permanent structure for human life (Oma, "Long House—Long Time," pp. 11-12). Even then, agriculturalists cannot always withstand floods, droughts, and other disasters, and they can't simply pack up and get out of the way without massive social disruption. Agricultural people develop concepts of powerful, yet humanlike deities who are able to bless and reward human efforts—but who might always decide not to do so. The focus shifts to cultic practices to gain the deities' blessings, although certain shamanistic elements may survive. Permanent holy sites take on much greater importance, deities are increasingly depicted in art, and offerings increase dramatically in number and value. The cult of the dead also becomes important, now that settled communities are staying close to their ancestors' graves. This process can be seen in the Near East, where, right as agriculture and animal domestication were being developed, art shifts from representing diverse animals to representing mythic beings, notably a Great Goddess figure and a male figure associated with, or appearing as, a great bull (Cauvin, *The Birth of the Gods*, pp. 29-33, 69-72). A similar "Revolution of Symbols" would have happened in northern Europe: as people adopted agriculture, they adopted this new mentality.

Bogs and Mounds

One sign of this new way of thinking is the intensification of bog sacrifices in Scandinavia. Animal bones had been deposited in Scandinavian bogs since the days of the earliest humans, but people began making more diverse sacrifices in the Neolithic. Wooden platforms and gangways were built to allow people to deposit offerings away from solid land. In addition to food, bog offerings included fine stone axes, sometimes in sizable hoards, like the ten axes found together at Maglehøjs Vange in Denmark. Treasures such as imported copper axes and amber necklaces were also offered; a ceramic vessel filled with 13,000 small amber beads was laid in a bog at Mollerup, Denmark, while a hoard of 4000 larger beads weighing a total of 8.5 kg (18.7 pounds) was laid in another bog, at Læsten (Kaul, "The Bog," pp. 23-25).

Amber hoard from a bog. Sortekærs Mose, Denmark. National Museum of Denmark, CC BY-SA 2.0.

People also ended up in bogs. The oldest "bog bodies," two young women from Sigersdal in Denmark, date to around 3500 BCE. At about the same time, a man who'd been shot in the face and chest with arrows was laid in a bog at Porsmose in Denmark (Price, *Ancient Scandinavia*, pp. 138-139, 156). At least some of the Neolithic bog bodies had cords around their necks and may have been strangled, a practice that returned in the Iron Age. Other human remains in bogs may be remains that were deposited some time after death, not sacrifices of still-living victims (Kaul, p. 40).

A sign of new attitudes toward the dead is a major change in burials. Around 4000 BCE, agriculturalists in western Europe, from Spain and Portugal to the British Isles and eastward to Denmark and south Sweden, began to entomb their dead in great enclosures of stone slabs, heaping earth over them to make mounds with chambers inside, and sometimes ringing the mounds with circles of stones. By 3000 BCE, these houses had developed into huge *gallery graves* and *passage graves* which might house several generations of a family, all buried with tools, weapons, jewelry, and food and drink. DNA analysis of human remains from passage graves shows that the males buried in a passage grave or other megalithic site were often related through the male line, suggesting that they belonged to one patrilineal family (Sánchez-Quinto et al., "Megalithic Tombs"). Such tombs may have been thought of as homes for the dead, with offerings of food and tools to allow them to live on (Schutz, *The Prehistory of Germanic Europe*, pp. 97-98). Aside from housing the dead,

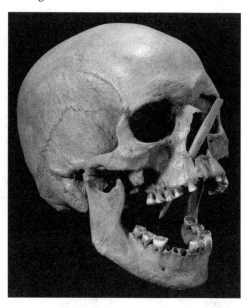

Skull of a Neolithic man deposited in a bog. Porsmose, Denmark. National Museum of Denmark, CC BY-SA 2.0.

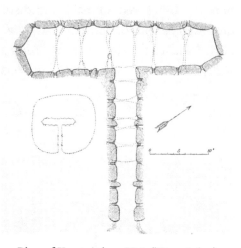

Plan of Kong Askers Høi, "King Asker's Mound", Møn, Denmark. The grave chamber is 10 meters long and 2 meters wide. Müller, *Vor Oldtid* (1897)

23

mounds and monuments like this provide a permanent record that every-one can see "inscribed" on the landscape, attesting that a tribe or clan has claimed the surrounding land. On a spiritual level, the dead may have been asked to bring good harvests and crops; a powerful clan leader might be expected to continue blessing the people even after death.

People of this time built other *megalithic* (made of large stones) mon-uments: standing stones (*menhirs*) and earth enclosures with or without stones or timber posts (*henges*). The earliest stages of construction of the most famous megalithic monument, Stonehenge in south England, date from this time frame; so do many of the monuments of Orkney Mainland and Carnac in Brittany. While some of the monuments from this time are actually grave-mounds from which the earth has eroded, others were built as free-standing structures. Stone was not the only building material: in Britain and Germany, people built circular banks and ditches with palisades of wooden posts, like Woodhenge (discovered near Stonehenge in 1923) and the great circles at Goseck, the Goloring, and other sites in Germany (Price, *Europe Before Rome*, pp. 182-212). At Pömmelte, dubbed "Germa-ny's Stonehenge," a double circle of wooden posts was raised within a ring-shaped mound. Offerings were left in pits dug into the ring mound: pots, bones of butchered animals, and dismembered bodies of women and chil-dren were all placed in the pits. A few men, presumably of high rank, were buried within the ring in more ordered graves (Spatzier and Bertemes, "The Ring Sanctuary of Pömmelte," pp. 655-668).

Reconstructed ring sanctuary (Ringheiligtum) at Pömmelte, Sachsen-Anhalt, Germany.
Photo courtesy of John Hyatt.

Debate still rages regarding how these monuments were built and what they were used for. Some have made them out to be centers of Neolithic "Great Goddess worship," but the evidence is ambiguous, to say the least (see Twohey, "A 'Mother Goddess' in North-West Europe?"). Others are aligned with points on the horizon such as the rising and setting of the sun on equinoxes and solstices; the gaps in the Pömmelte ring are aligned with sunrises and sunsets at the midpoints between the equinoxes and solstices. Whatever the reasons why they were built, their holiness was remembered by later folk. As late as the 1800s, the people of Orkney carried out rituals at stone circles and megaliths, especially at a megalith with a hole in it that they called the "Odin Stone" (Marwick, *The Folklore of Orkney and Shetland*, pp. 59-60). The stones from a Neolithic long barrow in Berkshire, England have long been remembered as "Wayland's Smithy." Megalithic grave mounds are still known in Danish as *jættestue*, "jotun's hill," and some are named for legendary giants or kings.

Feasting, Art, and Music

Stone Age sites in Scandinavia have yielded evidence of ceremonial feasts, with pottery vessels of food and drink together with evidence of animals slaughtered for food. Bog offerings from this time include bones of meat animals, sometimes split for their marrow, and ceramic pots in which food had been cooked; residues in the pots show that they had been used to cook fish stew (Kaul, "The Bog," p. 23). Occasionally, human flesh was on the menu: at Jettböle

"Face pot" (*ansigtskar*) from the Neolithic. Svinø, Denmark. National Museum of Denmark. CC BY-SA 2.0.

in the Åland Islands, for example, the bones of at least fourteen men, women, and children show cut marks from butchering, with long bones broken to get at the marrow (Götherström et al., "The Jettböle Neolithic Site," pp. 48-51). A distinctive feature of Neolithic feasts in Scandinavia is the deliberate breaking of pottery at graves and on causeways through bogs. Some passage graves show a buildup of broken pots before the entrance, deposited over many generations (Müller and Peterson, "Ceramics and Society," p. 584). A reasonable guess is that the pots and their contents were being given to the dead. With the appearance of the Single Grave Culture, communal passage graves were no longer built, and bog sacrifices stopped being made, suggesting a major change in religious practice.

Musical instruments provide another clue to Stone Age religion. Bone flutes continued to be made in Scandinavia all the way into medieval times. Some Neolithic bone flutes from Scandinavia, relatively short and pierced with one to three holes, may have been used as animal or bird calls in hunting, or conceivably in ritual; Norwegian hunters made such calls until the early 20th century (Lund, "Animal Calls"). Clay drums have been found at Funnel Beaker sites (4000-2700 BCE); some of these have a "chalice" shape similar to the Middle Eastern *doumbek* (Megaw, "Problems and Non-Problems in Palaeo-Organology," pp. 335-336, pl. XV.a-c). A pig's jawbone with thirty pierced shells that had been strung on it was found associated with three Neolithic graves in Gotland; it may have been playable as a combined rattle and scraper (Lund, "Archaeomusicology," p. 249). A probable bull-roarer was found at Kongemose, Denmark, dated to 6000 BCE; this is a long flat object tied to a cord and swung in a circle to produce a roaring sound (Lund, "Archaeomusicology," pp. 256-257). The largest percussion instruments of all are huge stones from the late Stone Age and Bronze Age, concentrated in Sweden, which resonate when struck. Many of them still have names like Sångsten or Sangelstainen, "singing stone," and Ballersten, "noisy stone." To this day, there are local folk stories to explain why they ring. Many of them are marked with carved or ground depressions known as cupmarks. It's likely that they were used in ritual (Lund, "Early Ringing Stones," pp. 180-189).[2]

Neolithic people wore strands of animal bones, teeth, and claws, pierced and strung together. Canine teeth of seals, dogs, and foxes, and incisor teeth of wild boars were commonly used. These could be strung or sewn in overlapping rows onto belts, aprons, clothing hems, pouches, or other ac-

---

2. The album *Fornnordiska klänger* by Cajsa Lund, on the Naxos label, is out of print at this writing. If you can find a copy, it is worth listening to: you hear instruments and soundscapes from the Stone Age to the early medieval period, including a "singing stone."

cessories; some Pitted Ware graves contain over a hundred teeth and bones strung like this. We might speculate that ornaments like this showed a special connection between the animal and the person who wore the animal's teeth; perhaps the animal was a spirit guide or clan totem. Whatever the case, strands of pierced teeth, bones or shells also served as rattles, especially when the wearer was dancing or running. Analysis of wear patterns on tooth pendants suggests that they did frequently knock against each other and were almost

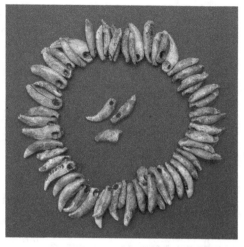

Bear teeth pierced for stringing together. Västerbjärs, Gotland, Sweden. Swedish Historical Museum 429728.

certainly intended to make sounds (Rainio and Mannermaa, "Tracing the Rattle," pp. 333-345).

People also carried or wore carvings and figurines of stone and bone, but possibly the most prized material was amber, which was made into amulets and offered in bogs. As early as 7500 BCE in Denmark, amber and bone pieces were carved into shapes or engraved with designs, and this custom persisted all the way to the Viking Age and beyond. Carvings of bears, birds, and other animals might have been made for luck in hunting, although

they could have had other symbolic meanings: as discussed above, we should not assume that every depiction of an animal was made because someone wanted to eat it. Amber and stone were also carved into miniature axe-heads or mace-heads, which have been found especially in megalithic passage graves (Larsson, "The Sun from the Sea," pp. 71-73). It is tempting, if unprovable, to see these as the weap-

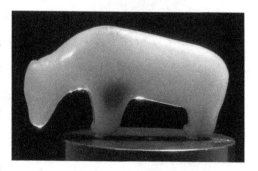

Amber carving of a bear. Lild Strand, Denmark. National Museum of Denmark, CC BY-SA 2.0.

One of over 300 amber axe-heads from the passage grave at Gantofta, Skåne, Sweden. Actual size 35 mm. Swedish Historical Museum 425898. CC BY 2.5.

Amber head from Norra Asarp, Swedish Historical Museum 425898. CC BY 2.5.

on of a sky-god who would contribute to the image of Thor. Amber carvings of human heads are also known, and both bones and amber pieces were sometimes carved with abstract patterns of lines, dots, and pits, whose meaning is unknown.

Why Does This Matter?

Some Heathens have claimed that Ásatrú can be traced all the way back to the earliest Europeans. Stephen McNallen wrote that "since Asatru is the religion which springs from the specific spiritual beliefs of the Northern Europeans, it is as old as this branch of the human race which came into being some 40,000 years ago" (*What Is Asatru?*, p. 1). This is fundamentally wrong. The people of northern Europe never did form one single "branch of the human race." Populations with different genetic backgrounds, physical appearances, cultures, and spiritual beliefs have migrated, mixed, and mingled all through Europe's prehistory. Nor can we assume that the Stone Age people of northern Europe possessed a single common "spirituality," or that their spiritual beliefs were fundamentally the same as the Viking-era Norse. As we shall see, Indo-European-speaking cultures probably did not appear in northern Europe until roughly 3000 BCE, and it would take over two millennia more before anything like a distinctive Germanic language would appear.

Yet it is important to understand something about these early cultures of northern Europe. Neolithic peoples knew the same plants and animals that

28

live there to this day, many of which had mythologic or symbolic meaning all the way through the Viking Age. They made music and art, buried their dead with complex rituals, and offered grave-goods at and after the burial. They made offerings to the powers around them, including precious objects such as amber and weaponry. The shamanistic worldview of the Sámi and Siberian peoples may well have its deepest roots in the Stone Age, and this would go on to influence Norse religion. And by the end of the Stone Age, the genetic mixing of three major waves of migration—the early foragers, the farmers from the Near East, and the Yamnaya people from the steppes— had created the roots of most European populations today. It is well to remember the earliest layers of our *ørlǫg*.

Contributors:

1st edition: Kveldúlfr Gundarsson.

2nd edition: Revised and expanded by Diana Paxson and Ben Waggoner.

3rd edition: Reorganization and new material by Ben Waggoner.

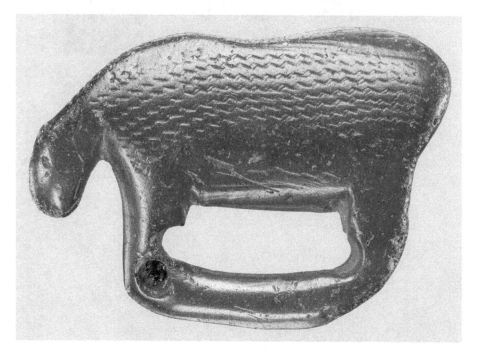

Miniature amber carving of a female elk. Næsby Strand, Zealand, Denmark. National Museum of Denmark, CC BY-SA 2.0.

Bell beaker from Paha Holešovice, Czech Republic.
City of Prague Museum. Photo by Zdeněk Kratochvíl,
Wikimedia Commons, CC BY-SA 4.0.

CHAPTER TWO

The Indo-Europeans

ca. 4000-2500 BCE

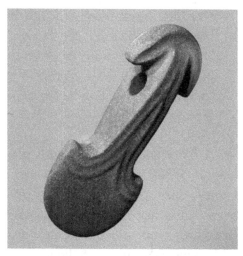

Most of the languages spoken in a great swath of land, from Iceland and Britain to northern India and Bangladesh, show consistent similarities in their vocabulary and grammar. All these languages make up the great Indo-European language family, and all have descended from a common ancestral language. Although it was spoken long before the invention of writing, it is possible to reconstruct Stone battle-axe head from Vrou Hede, Denmark. National Museum of Denmark, CC BY-SA 2.0.

much of its vocabulary and grammar—and through those, we can learn something of the minds of those who spoke it, and even tentatively identify the speakers.

In 1785, Sir William Jones, a British judge on the Supreme Court of Bengal under the rule of the British East India Company, began learning Sanskrit in the course of studying Indian law. Jones not only knew English and his native Welsh, but had studied twenty or so other languages, including Greek, Latin, Persian, Arabic, and Hebrew (Lincoln, *Theorizing Myth*, pp. 192-193) He was so struck by the similarities among all these languages that he declared, in a famous speech to the Royal Asiatic Society of Bengal in 1786:

> The Sanscrit language, whatever be its antiquity, is of a wonderful structure; more perfect than the Greek, more copious than the Latin, and more exquisitely refined than either, yet bearing to both of them a stronger affinity, both in the roots of verbs and the forms of grammar, than could possibly have been produced by accident; so strong indeed, that no philologer could examine them all three, without believing them to have spring from some common source, which, perhaps, no longer exists:

there is a similar reason, though not quite so forcible, for supposing that both the Gothick and the Celtick, though blended with a very different idiom, had the same origin with the Sanscrit, and the old Persian might be added to this family, if this were the place for discussing any question concerning the antiquities of Persia. (Jones, *The Works of Sir William Jones*, vol. 3, pp. 34-35)

A few scholars had previously come close to this realization (see Mallory, *In Search of the Indo-Europeans*, pp. 9-13), but Jones's announcement is often taken as the founding of historical linguistics. Jones was the first to recognize that most of the languages spoken from Iceland to India were related by common descent from a distant ancestral language. Jones himself tried to interpret this in the light of Biblical history, suggesting that all these languages descended from the language of Noah's son Ham. Later scholars quietly dropped the Biblical theorizing, and in 1813, Thomas Young proposed the name *Indo-European* for this language family—although the alternate name *Indo-Germanic* was also popular, especially among German linguists (Arvidsson, *Aryan Idols*, pp. 17-20).

There is more to the story than just similarities between words. Early 19th century linguists showed that Indo-European languages shared not only vocabulary, but grammatical structures as well. They also showed that sound changes followed consistent rules that affect all words in the same way. For example, Jacob Grimm and Rasmus Rask showed that the sounds *p, t, k,* and *kw* in other Indo-European languages corresponded to the sounds *f, th, h,* and *hw* in the Germanic languages. The sounds *b, d, g,* and *gw* in other languages "fill the gap" and become *p, t, k,* and *kw* in Germanic. This pattern is still called Grimm's Law. Thus Latin *pater* corresponds to English *father, cordis* corresponds to *heart, quod* corresponds to *what, duo* corresponds to *two,* and *pedis* corresponds to *foot*; hundreds more examples could be given. The same pattern appears using other languages than Latin: for example, *father* corresponds to Greek *patēr* and Sanskrit *pitā* as well as Latin *pater.* Allowing for sound changes in other language branches, *father* also corresponds to Persian *pedar,* Irish *athair,* Armenian *hayr,* archaic Russian *batja,* and Albanian *äte.* Taking all these regular sound shifts into account, we can reconstruct what the earliest forms of these words would have been in an ancestral language: *pəter, *ker-, *kwod, *dwo, and *pods.[3]

This common root of most of the languages spoken in Europe and southwestern Asia, including the Germanic language family as well the Celtic, Italic, Slavic, Greek, Iranian, and Indian families (among others), is now called *Proto-Indo-European* (PIE). Even though PIE was never written, we can reconstruct PIE vocabulary and grammar, in considerable detail by comparing languages in the Indo-European family. But languages don't evolve in a vacuum—the proto-language must have been spoken by real people, whose culture must have been reflected in the language they spoke. Reconstructing PIE allows us to discover aspects of this culture: if PIE had a word for a thing, presumably the people who spoke it knew that thing. (Calvert Watkins's essay "Indo-European and the Indo-Europeans" in *The American Heritage Dictionary of Indo-European Roots* is probably the most readable account of how this "linguistic paleontology" is done.)

Some Cautions

It's important not to push the linguistic evidence farther than it will go. For example, we cannot reconstruct a PIE root for "eyelash," but that does not mean that PIE speakers didn't have eyelashes; it just means that whatever word they used has not survived in enough descendant languages that we can be sure of what it was. On the other hand, we can reconstruct not one, but two PIE roots for "fart"—*perd- for a loud one, which perfectly corre-

---

3. Asterisks show that a word is a reconstruction, not known directly from a text. PIE had a large inventory of sounds, some of them unfamiliar to English speakers, and some of them not reconstructed with certainty. For example, there were three *laryngeals*—consonants produced at the back of the throat—which vanished from most descendant languages. Since their exact pronunciation is not clear, they are written h_1, h_2, and h_3. Other reconstructed sounds have to be written with diacritical marks above and below the letters. The upshot is that a reconstructed Indo-European root often looks more like a calculus equation than like anything pronounceable. Such roots are also difficult to typeset, especially on e-book platforms that may not be able to display the correct fonts or character encodings. Thus, although professional linguists might wince, the editors have chosen to use the simpler reconstructions of PIE roots found in *The American Heritage Dictionary*. For more modern reconstructions, Mallory and Adams, *Oxford Introduction to Proto-Indo-European*, is handy. Serious students of linguistics who want a detailed explanation of PIE and how it evolved into Proto-Germanic should consult Ringe, *From Proto-Indo-European to Proto-Germanic*.

sponds to English "fart," and *pesd-* for a soft one, which by various twists and turns is the root of both "fizzle" and "feisty." This is linguistically interesting, but it does not tell us much about the PIE speakers, except that their digestive systems worked pretty much like ours do. We also can't assume that a PIE root would have had the same meaning as its modern cognates, because meanings shift over time; to give a younger example, French *court* and Spanish *corte* both mean "royal palace and/or the king and retainers who live there," but their common ancestor, *cohors*, originally meant "farmyard" in Latin. Working out the meanings of PIE roots can be a fuzzy business even when the roots themselves are firmly supported.

Furthermore, any language spoken by more than a few people will show dialect variation; any language spoken for more than a few years will change over time; and any language spoken by people with neighbors will absorb influences from the neighbors' languages. This is simply what languages *do*. There never was a single, unified, standard Proto-Indo-European language; it is probably best to think of PIE as a bundle of shifting dialects, spoken by peoples with shifting cultures over a wide span of time. Reconstructed PIE unavoidably contains a mixture of word forms from different times and places. I [BW] suspect that if we could travel back in time and speak our reconstructed PIE to an actual speaker from the past, it would come across as something like "Prithee, hwæt! 'Owyagoin', moste plesaunt old chap, LOL?" Nor was PIE at any stage of its development a "pure" language (which is something that doesn't exist and never has). Several reconstructed PIE roots look to be borrowings from Afro-Asiatic (the language family that includes Hebrew and Arabic); Uralic (the family that includes Finnish, Hungarian, etc.); and languages spoken in the Caucasus Mountains (Anthony and Ringe, "The Indo-European Homeland," pp. 206-207; Bjørn, "Foreign Elements"). A few scholars have tried their hand at writing complete texts in reconstructed PIE, and some modern pagans have even created rituals in the reconstructed language (e.g. Ceisiwr Serith's fascinating book *Deep Ancestors*). But we can never know if these would have been intelligible to someone living on the Caspian steppes around 3000 BCE.

Finally, this is very important: Languages, cultures, and genes all tend to be passed down in family groups, from older members to young children. All three of them change over time, and sifting through evidence of these changes has allowed us to identify probable traces of ancient people who were genetically related to each other, spoke PIE languages, and shared cultural features. But a linguistic group, a cultural group, and an ethnic group are *not* the same thing. While their histories will often be associated, it's very common for them to diverge. There are well-documented examples all over the world of members of different genetic groups adopting a common culture and/or language—and members of one genetic grouping adopting different cultures and/or languages. Cultural innovations, ideas, words, and languages can and do diffuse among populations in ways that genes do not. Nor do cultures or ethnicities ever remain "pure": people can and do mingle their genes, cultures, and languages all the time, and all the evidence suggests that this has been common for as long as humans have existed. We should never assume without evidence that the histories of genes, languages, and cultural practices will match. (As archaeologists say: "Pots aren't people.") The linguist Max Müller made the point well when he complained:

> To me an ethnologist who speaks of Aryan race, Aryan blood, Aryan eyes and hair, is as great a sinner as a linguist who speaks of a dolicho-cephalic dictionary or a brachycephalic grammar.[4] It is worse than a Babylonian confusion of tongues—it is downright theft. We have made our own terminology for the classification of languages; let ethnologists make their own for the classification of skulls, and hair, and blood. (*Biographies of Words and the Home of the Aryas*, pp. 120-121.)

Prehistory simply does not look like a game of Risk™ in which ethnically "pure" waves of people push each other across the map. Prehistory is *messy*.

The 19th century French scholar Arthur de Gobineau came up with the idea of an "Aryan race" of light-skinned people with a superior physical type, language, and culture, who had created the world's great civilizations (*The Inequality of Human Races*, pp. 205-212).[5] Parroted by scholars and

---

4. *Dolichocephalic* and *brachycephalic* mean "long-headed" and "short-headed," referring to physical measurements that were once used in attempts to classify human races.

5. Gobineau, and countless racists who have followed him, used "Aryan" to mean "non-Jewish white people." The only people who are documented as calling themselves "Aryans" were the Vedic Indians and the Persians—the name of Iran means "land of the Aryans"—and they originally used the term to mean "those who perform ritual correctly," not for a race or ethnicity at all. The oldest written lists of "Aryans" include people with non-Indo-European names (Anthony, *The Horse, The Wheel, and Language*, pp. 9-11).

demagogues for years, his ideas would yield bitter fruit, especially in Nazi Germany. And not only there: The British economist Roger Pearson (p. 1924) has spent much of his career advocating for white supremacy and the inferiority of Africans and Jews. A group he founded in 1958, the Northern League, openly advocated for Nazi "racial hygiene" and drew a number of actual Nazis, including Hans Günther, the top "racial theorist" in Germany under the Third Reich. Supported by the Pioneer Fund, a nonprofit foundation organized and funded by wealthy segregationists, eugenicists, and Nazi sympathizers (Lombardo, "'The American Breed'," pp. 754-815), Pearson slipped into mainstream conservative circles in the 1970s and founded the Institute for the Study of Man, a publishing company. The ISM took over the publication of an academic journal called *Mankind Quarterly*, which had been founded in 1961 expressly to disseminate "scientific" white supremacy (Schaffer, " 'Scientific Racism Again?'," pp. 269-278). The ISM published *Mankind Quarterly* until 2015, and it continues to publish another academic journal called the *Journal of Indo-European Studies* (*JIES*). The vast majority of what this editor [BW] has seen published in the *JIES* is not detectably racist, and much of it is too abstruse to have any obvious connection with contemporary politics. In fact, this chapter cites articles in both *Mankind Quarterly* and the *JIES*; it is hard to do research in this field without consulting the *JIES*, and even *Mankind Quarterly* has been known to run sound articles on anthropology and comparative religion. All the same, it should give the reader pause to reflect that much modern research in Indo-European studies has been funded and promoted by groups with a well-documented white supremacist agenda (Sussman, *The Myth of Race*, pp. 242-248; Schnurbein, *Norse Revival*, pp. 283-285; Lincoln, *Theorizing Myth*, pp. 122-123). It should be unnerving that the same nonprofit that funded the *JIES* was also underwriting books like *America's Bimodal Crisis: Black Intelligence in White Society*, which argued for African genetic inferiority and called for sterilizing "welfare mothers" (Lombardo, pp. 816-818).

So let it be said here, loudly and clearly: The people who spoke PIE languages thousands of years ago were not a "race," to the extent that the word means anything at all. They were probably not conscious of any common

---

"Indo-Aryan" is sometimes used for the Indo-Iranian branch of the IE language family, which includes Avestan, Persian, Sanskrit, and related languages. By this definition, the only Aryans in Europe are the Roma people.

"ethnic identity." Nor did they necessarily share exactly the same cultural patterns. Nor did they necessarily come from one genetic stock. Nor did they keep themselves "pure" of genetic, linguistic, and cultural influences from other peoples. When we speak of "the Proto-Indo-Europeans," we mean a very general average of the speakers of a set of related, yet diverse and changing languages, used across hundreds of thousands of square miles and over a time span of roughly two thousand years. To treat them as if they were a unified ethnic grouping is, at best, a simplification, and it's very easy to misuse. Even modern geneticists sometimes make this mistake and end up communicating misleading information to the general public (Hakenbeck, "Genetics, Archaeology and the Far Right," pp. 520-523).

With all those disclaimers in mind: By carefully cross-checking linguistic, archaeological, and genetic data, we can reconstruct a testable story of where and how probable speakers of PIE languages lived, where and how they migrated through the world, and where and how they interacted with other peoples. In some cases, we can reconstruct important words for mythic and ritual concepts they may have held—even the names of deities. Myths and legends across the Indo-European cultural sphere share enough common features that we can infer something about the belief systems of the people who spoke PIE languages. William Jones himself realized this when he pointed out to his audience in India that "we now live among the adorers of those very deities, who were worshipped under different names in old Greece and Italy. . . The Scythian and Hyperborean [far northern, i.e. Norse] doctrines and mythology may also be traced in every part of these eastern regions." (Jones, *The Works of Sir William Jones,* vol. 3, pp. 37-38) But this is a field of study where it is wise to remember *Hávamál* 1; what we think we know can be shaped by our biases, and it is never a bad idea to use critical thinking here.

The Indo-European Homeland

Areas from Siberia to the North Pole have been seriously proposed at one time or another as the land where the Proto-Indo-European speakers lived. Today, there is fairly widespread consensus, if not universal agreement, that the Kurgan peoples (from Russian *kurgan*, a burial mound), who lived on the steppes and steppe-forests north of the Black Sea and west of the

Ural Mountains between six and four thousand years ago, were speaking early Indo-European languages. The archaeological remains of these cultures closely match what can be reconstructed of the Proto-Indo-European language. For example, as will be discussed further, PIE has many words for parts of wagons—and wagons were used by the later steppe cultures, and sometimes turn up in their graves. (See Mallory, *In Search of the Indo-Europeans*, and Anthony, *The Horse, The Wheel, and Language*, for overviews.) A competing hypothesis, that the PIE speakers were identical with the Near Eastern farmers who introduced agriculture into Europe, has been criticized on several grounds (e.g. Mallory, pp. 177-181; Haak et al., "Massive Migration," p. 211; Anthony and Ringe, "The Indo-European Homeland," pp. 202-210). The Kurgan hypothesis is still being debated and revised (e.g. Klejn et al, "Discussion"), but as of this writing, it seems to give the best explanation of the facts.

One brief note: where did the PIE speakers themselves come from? The speakers and the language they spoke didn't just fall out of the sky; both must have had ancestors of their own. Analysis of ancient DNA suggests that the Kurgan peoples themselves originated from the fusion of two groups: a population from the northeast (the Ancient North Eurasians or ANE, which also has distant genetic links with Native Americans), and another population from somewhere in the Near East or the Caucasus Mountains (Haak et al., "Massive Migration," pp. 209-210). As for their language: one hypothesis has the Indo-European language family sharing a distant common ancestor with Uralic (including Finnish, Hungarian, Sámi, and many languages of the Urals and Siberia), Altaic (including Turkic and Mongolian), various Siberian languages, and possibly Japanese and Korean, in a "superfamily" called Eurasiatic. A similar hypothesis proposes that most of the Eurasiatic languages share a common ancestor with Kartvelian (including Georgian), Dravidian (the main language family of southern India), and Afro-Asiatic (including Arabic, Hebrew, ancient Egyptian, and many languages of north and east Africa), defining an even larger superfamily called Nostratic. While neither hypothesis has really been disproved, most linguists feel that not enough solid evidence exists to support either one. Logically, PIE itself must have evolved from even earlier languages, and must have more distant relatives—but we may never be certain what those were (Mallory and Adams, *Oxford Introduction*, pp. 83-85; see Campbell, *Historical Linguistics*, pp. 346-361 for a detailed critique of Nostratic).

Clues to where the Proto-Indo-European speakers lived come from the words that can be reconstructed. PIE had words for birch and willow trees, and probably also alder, elm, maple, oak, and firs or other conifers (Mallory and Adams, *Oxford Introduction*, pp. 156-161). The speakers knew wolves, bears, foxes, elk, red deer, hares, otters, beavers, mice, and hedgehogs; they seem to have known eagles, cranes, ravens, owls, sparrows, woodpeckers, geese, and ducks; and they had salmon, carp, eels, and minnows in their streams (Mallory and Adams, pp. 134-148). Their landscape had mountains (or at least big hills), rivers, and large bodies of water, although whether the root meaning was "ocean" or "lake" is not entirely clear. They knew winter, spring, and summer, and they had snow and rain. This is consistent with the ecology of the steppes and steppe-forest zones, including the valleys of the Don, the Volga, and other rivers which drain the steppe country.

Proto-Indo-European terms for agriculture (such as *se- "to sow," *peis- "to thresh," and *egro- "field"); agricultural tools (such as *er- "plough," *ek- "rake," *srpo- "sickle," and *gwern- "quern"); crops (*dʰone- "harvested grain," *ieuos- and *grnom- "grain"; *rughis- "rye"); and domesticated pigs (*su-), which cannot be herded by nomads, all suggest that the speakers were familiar with settled agriculture, at least for stockbreeding and growing cereal crops (Mallory and Adams, *Oxford Introduction*, pp. 163-169, *Encyclopedia of Indo-European Culture*, pp. 7-8). Archaeology confirms that the steppe cultures practiced agriculture, although their dependence on it varied—global climate shifts between 5000 and 3000 BCE affected the steppes strongly, and the people had to adapt during times when agriculture was less favorable. Pig bones, grindstones, and remains of grains have been excavated from steppe sites, although some steppe peoples gathered wild grains as well. Archaeology also confirms that they hunted, fished, and gathered freshwater clams and wild plants (Shishlina, *Reconstruction of the Bronze Age*, pp. 222-236).

However, the basis of steppe culture was cattle raising. Cattle *(*gʷou-)* could turn the tough steppe grasses into nutritious milk and meat and useful leather, bones, and horns. Cattle also provided the muscle power to pull wagons. Thus, cattle were immensely important to PIE speakers; *peku- meant both "cattle" and "wealth," and we can reconstruct a sizable number of roots for "milk," "sour milk," "curds," and other dairy products (Mallory and Adams, *Oxford Introduction*, pp. 261-262). The basic lifestyle of the PIE speakers seems to have been *transhumance*: moving herds of livestock in a seasonal cycle to places with good forage. They would have pastured their livestock on the lower river terraces in winter. In the summer, some hunting, fishing, and agriculture might be carried out in the river valleys, while the herds grazed on the vast expanses of the open steppe, watched over by groups of young men, the *koryos* (cognate with ON *herr*, OE *here*, OHG *heri*, "raiding party," as well as Modern English *to harry*; it is also found in ON *einherjar*, "best of the war-band," and Odin's name *Herjan*, "master of the war-band"). Some insight into what these *koryos*-bands got up to may be gained by the fact that a Sanskrit word for "war," *gavisthi*, literally means "desire for cows". Cattle-rustling features prominently in the myths and tales of most Indo-European peoples, from Indra challenging the Panis over stolen cattle in the *Rig-Veda*, to Nestor's cattle raid in the *Iliad*, to the Irish *Tain Bó Cualgne*. The *koryos* was made up of young warriors who were not yet initiated as men, living on the margins of society, with a certain license to raid and plunder. These bands were identified totemically as "wolves"; not only did they engage in scouting, raiding, and low-intensity guerrilla warfare, but they took part in ecstatic masked processions, incarnating the dead ancestors, at certain times of the year. These *koryos* bands were the cultural root of the warrior-societies known to the various Indo-European peoples. (See Kershaw, *The One-Eyed God*, for a full overview.)

Besides cows, the PIE speakers kept domesticated sheep (*owi-*), horses (*ekwos*), pigs (*su-*; also *porko-*, "piglet"), and dogs (*k^won-*). Sheep and goats provided milk, hides, meat, and horn, and sheep and goats also gave wool (*wln-*). Horses may have been originally raised for meat and hides, but were used for transportation very early: at Botai in present-day Kazakhstan, dated to around 3700 BCE, horse teeth show distinctive signs of wear from a bit in the mouth. The settlement at Botai also preserved layers of horse dung dumped in a pit, evidently shoveled out of a stable (Anthony, *The Horse, The Wheel, and Language*, pp. 195-224). Pieces of horse harness are also found in steppe burials (Mallory, *In Search of the Indo-Europeans*, p. 200) and bridled horses are depicted in steppe culture art. Domesticated horses probably reached the Pontic-Caspian steppes through contact with the Botai people. Horses made it possible to hunt from horseback and drag large animals home. They also allowed the steppe dwellers to keep much larger herds—as any cowboy knows, you can herd far more cattle on horseback than on foot.

The PIE speakers had a technical vocabulary for wheeled vehicles: words for "wheel" (*k^wek^wlo-*, *roto-*) can be reconstructed, as well as words for "axle," "wheel hub," "wagon-pole," "linchpin," "yoke," "reins," and "to carry by wheeled vehicle". They knew boats (*nau-*) with oars (*ertrom-*), but no words for "sail," "rudder," or other nautical technology have survived. Archaeology shows that the steppe people made baskets and pots, decorating their pottery with geometric patterns of lines and dots. They spun and dyed fibers, wove and sewed cloth, and wove reeds or sedges into tough mats and carpets. They also knew gold (*auso-*), silver (*arg-*), and copper or bronze (*aios-*), and were sometimes buried with ornaments made of these metals, bone, or shell. No PIE word for iron can be reconstructed, which is consistent with the lack of evidence for iron smelting among the Kurgan cultures.

Proto-Indo-European societies were probably organized into extended families (*dems-*). The rite of naming a child was important; the phrases "to place a name" and "to bear a name," *nomen-dhe* and *nomen-bher*, have cognates in several languages. Indo-European society is usually considered to be patrilineal (descent and clan membership were traced through the male line) and patrilocal (a wife came to live with her husband's family). After all, the PIE word for "marriage," *wedh-*, literally meant "to lead [a bride] home." PIE expressions such as "master of the household" (*dems-potis*—cognate to our word "despot") are grammatically masculine; and we can reconstruct several specific words for a husband's or father's relatives (such as *swekru-*, "husband's mother," *daiwer-*, "husband's brother," and even *ienəter-*, "husband's brother's wife") but fewer for a wife's or mother's relatives. But there is one major exception: PIE used the same word for "grandfather" and "mother's brother" (*awos* or *awyos*), and the same word for "grandson" and "nephew" (*nepots*). This suggests a close relationship between maternal uncles and nephews, a relationship found in several later Indo-European traditions.[6] The mother's brother is the closest male relative whose status cannot be questioned—without DNA testing, it's impossible to be certain of who

---

6. For example, Tacitus mentioned it among the Germans: "sisters' children mean as much to their uncle as to their father" (*Germania* 20, transl. Hutton, pp. 162-163). In literature we have Sigurd and his maternal uncle Gripir, Beowulf and his maternal uncle Hygelac, Sigmundr and Sinfjǫtli, Roland and Charlemagne (in medieval legend), and so on.

one's father is, but there's never any doubt about one's mother. Furthermore, in patrilineal societies, the father is usually an authoritarian figure; since one's mother's brother is the closest male relative who is outside the patri-lineage, he can afford to be a kinder, friendlier figure. (In matrilineal societies, in which one's descent and family membership is reckoned through the maternal line, the situation is usually reversed: the maternal uncle is the disciplinarian, and relations with the father are more relaxed.) Anthropologists call this the "Omaha kinship system," after a Native American tribe that used it. Although the PIE data doesn't fit the Omaha pattern perfectly, and some scholars have expressed skepticism, Omaha kinship seems to be closest to what we can reconstruct for PIE speakers (Mallory and Adams, *Encyclopedia of Indo-European Culture*, pp. 332-335).

Words for "head of the household; family leader" (*dems-potis*) and "village or clan leader" (*wik-potis*) can be reconstructed with high probability. Olmsted ("Archaeology and Social Evolution") has argued, based on comparisons of social structures in early IE societies, that Proto-Indo-European society was based on clientship, in which groups of free farmers and producers were led by a relatively small elite. The highest-ranking leaders bore the title *regs*, which seems to be derived from a root meaning "to straighten, to set right," or possibly from a root meaning "to have power". The tribes they ruled (*teuto-*) were presumably made up of several clans which had allied with each other for mutual benefit. We can reconstruct legal terms such as *oitos-* "oath," *bʰendʰ-* and *leig-* "to bond together," *mei-* "to tie; to make a contract," *weghw-* "to vow," *uadʰ-* "to pledge," and *kʷei-* "to pay compensation," as evidence for how PIE alliances were maintained. Gift-giving was important in maintaining social bonds; words for gifts (*de-*), rewards (*mis-dʰos-*), and exchange (*mei-*) can be reconstructed. The root *ghos-ti-* gave rise to our word "guest" and to the Latin words for both "guest" (*hospes*) and "stranger, enemy" (*hostis*), from which English later borrowed both "hospitable" and "hostile". This suggests an ambivalent attitude towards strangers; Proto-Indo-European speakers may have had a tradition of ritualized hospitality as a sacred obligation, similar to the ancient Greek custom of *xenia* (which is also derived from *ghos-ti-*). For the times when hospitality went wrong, words for "fortified high place" (*pele-*, *dʰuno-* and *bʰergh-*), "war-band" (*lawa-*), "battle" (*katu-*), "fight" (*weik-*), "throwing spear" (*gaisos*), and "bow" and/or "arrow" (*erkwos*) show that warfare was not unknown.

Burial customs varied somewhat in space and time. In general, the steppe peoples buried their dead in rectangular pits with wooden floors, sometimes with wooden ceilings and posts. Woven mats of reeds or grasses were laid on the floors and sometimes hung on the walls, and folded animal skins, or pillows stuffed with dried grasses, were placed under the head of the deceased. The dead were placed in these graves individually, or sometimes in small groups; in Yamnaya culture burials most were buried on their backs with their knees flexed and their heads to the east. The living raised a circle of stones and a low mound (now referred to by the Russian name *kurgan*) over the grave. Kurgans were built in long rows, probably marking out seasonal travel routes. Yamnaya kurgans were topped with a stone slab carved with a humanlike figure, possibly a representation of the deceased. The dead were provided with grave goods, including weapons, pottery (including small wide bowls that are thought to be incense burners), jewelry for women (including ornamented headdresses and distinctive hammer-headed bone pins), and in a few cases entire wagons. There's also evidence of animal sacrifice associated with

Yamnaya burial from the Volgograd region. Photo by Xvoladzx, Wikimedia Commons, CC BY 2.5.

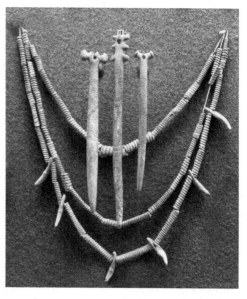

Yamnaya jewelry from a grave. Photo by Xvoladzx, Wikimedia Commons, CC BY 2.5.

burials, notably of sheep, cows and horses. In a few cases, the dead were buried with other humans who appear to have been slain (or committed suicide) as part of the funeral rites. Red ochre is common in steppe graves, often found powdered and sprinkled on the body (Shishlina, *Reconstruction*, pp. 43-82).

Incidentally, analysis of ancient DNA shows that the steppe people who probably spoke Proto-Indo-European languages had a range of skin tones, but were generally darker than most Europeans today (Wilde et al., "Direct Evidence for Positive Selection"). Sorry, bigots.

Indo-European Religion

There has been much debate over what the religion of the Proto-Indo-European speakers might have looked like, and scholars have devised several different reconstructions. For reasons of space, we can't get too deeply into the controversies.

Three Functions?

The scholar Georges Dumézil and his followers have made the most sweeping attempts to reconstruct an original structure for PIE religion.[7] In Dumézil's view, Proto-Indo-European society was structured as a tripartite hierarchy, reflected both in the roles of the gods and goddesses and the society of Germanic folk. There are three divine "functions": Ruler (magician, priest, judge), Warrior, and Provider. According to Dumézil, the Proto-Indo-Europeans' deities filled three main functions, mirrored in three main social roles: sovereignty, force, and abundance. Deities of the first function are divine rulers: Dumézil subdivided this role into a deity of law and justice, and a deity of magic and cosmic order. (In the Vedas of India, these would be Mitra and Varuna; in Norse mythology, they would be Tyr and Odin.) Deities of the second function are warriors who defend the cosmic order; the Norse god in this function would be Thor. Finally, third-function deities provide

---

7. Dumézil's ideas are spread through multiple books, and they changed over the course of his career. Thus the handiest guides to Dumézil's thought are not by Dumézil: Jaan Puhvel's *Comparative Mythology* is probably the best reference, while C. Scott Littleton's *The New Comparative Mythology* covers the changes in Dumézil's ideas over the course of his career, and his introduction to *Gods of the Ancient Northmen* is a handy overview.

fertility, healing, and prosperity, and provide for the common people; often they are seen as a pair of twins. The third-function deities in Norse mythology would be the Vanir. Dumézil argued that this three-fold division affected almost every aspect of society. Indo-European descendant cultures tend to emphasize tripartism in ritual and social structure. For instance, there are comparative suggestions that at rituals, a constellation of three different types of animal was sacrificed. Healing was carried out in three ways, each reminiscent of one of the functions: magical spells, surgery, and herbs (Watkins, *How to Kill a Dragon*, pp.

Details of the tapestry from Skog Church, Hälsingland, Sweden. These three figures have been identified by some scholars as (L to R) Odin, Thor, and Freyr, embodying Dumézil's three functions. Alternately, they could be three saints. Swedish Historical Museum 96352, CC BY 2.5.

537-539). Human sacrifices were generally done in three different ways: hanging, stabbing, and drowning, also corresponding to the three functions.

Dumézil's theories have been extremely influential in academia and remain influential among Heathens today. Edred Thorsson has championed Dumézil in particular, explaining the functions in *A Book of Troth* (p. 72):

[The hierarchy] must be arranged in just this way: sovereignty must rule over force, and generation must serve the interests of the whole again under the direction of sovereignty. The king commands the warrior, and the farmer, or worker, provides for all.[8]

However, while Dumézil assembled an impressive range of information, his theories came to reflect an idealized Indo-European society rather than

---

8. The most perfect example of a Dumézilian trifunctional society is Equestria in *My Little Pony: Friendship is Magic*, populated by magic-wielding unicorns, warrior pegasi, and hard-working earth ponies. All are governed by the rare alicorns: semidivine rulers who, like Konr ungr in *Rígsþula*, incorporate all the functions in themselves.

known societies, especially in the later part of his career (cf. Page, "Dumézil Revisited"; Lincoln, *Death, War and Sacrifice*, pp. 244-258; Arvidsson, *Aryan Idols*, p. 243). On the one hand, most agrarian societies, Indo-European or not, develop very similar threefold class systems (or fourfold, if merchants are considered a separate class), with similar roles and expectations for each class (Priestland, *Merchant, Soldier, Sage*, pp. 20-28). Dumézil's tripartite system also ignores two classes of folk who are important in actual societies: the crafters, who are sometimes classed as "third function" but who, especially as smiths, were thought to have magical powers; and the marginal figures of the thrall and the outlaw. On the other hand, the structures which Dumézil claims to be common to the Indo-European folk are not complete within any individual branch, and so it's unclear how well they might apply to the Proto-Indo-Europeans.

Among most of the Germanic-speaking tribes, people simply did not occupy roles corresponding to a single function. A ruler was expected to bring fruitfulness to the land; every free person should be able to serve as a warrior; and the sovereign gifts of magic and poetry were never restricted to nobles—the free farmers of Iceland produced the greatest poets of the Viking Age. Nor can any of the deities be limited to a single primary function: our gods and goddesses have a habit of walking right through the walls between the neatly defined functions we construct for them (Gunnell, "Pantheon? What Pantheon?," pp. 67-68). The supposedly third-function Freyr, for instance, is also a founder of a royal dynasty, and appears together with his father Njǫrðr in the priestly role (first function). In *Ynglinga saga*, Snorri specifically refers to these two as being not only *blótgoðar* (blessing-godmen) but also priests (*díar*) among the gods. Freyr is also called "battle-wise" and "leader of the host" in skaldic poetry (second function). We have many more references to Thor as a god of hallowing (first function) than as a patron of warriors, and he could also be invoked for fertility (third function). Odin himself was the chief battle-god (second function) of the Germanic peoples at least in the late Iron Age; and his original function was probably that of death-god, a role which has no clear place anywhere in the tripartite system. Although Snorri Sturluson's *Prose Edda* calls Óðinn the ruler of the pantheon, older sources show that the god who was seen as highest varied from tribe to tribe: Freyr was particularly worshipped among the Swedes, for example, while Thor was most generally the chief god in the Norwegian hofs.

Saga accounts, place names, and personal names provide far more evidence for devotion to Thor, Freyr, and Njord among the settlers of Iceland than to Odin (Gunnell, "How High was the High One?," pp. 105-114). There is no evidence in any source older than Snorri, who was writing two hundred years after the conversion of Iceland, that Odin, or any single deity for that matter, was ever seen as having authority over any of the others. In short, for the Dumézilian system to stand up within Germanic religion, one must ignore sizable amounts of evidence and focus only on the latest and most literary renditions of the tales.[9]

With all that said, many Heathens continue to find Dumézil's threefold model to be powerful for ritual and belief. Yet sticking too closely to structuralist literalism may not be helpful in understanding how our forebears really saw the world, the gods, and their relationship to both.

Proto-Indo-European Religion

What we can know of Proto-Indo-European religion from reconstructed vocabulary suggests a rich tradition of religious thought. Their language seems to have had two words for "sacred," one meaning "filled with power" (*spent-) and one meaning "set apart from the world" (*yag-); this distinction is made in several Indo-European traditions even when the words are not preserved. Proto-Indo-European had roots for "good" and "bad," *esu- and *dus-, but these probably just meant "favorable" and "unfavorable," without moral connotations. What was moral was to follow the social and cosmic order (*ertus), religious laws (*yewes-), and human laws (*dhemi-, derived from *dhe- "to place; to lay down"). The metaphor of law as something "laid down" survived even when the word itself was replaced; English *law* and Latin *lex* both come from *legh-, "to lay down." A lawbreaker was a *wergh, an outcast, cognate with Norse *vargr* (Mallory and Adams, *Oxford Introduction*, pp. 276-277). "To believe" was *kred-dhe-, literally "to place one's heart"; to be "holy" was to be "complete, whole" (*kailo-). The root

---

9. In the 1920s and 1930s, Dumézil was a supporter of the Fascist organization Action Française, and several of his closest colleagues also had ties to Fascist or outright Nazi groups. Dumézil's theory of Indo-European tripartite organization bears an uncomfortable resemblance to the ideal society proposed by French and Italian Fascists, divided into castes of leaders, soldiers, and commoners. See Arvidsson, *Aryan Idols*, p. 241; Lincoln, *Death, War, and Sacrifice*, pp. 231-243; *Theorizing Myth*, pp. 121-127).

deru- meant "firm, solid, strong"; from this root come our words "true," "trust" and "troth" (as well as "tree"). There is debate over whether we can reconstruct a PIE word for "priest," but whoever worshipped in Proto-Indo-European society did so in familiar ways: we can reconstruct roots *prek- and *meldh-, "to pray"; *gheuə- "to invoke"; *sengʷh- "to sing"; *gʷerə- "to praise"; *peu- "to purify"; *dap- "sacrificial meal"; and *spend-, *leib-, and *gheu- "to libate; to make an offering" (Dowden, *European Paganism*, pp. 250-251). The root *gheu-, "to pour," is especially interesting, because it is probably the source of our word "god"; etymologically, a "god" is "one who receives what is poured out" (Watkins, *The American Heritage Dictionary*, pp. 30-31). We can also reconstruct *aiw- for "vital force" or "spirit." The root *wet- meant "to inspire, spiritually arouse." In this sense it survives in Latin *vates* and Irish *fáith*, both meaning "soothsayer," and in two Old English words, *wōd*, "madness," and *wōþ*, "song." The combination of this root with a PIE-derived suffix meaning "master of," *-ono-, is the source of the Proto-Germanic name *Woðanaz—Woden, Wotan, Óðinn.

Several religions derived from Indo-European culture posit two tribes of godly beings, one of which upholds cosmic order and receives worship. The other is identified with the forces of chaos and destruction, and may be appeased or banished in ritual, but is never asked for blessings. In Vedic India, the divine "good guys" are *devas* opposed to the demonic *asuras*; in Persia the situation is reversed, and the good *ahuras* are opposed to the demonic *daevas*. Both derive from Proto-Indo-European; the PIE word for "god" (*deiwos*) is related to the word for "bright" (*dyeu-*). The word *ansu- meant something like "ruler" or "governor"; it survives in Sanskrit *asura*, Persian *ahura*, the Gaulish god's name *Esus*, the Gothic word *anses* (defined as "demigods" by the historian Jordanes), and the ON *Æsir* (Watkins, *How to Kill a Dragon*, pp. 8-9). While the linguistic roots have shifted, the Greek Titans and the Norse Jǫtnar, or possibly Muspili, seem to fit the role of destructive forces (York, "Towards a Proto-Indo-European Vocabulary of the Sacred," pp. 235-237). Also common to PIE cultures is a myth of the "War of the Functions," in which the gods of rulership and force fight against the gods of fertility and abundance, ending in the integration of the two groups; the Norse version of this myth is the war between the Æsir and Vanir. Lastly, the Proto-Indo-Europeans knew a myth concerning a cataclysmic battle between two cosmic armies, with the Gods and/or heroes fighting the personified forces of chaos, ending in total destruction and the beginning of a completely new order of things. In some Indo-European traditions this battle has already occurred, in the mythic past, such as the Irish Second Battle of Mag Tuired and the Indian Kurukshetra War. In others, such as the Norse Ragnarǫk, it lies in the future (Puhvel, *Comparative Mythology*, pp. 284-285).

Judging by practices preserved in early Indo-European descendant cultures, the greater gods received their offerings from priests who inherited the knowledge of the correct ritual procedures and hymns, passed down through certain families. The horse sacrifice (*ekwo-medhyo-*, literally "horse-drunkenness") was the most elaborate ritual, associated with kingship and kingly power. If properly worshipped, the gods would grant prosperity to the people; we can reconstruct the phrase *dotores weswam*, "givers of goods," as a term for the gods. (Lincoln, *Death, War, and Sacrifice*, p. 6) From phrases common to several languages, we can even reconstruct a prayer showing what the gods were asked to do: *pah- uiro- peku-*, "protect men and cattle!" (Watkins, *How to Kill a Dragon*, p. 212)

The steppe peoples built no temples; as far as we can tell, worship was centered on the household. Proto-Indo-European had two words for "fire": one was grammatically an inanimate noun, *paǝwr-*. The other, *egni-*, was grouped with nouns for animate objects, suggesting a PIE belief in fire as a living being; this is the root of the Vedic god Agni, who was seen as accepting sacrifices and distributing shares to the gods. In India in the Vedic period, sacrifices were made to fires kindled on the altars. A round altar, the *garhapatya*, was and still is stationed in the west and represents the earth and the family, while a square altar, the *ahavaniya*, represents the sky and the gods. The Greeks and Romans had a similar duality of shape, with the family hearth fire maintained on a round altar and the offerings to the gods made on a rectangular altar (Della Volpe, "From the Hearth," pp. 165-167). Square and round arrangements of burned stones and bones, almost certainly fire altars, have also been excavated from the Bronze Age and Iron Age of Scandinavia. This similarity between cultures at nearly the opposite ends of the Indo-European world implies that the Proto-Indo-Europeans sacrificed at similar altars. These may have been made on top of kurgans; the mound may have functioned as an altar, where sacrifices could be made to the gods and the ancestors (Kaliff, *Fire, Water, Heaven and Earth*, pp. 75-84, figs.

3-9). The father and mother of each family or clan probably made offerings at their hearth fires to their ancestors, and perhaps to the minor deities of the household as well: the powers of the courtyard, the livestock, the trees and groves, all the host of godlets who protected the people from calamity (Della Volpe, pp. 157-167).

We can reconstruct an Indo-European myth of the origin of the world, which began with two primal beings: "Man" (*Manu) and "Twin" (*Yema or *Hiemos). Man, the first priest, had sacrificed Twin, the first king, who went on to become lord of the dead, the first to find the path that all others would have to follow. Man then created the world from the body of Twin, making stones from his bones, soil from his flesh, wind and water from his breath and blood, the sun from his eye, the moon from his mind, and the vault of the sky from his skull. Whenever a priest sacrificed, he was re-enacting the primal sacrifice, and his sacrifice upheld and renewed the cosmic order. Each death was also a recreation of the original sacrifice. Those who know the Norse myth of Ymir should compare it with a funeral hymn in the *Rig-Veda*, sung to the dead man:

> May your eye go to the sun, your life's breath to the wind. Go to the sky or earth, as is your nature; or go to the waters, if that is your fate. Take root in the plants with your limbs. (*Rig-Veda* 10.16.3; transl. O'Flaherty, p. 49)

Different social classes of humans had come from different parts of Twin—rulers from the head, warriors from the arms, workers from the legs—and so the myth and the sacrifices based on it upheld the social as well as the cosmic order (Puhvel, *Comparative Mythology*, pp. 286-290; Lincoln, *Death, War and Sacrifice*, pp. 167-175).

There seems to have been a PIE myth about a warrior named *Trito, "Third"—possibly the younger brother of *Manu and *Yema, and possibly the paradigm of warriors, just as *Manu's sacrifice established the priestly role. The cattle of *Trito were stolen by a three-headed serpent. With divine help, *Trito killed the serpent and recovered the stolen cattle. The phrase "he slew the serpent," *$g^w hen$- $og^w hi$-, has been reconstructed from appearances in several descendant languages (Watkins, *How to Kill a Dragon*, p. 365). The story is not preserved in Germanic texts, but it may be depicted

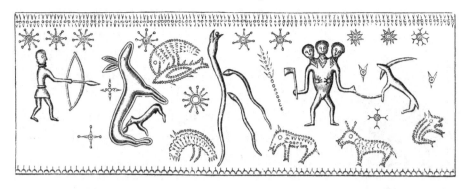

Design on one of the now-lost Golden Horns of Gallehus, Denmark.
Stephens, Stephens, Old-Northern Runic Monuments, 1866-7.

on one of the Golden Horns of Gallehus, from the Iron Age of Denmark, albeit with the serpent changed into a giant. References in skaldic poetry to Thor defeating a giant named Þrivaldi, "Three Powers," might also point to the ancient tale. (See Lincoln, "The Indo-European Cattle-Raiding Myth.")

There is reasonably good linguistic evidence that the Indo-Europeans worshipped a Sky-Father or Bright Father, *Dyeus pəter,* whose name survives in the Latin *Jupiter* and Sanskrit *Dyaus-pita*, and, minus the "father," in Greek *Zeus* and Norse *Týr*. He may have had a female consort, *Diuone* (Jackson, "Light From Distant Asterisks," p. 73). Jackson further suggests that *Dyeus* may have had a counterpart god of the night sky, whose name would have been something like *Uorunos,* "the one who covers." Dumézil theorizes a double sky-rulership, in which the Bright Father (who may have been seen as one-handed) governed human law, the day, and light, while his counterpart, the "Seer" (perhaps seen as one-eyed), represented the powers of magic, night, and darkness ("'Le Borgne' and 'Le Manchot,'" pp. 17-28).

The Indo-Europeans probably also knew a thunder and storm god, *Perkʷons* (a name which survived in Old Norse as *Fjǫrgynn*, the mother of Thor). The Storm Lord brought the life-giving rains and protected his people and their herds from enemies, wielding a great axe, hammer, or mace—his very name is derived from *perkʷ-*, "to strike". Some sculptures from the steppe cultures depict a powerful, mustached male figure carrying axes, clubs or hammers (Telegin and Mallory, *The Anthropomorphic Stelae of the Ukraine*, especially figs. 8, 9, 10-1). Although it is difficult to be certain who is portrayed, these sculptures could well represent the Storm Lord.

Replica of the Kernosovsky Stele, Photo by Denis Vitchenko, Wikimedia Commons, CC BY-SA 3.0.

In myth, the Storm Lord was known for fighting and slaying a monstrous dragon or serpent, the embodiment of chaos and devastation (Watkins, *How to Kill a Dragon*, pp. 297-303).

Other important celestial deities included the Sun Goddess (*Swel-*), the daughter of the Bright Father; the expression *suens kʷekʷlos,* "the wheel of the Sun" can be reconstructed for PIE. The name of the Moon (*Men-*) was derived from a root meaning "to measure" (*me-*), since his cycle of phases measured time. We can also reconstruct the Dawn Goddess (*Ausos*) and the Twins (*Diuos sunu),* who were often considered to be the daughter and the sons or grandsons of the Bright Father. In some Indo-European traditions, the Twins are identified with the Morning and Evening Stars; in others, they are identified with the horses that pull the Sun. They were seen as horsemen or closely associated with horses, and were known to be helpful, bringing wealth and rescuing persons in distress (Mallory and Adams, *Oxford Introduction,* p. 432). Artifacts from the steppe cultures depicting twinned figures of humans or horses may well be depictions of the Twins (Mallory, *In Search of the Indo-Europeans,* figs. 121-122; Telegin and Mallory, *The Anthropomorphic Stelae of the Ukraine,* especially figs. 23-1,2, 24-3).

Death was personified by a female figure, *Kolyo,* "The Coverer" (same root as the name of the Norse goddess Hel), who was seen as half living and half decaying, and who bound the dead in unbreakable bonds (Lincoln, *Death, War and Sacrifice,* pp. 78-80). The dead were thought of as choosing to cross one of two different bridges, each of which led to a different afterlife (Lincoln, pp. 119-127). Several Indo-European traditions also show the dead being ferried across a river by an aged ferryman (Lincoln, pp. 62-75). However, Bruce Lincoln has argued that all of these myths were metaphors for physical aging and death, rather than actual descriptions of afterlife events; he questions whether the Proto-Indo-Europeans believed in any real survival of the soul after death.

The two most important deities of the land were the Lord of Water and the Moisture Mother. The Lord of Water (*Nepto-no-*) was god of the waters beneath the earth. Paradoxically, he was also the ancestor of Fire, seen as a kind of radiance or vital energy within the water. Fire is poetically called "descendant of water" in several IE traditions—including Old Norse poetry, which preserved the kenning *sævar niðr*, "descendant of seas," for fire (*Ynglingatal* 7, in *Ynglinga saga* 14, ÍF 26, p. 31; see Puhvel, *Comparative Mythology*, pp. 277-283; Mallory and Adams, *Oxford Companion*, p. 438). The Moisture Mother was the goddess of the fertile earth that sustained the people's crops and the grasses for their livestock. In several Indo-European traditions, she is the spouse and/or sibling of the Sky-Father; in others, she is the counterpart of the Striker, *Perk^wons*. The Indo-European word *dhg^homyo-*, which ultimately gave rise to the English "human," is derived from *dhg^em*, "earth"—perhaps reflecting the return of human bodies after death to the Moisture Mother's keeping. One version of the Moisture Mother was the goddess *Donu*, "River." She may have been regarded as the ancestress of many tribes: the *Danavas* of Persia, the *Danaans* of Greece, the *Tuatha de Danaan* of Ireland, and possibly the *Danes* of Denmark, all seem to preserve her name. On the other hand, she sometimes appears as a hostile force, or as the mother of a water monster that a hero slays. Many rivers of the steppe country still bear her name, including the Don, the Donets, the Dniepr ("River to the Rear"), and the Dniestr ("River to the Front"). The Danube ("Holy River") is also hers (Dexter, "Reflections on the Goddess *Donu*").

Comparative studies of magic and spells in Indo-European cultures, together with alterations of "taboo" words in PIE, show that the Proto-Indo-European speakers knew and feared spoken curses and spells (Huld, "Magic, Metathesis and Nudity"). The Proto-Indo-European speakers also used magic for healing; various healing charms known in Old English and Old High German have analogues throughout the Indo-European sphere (Watkins, *How to Kill a Dragon*, pp. 519-536). Wolves and bears are thought to have been sacred or taboo, because their original names (*vlkos* and *rktos*) ended up either respelled, or replaced by euphemistic names, in many Indo-European languages. (For example: the words "bear" and "bruin" and their Germanic cognates mean "the brown one," while the Russian word *medved*' literally means "honey-knower.") No evidence for Indo-European shamanistic practices has yet been put forward, but there is evidence for the use of intoxicating plants or brews: the people made an alcoholic drink for ritual (and perhaps other) use, *medhu*, probably mead or much like it. Some cultures used different intoxicants in ritual, notably *soma* in Vedic India.

History, law, rituals, myths, and other forms of knowledge were transmitted orally by poets, whose training might take many years. Indo-European poetry involved the use of complex meters and rhythms, various stylistic devices, and special vocabulary. Many of these features are shared in detail by medieval Irish, ancient Greek, Germanic, Vedic, and other Indo-European poetic traditions. A poet—or *wek^wom tekson*, "weaver of words," as he would have called himself—would have been rewarded by chieftains and warriors for making songs of praise. His poems, in turn, would confer *klewos ndhg^whitom*, "undying fame," upon their subjects. This symbiotic relationship between rulers and the poets who praised them is widespread in Indo-European cultures (Watkins, *How to Kill a Dragon*, pp. 12-14, 68-84). Whatever beliefs the Proto-Indo-Europeans may have held about an afterlife, the only immortality that warriors seems to have cared about was *klewos ndhg^whitom*. (Lincoln, *Death, War, and Sacrifice*, pp. 14-15) We see this attitude in the careers of Achilles, Cú Chulainn, and the Nart heroes of the Caucasus, who are all depicted as deliberately choosing a short life with undying fame over a long life in obscurity (Homer, *Iliad* IX.410-416, transl. Murray, pp. 410-413; Gantz, *Early Irish Myths and Sagas*, p. 141; Colaruso, *Nart Sagas*, p. 11). We see this also in Beowulf, who is praised after his death as *lofgeornost*, "the most eager for fame" (*Beowulf* 3182), and in Magnús Barefoot's aphorism *til frægðar skal konung hafa, en ekki til langlifis*: "kings are meant for fame, not for long life" (*Magnúss saga berfœtts* 26, ÍF 28 p. 237).

Indo-European Speakers in Europe

The steppe cultures migrated away from the steppes in three directions. The earliest entered Asia Minor, giving rise to the Anatolian languages such as Hittite, the earliest branch of the Indo-European language family. (Ancient DNA analysis has shown that the people who spoke Hittite were not closely related to the steppe people. In this case, there's no evidence for a mass migration. Perhaps Anatolian populations adopted an early Indo-European language for trade purposes, or perhaps a small IE-speaking elite managed to dominate a large local population. See Mathieson et al., "The Genomic History of Southeastern Europe," p. 201; and Damgaard et al., "The First Horse Herders.") The second branch moved westwards into the Altai Mountains, giving rise to the extinct languages now known as Tocharian (and possibly to the famous "red-haired mummies" of China's Tarim Basin). And the third branch, speaking what are now called "Core Indo-European" languages, moved into southeastern Europe, heading up the Danube valley and around the Carpathian Mountains (Anthony and Ringe, "The Indo-European Homeland," pp. 210-212).

Steppe migrants following the Danube up into Europe would have found themselves in another world. Although the adoption of farming had already deforested some areas, much of Europe was still covered with vast forests. It was also full of people: in the Danube valley and Carpathian foothills, the migrants came into contact with the Cucuteni-Trypillia (or Cucuteni-Tripolye) culture, one of several cultures descended from the migrating Near East farmers.

These farming cultures of what Marija Gimbutas called "Old Europe" extended from present-day Czechia and the western Ukraine south to the Balkans and Greece, and they had reached a high level of sophistication (Gimbutas, *The Gods and Goddesses of Old Europe*, pp. 17-35). The people lived in clay and timber houses, many with two stories, in sizable towns located on high plains, defended by palisades and surrounded by crop fields. They made sophisticated ceramics with painted geometric and swirling designs. They smelted copper from ores to make tools and jewelry, although they had not yet started adding tin to their copper to make bronze.[10] They mined and worked gold, and made ornaments from colorful *Spondylus* clam shells, traded from the Mediterranean (Séfériadès, "Spondylus and Long-Distance Trade," pp. 178-189). One Balkan culture of "Old Europe," the Vinča culture, made markings on ceramics that could be an early form of writing, although whether it truly represented language is unclear. While these cultures are often claimed to be egalitarian, some definitely had elites; the cemetery at Varna, Bulgaria, dated from 4600 to 4200 BCE, included graves

---

10. The time frame when copper was smelted but bronze was not made is known as the Eneolithic or Chalcolithic.

Figurine of the Vinča culture, Serbia, 4000–3000 BCE. Cleveland Museum of Art. Public Domain.

rich in gold jewelry, including one man who was buried with over three pounds (1.5 kg) of gold. And most households had clay figurines, usually of broad-hipped females, often incised with geometric patterns. Marija Gimbutas famously interpreted these figurines as representing a Great Goddess (e.g. *The Language of the Goddess*, pp. 316-321). This interpretation has been questioned—some of them are clearly male, and a few figurines even seem to show a mix of gender signs. Nor did all figurines necessarily represent the same deity or have the same function. They may have represented ancestors or other spirit beings, or symbolized group identity or individual status (Tringham and Conkey, "Rethinking Figurines"; Bailey, "The Figurines of Old Europe," pp. 117-125).

The "Old Europe" cultures changed dramatically between around 4200 and 3800 BCE. Towns were burned and abandoned, fields ceased to be cultivated, and craft traditions were abandoned or modified. Despite this disruption, the Trypillia culture survived the stress and actually expanded eastward, adopting certain features of the steppe cultures, such as pottery styles, as they went (Anthony, *The Horse, The Wheel, and Language*, pp. 229-230).

Meanwhile, more cultural innovations were entering the steppes from the south, around or across the Caucasus mountains—creating a wealthy mixed culture in the north Caucasus called the Maikop culture, who made and exported arsenic bronze, used heavy ox-drawn wagons, and traded with the Sumerians to the south. Probably by way of the Maikop culture, the steppe peoples gained wheeled vehicles. By about 3300 BCE, the steppe peoples had shifted from partial reliance on herding to an almost completely nomadic herding existence, using both horses and ox-drawn wagons for increased mobility (although they still seem to have maintained some agricultural bases). They were still buried under kurgans, but often laid in their wagons and buried in them. For the first time, kurgans appear not only in the river valleys, but on the open steppes themselves, implying that people were able to spend extended periods away from the rivers by using their wagons as bases. Graves on the open steppes suggest that clans or tribes were now claiming ownership of territories that had not been claimed before. The resulting culture is now called the Yamnaya or "Pit-Grave" people (Baumer, *History of Central Asia*, pp. 89-97).

Branches of the Yamnaya culture moved rapidly into northern Europe along several routes around 3200 BCE. One branch of them seems to have moved up the Dniestr and absorbed the remains of the Trypillia culture, forming a hybrid culture known as the Usatovo culture (Baumer, *History of Central Asia*, pp. 78-79). These people then seem to have spread northwards. Joining with other people, including the Funnel Beaker culture in what is now Poland, they formed a new culture around 3000 BCE that expanded rapidly across eastern and central Europe, now called the Corded Ware culture. The Corded Ware culture is thought to have been created by people who included the ancestors of the later Baltic, Slavic, and Germanic-speaking peoples (Anthony, pp. 340-370).

Marija Gimbutas, and other writers who followed her, have concluded that the peaceful, egalitarian, Goddess-worshipping peoples of "Old Europe" were wiped out or subjugated by a wave of invasions by the violent, patriarchal Indo-European steppe horsemen (e.g. Gimbutas, *The Language of the Goddess*, pp. 318-320; Eisler, *The Chalice and the Blade*, pp. 42-58; see critique in Eller, *The Myth of Matriarchal Prehistory*, pp. 48-49, 89-90, 157-179). There's no question that violence was part of the drastic cultural change at this time: for example, the towns at Hotnitsa and Yunatsite in present-day Bulgaria were destroyed by fire, with their inhabitants buried under the ruins. At times of greatest stress, Trypillia towns built or expanded their defensive earthworks and palisades; violence was clearly a threat (Anthony, *The Horse, The Wheel, and Language*, p. 228). Analysis of ancient DNA shows that Y-chromosome DNA markers (inherited only through the male line) associated with the steppe cultures almost completely replaced markers associated with Neolithic farmers (Haak et al., "Massive Migration," p. 210). It's easy to interpret this as evidence for invading hordes killing off the native men and taking their women, even though this is not the only possible explanation (Hakenbeck, "Genetics, Archaeology and the Far Right," pp. 520).

The truth seems to be more complicated. A sweeping invasion of Indo-European horsemen, like the Mongol hordes over four thousand years later, is extremely unlikely: the steppe nomads were not organized into huge armies, and they lacked the short composite bows that made later steppe nomads like the Mongols so effective at fighting from horseback (Anthony, *The Horse, The Wheel, and Language*, pp. 236-238). There is genetic evidence for intermarriage between the Cucuteni-Trypillia people and the steppe people for at least a thousand years before the Trypillia culture came to an end (Mathieson et al., "The Genomic History of Southeastern Europe," p. 200), and there is archaeological evidence for cultural exchange as well, in the form of shared artifact styles (Anthony, pp. 231-225). Right as the steppe peoples were making contact, the farming cultures were also hit hard by climate change; a global cold spell between about 4200 and 3760 BCE, coupled with deforestation leading to increased flooding and erosion, and possibly exhaustion of soil fertility, put heavy stress on the food supply (Anthony, pp. 227-228). We can now add plague to the list of stressors: ancient DNA from plague bacteria has been recovered from Neolithic human remains, and the large towns of the Trypillia culture are a likely point of origin, from which plague could have spread along trade networks (Rascovan et al., "Emergence and Spread," pp. 299-301). Finally, some of the violence that afflicted the cultures of "Old Europe" was internal: the people had weapons, and they sometimes turned them on each other. One town was attacked by people firing arrows tipped with arrowheads made of the local flint: the attackers were neighbors, not roving nomads (Anthony, p. 223).

David Anthony has suggested that Indo-European speakers spread into Europe, not usually through conquest, by establishing a system of patronage. Towns under stress, running out of resources and increasingly coming into conflict with each other, may have sought out alliances with bands of steppe migrants. The migrants, for their part, may have hoped to acquire land, which is harder to steal than livestock. Such alliances would have been maintained through trade, hospitality, feasting, gift exchanges, ritual oaths, and intermarriage, all of which are well represented in PIE vocabulary. Of course, the relationship may not always have been peaceful. There would always be temptation for a band of steppe herders to rustle some of their allies' cattle, or even to abandon their allies if they saw the opportunity for a better deal elsewhere. Yet the PIE-speaking nomads almost certainly didn't carry out anything like the mass genocide that they are sometimes accused of (Anthony and Ringe, "The Indo-European Homeland," pp. 210-214).

The migrations of the Corded Ware people may have caused the first major linguistic division, between the *centum* branch in the west and the *satem* branch in the east. *Centum* and *satem* are the words for "one hundred" in Latin and Avestan respectively, both derived from PIE *kmtom; centum* languages retain the old PIE *k-, whereas in *satem* languages the *k- shifts to an *s-. Balto-Slavic and Indo-Iranian are the major *satem* branches, while Italo-Celtic, Greek, and Germanic are the main *centum* branches. That being said, the history of Indo-European languages is more like a network than a simple branching tree, since different Indo-European groups have always moved around, mingled, and influenced each other. For every nice, neat grouping of Indo-European language families, one can find similarities that cut across group boundaries. Germanic, for instance, borrowed many words from Celtic at an early stage (see the chapter on the Iron Age). Slavic is a *satem* family but shows many similarities to Germanic (a *centem* family) in vocabulary and grammar. Whether similarities like these reflect common linguistic ancestry or extensive borrowing is often very difficult to determine.

Coming into Northern Europe

The Corded Ware people are known to have shared genetic markers with the Yamnaya people, and some aspects of their culture were retained from their steppe ancestors. For example, the dead were buried in individual pit graves covered by mounds and surrounded by rings of stones, often arranged in lines on the landscape. Bodies were laid in these graves lying on their sides and facing south, with men's heads to the west and women's heads to the east. Such burials rapidly replaced the older Neolithic customs of communal burial sites such as long barrows and passage graves. Genetic and chemical analyses of human remains show that the founders of the Corded Ware culture were primarily males related to the Yamnaya, who commonly married women from surrounding farming cultures. How often such marriages were peaceful or forcible is not entirely clear, but there are several burials of Corded Ware men who died violent deaths. At Eulau, Saxony-Anhalt, Germany, around 2600 BCE, four families—including Corded Ware men, women who had grown up outside the region, and their children—were killed by another tribe (Haak et al., "Ancient DNA," pp. 18226-18231; Kristiansen et al., "Re-Theorising Mobility," pp. 337-340). Most modern European populations are genetic admixtures of three main source populations: western European hunter-gatherers (WHG), Near Eastern farmers, and Yamnaya/Corded Ware migrants (Lazaridis et al., "Ancient Human Genomes," pp. 409-413; Haak et al., "Massive Migration," pp. 210-211).

The Corded Ware people adapted as they intermarried with the Neolithic farmers and moved into new climates and conditions. They developed more sophisticated ceramics than their Yamnaya predecessors, decorating pots by pressing cords into the wet clay (hence the name "Corded Ware"). They seem to have adopted ritual drinking, reflected in the appearance of new forms of cups and bowls derived from the Funnel Beaker culture. They also learned more about agriculture from their new neighbors. European IE languages share a set of words for crops and agriculture that none of them share with the Asian IE languages, probably because Indo-European speakers in Europe borrowed these words from Neolithic farmers: *b^haw- or *b^hab^h- "bean," *lin- "flax," *orw-/erw- or *$ereb$- "pea," and *rap- "turnip," for example. Borrowed words for "shrimp" (*rek-), "walnut" (*$rais$-), "water bird" (*rod-),

Corded Ware vessel from Germany. National Archaeological Museum, Saint-Germain-en-Laye, France. Photo by DeuxPlusQuatre, Wikimedia Commons, Public Domain.

"blackbird" (*mesl-*), and "sturgeon" (*setr-*) further hint at the new world that IE speakers found as they migrated north and west (Iversen and Kroonen, "Talking Neolithic," pp. 511-525). The languages of the Neolithic farmers eventually died out, but they left a sizable heritage in the vocabulary of the new cultures.

Not only did the European IE languages borrow vocabulary from the non-IE peoples they encountered, the speakers of the ancestors of the Germanic branch specifically borrowed more vocabulary on top of that; some of these words are shared with Celtic, but none appear in other branches. These borrowings from an unknown "substrate" language include most of the Germanic nautical terms—words like "sea," "shore," "mast," "rudder" and "keel" (Sausverde, "*Seewörter* and Substratum"). The ancestral language to Germanic also borrowed words for local plants (such as apple, hemp, woad, dill, and clover) as well as animals (such as cat, heron, lark, teal [duck], and dove) and tools (axe, mattock, plough) (Polomé, "Who are the Germanic Peoples?"; Huld, "Linguistic Typology"; Schrijver, "Animal, Vegetable, and Mineral"). The linguist Theo Vennemann has suggested that all northern European IE languages have borrowed words, place names, and structures from indigenous languages which were related to Basque—and that later, the Germanic branch borrowed more words from a language related to Semitic, reflecting interactions with traders migrating up the Atlantic coast ("Languages in Prehistoric Europe," pp. 319-332; for a much more comprehensive and technical overview, see his book *Europa Vasconica—Europa Semitica*). His theory is controversial among linguists, but hasn't been conclusively disproven either, and is consistent with known prehistoric migration and trade routes. It has also been suggested the sound-shifts that are unique to the Germanic languages resulted from a non-IE people's accent when trying to speak a pre-Germanic language. Peter Schrijver (*Language Contact*, pp. 158-196) has argued that speakers of Balto-Finnic languages, ancestral to modern Finnish and Sámi, adopted early Germanic and triggered its unique sound shifts, at a time when both Germanic and Finnic were spoken on the south Baltic coast. It is certain that many words entered Finnish from very early Germanic during this time frame, and surely the influence wasn't one-way.

Polished flint "boat-axe." Granerud, Akershus, Norway. Kulturhistorisk Museum
C5365, University of Oslo. CC BY-SA 4.0.

The Corded Ware peoples may have adopted from the Funnel Beaker
people the custom of making distinctive stone axes with a boat-shaped outline, generally with one sharp end and one blunt hammer-like end. These
were left in male graves. These "Battle Axe" or "Boat Axe" cultures, also
known as the Single Grave culture because they retained the steppe cultures'
practice of burying their dead singly under small mounds, appeared in Scandinavia by 2800 BCE and soon spread north of the Arctic Circle (Østmo,
"The Indo-European Question"). Meanwhile, around roughly 2600 BCE,
the Corded Ware cultures of central Europe came into contact with the
Bell Beaker culture, which had appeared in what is now Portugal and was
spreading west, as discussed in Chapter 1. It's not yet clear whether, or to
what extent, the Corded Ware people were replaced or joined by Bell Beaker
migrants, or simply adopted Bell Beaker technologies. Whatever the case,
various branches of the Bell Beaker culture spread into central and northern
Europe, including Denmark. Around 1800 BCE, as bronze came into widespread use, the Stone Age "officially" came to an end.

The story that this chapter tells is not fixed. New discoveries are still
being made, old evidence is always being re-evaluated, and many points of
this story will be revised in the future. But this much seems certain: the
roots of our Troth run deep indeed. At their core, the cultural and spiritual
traditions of the Germanic-speaking peoples show strong kinship with the
ways of other Indo-European speakers. Yet what we can see of their history
shows a complex interweaving of peoples and ideas across the millennia.

Contributors:

1ˢᵗ edition: Sunwynn Ravenwood, with contributions from Gert McQueen.

2ⁿᵈ edition: Revised by Ben Waggoner, with help from Daniel Flores and Rich Riedlinger.

3ʳᵈ edition: Reorganization and new material by Ben Waggoner.

Corded pot from the Single Grave culture. Ny Ågård, Denmark. National Museum of Denmark. CC BY-SA 2.0.

Boats with rowers, an axe-wielder, and a lur-player. Tanum, Bohuslän, Sweden.
Photo by Erlend Bjørtvedt, Wikimedia Commons, CC BY-SA 3.0.

CHAPTER THREE

The Bronze Age

1800-500 BCE

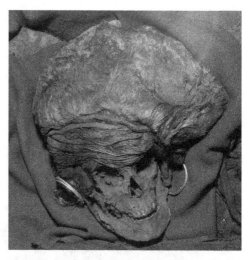

During the period known as the Bronze Age, cultures emerged in Scandinavia and on the Continent which were, if not the "Mothers," at least the "Grandmothers" of the religious traditions we follow now. Archaeology provides a rich testament to their lives and beliefs.

Head of the Skrydstrup Girl. National Museum of Denmark. CC BY-SA 2.0.

Diversifying Cultures

In the second millennium BCE, Bronze Age societies across Europe grew more diverse and complex, as compared to the relatively homogeneous Stone Age cultures. In Scandinavia, the Bronze Age is said to have begun around 1800 BCE and ended around 500 BCE, when iron came into common use. In central Europe, a slightly different division of time is used; the first stage is the Únětice Culture (2300-1600 BCE), which grew up around the largest source of tin in central Europe, the mountains on the present-day German-Czech border still known as the *Erzgebirge*, the Ore Mountains. The Únětice Culture was followed by the Urnfield Culture, or more accurately a group of related cultures (1300-900 BCE)—reflecting a major shift in burial practices, from burials in mounds to cremation burials in urns placed in gravefields. The Urnfield group expanded west and south all the way to eastern France and northern Italy, and is suspected of having influenced the later Etruscan culture (Price, *Europe Before Rome*, pp. 245-248).

In the far north, where agriculture was difficult, Stone Age ways continued with little change. There is some evidence for coastal settlements of farmers, who probably raised livestock and pastured them in the mountains during the summer. The interior, however, remained populated by foragers. Farther south, mixed agriculture was the norm; hunting and fishing never died out, but became less common, possibly because of human-induced environmental changes such as forest clearing (Harding, *European Societies in the Bronze Age,* p. 136). With the climate slightly warmer than today, crops like millet could be grown. Spinning, sewing and weaving were sophisticated arts (Harding, pp. 254-265). Ceramics continued to be made but were not especially decorative; for purposes of prestige and display, people seem to have preferred metal containers.

Reconstructed Bronze Age house, Borum Eshøj, Denmark.
Photo by Erik Christensen, Wikimedia Commons, CC BY-SA 4.0.

Relatively little is known about the lives of ordinary people in the Scandinavian Bronze Age; most of our knowledge comes from rich hoards and burials. We do know that throughout the Bronze Age in both Scandinavia and north Germany, people lived in long rectangular timber houses. In the earliest Bronze Age, houses were held up by a single central row of posts, but a new type of house soon developed, with two rows of posts dividing the interior into three aisles. Wattle and daub—woven twigs plastered with clay—was used for the walls and interior partitions. Cattle could be stalled at one end; in winter, not only would the cattle have been protected, but their body heat would have warmed the human inhabitants. Such great three-aisled houses continued to be built all the way to the end of the Viking Age (Oma, "Long Time—Long House," pp. 12-17). Houses were usually not clustered tightly in the Bronze Age, but at some sites, such as Forsandmoen in Norway, houses were grouped closely enough to create what might be called a village. Some of these houses could be huge: the house at Skrydstrup in Denmark was 50 meters by 10 meters, covering an area larger than a basketball court (Price, *Ancient Scandinavia*, pp. 236-238).

Trade Networks

As the name suggests, the Bronze Age peoples of Germany and southern Scandinavia worked in bronze and copper, and these had to be imported. Scandinavia does have some copper ores, but they were not used at this time, probably because they are difficult to smelt. Tin, the other component of bronze, is only found in isolated spots, not necessarily in the same places where copper can be mined—and not in Scandinavia at all. The need to have both copper and tin drove the development of large-scale trade networks, and the Scandinavian people plugged right into these networks when they adopted bronze. The oldest Scandinavian bronze came from the Tyrol region in central Europe—but by 1500 BCE, significant amounts of bronze were coming from as far as Britain, the Italian Alps, and Iberia, and some came all the way from Sardinia and Cyprus (Ling et al., "Moving Metals II," pp. 125-129; Melheim et al., "Moving Metals III," pp. 100-103). The extent of these trade networks is corroborated by rock art from Sweden that depicts the distinctive "oxhide" bronze ingots that were produced on Crete (Ling and Uhnér, "Rock Art and Metal Trade," p. 27, figs. 8-9). Some bronze objects, such as the Balkåkra bronze "drum," found at Skåne in Sweden and dated to 1500 BCE, were made in central Europe and imported as finished works. Nonetheless, many Scandinavian bronze artifacts were made in local workshops, as shown by finds of molds for casting. Many of these objects show exceptional craftsmanship, from fine axes and swords, to the great *lurs*—blowing horns probably used in ritual.

Bronze casting mold for an axehead. Bregnemøse By, Denmark. National Museum of Denmark, CC BY-SA 2.0.

High-status female buried in an oak tree trunk coffin, Ølby, Denmark. The beads by her left shoulder include a blue glass bead that has been traced to a workshop in Amarna, Egypt, around the time of Tutankhamun. Müller, *Vor Oldtid* (1897).

What the people were trading in exchange for bronze was amber, which was highly prized as a gem and for making perfumes and medicines (Singer, "Amber Exchange," pp. 253-256). The richest Baltic amber deposits are located on the Sambia Peninsula (now part of the Kaliningrad region of Russia), and there is also amber in Jutland. Erosion of coasts and riverbeds releases amber pieces into the ocean, and because amber floats in salt water, pieces wash up on shores all over the Baltic. A network of Bronze Age trade routes, collectively called the "Amber Road," led from the Baltic coast southwards. Caches of amber found near mining regions in Italy and Germany suggest that the Únětice people of central Europe were the middlemen, trading amber for bronze (Ling et al., "Moving Metals II," fig. 19; Melheim et al., "Moving Metals III," p. 103). From there, amber was brought south to the Adriatic coast, entering the rich trade among the Mediterranean Bronze Age kingdoms. A Bronze Age shipwreck off Uluburun, Turkey was found to be carrying cargo from all over the Mediterranean and beyond: copper from Cyprus, tin mined in Afghanistan, ebony and ivory from Africa, aromatic resin from the Middle East, glass, spices, ceramics—and Baltic amber (Mukherjee et al., "The Qatna Lion," p. 56; Cline, *1177 B.C.*, pp. 73-79). Splendid necklaces made from Baltic amber have been found in Mycenaean tombs on Crete (Harding, *European Societies in the Bronze Age*, p. 189-191), and an amber seal carved with Linear B signs—the oldest written form of Greek, used by the Mycenaean civilization—turned up at Bernsdorf, Germany, which seems to have been a trading depot (Price, *Ancient Scandinavia*, p. 199). Even a few Egyptian artifacts have been tentatively identified as Baltic amber—notably, necklaces and a scarab from the tomb of Tutankhamun (Serpico, "Resins, Amber and Bitumen," pp. 451-454). A royal burial at Qatna, Syria, from ca. 1340 BCE, contained beads and a lion's head carved from amber that definitely came from the Baltic (Mukherjee et al.). Goods traveled the other way: blue glass beads from Egypt and the Middle East reached Scandinavia. One blue glass bead from a rich female burial at Ølby, Denmark was analyzed chemically, and turned out to come from the same workshop as the glass from the tomb of Tutankhamun. Other blue glass beads from Denmark and northern Germany matched glass excavated at Nippur, southeast of present-day Baghdad (Varberg et al., "Mesopotamian Glass"; Varberg et al., "Between Egypt, Mesopotamia, and Scandinavia"). Thus, amber linked Bronze Age Scandinavia to a trade network that spanned three continents. As we will see, not only goods were transported along the trade routes, but ideas as well.

The Mound People

Bronze Age trade led to social inequality compared to the relatively egalitarian Neolithic. We see signs of a warrior aristocracy in the Bronze Age, including bronze swords that were often repaired and resharpened, and the oldest evidence in Scandinavia for chariots. (Keeping other people's hands off your gold was a full-time job, it seems.) When the battle was done, there was plenty of alcoholic drink;

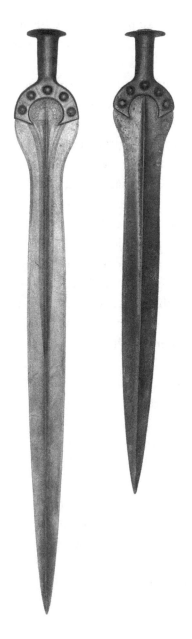

Bronze Age swords from Åmose (L) and Stengård (R). National Museum of Denmark, CC BY-SA 2.0.

for example, a high-status man was buried at Nandrup on northern Jutland, around 1500-1300 BCE, with a jar of mead. By the late Bronze Age, the elite were drinking wine imported all the way from the Mediterranean: a strainer found at Kostræde, Denmark retained chemical residue of grape wine, flavored with honey and herbs, and mixed with pine resin to keep it from spoiling, like modern Greek *retsina* (McGovern et al., "A Biomolecular Archaeological Approach to 'Nordic Grog'").

For a relatively short time in the early Bronze Age, burial mounds grew huge, as magnates gained the power to command large numbers of people to build them. These mounds were built of layers of turf, stripped from the soil and piled high. A typical mound required 0.5 to 10 hectares (1-25 acres) of turf, which would have ruined the land for livestock grazing for years to come. Evidently, the people who ordered these mounds controlled enough land that they didn't think they had to worry about things like that. In fact, in the early Bronze Age, an estimated 1200–1500 km^2 of grassland (460–580 mi^2)—an area roughly the size of the city of Los Angeles—was destroyed in order to build 50,000 mounds in southern Scandinavia (Holst et al., "Bronze Age 'Herostrats', p. 1). Building each mound must have required considerable collaborative effort among people living over a wide area. This effort may reflect competition among groups from different areas (Holst et al., pp. 23-25).

People were buried in these mounds, singly or in small groups, in coffins made from hollowed sections of oak tree trunks. Because the growth rings are well preserved, we can date these burials precisely: most of the coffins in the great mounds were made between 1396 and 1260 BCE, an interval of only 164 years (Price, *Ancient Scandinavia*, pp. 218-221). In these coffins, the dead were buried fully dressed and equipped with grave goods. Where these coffins were buried in waterlogged soils with no oxygen present, clothing and hair were often preserved remarkably well. (P. V. Glob's book *The Mound People* is an old but still useful and accessible summary of these burials.) Burial within a mound is also the norm in the early Bronze Age in central Europe and England, although the preservation of the bodies is much less spectacular than in the waterlogged soils of Denmark. For example, the great mound at Leubingen in central Germany, dated to 1942 BCE and thus belonging to the Únětice Culture, covered a wooden burial chamber. Inside was the body of a man who had died at about 50 years of

Log coffin excavated in 1883 from Muldbjerg mound, with the coffin covered by
an outer "shell" made from a hollowed log. Müller, *Vor Oldtid* (1897).

age, buried with bronze axes and daggers and gold jewelry (Price, *Europe
Before Rome*, pp. 245-246).

The dead in the great mounds were buried with bronze and gold treasures, from small personal items like razors and tweezers, to swords. P. V.
Gløb points out that this created a huge need for metal: "Not only was
enough required to counteract the wastage of tools in constant use; it was
also needed for new weapons and ornaments for each succeeding generation
since so many personal belongings of bronze and gold accompanied their
owners to the grave. Sacrifices to the powers watching over the life and fortune of the Mound People swallowed up a large proportion of metal imports
as well" (*The Mound People*, p. 134). Besides treasures, the dead received
food and drink, and sometimes human sacrifices as well. At the great mound
of Guldhøj, a child was buried with three crabapples; beside him, a man was
buried with six split sticks of hazel, possibly a magical grave-gift (*The Mound
People*, pp. 92-94). The famous "Egtved Girl," who died around 1380 BCE,
was found wearing a blouse, a belt with a large bronze disk over the stomach,
and a "string-skirt"—a short skirt made of many cords hanging down from
the waist, weighted at the ends with metal fittings. Such skirts are seen on
carvings and bronze figures of women, who are often striking acrobatic poses, suggesting that the Egtved Girl may have been a ritual dancer or acrobat.
The Egtved Girl was also buried with the burned bones of a young girl at
her feet—probably a serving-maid sent into the mound with her mistress.
Fresh yarrow flowers were laid in her coffin, and she was also given a bucket

The Egtved Girl's clothing.
National Museum of Denmark,
CC BY-SA 2.0.

of wheat beer flavored with honey, cranberries, and bog myrtle (Gløb, pp. 60-63). The tremendous effort and expense of building the mounds, and supplying the living and the dead with their treasures and beverages, suggests a high level of social stratification and probably considerable worship of the dead.

Something changed in northern Europe around 1100 BCE. Houses got smaller, and burial mounds stopped being raised. Cremation and urn burials became the common practice; sometimes these remains were buried in the sides of older mounds (Price, *Ancient Scandinavia*, pp. 249-250). The cause may have been environmental degradation. Building large houses (and rebuilding them every fifty years or so) consumed large amounts of timber, and forests were also cleared to accommodate agriculture; houses may have shrunk as the supply of timber did. Loss of forests, together with loss of turf from mound building, may have led to soil erosion and decreased productivity (Holst et al., "Bronze Age 'Herostrats'", p. 25).

The old trade networks were also disrupted. In the Mediterranean, the civilizations of the Mycenaeans, Babylonians, Hittites, and Egyptians declined or collapsed in a "perfect storm" of earthquakes, droughts, internal turmoil, and invasions, soon after 1200 BCE (Cline, *1177 B.C.*, especially pp. 139-170). With the main consumers of Baltic amber no longer open for business, fewer goods came north. Not only did less bronze enter Scandinavia, but the routes by which it came shifted: less bronze came from the eastern Mediterranean and the Italian Alps, and more from the Atlantic and eastern Europe (Mehlheim et al., "Moving Metals III," pp. 100-103). Artifacts and rock art from the later Bronze Age of Scandinavia shows similarities with designs from southern Spain, one of the most important sources of bronze. Other artistic designs show connections between Scandinavia and central Europe, probably reflecting trade in less luxurious goods (Ling and Uhnér, "Rock Art and Metal Trade"). By the late Bronze Age, there was enough trade for powerful people to accumulate hoards of gold, such as the five gold rings and six beau-tifully crafted golden bowls found at Borgbjerg Banke, and eleven gold bowls found at Mariesminde, both sites dating from the later Bronze Age of Denmark (Price, *Ancient Scandinavia*, pp. 244-245).

Golden cup with animal-headed handle. Borgbjerg Banke, Denmark. National Museum of Denmark, CC BY-SA 2.0.

Ritual and Religion

Bronze Age buildings intended for religious rituals are rare and difficult to interpret. A square setting of upright posts roofed by cross-beams with curved ends, preserved in a bog at Bargeroosterveld, Holland, may be a ritual enclosure, and a few other possible ritual structures are known from Scandinavia (Harding, *European Societies in the Bronze Age*, pp. 309-312). But the religious rites of the Bronze Age people were usually conducted out-doors. The practice of leaving offerings in bogs was widespread, and people in present-day Germany also left offerings in shafts, wells, and caves. Over a thousand offering hoards have been found in southern Scandinavia and northern Germany, mostly placed into lakes or bogs, but sometimes left on dry land. These offerings included precious bronze and gold objects. The fa-mous "sun wagon" from Trundholm was a bog offering; so were the horned helmets from Veksø, which resemble those depicted on statues and in rock art. Jewelry, weapons, and shields were also deposited as offerings. Bronze shields from offering deposits show no sign of having been used in combat, and may have been made solely for ritual use (Price, *Ancient Scandinavia*, pp.

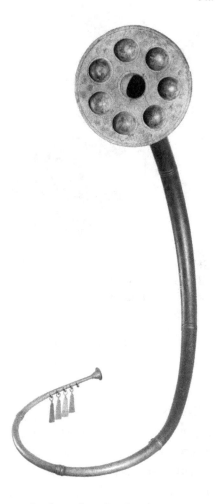

Lurhorn from Brudevælte mose,
Denmark. National Museum of Denmark,
CC BY-SA 2.0.

212-213). The great bronze horns known as lurs were also sunk in bogs as holy gifts, and also appear in rock art, sometimes in scenes of what look like processions or other rituals. They seem to have been made and played in matching pairs tuned to the same pitch, with one horn curving left and the other curving right. Older ones tend to be C-shaped, while later ones have a prominent S-curve. Although they lacked valves, modern brass players have found that they can produce a surprising range of notes; the tone is somewhat similar to the modern trombone. Their musical character was enhanced by the use of rattle-ornaments which tinkled as the player walked.

Noteworthy for reconstructing a different sort of Bronze Age belief are bags or boxes containing odd selections of objects, buried with bodies. The man buried at Hvidegård, for example had a leather bag containing seashells, dried roots, animal bones, a flint knife, and small bronze items including a razor and tweezers (Gløb, *The Mound People*, pp. 114-117). A woman buried at Maglehøj had a bronze box containing animal bones and teeth, pieces of quartz and pyrite, bits of bronze, a twig of mountain ash wood, and other small objects (Gløb, p. 162). Similar bags of bones, teeth, stones, and other odd objects are known from Iron Age and even later burials in Europe, and are mentioned in early medieval accounts as being used in healing magic (Flint, *The Rise of Magic*, pp. 247-249).

Art on the Rocks

Probably the closest we can get to understanding Bronze Age mentality and spirituality is through the study of rock art. While there is Bronze age rock art all over Scandinavia, the richest region is Bohuslän in southeast Sweden, where over 1500 sites are known, including 450 sites in a 45 km² (17 mi²) region at Tanum (Price, *Ancient Scandinavia*, p. 196). Rock art was made in the Stone Age as well, but where Stone Age and Bronze Age rock art coexist, the differences are obvious. Stone Age rock art emphasizes wild animals, especially elk, reindeer, and whales, and panels of Stone Age rock art are often visible from a distance. Bronze Age rock art emphasizes different motifs: ships, wagons, ploughs, footprints, sun-wheels, spirals and concentric circles, armed and phallic men, and mating couples. Bronze Age rock art is often placed on nearly horizontal surfaces, where it can't be seen until the viewer is close to it—it was not made for passers-by to see, but for people who already knew the landscape well, and who marked their owner-ship of it with burial mounds and cairns (Sognnes, "Symbols in a Changing World," pp. 154-161).

The simplest rock art motifs are the little cup-shaped depressions or cupmarks, which the Swedes still call *älvkvarnar*, "alf-mills." Sometimes these are elements on much larger panels. In other cases, large rocks are covered with these depressions but have no other obvious carv-ing. In Sweden, offerings of milk and drink have been made in these cups up to recent times (Ellis, *The Road to Hel*, p. 114), and there is a report from the 1840s of human semen and seeds ground up to-gether in a cup-mark and sown on the fields in an attempt to improve their fertility (Jonsen, *The Cosmic Wedding*, pp. 33-34; discussed fur-ther below). In the Baltic region in recent times, seeds were also placed (and occasionally burned) in cup-

Stone with ground depressions where of-ferings were left to the elves. Skattegärden, Västergötland, Sweden. Photo courtesy of Vänsresborgs Museum, CC BY-SA 4.0.

marks. On larger rock art panels, cupmarks sometimes appear between the legs of human figures with long hair, and these have been interpreted as vulvas and/or the heads of babies in birthing scenes. That said, cupmarks are sometimes seen between the legs of phallic figures (and some phallic figures have long hair), which suggests that neither cupmarks nor long hair are simple markers of biological gender. In still other contexts, cupmarks may represent human heads, perhaps as a kind of graphic shorthand for ancestors (Horn, "Cupmarks," pp. 33-38; "It's a Man's World," pp. 238-240).

Many Bronze Age rock art panels show what look like religious rituals and processions. Several stones show boats with lur-players or acrobats doing back-bends. The acrobats resemble a little bronze figurine of a woman in a string-skirt, laid in a bog at Grevensvænge, Denmark, along with several other figurines. It's been speculated that these figurines were fitted to a model of a ship which was carried in a procession (Gløb, *The Mound People*, pp. 163-167, fig. 71). Figures with upraised arms and hands, known as *adorants*, may represent worshippers or participants in ecstasy. At Bredarör, a mound at Kivik in Sweden, slabs of rock were used to build the walls of a burial chamber, which was then covered by a mound of stones. Carvings on these slabs show geometric figures, sun-wheels and crescent de-

signs, animals, weapons, and people in single file, including a charioteer, robed and hooded figures, lur-players, and possible sacrificial victims with hands tied. At least five people were buried here, with rich grave goods (mostly lost to looting), between about 1400 and 1000 BCE (Goldhahn, "Bredarör on Kivik," pp. 359-370). It's a reasonable guess that the Kivik panels depict rites connected with the cult of the dead.

Panel from the chambered rock cairn at Kivik, Sweden. Photo by Sven Rosborn. Wikimedia Commons, CC BY-SA 3.0.

The location of rock art panels by the sea, as well as the many carvings of ships, hints at a pivotal role for the sea and ships in Bronze Age

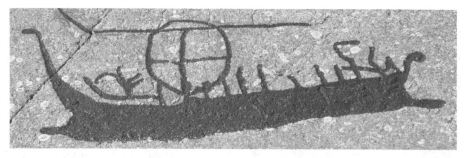

Solar ship petroglyph at Himmelstalund, near Norrköping, Sweden.
Photo by Harri Blomberg, Wikimedia Commons, CC BY-SA 3.0

religion. From a purely practical point of view, Scandinavians depended on trade for their supply of bronze and gold, and ships had to bring these treasures across the Baltic Sea at the least. The ship was also important mythically: Bronze Age art frequently depicts ships bearing sunwheels. Flemming Kaul has analyzed the positions of ships on both rock art and portable items, and concluded that they depict the sun's journey through the sky by day, and through the underworld at night. When the sun-ship is depicted moving left to right, it is in the day sky, and appears next to figures

Bronze single-edged razor (*ragekniv*) with ships sailing left to right. Solbjerg, Denmark. National Museum of Denmark, CC BY-SA 2.0.

of horses; when it is depicted moving right to left or upside down, it is in the night sky and appears with fish or serpents. The animals seem to be helpers, and some depictions of the sun-ship appear next to the horse pulling the sun, suggesting that the sun-ship image coexisted with the sun-chariot (see below; Kaul, "Tripartite Cosmologies," pp. 138-139; "Left-Right Logic," pp. 236-242). The symbolism of the solar ship seems to have been shared by the people of what is now central Germany. The oldest star map, the famous Nebra Sky Disk made around 1600 BCE, was originally made to help determine the calendar, but later had a golden arc added to it that probably represents the sun-ship at night (Price, *Europe Before Rome*, pp. 256-259).

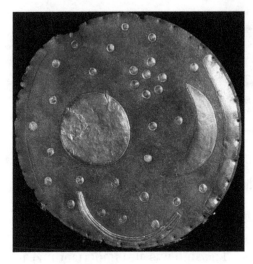

Nebra Sky Disk. Photo by Anagoria,
Wikimedia Commons, CC BY 3.0.

Bronze and amber staff head showing
sunwheel design. Unknown location.
National Museum of Denmark,
CC BY-SA 2.0.

The sunwheel design, an equal-armed cross inside a circle, may represent the sun's circular course through the sky. The horizontal line of the cross would be the horizon, and the sun's path would intersect it at dawn and dusk, with the vertical line connecting the sun's positions at noon and midnight (Kaul, "Tripartite Cosmologies," pp. 145-147). Amber may have been linked with the sun, because of its golden color, warm feeling in the hand, and ability to burn. A staff head from Denmark bears an amber disk in a bronze frame shaped like a sunwheel, making the link clear between amber and the sun. Amber disks and axes from this time may also be symbols of the sun's might (Herva and Lahelma, *Northern Archaeology and Cosmology*, pp. 156-162).

The ship not only bore the sun, it may have ferried the dead. The custom of "ship-settings," in which a burial was enclosed in a ship-shaped ring of stones, began in the middle Bronze Age and continued into Viking times. About thirty examples of Bronze Age "ship-settings" are known from northern Germany and Scandinavia (Harding, *European Societies*, pp. 109-111; Price, *Ancient Scandinavia*, p. 222). In artistic depictions of the sun-ship, it's been suggested that the rowers are the dead, traveling to the Underworld and assisting the sun (Kaul, "Tripartite Cosmologies," pp. 139-142; "Left-Right Logic," p. 242). Some rock art panels depict an entire procession with dancers and lur-players accompanying a ship. This might depict rites meant to honor and strengthen the sun on its course, to carry the dead into the afterlife—or possibly both, if the dead were thought of as sinking into an Underworld and then rising again with the sun.

The wagon is also necessary for trade and transport, and both the wagon (or chariot) and the ship appear in Bronze Age art as bearers of the sun. One of the most famous Bronze Age artworks is the model wagon or chariot recovered from a drained bog at Trundholm, Denmark. A bronze disk, ornamented with spirals all over, has been mounted on wheels and is drawn by a horse with sunray-like decorations around its eyes. The side of the disc visible when the chariot is seen moving left to right is gilded, while the other side is not. This matches the directional symbolism of ships on Bronze Age art, and probably represents both the day-sun and the night-sun (Kaul, "Left-Right Logic," pp. 236-238). The solar wagon or chariot was remembered through the Viking Age; the *Poetic Edda* mentions the horses

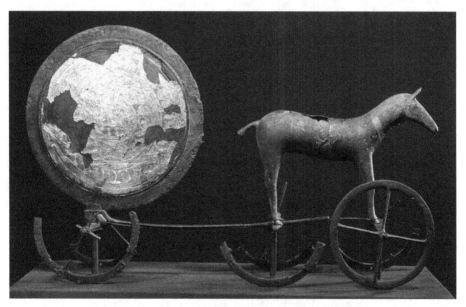

Solar wagon (*solvognen*) from Trundholm, Denmark.
National Museum of Denmark, CC BY-SA 2.0.

Árvakr and Alsviðr that draw the sun (*Grímnismál* 37). On the other hand, the solar ship seems to have been forgotten by the Viking Age, although ships and solar symbols occur together on the earlier Migration Age picture stones of Gotland, strongly suggesting that the Bronze Age myth of a ship carrying the sun by night survived until then (Andrén, *Tracing Old Norse Cosmology*, pp. 136-139).

Rock art suggests that the sun was seen as masculine, which is an interesting departure from both reconstructed Proto-Indo-European myth and from later Norse mythology. In the late Bronze Age, stags are sometimes depicted drawing the sun-wheel or bearing the sun-wheel in their antlers (Green, *The Sun-Gods of Ancient Europe*, pp. 80-81), a motif that seems to

Phallic figures with sunwheel bodies.
Aspeberget, Tanum, Bohuslän, Sweden.
Sven Rosborn, Wikimedia Commons,
CC BY 3.0.

have come from the east (Gelling and Davidson, *The Chariot of the Sun*, pp. 92-94). Other rock art panels show circles giving forth rays that resemble antlers. Phallic figures with sunwheel-shaped bodies are fairly common at several rock-art sites, although some of these may simply depict men carrying round shields. Some of these wheel-bodied phallic males are shown approaching female figures or copulating with them (e.g. Gløb, *The Mound People*, fig. 74).

In fact, mating couples in general, wheel-bodied or not, are another notable rock-art motif; over twenty examples have been documented (Horn, "'It's a Man's World'?," p. 242). It is tempting, if speculative, to see the solar-bodied men mating with women as depictions of a male sky-god or sun-god mating with an earth-goddess. On the other hand, the depictions of mating couples might represent public rituals that were actually carried out, a *hieros gamos* or "sacred marriage." This was actually done as late as the 1840s in Dalsland, Sweden; there is a report that, after several years of bad harvests, the old people "who knew what should be done in such situations" took a virgin girl and boy to a rock art panel at Råvarpen, had them have sex on the rock, placed the boy's semen in a cupmark, ground it together with seeds, and sowed the mixture on the fields (Johnsen, *The Cosmic Wedding*, pp. 33-34). It may be tempting to interpret this as a pagan ritual survival, but most folklorists today would be skeptical that any ritual could survive in anything like its original form for 3500 years. But certainly sex and reproduction were spiritually important, as also attested by a few panels depicting childbirth. There are a few instances of male homosexual intercourse depicted in rock art, a few other depictions of intercourse where the genders are ambiguous, and at least one panel showing a man mating with a cow (Gløb, *The Mound People*, fig. 56). However, the stylized nature of rock art images make it hard to conclude anything definite about the role of homosexual or "third gender" persons in Bronze Age society, although such persons certainly existed, as they did and do in every human society (Horn, "'It's a Man's World'?," pp. 246-247).

Urn lid depicting sexual intercourse within a wreath. Maltegårdens Mark, Denmark. National Museum of Denmark. CC BY-SA 2.0.

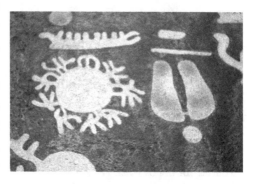

"Antlered" solar disk, footprints, ship, and cupmark. Tanum, Bohuslän, Sweden. Photo by Rainer Knäpper, Wikimedia Commons, CC BY-SA 2.0.

Bare footprints and shod footprints are frequent motifs in rock art, and some have linked them with the myth of Skaði choosing her husband by his feet. However, we cannot know whether the Bronze Age people knew this myth in anything like the form in which we have it. The bare footprints may have shown the passing of a god, or perhaps the continued presence of an unseen god. Since many Bronze Age rock art panels with footprints are nearly horizontal, it's also been suggested that the footprints mark where human participants in a ritual were supposed to stand. These footprints point northeast or northwest, southeast or southwest, but rarely due east or west, and never due north. This suggests that anyone standing in them would have been facing the sunrise or sunset around the winter solstice (southeast/southwest) or the summer solstice (northeast/northwest) (Bradley, "Midsummer and Midwinter," pp. 226-230).

One more common rock art motif is men wielding weapons. We cannot know whether these represent deities, but it's at least possible that the figures wielding hammers or axes may represent a version of the Indo-European thunder-god. The Vitlycke stone at Tanum shows a large man standing beside a mating couple and raising his axe over them. de Vries draws on an episode in *Þrymskviða*, in which Thor's hammer is used to hallow the bride, and interprets this scene as a ritual mating (*Altgermanische Religionsgeschichte*, I, p. 106). On the other hand, axe-wielding figures often come in pairs,

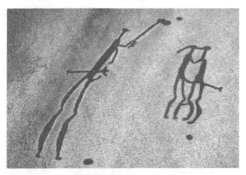

"Sacred marriage" from Vitlycke, Bohuslän, Sweden. Photo by Bengt A. Lundberg, courtesy of the Swedish National Heritage Board (Riksantikvariembetet), CC BY 2.5.

Twin figures with axes from Vitlycke, Bohuslän, Sweden. Photo by Bengt A. Lundberg, courtesy of the Swedish National Heritage Board (Riksantikvariembetet), CC BY-SA 2.5.

such as the paired bronze figurines of kneeling men in horned helmets from Grevensvænge, Denmark (now mostly lost; see Gløb, *The Mound People*, p. 165, fig. 70) and the figures on rock art panels from Fossum in Sweden. These twinned axe-wielders are associated with ships, horses, and sun-wheels, which are themselves often twinned (Kristiansen, "Rock Art and Religion," pp. 96-112). It's been suggested that these paired axe-wielders were the Divine Twins of Indo-European mythology, mentioned briefly in Chapter 2. In Indo-European mythologies, the Twins (the Greek *Dioskouroi*, Vedic *Aśvinau*, Roman *Gemini*, Latvian *Dieva dēli*, and possibly the Roman-era Germanic *Alci*), brothers of the Sun, are superlative horsemen and charioteers, rescuers of sailors and warriors in peril, and rescuers of the Sun from nighttime captivity. Whoever the Bronze Age twinned figures were, their axes generally have short handles and broad, crescent-shaped blades. Axes exactly like this have been found in Denmark and Sweden. The bronze axe from Västerås in Sweden is a foot long and weighs eight pounds; too unwieldy to use effectively in battle, it was probably used in ritual (Andersson and Jansson, *Treasures of Early Sweden*, p. 38). Other axes were made of very thin bronze over a clay core, and would not have been suitable as weapons.

Ritual bronze axe with the blade cast over a clay core. Skogstorp, Södermannland, Sweden. Swedish Historical Museum 96956. CC BY-SA 2.5.

In Viking-era mythology, Odin bears a spear; thrown over the heads of enemies, it dedicates them as sacrifices to himself. It's not clear whether the Bronze Age people worshipped Odin in a recognizable form, but there are certainly spear-wielding figures depicted in rock art, although they usually bear thrusting-spears, not throwing-spears. One of the largest is "Litsleby Man," carved about the size of an actual human and shown wielding a great spear. Human figures carrying bows and arrows are also known, and these

Rock art from Litsleby, Bohuslän, Sweden. Sven Rosborn, Wikimedia Commons, CC BY 3.0.

Rock art from Litsleby, Bohuslän, Sweden.

could conceivably represent a deity like Ullr. Anoter carving from Litsleby shows a phallic man behind a plough, holding a branch in one hand and a hammer in the other. The ploughman has made two furrows and is starting a third. P. V. Gløb links this to an old saying on the island of Bornholm, "Three furrows in Thor give a green spring," (*The Mound People*, p. 150), suggesting that we might be seeing the thunder-god in the role of giver of fertility. Finally, both in rock art and in metalwork of the Late Bronze Age, there seems to be an association between female figures, horses, and chariots. These could represent priestesses carrying out ritual acts; they could also represent a goddess associated with battle and horses. Understanding her any further gets increasingly speculative, but on the one hand she might be reminiscent of Mediterranean goddesses such as Ishtar and Athena, and on the other hand she might be related to the Viking Age figure of Freyja (Varberg, "Lady of the Battle and of the Horse," pp. 147-167).

Cultural Exchange

Few Bronze Age Scandinavians, if any, actually traveled between Scandinavia and the Mediterranean: trade goods exchanged between these places would have passed through several middlemen. Nevertheless, ideas tend to follow trade routes, and it is now thought that some social and religious concepts, associated with the warrior aristocracies of the Mediterranean kingdoms, influenced the Scandinavian elites at the other end of the trade network.

One common item in Scandinavian male graves is the single-bladed bronze razor, with a handle shaped like a spiral or a horse's head. This style closely resembles razors from Crete. Flemming Kaul suggests that although Scandinavians did not import any actual razors from Crete, they absorbed not just the shape of the razor, but an ideal of masculinity, from contact with Crete, including a concept of noble warriors as clean-shaven ("The

Nordic Razor," pp. 467-470). Perhaps surprisingly, folding stools are another Mediterranean item that filtered northwards. King Tutankhamun and other Middle Kingdom Egyptian nobles owned folding stools, and Mycenaean murals from Crete depict women seated on them at banquets. The man buried in the mound at Guldhøj, Denmark around 1500 BCE owned a finely made folding stool, originally with an otter fur seat. Fragments of other such stools are known from Denmark, Sweden, and Germany, all from the same time frame as the Egyptian and Mycenaean stools (Wanscher, *Sella Curulis*, pp. 75-82). This is more significant than it seems: folding stools were symbols of authority in the Mediterranean world, and they probably had a similar meaning in Scandinavia (Wanscher, pp. 12-16). Folding stools would continue to be prestigious: known as the *sella curulis*, they were used by Roman magistrates, placed in rich Anglo-Saxon graves, and depicted in medieval artworks as seats for royalty until well into the Middle Ages (Wanscher, pp. 121-144, 191-278).

There are other hints at Mediterranean influence on Nordic Bronze Age culture, and even mythology. The "sun-ships" in Scandinavian art resemble Egyptian depictions of the solar boat of Ra, which was also crewed by the soul of the dead pharaoh, and which traveled with various animal helpers (Kaul, "Bronze Age Tripartite Cosmologies," pp. 139-141). While it is hard to be certain just how much influence Egypt had on Scandinavian myth, we can-

Left: Folding stool frame from the mound at Guldhøj, Denmark. National Museum of Denmark, CC BY-SA 2.0. Right: Egyptian folding stool, 2030–1640 BCE. Metropolitan Museum of Art, New York City, 12.182.58. Public domain.

Double-bladed axe miniature from Lundsbakke, Denmark. National Museum of Denmark. CC BY-SA 2.0.

not rule out that some existed. While most axes depicted in Scandinavian art are single-bladed, double-bladed miniatures are sometimes found, such as the man buried at Lundsbakke in Denmark with two miniature bronze double-bladed axes, and the double-bladed amber axe pendants from Låddenhøj in Denmark. The double-bladed axe or *labrys* is a well-known symbol from the Minoan civilization of Crete. A figurine from Grevensvænge, Denmark, as well as rock art associated with carvings of ships, depict topless women, wearing short skirts, doing back-bends. Exactly the same pose is seen in Egyptian and Minoan art of the same age (Iversen, "Bronze Age Acrobats"). The association between female figures and snakes, famous from the Mycenaean goddess statues, appears at Fårdal in Denmark, where a bronze statue of a kneeling female figure in a string skirt was associated with figures of bull's heads and a serpent.

Left: Acrobatic dancer drawn on a potsherd, Egypt, 19th Dynasty, ca. 1300 BCE. Museo Egizio, Turin. Wikimedia Commons, Public Domain.
Right: Bronze figurine of an "acrobat" in a string skirt, once part of a larger set of figurines. Grevensvænge, Denmark. National Museum of Denmark, CC BY-SA 2.0.

To summarize: Bronze Age Scandinavia was home to a wealthy elite, connected with a much wider world through an extensive trade network. Not only material goods, but symbols, ideas, and even myths entered the Northlands—and some of these may have left traces in the myths that have come down to us.

Contributors:

1st edition: Kveldúlfr Gundarsson, mostly from "Rock Carvings and Rites of Spring," *Idunna* no. 14 (1992), pp. 45-47.

2nd edition: New material by Ben Waggoner.

3rd edition: Reorganization and new material by Ben Waggoner.

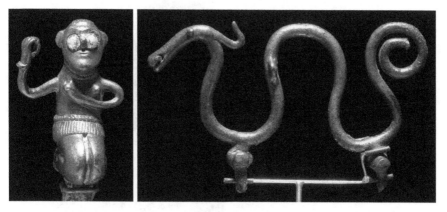

Bronze figures of a female figure and a serpent (not to the same scale). Fårdal, Denmark. National Museum of Denmark. CC BY-SA 2.0.

Iron Age phallic idol from Broddenbjerg, Denmark.
National Museum of Denmark CC BY-SA 2.0.

CHAPTER FOUR:

The Iron Age

500 BCE-350 CE

In the first millennium BCE, groups of people who probably spoke Germanic languages appear. As these peoples came into contact with peoples who had developed writing, the historical record begins, adding its evidence to that of archaeology. Contact with the Roman Empire sometimes brought violence, but more often brought trade and cultural exchange, transforming the tribal societies beyond the Rhine and the Danube Rivers.

Griffin head, probably once part of a Roman parade helmet. National Museum of Denmark. CC BY-SA 2.0.

Celts and Germans

Iron came into common use in central Europe around 900 BCE. The culture bridging the Bronze and Iron Ages in central Europe between 900 and 300 BCE, overlapping with the earlier Urnfield cultures, is known as the Hallstatt culture, named after the great burial site at Hallstatt in Austria. The Hallstatt culture is often considered "proto-Celtic." Although we cannot know what languages the Hallstatt people spoke, their culture develops, with considerable change but no real cultural break, into the La Tène culture, which in turn was shared by historic cultures that are known to have spoken Celtic languages (Cunliffe, *The Ancient Celts*, pp. 63-67).

By around 500 BCE, iron reached northern Europe, and the old bronze trading networks came to an end. The earliest remains of the Jastorf culture, in Denmark and northern Germany, date from about this time. This is the oldest culture that most assign to a Germanic-speaking people, because it develops without a major break into Roman-era cultures that we know spoke Germanic languages. The Jastorf culture developed from earlier Bronze Age cultures, but it isn't certain whether these earlier groups had yet differentiated into separate Baltic, Celtic, Slavic, or Germanic branches (Mallory, *In Search of the Indo-Europeans,* pp. 84-87). Dating changes in language is tricky if there are no written texts, but the sound shifts of Grimm's Law, discussed in Chapter 2, are thought to have taken place at some time in the first millennium, so the Jastorf people were probably speaking Proto-Germanic dialects.

The Jastorf people and their successors were primarily farmers. In the early Iron Age, their fields were plowed with ards ("scratch-ploughs"), which cut furrows in the heavy clay soil but did not turn it over. This meant that weeds and stubble did not decay, which in turn meant that the soil lost its fertility fairly quickly. Settlements were small and needed large fields to sustain themselves. They tended to last only a few generations before people had to move on; as late as the first century CE, Tacitus noted that the German tribes regularly had to reapportion their fields (*Germania* 26, transl. Hutton, pp. 168-171; Heather, *Empire and Barbarians*, pp. 48-52).

In the early Iron Age, possibly Celtic-speaking groups to the south and east of the Jastorf culture were wealthier and more centralized; the name "Celtic Iron Age" is sometimes applied to the sixth through first centuries BCE. The late Hallstatt culture dominated central Europe, centered around powerful chieftains occupying large hillforts—known in German as *Fürstensitze,* "princely seats." One of the most famous, the Heuneburg overlook-

Aerial view of the hillfort on the Ipf, a hill near Bopfingen, Germany, occupied between 1200 and 300 BCE. Photo by Enzyerklopaedie. Wikimedia Commons, CC BY-SA 3.0.

ing the Danube River, began to be occupied around 700 BCE. The largest *Fürstensitz*, the somewhat younger Heidengraben to the west, enclosed an area of 17 km² (6.5 mi²). Hallstatt chieftains were buried in great mounds; most of them were looted centuries ago, but the mound at Hochdorf was not disturbed until archaeologists excavated it. Here, around 530 BCE, a Hallstatt chieftain was buried in a chamber with double wooden walls, under a great circular mound. He was dressed in silk-embroidered clothes and gold-encrusted shoes, laid on a bronze couch, and given

Gold foil ornaments from the shoes of the chieftain buried at Hochdorf. Photo by Rosemania, Wikimedia Commons, CC BY 2.0

a 400-liter cauldron of mead, a gold drinking bowl, nine drinking horns, bronze dishes, a horse-drawn cart, and a gold-hilted dagger (Price, *Europe Before Rome*, pp. 307-311). By 600 BCE, the Greeks had established trading stations on the Mediterranean coast, such as Massalia (Marseilles) and Monoikos (Monaco), and were trading extensively with the Hallstatt people, especially wine and fine vessels for serving and drinking wine at feasts. By about 450 BCE, there was additional luxury trade across the Alps, between the Hallstatt culture and the Etruscans (Cunliffe, *The Ancient Celts*, pp. 44-67).

In contrast to the Hallstatt culture, Jastorf settlements show less evidence for differentiation based on wealth. While each farmstead or village presumably had a headman or council, the early Iron Age Germans were much less socially stratified (Cunliffe, *Extraordinary Voyage*, pp. 150-151). Compared to their Bronze Age predecessors, they produced much less art: in most areas the tradition of carving rock art ended around 500 BCE, although it was maintained in a few areas. After 200 BCE, very few symbols and designs appear on artifacts, probably because the elites who formerly would have used such things no longer existed (Andrén, *Tracing Old Norse Cosmology*, pp. 132-136). This difference in social organization is reflected in the language: a number of Germanic words dealing with warfare and politics were borrowed from Celtic, notably the words for "ruler," *rikaz* (German *Reich*/English "rich"/ON *ríkr*, "powerful") and the word for "servant," *andbat* (German *Amt*/ON *ambatt*; related to English "ambassador"). Words like English *oath, feud, free*, and *byrnie* (mailcoat), and German *Beute* (loot), *Erbe* (inheritance; OE *yrfe*), *Ger* (spear; OE *gar*), and *Geisel* (hostage; OE *gīsel*), ultimately descend from Celtic borrowings into Proto-Germanic. Germanic speakers also borrowed the name of a Celtic tribe, recorded in Latin as the *Volcae*, as their word for foreigners in general: Proto-Germanic *Walhaz* gave rise to OE *Wealh* and ultimately modern English *Wales* and *Welsh*, the predominant "foreigners" that the Anglo-Saxons knew (Wells, *German*, p. 54). One more borrowed word was *iron*, thought to come from Proto-Celtic *isarno*. The ancestors of the Jastorf people were probably dependent on Celtic-speaking peoples for iron until around 500 BCE, when they learned to smelt it themselves. Chemical processes in bogs create deposits of "bog iron;" these are fairly easy to dig up, and they were exploited through the Viking Age.

Some fine goods did find their way north along the trade routes. The most spectacular of these pieces is the huge silver Gundestrup Cauldron, probably made in central Europe around 100 CE, but placed in a Danish bog as a sacrificial offering. Almost as spectacular are the remains of two wagons, decorated in Celtic style, found in a bog near Dejbjerg in Denmark; and the bronze cauldron from central Europe found at Brå in Jutland, with a capacity of 130 gallons (Todd, *The Early Germans*, pp. 20-21). Social stratification

The Gundestrup Cauldron.
National Museum of
Denmark, CC BY-SA 2.0.

of Germanic tribes became much more pronounced in the later Iron Age: the institution of the warband probably grew up around this time, perhaps following Celtic models (Enright, *Lady with a Mead Cup*, pp. 169-282). Still, in the first century BCE, Julius Caesar noted the greater wealth and more complex organization of the Gaulish tribes, compared to the relatively sparse lifestyle of the Germans. According to Caesar, the Germans had no priestly caste to compare with the Gaulish druids; they spent their lives eager for hunting, warfare, "toil and hardship," and avoided social stratification because "it is their aim to keep common people in contentment, when each man sees that his own wealth is equal to that of the most powerful" (*De bello gallico* 6:21; transl. Edwards, pp. 344-347).

Despite these differences, Celtic speakers and Germanic speakers were evidently in close cultural and political contact, trading, intermingling and probably intermarrying, along the zone of contact in northern Europe. Celtic speakers borrowed a number of Germanic words, notably Proto-Germanic *brokez*, "breeches," which became *braca* in Gaulish. Several Roman references to "Germans" include very Celtic-sounding personal and tribal names; perhaps the most famous is Veleda, whom Tacitus calls a seeress among the Germanic Bructeri, but whose name probably came from a Celtic root meaning "to see," preserved in Gaelic *fili / filidh*, "seer," and Welsh *gweled*, "to see" (Enright, *Lady with a Mead Cup*, pp. 170-171). A number of ritual practices, notably the sacrifice of humans in bogs and the sacrifice of riches in holy wells, are common to both peoples. As late as the sixth century CE, Celtic-style carvings of deities, and inscriptions of unmistakably Celtic god-names, were being made in Denmark—one inscription from Jutland reads "LUGOS," a god well-attested from Irish, British and continental European Celts alike (Ross and Robins, *Life and Death of a Druid Prince*, pp. 157-167).

Julius Caesar and other Roman writers referred to all peoples beyond the Rhine as "Germani," a designation which has stuck. We have to be careful in using this term, because as far as we can tell now, the people of northern Europe did not call themselves "Germans"; the name was imposed by a colonizing power. They belonged to a multitude of tribes, followed different customs, and as far as we can tell were not conscious of belonging to any greater "German nation." Nor did they all speak languages in the Germanic family; Tacitus, for example, noted that some of the tribes in "Germania" spoke languages that were unrelated to their neighbors' languages. No one before the 800s CE seems to have realized that the languages of groups like the Franks and the Goths were actually related (Goffart, *Barbarian Tides*, pp. 41-42). While we can trace some shared cultural practices among them, the people that the Romans called *Germani* did not necessarily form a linguistically and culturally well-defined group, nor did they think of themselves as parts of one larger "nation" (Goffart, pp. 1-22).

The Germans Enter History

Beginning in the first century CE, the isolated farmsteads of the Jastorf culture began to grow into larger, more permanent settlements. These towns, like those excavated at Hodde and Vorbasse in Denmark and Feddersen Wierde in Germany, consisted of clusters of longhouses and outbuildings, all surrounded by palisade walls. The dead were cremated and their remains placed in urns, which were buried in large cemeteries or urnfields (Price, *Ancient Scandinavia*, pp. 262-266). This new settlement type is probably connected with the development of iron ploughs that turned the heavy soil over more effectively, as well as more efficient use of fertilizers such as manure. Now that fields could be used for much longer before their fertility was exhausted, settlements became more stable. Agriculture could now produce surplus crops, which could be traded and/or used to support specialized craftsmen such as smiths and potters. Surpluses could also be used to support warbands led by increasingly powerful chieftains. Thus we see signs of slow and gradual but steady social transformation in Germania during the Roman Iron Age (Heather, *Empire and Barbarians*, pp. 48-55).

The first historical records of probable Germanic-speaking peoples date from approximately 320 BCE. The Greek explorer Pytheas of Massilia journeyed up the Atlantic Coast, where he circumnavigated Britain, probably reached Iceland (which he called Thule), and may also have explored the North Sea coast of present-day Jutland, Germany and the Netherlands. His writings have been lost, but selections are quoted in the works of later authors. What has survived includes tantalizing notes on how amber was collected by the inhabitants of a North Sea island (probably present-day Heligoland) and sold to the neighboring Teutoni. He described the "midnight sun" and Arctic ice, and made astronomical observations that were later used to determine the latitudes of the places he visited. He also mentions that the inhabitants of the North live on honey and burn amber, which could be references to mead and to the use of incense. Although later Greek and Roman scholars doubted his truthfulness, Pytheas appears to have been an accurate observer. For nearly two centuries his work was the only source of information on the Northlands (Cunliffe, *Extraordinary Voyage*).

According to later historians such as Jordanes (*Gothic History* IV, transl. Mierow, p. 57), the Goths originated in Scandinavia and migrated south, crossing the Baltic into present-day Poland around the start of the first century CE. Scholars have debated the accuracy of this account (for a detailed critique, see Goffart, *Barbarian Tides*, pp. 45-71). But place-names and Greek historical accounts suggest that at least some people moved southwards from Scandinavia around this time—probably just individuals or small bands, rather than a mass migration. These people would have mingled with existing tribes on the Baltic coast to give rise to the Goths and other peoples who spoke East Germanic languages (Wolfram, *History of the Goths*, pp. 36-40). These early Goths are probably represented in archaeology by the Wielbark culture, which appeared in the 1st century CE around what is now Gdansk, Poland. By 180 CE, they had begun moving into the steppes of Eastern Europe. Jordanes makes this a single large-scale migration of the entire tribe (*Gothic History* IV, transl. Mierow, p. 57), but there's no support from archaeology for any mass migration. What seems more likely is that over many years, various bands began breaking away and drifting southward into the present-day Ukraine, Moldova, and Romania. They reached the Dniepr River around 200 CE, and seem to have taken over rulership from the Alans and Sarmatians, confederations of Iranian peoples. Ruling the steppes north of the Black Sea, they mingled with the peoples already in the region, including Slavs, Alans, Sarmatians, Scythians, Dacians, and others, forming a distinctive cultural grouping that archaeologists refer to as the Chernyakhovo (or Chernyakhiv) culture. The Gothic language predominated; the Slavic languages contain a sizable number of Gothic loan-words for domestic items, weapons, and financial affairs (Gimbutas, *The Slavs*, p. 77). Sarmatian goldsmiths among the Goths continued to produce their traditional style of gold jewelry set with garnets. This style, adapted to Gothic tastes, would spread all over Europe as far as Anglo-Saxon England (Sulimirski, *The Sarmatians*, pp. 162-164, 183-186). By the third century CE the Goths were a major military power on the Danube frontier of the Roman

Empire. In 238 CE they first raided across the Danube; by the 250s, they were sailing across the Black Sea and inflicting devastating raids on Asia Minor and even Greece (Heather, p. 135; Todd, *The Early Germans*, pp. 140-142).

Runes and Deities

It is in this time frame that we find the oldest evidence of runes. The origin of the rune letter shapes is still debated, but the leading theory at this time derives them from a variant of the Etruscan alphabet that was used in north Italy and diffused northward from there. The Etruscan alphabet itself originated from a variant of the Greek alphabet, and it also gave rise to the Latin alphabet and other alphabets used to write various languages. The closest match to the rune letters is the variety of the Etruscan alphabet used to write an obscure north Italian language called Camunic (Markey, "A Tale of Two Helmets," pp. 78-103).

A hoard of twenty-six Etruscan crested helmets was found in 1811 in the village of Ženjak, in what was then the district of Negau in Austria (it's

The Negau B helmet, now in the Kunsthistoriisches Museum, Vienna. Photo by Peter1936F, Wikimedia Commons, CC BY-SA 4.0.

now part of Slovenia). These were made between 500 and 400 BCE, but ritually deposited much later, probably around 50 BCE. Of the twenty-three helmets that survive, two bear readable inscriptions in the Camunic alphabet. One has several names in a Celtic language, and the other, Negau B, reads **harigasti teiwa**, "Army-Guest, Tei-wa[z]." Teiwaz is certainly the god later known as Tyr or Tiw; Hari-gasti is a personal name, possibly a by-name for a god, but more likely to be a person's name, possibly a priest of Teiwaz (Markey, "A Tale of Two Helmets," pp. 118-127). This is the oldest direct evidence

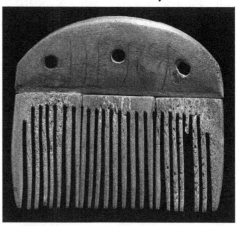

for Germanic deity names. It also shows that at least some Germanic speakers had learned versions of the Etruscan alphabet and drew on it in developing the runic system.

The oldest known inscription that could be runic, on a fibula from Meldorf, is dated to 50 CE, but it consists of only four letters of unclear meaning. The next oldest inscriptions date to the second century CE, such as the comb from Vimose, Denmark, dated to 160 CE and inscribed **harja**, "warrior." As far as can be understood from the short and sometimes obscure inscriptions, the language of the oldest inscriptions shows similarities with both North and

Comb from Vimose, Denmark, with a tracing of the rune letters. National Museum of Denmark, CC BY-SA 2.0.

West Germanic, but not Gothic, suggesting that the East Germanic groups had parted company with their kin by this time. Although the language of the oldest runic inscriptions is often called Proto-Norse, it does not show uniquely North or West Germanic features until the sixth century, suggesting that the division between North and West Germanic was surprisingly late (Robinson, *Old English and its Closest Relatives*, pp. 94-97).

Now that we have written evidence for Germanic languages, we can trace something of the evolution of the gods that would come to be known as Odin, Thor, Tyr, and other familiar names. As mentioned, the Negau helmet mentions Teiwaz (Tyr). Tacitus, writing in the first century CE, calls the Germanic tribes of present-day Denmark, the Low Countries, and northwestern Germany the "Ingaevones," a name clearly derived from *Ingwaz (i.e. Freyr) He also records the personal name *Inguiomerus*, meaning "glory of *Ingwaz," confirming that this god was known among the Cherusci; and he mentions a "Mother Earth" by the name of Nerthus (who is related to, or developed into, the Norse god Njǫrðr). The Gothic alphabet (invented around 350 CE, but drawing on earlier runic traditions) preserves the letter-names *enguz* (*Ingwaz) and *tyz* (*Tiwaz—Tiw or Týr). It seems likely that the Germanic folk also knew *Wōðanaz (Odin), *Frijjo (Frigg), and *Þonaraz (Thor), as well as the personified Sun-goddess and a corresponding Moon-god. A piece of a scabbard from about 200 CE, found at Torsbjerg in Denmark, bears a rune inscription with the personal name *owlþuþewaR,* "servant of Wolthur," i.e. Ullr. Finally, a third-century buckle from Vimose in Denmark has the inscription *asau wija,* "I dedicate [this] to the Æsir" (Simek, *Dictionary*, p. 3), and the Gothic alphabet retains the letter *azu* (*Ansuz – a god; one of the Æsir). The historian Jordanes recorded that the Goths used the name *anses* for "demigod; deified ancestor," a word cognate with ON *Æsir* (*Gothic History* XIII; transl. Mierow, p. 73).

Iron and Warriors

The adoption of iron had advantages for the Germanic peoples. Iron is much more abundant in the Earth's crust than copper or tin. Scandinavian bog iron made the people there increasingly self-sufficient, while to the east, new mines were opened up in what is now Polish territory, producing an estimated eight million kilograms of iron ore throughout the Roman period (Heather, *Empire and Barbarians*, pp. 52-53). Not only did this improve agriculture, since iron-tipped plows could turn the soil far more effectively, it also made weapons more available; unlike the Bronze Age when a bronze spearhead or knife was a significant expense, almost anyone could get enough iron for a spearhead. The Roman historian Tacitus's assertion that the Germans had little iron (*Germania* 6; transl. Hutton, pp. 138-139) was out of date; by the time of the Battle of the Teutoburg Forest in 9 CE, the Germanic peoples were making, importing, and using good steel weapons. Thrusting and throwing spears were the usual weapons, while swords were relatively uncommon and probably worn only by the elite. Shields were common, but armor was rarely worn (Todd, *The Early Germans*, pp. 35-43).

The increasing frequency of burials with weapons and rich grave-goods suggests that Germanic society generally became more centralized, stratified, and militaristic throughout the Roman Iron Age. In part, this was caused by cultural influence from Germans who had served in the Roman armies, and who brought Roman arms and military knowledge back to their own people. Arminius, for example, who led the Germans in inflicting one of Rome's worst defeats, had grown up in Rome as a hostage, received Roman military training and rank, and commanded troops from his own tribe of Cherusci in Roman service (Wells, *The Battle that Stopped Rome*, pp. 111-124). Together with the worsening of the climate, this social change set the stage for the events of the Migration Age, which would in turn play such a huge part in shaping European history and culture.

A metal as important as iron was inevitably assimilated into the mythology of the Germanic peoples. Bronze weapons were prized in the Bronze Age, and in some cases were made solely for ritual use, like the elaborately ornamented but militarily useless bronze shields, axes, and swords found in Denmark. Iron weapons had no place in that sphere, and iron became associated with giants, who still bear names like Járnhauss (Iron Skull) and Járnsaxa (Iron Knife) in Norse legendary sagas. At the same time, iron was also recognized as a defense against hostile magic and wights; the belief that fairies or similar landwights hate cold iron is widespread in Europe, as is belief in the luck-bringing properties of the iron horseshoe. The association of iron with giants, however, suggests that the early Germanic speakers viewed it with a certain ambivalence: although humans could wield its power, it was not without its dangers. The Finnish *Kalevala* tells how iron was born "in the swamp. . . . in the slack place": the sky god Ilmarinen is the first to forge iron. He calls for the bee to bring honey to temper it—but instead, the wasp treacherously brings him venom. Tempered in venom, iron forgets its oath to do no harm, and ever since then iron has "freed the blood to spill, the gore to gush forth" (canto 9, transl. Bosley, pp. 88-95). This hints at a deep awareness of the new metal's potential both to benefit and to harm.

The Evidence of the Bogs

Peat is made of layers of *Sphagnum* moss, which grows abundantly in northern European wetlands, creating unique environments known as peat bogs. Compacted peat can be dug out of a bog, dried, and used as fuel. Peat bogs also chemically generate iron-rich precipitates, so-called "bog iron," which can be used as ore. Bogs provided life-giving resources, and evidently the powers that dwelled in them accepted offerings in return. In the early Iron Age, between about 500 BCE and 100 CE, pots of food, wooden carvings, white quartz stones, and bones of butchered animals were fairly common bog offerings, often deposited in water-filled pits that were left by older peat cutting. Live animals were sometimes offered; at Hedelisker on Jutland, thirteen dogs had been sacrificed in a bog, including two that had been tied to a stone with a rope (Asingh, "The Magical Bog," pp. 283-286)

Humans were also sacrificed in bogs, and are one of the most famous types of archaeological discoveries from the Iron Age. Over five hundred "bog people," and possibly as many as two thousand, have been found in Denmark, northern Germany, the Netherlands, Britain, and Ireland, although many of these were not well preserved and/or were never documented well (Asigh, "The Bog People," pp. 291-292). The tannins in the peat and the lack of oxygen in the water can preserve the skin and soft tissues of these bodies amazingly well, even down to the contents of their stomachs (although the acidic water often destroys or considerably reduces the skeleton, and the pressure of overlying peat layers can crush or severely distort bodies). The clothing of the "bog bodies" (when they were wearing any) is often well preserved as well. Some of these sacrificed people may have been lawbreakers; Tacitus mentions that the Germans executed cowards and sex criminals by drowning them marshes (*Germania* 12, transl. Hutton, pp. 148-149). Yet many seem to have been persons of high social standing; several bog bodies, including the most famous bog bodies from Denmark, Tollund Man and Grauballe Man, were men in their 30s with no calluses on their hands. Several Danish bog bodies, including both Tollund Man and Grauballe Man, had eaten a last meal of gruel, including copious weed seeds as well as cultivated grain. P. V. Gløb suggested that the gruel

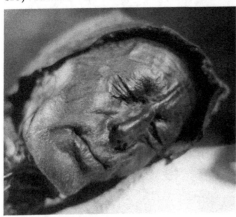

Head of Tollund Man. Photo by Sven Rosborn, Wikimedia Commons, Public Domain.

may have been a symbolic mixture to encourage the spring return of a goddess who would make the seeds sprout (*The Bog People*, pp. 163); however, it is more likely to have resulted from ordinary methods of growing grain and sorting the seeds at the time, which would have incorporated seeds from many plants now considered weeds. Re-creations of the gruel recipe have generally been judged unpalatable, but nutritious enough (Harild et al., "New Analyses," pp. 178-181). Grauballe Man's porridge included ergot, a common fungus growing on stored grain. Ergot is hallucinogenic in high doses; while it was once thoughts that Grauballe Man was deliberately dosed with a hallucinogen before being sacrificed, the actual dosage he received was probably far too low to have any effect (Harild et al., pp. 175-176). Bog bodies were deliberately killed, and sometimes violently treated around the time of death; Tollund Man was hanged, Grauballe Man's shin was broken and his throat was slashed from ear to ear, one of the men from Weerdinger in the Netherlands had been stabbed in the heart, and the man from Dätgen, Germany had been stabbed in the chest and then beheaded (Asingh, "The Bog People"). Gløb speculated that the rope nooses found around the necks of several bog bodies were analogous to the twisted neck-rings worn by the goddesses who received them, "the pass which carries (the bog man) over the threshold of death and delivers him into the possession of the goddess, consecrating him to her for all time" (*The Bog People*, pp. 165-166). However, hanging or strangulation, especially when combined with stabbing, is also reminiscent of the cult of Odin, or *Woðanaz as he would have been called at this time.

The most spectacular bog sacrifices of all involved the sacrifice of an entire defeated army. Horses and men were killed, weapons were bent or broken, and all their gear was laid in a bog or lake. The late Roman historian Orosius, quoting a much earlier account, describes the Cimbri sacrificing an entire defeated Roman army with all their gear in 105 BCE (*Seven Books of History* V.16; transl. Deferrari, p. 202):

> The enemy, after gaining possession of both camps and great booty, by a certain strange and unusual bitterness completely destroyed all that they had captured; clothing was cut to pieces and thrown about, gold and silver were thrown into the river, corselets of men were cut up, trappings of horses were destroyed, and the horses themselves were drowned in whirlpools, and men with fetters tied around their necks were hung from trees, so that the victor laid claim to no booty, and the conquered to no mercy.

Sacrificed sword, deliberately bent, from Kragehul Mose. National Museum of Denmark. CC BY-SA 2.0.

Tacitus tells how in 58 CE, the Hermunduri fought the Chatti over control of a salt spring, with each side vowing to sacrifice their enemies to "Mars and Mercury": "a vow implying the extermination of horses, men, and all objects whatsoever" (*Annales* XIII.57; transl. Jackson, vol 4, pp. 90-101). The Hjortspring find (4th century BCE) is the oldest evidence for this kind of sacrifice: 169 spear-points, 11 swords, several byrnies, and a large canoe-like war-boat very similar to the ships in Bronze Age rock art were all deposited together in a bog. A similar, though much larger, deposit was made at Illerup around 200 CE, with the gear of about 350 soldiers recovered so far. Several deposits were made at Nydam Mose (including three boats), Ejsbøl Mose, and Kragehul, all in Denmark, between about 200 and 500 CE. Smaller finds of this sort are relatively common through the sixth century CE (Ilkjær, "Danish War Booty Sacrifices," pp. 44-65). The Hermunduri dedicated their sacrifice to "Mars and Mercury," who would be *Teiwaz and *Woðanaz in the standard *interpretatio romana*, the system that Romans used to translate foreign god-names into equivalents in their own mythology.

Bogs were also the place where sacred images were kept in Denmark and northern Germany. At Foerlev Nymøllen, a forked oak branch, three meters long, only had to have minimal carving to be transformed into a tall, slender female form. She was laid in a cairn of stones, surrounded by pots of food, bones of butchered animals, and white quartz stones, all of which are typical bog offerings (Asingh, "The Magical Bog," pp. 284-286). We cannot know if she was the same deity as Nerthus in Tacitus's account, but her cairn is reminiscent of Tacitus's description of Nerthus in her "sacred precinct" (*Germania* 40; transl. Hutton, pp. 196-197). Tacitus also mentions the sacred wagon that carried Nerthus's image—and the remains of two wagons were found in a bog at Dejbjerg on west Jutland, dated to the first century BCE. These had been imported from central Europe, used and repaired locally, and carefully disassembled and laid within a fenced-in enclosure. At another site, Rappendam Mose on Zealand, remains of at least seven wagons were found in a bog, along with a human skeleton and animal bones (Gløb, *The Bog People*, pp. 166-170). Other figures are male; the idol from Brodden-bjerg is a branch with three forks, cleverly worked by minimal carving into a male with a head, two legs, and a huge phallus. Still other idols seem to have been paired males and females; two idols cut from planks were found alongside a trackway over the Wittemoor, near Oldenburg, one with a rect-angular body and one with three curves, presumably breasts, belly, and hips. Another pair of idols, anatomically male and female, was found carved from branches at Braak, in Schleswig-Holstein. At Oberdorla in Thuringia, many figures once stood around a marshy pool, and another idol with raised arms was found at Possendorf in 1859 (Todd, *The Early Germans*, pp. 108-109). Schutz comments that, "In spite of [the Germanic peoples'] sophis-ticated tools and skill as craftsmen, the awkward crudeness of all these figures is striking and must have been deliberate" (*The Prehistory of Germanic Europe*, p. 333).

Because bogs preserve ritual offerings so well, we know far more about ritual practices from bog evidence than for any other type of holy site. Yet Tacitus reports that the Germans "consecrate groves and coppices" (*Germania* 9, transl. Hut-ton, pp. 144-145), and he also describes the holy grove of the Semnones (*Germania* 39, pp. 194-195); the sacred grove of the Frisians consecrated to the goddess Baduhenna (*Annals* IV.73; transl.

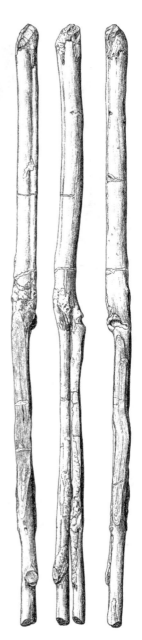

Three views of the idol from Forlev Nymølle. National Museum of Denmark.
CC BY-SA 2.0.

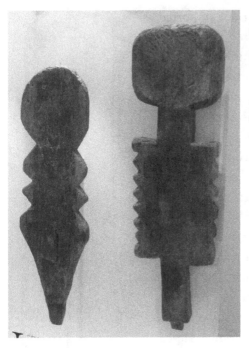

Iron Age idols from the Wittemoor, near Oldenburg, Niedersachsen, Germany. Landesmuseum für Kunst und Kulturgeschichte, Oldenburg. Image by Bullenwächter, Wikimedia Commons.

Jackson, vol. 3, pp. 130-131); and the grove where the prisoners from the Battle of the Teutoburg Forest were sacrificed (*Annals* I.61; transl. Jackson, vol. 2, pp. 346-349). For that matter, worship in sacred groves is recorded all over Europe and elsewhere; the Greeks and Romans had their own tradition of the sacred grove (Greek *nemos*, Latin *lucus*), and groves are also recorded among the Celts, Balts, and Slavs. Remains of sacred groves, usually preserved by being flooded as a nearby bog expanded, have been found from this time frame in Denmark and central Germany (Dowden, *European Paganism*, pp. 91-116). Sites that look very much like sacred groves have turned up from later time periods, notably at Lunda in Sweden (Andersson, "Among Trees, Bones, and Stones," pp. 195-198), and there are accounts of Viking-era sacred groves such as *Coll Tomair* ("Grove of Thor") in Ireland. Thus the custom of sacred groves continued from at least the Roman Iron Age (and probably farther back) until the coming of Christianity. The Roman poet Lucan described a "barbarian" sacred grove in his *De Bello Civili* (III.399-425; transl. Duff, pp. 142-145). While the actual grove he described is in southern France, German sacred groves could not have been very different:

A grove there was, untouched by men's hands from ancient times, whose interlacing boughs enclosed a space of darkness and cold shade, and banished the sunlight far above. No rural Pan dwelt there, no Silvanus, ruler of the woods, no Nymphs; but gods were worshipped there with savage rites, the altars were heaped with hideous offerings, and every tree was sprinkled with human gore. . . . The images of the gods, grim and rude, were uncouth blocks formed of felled tree-trunks. Their mere antiquity and the ghastly hue of their rotten timber struck terror; men feel less awe of deities worshipped under familiar forms; so much does it increase their sense of fear, not to know the gods whom they dread. . . . The people never resorted thither to worship at close quarters, but left the place to the gods. For, when the sun is in mid-heaven or dark night fills the sky, the priest himself dreads their approach and fears to surprise the lord of the grove.

Germans and Romans

Roman records of probable Germanic peoples begin abruptly, with the invasion of Gaul and northern Italy by the Cimbri (whose name may be preserved in the name of Himmerland, a region of Jutland in Denmark), Teutoni, and Ambrones in 113 BCE. While Roman records and place-name evidence suggest that they came from Jutland, they may have been at least partly Celtic; the last king of the Cimbri bore the very Celtic-sounding name Boiorix. Whoever they were, they invaded the lands of Rome's allies the Taurisci, and defeated the Romans at Noreia (probably in southern Austria) in 112 BCE. Turning westward into Gaul, they defeated two Roman consular armies at Arausio (Orange, France) in 105 BCE. After several years of wandering, they entered northern Italy and were crushed by the Romans at Vercellae (Vercelli, northern Italy) in 101 BCE (Rawlings, "The Roman Conquest of Southern Gaul").

Julius Caesar encountered other Germanic-speaking peoples during his Gaulish campaigns. In fact, the cause of his first campaign was an alliance between Gaulish tribes, the Sequani and Arverni, and the Germanic Suebi against their rivals the Aedui. Under their war-leader Ariovistus, the Suebi crossed the Rhine into Gaul and defeated the Aedui in 63 BCE—biting off a sizable chunk of Gaulish territory for themselves into the bargain. The Aedui begged for help from their Roman allies (Julius Caesar, *De bello gallico* I.31-36, transl. Edwards, pp. 46-57). In his account of the resulting wars, in which he drove the Suebi back across the Rhine, Caesar left some notes on the Germans' culture. The Suebi were not the only Germanic people crossing the Rhine; another of the tribes that Caesar fought, the Belgae, claimed kinship with the "Germans," and may have been a mix of Germanic and Celtic speakers (*De bello gallico* II.4, pp. 92-97).

Rome's push into Gaul and beyond soon brought more conflict with the Germanic peoples. An invasion in 16 BCE by the Sicambri or Sugambri, with their allies the Tencteri and Usipetes, wiped out an entire Roman legion (Cassius Dio, *Historia Romana* LIV.20, transl. Cary, vol. 6, pp. 332-333). Rome responded by strengthening the Rhine border and mounting military campaigns beyond it, as far as the Elbe River (Cassius Dio, LV.1, pp. 380-381, LV.28, pp. 466-469). The historian Velleius Paterculus reported that "All Germany was traversed by our armies; races were conquered hitherto almost unknown, even by name" (*Compendium of Roman History* II.106; transl. Shipley, pp. 268-271). In fact, a surprising number of Roman military bases has recently been excavated on the eastern side of the Rhine; the most distant ones are at Marktbreit in Bavaria, Hedemünden in Lower Saxony, and Hachelbich in Thuringia, while the base at Oberaden covered 56 hectares (138 acres), the largest Roman military base ever found. The large base at Haltern shows signs of local industry and civilian-style buildings, and was beginning to look like a town when it was abandoned (Schnurbein, "Augustus in Germania," pp. 95-97; Wolters, "Emergence of the Provinces," pp. 30-35; Küßner and Schüler, "Truppen in Thüringen," p. 6). In fact, at Waldgirmes, near present-day Frankfurt and 100 km away from the Rhine, construction began in 4 BCE on a Roman city. Excavation has revealed the remains of Roman-style homes and public buildings, a water and sewage system, a central forum, and a gilded bronze equestrian statue of Emperor Augustus (Curry, "The Road Almost Taken"; Schnurbein, pp. 98-104). Cassius Dio had reported that Rome was beginning to build cities deep in German territory, and although scholars were long skeptical, the excavations at Waldgirmes have confirmed his accuracy. Had the Romans been able to push their boundaries this far, at least half of present-day Germany would have become part of the Empire.

But in 9 CE, Arminius the Cheruscan[11] deceived the Roman commander Varus into marching his troops into a deathtrap. As the Romans were spread out along a narrow track between hills and marsh, vulnerable to ambush

---

11. Arminius's name was Germanicized to "Hermann" by Martin Luther and authors that followed him. This may not be historically accurate, but he is still commonly known as Hermann.

and unable to concentrate their forces, the Germans attacked and destroyed three legions at the Battle of the Teutoburg Forest. The survivors retreated to a fort called Aliso, which the Germans besieged; the Romans eventually abandoned the fort and escaped while the Germans were pillaging it (Cassius Dio, *Historia Romana* LVI.20-22, transl. Cary, vol. 7, pp. 42-50; Velleius Paterculus, *Compendium of Roman History* II.cxx.3-4, transl. Shipley, pp. 304-305; see Wells, *The Battle that Stopped Rome*). Aliso is strongly suspected to be the Roman base at Haltern, which was burned and abandoned at this time (Todd, *The Early Germans*, p. 51). Rome mounted a reprisal expedition in 15-16 CE, and after several inconclusive battles, defeated Arminius's forces at Idistaviso, somewhere on the Weser River. But as the Roman army was returning to its Rhine bases, sailing down the Ems River to the North Sea, a sudden storm destroyed part of the transport fleet and scattered the rest (Tacitus, *Annals* I.49-II.26; transl. Jackson, vol. 2, pp. 324-419). Emperor Tiberius put an end to further campaigns across the Rhine, and the city at Waldgirmes was abandoned. There were raids and revolts to come—such as the tax revolt of the Frisians in 28 CE, when they defeated a Roman force at Baduhenna Wood (Tacitus, *Annals* IV.72-74, transl. Jackson, pp. 126-133); and the

Statue of Arminius atop the *Hermannsdenkmal*, near Detmold, Germany (about 100 km away from the probable site of the Battle of Teutoberger Wald), sculpted by Ernst von Bandel and completed in 1875. Photo by Tsungam, Wikimedia Commons, CC BY-SA 4.0.

Batavian revolt in 69 CE led by a Romanized German known as Julius Civilis (Tacitus, *Histories* IV.12-86, V.14-26, transl. Moore, vol. 2, pp. 20-171, 199-219). Still, aside from a few Roman bridgeheads on the east bank, the Rhine remained the western border between the Roman Empire and the Germanic tribes until the Migration Age.

In the meantime, the Romans had occasionally sent military expeditions northeastward over the Alps into Pannonia (present-day eastern Hungary), but began serious campaigns against the tribes there in 15 BCE, formally annexing it in 11 BCE and putting down rebellions until 8 CE (Mócsy, *Pannonia and Upper Moesia*, pp. 31-41). Rome pushed its territorial claim as far north as the Danube River, where Roman settlers came into contact with other Germanic-speaking peoples, notably the Marcomanni ("border-men") and Quadi (possibly "speakers," i.e. people who speak a common language). The king of the Marcomanni, Maroboduus, had spent years living in Rome (like his rival Arminius) before returning to his people and moving them beyond the Danube. Augustus considered him a threat to Rome. Emperor Tiberius prepared a massive campaign against the Marcomanni by no fewer than twelve legions in the year 6 CE, but a revolt in Pannonia forced its cancellation, and Rome made a treaty with Maroboduus instead. Rivalry between Arminius and Maroboduus led to Arminius's killing and Maroboduus's exile back to Rome. Yet despite periodic unrest on the Danube frontier, the Romans did not push beyond the Danube (until a century later, when they annexed Dacia, present-day Romania, east of the German-speaking region).

To maintain the border across the gap between the two rivers, the Romans cleared the forest and built a line of forts, beginning in 90 CE. They also maintained large military bases along both rivers, some of which grew to be important cities: *Castra Bonnensis* (Bonn), *Colonia Claudia Ara Agrippinensium* (Köln/Cologne), *Confluentes* (Koblenz), *Mogontiacum* (Mainz), *Augusta Treverorum* (Trier), *Castra Regina* (Regensburg), *Vindobona* (Vienna), *Lentia* (Linz), *Aquincum* (Budapest), and *Singidunum* (Beograd/Belgrade). Thus the Roman *limes*, the frontier, was created.

Germania Beyond the Frontier

Around 98 CE, Publius Cornelius Tacitus wrote his account of the Germanic peoples, simply called *Germania*. Packed with information and vividly written, it remains a precious source of evidence for Germanic tribal culture and customs. Many of its details can be confirmed by archaeological and

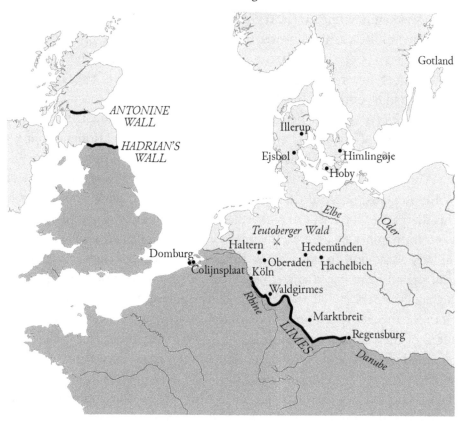

linguistic evidence. Yet it must be taken with a grain of salt: there is no evidence that Tacitus ever visited Germania himself. We know that he drew on writings by people who had been there, such as Pliny the Elder's book on the German wars (which unfortunately has not survived), and he also might have talked to Germans living in Rome. But he also used the stereotypes that any Greek or Roman historian was expected to use when writing about "barbarians." For example, he called the Germans a unique people, "like no one but itself"—but other Roman authors had used the same figure of speech about the Egyptians and Scythians; this was the sort of thing a Roman author was expected to say to emphasize the gap between Romans and "barbarians." Tacitus had served in government during the reign of the tyrannical Emperor Domitian, and surely had to keep his mouth shut to advance his own career. But Tacitus started publishing his historical works as soon as Domitian was dead, and *Germania* is slanted accordingly: when Tacitus praises the Germans for their freedom and liberty, what he was really doing was commenting on the regime that he'd lived through. Domitian had celebrated military triumphs over the Germans, which were probably staged shams. Tacitus's reminder that the Germans were still free and dangerous was meant to smear Domitian's memory. His description of the Germans as simple, rough, uncouth, but honest and virtuous, is meant as a critique of Roman society—not as a neutral report of how the Germanic tribes actually lived. In short, *Germania* is as much a commentary on the Romans as it is a book about the Germans (Krebs, *A Most Dangerous Book*, pp. 37-50).

Although most of the Germanic-speaking tribes were never conquered by the Romans, many of their men joined the Roman army. In some cases this was part of the terms of an alliance; a tribe might be expected to supply a certain number of men each year, in exchange for gifts, trade deals, and military assistance. In other cases, Rome might take hostages to assure the tribe's good behavior; this was how Arminius came to Rome, for example. No doubt others joined the legions for the adventure, the chances to win glory, or the steady pay and rations. Roman army units called *auxilia* consisted of men from a specific tribe; such *auxilia* might retain their tribe's preferred weapons and be used in battle in roles that suited their tribe's expertise. To avoid testing their loyalty, *auxilia* were often stationed far from their homeland. As a result, evidence for Roman-era Germanic religion can be found across the Empire. For example, a cohort of Tungri, a tribe from what is now Belgium, raised altars to their god Mars Thincsus (probably equated with Tyr) along Hadrian's Wall in northern England. On the other side of the Empire, the staff of a 2nd century governor of Egypt included a seeress named Waluburg, of the Germanic tribe of Semnones (Spickermann, "Waluburg"). Waluburg wasn't the only Germanic woman whom the Romans valued for her prophetic ability: the Emperor (briefly) Vitellius had an unnamed woman of the Chatti tribe as his personal seeress (Suetonius, *Lives of the Caesars* VII.xiv.5, transl. Rolfe, pp. 270-271), and the Emperor Domitian rendered honors to the priestess Ganna, the successor of the famous seeress Veleda (Cassius Dio, *Historia Romana* LXVII.5.3, transl. Cary, vol. 8, pp. 346-347).

Both from hostile encounters and through military service, the fighting gear of various Germanic-speaking tribes came to be based on Roman designs. Pattern-welded swords, made from strips of iron and steel repeatedly folded or twisted together and then forge-welded repeatedly, may be an adaptation of a Celtic invention, but the oldest known pattern-welded blades are of Roman manufacture: at bog sacrifices such as Nydam and Illerup, the blades bear Roman names and smiths' marks, although the hilts were made by Scandinavian craftsmen (Ilkjær, *Illerup Adal*, pp. 76-78; Williams, *The Sword and the Crucible*, pp. 62-72). Evidently Roman weapons were traded beyond the frontier, although possibly not with the consent of the Roman government. Roman-style

Detail of a sword blade from the bog sacrifice at Illerup, with an inlaid figure of the Romn god Mars. National Museum of Denmark. CC BY-SA 2.0.

belts and baldrics were also adopted, like the bronze baldric mount from Illerup that bears the letters OPTIME MAXIME CON—short for OPTIME MAXIME OMNIUM MILITANTIUM CONSERVA, "O [Jupiter] Best and Greatest, preserve all fighters" (Ilkjær, p. 96). The magnificent helmets from Vendel-age Sweden were based on Roman cavalry helmets, which bore a central ridge over the head and hinged plates to protect the cheeks and neck (Coulston, "Late Roman Military Equipment Culture," pp. 470-474). Germanic tribes also adopted Roman tactics; while legends claim that the wedge formation, called the *svinfylking* or "swine-formation" in the sagas, was taught to heroes of old by Odin himself (e.g. Saxo Grammaticus, *History of the Danes* VII.248, transl. Fisher, pp. 226-227), the Germanic people actually learned it in the Roman legions. At the same time, late Roman military equipment may have been influenced by Germanic equipment: for example, the large curved rectangular shields (*scuta*) of the Roman army were replaced in the 3rd century by round or oval shields, more like those used by Germanic peoples. The Romans also seem to have picked up from the Germans their customary battle-cry, the *barritus*: a wordless roar, amplified by using the shield as a sounding board (Coulston, pp. 475-477). By the time of the Migration Age (next chapter), "Roman" and "barbarian" armies generally fought using much the same types of weapons.

There was also considerable trade across the border. Tacitus attests to Germanic tribes near the Rhine buying wine from the Romans (*Germania*

23, transl. Hutton, pp. 166-167). Wine, along with the buckets, strainers and ladles for serving it, made it all the way to southern Scandinavia (Mc-Govern et al., "Nordic Grog," pp. 125-126). Roman pottery, glass, and spices also found willing buyers. In exchange, the Romans purchased German grain, livestock, meat, fish, leather, timber, iron, and other goods. Although such perishable goods have left almost no traces for archaeologists to find, the trade must have existed; the Roman army needed plenty of supplies, and since bulk transportation was slow and difficult, its policy was to buy locally when possible. Romans also bought Germanic slaves and hired Germanic craftsmen. Some Germanic tribesmen may have resented the Roman forts and settlements on the *limes*, but others must have seen them as huge economic opportunities (Heather, *Empire and Barbarians*, pp. 70-74). Amber remained a prized commodity, still traded along the old Amber Road to the head of the Adriatic Sea; Roman authors recorded the German name *glaesum* for it, closely related to the English word *glass* (Pliny, *Natural History* XXXVII.xi.42-46, transl. Eichholz, pp. 194-199). Two other products of German lands found a ready market in Rome: *sapo*, a strong soap used for bleaching hair (Pliny, *Natural History* XXVIII.li.191; transl. Jones, pp. 128-131); and goose down for pillows (Pliny, X.xxvii.53-54, pp. 326-327).

Roman diplomats gave Germanic chieftains prestigious gifts to maintain alliances and peaceful relationships. Roman bronze and glass vessels, some of them of high quality and probably prestigious gifts, have been found as far east as present-day Poland. Tacitus claims that "One may see among them

Silver dish from the Hildesheim hoard. Pernice and Winter, *Der Hildesheimer Silberfund* (1901).

silver vases, given as gifts to their envoys and chieftains, but treated as of no more value than earthenware" (*Germania* 5, transl. Hutton, pp. 136-137)—and indeed, the great hoard found at Hildesheim in northern Germany, far beyond the Rhine, included over seventy pieces of some of the finest Roman silverware found anywhere. The Hildesheim hoard may represent several generations of diplomatic gifts given over the first half of the first century (Todd, *The Early Germans*, pp. 89-92). Roman diplomacy extended as far as Denmark: an inscription from 14 CE, *Res Gestae Divi Augustae* (*Acts of the Divine Augustus*), relates how a Roman fleet sailed from the mouth of the Rhine eastward to the mouth of the Elbe and north to Jutland. There, says Augustus, the people "through their envoys sought my friendship and that of the Roman people" (V.20; transl. Shipley, pp. 386-389). In fact, some scholars have concluded that a realm centered on the island of Zealand was actually a Roman client state, not part of the Empire but formally allied with it (Storgaard, "Cosmopolitan Aristocrats," pp. 109-118).

Certainly, the Roman prestige goods deposited in graves attest to diplomacy as well as trade. A rich grave at Hoby, on the Danish island of Lolland, included a full Roman banqueting set: a bronze wine bucket, ladle, and pitcher, and two fine silver cups. The graves at Himlingøje on Zealand include more Roman treasures of silver and glass (Price, *Ancient Scandinavia*, pp. 282-284).

Roman silver cup depicting scenes from the *Iliad*. Part of a banqueting set from a chieftain's grave at Hoby, Lolland, Denmark. First century CE. National Museum of Denmark, CC BY-SA 2.0.

Yet another source of information on German-Roman contacts is the number of Latin words that were borrowed into Germanic languages at this time. Some of these words come from service in an army that marched everywhere it went and camped behind temporary stockades: English *street*, *mile*, and *wall* come from Latin *via strata* "paved road," *mille passum* "thousand paces," and *vallum* "row of posts." The legionary's sword belt, *balteus*, became English *belt*; his javelin, *pilum*, shifted meaning

Roman glass cup with wild animals. Himlingøje, Denmark. National Museum of Denmark, CC BY-SA 2.0.

and evolved into German *Pfeil*, "arrow;" and the *campus*, the field where he fought, evolved into both English *camp* and German *Kampf* "battle." Other words reflect trade: Latin *caupo*, "trader," gave rise to words such as German *kaufen* "to buy" and English *cheap*. Latin *mango*, "dealer," is the origin of the archaic English word *monger* (as in "fishmonger," "ironmonger," and so on). *Libra pondo* "a pound by weight" gave rise to *pound* in the sense of "unit of weight"; *teloneum* "customs house" became *toll* in the sense of "a tax"; and *moneta* became *mint* in the sense of "place where coins are made." As for what was traded: Latin *vinum* and *flascum* evolved into English *wine* and *flask*. Many words for ceramic household objects were borrowed: *catillus* "little bowl" became *kettle*, *discus* became *dish*, *cuppa* became *cup*, *tegula* became *tile*. One can imagine a retired German legionary, now married and settled down in the Rhineland, trying to keep up with the names of all the unfamiliar knick-knacks that his proper Roman wife keeps buying for their house. Perhaps she might expect him to buy her a *gem* (Latin *gemma*) for her birthday, or perhaps she might decide that the bedroom needs a new *pillow* (Latin *pulvinus*). She might also stock her *kitchen* (Latin *cucina*) with Roman ingredients: *cherry, plum, chestnut, peas, pepper, cumin, poppy, mint,* and even *butter* and *cheese* were borrowed from Latin *cerasus, prunum, castanea, pisum, piper, cuminum, papaver, menta, butyrum,* and *caseus* (Kastovsky, "Semantics and Vocabulary," pp. 301-304; Ringe, *From Proto-Indo-European to Proto-Germanic*, pp. 328-329).

German and Roman Religion

The Romans almost never tried to stamp out other polytheistic religions that they encountered. In fact, they had a formal religious rite, called *evocatio*, for inviting foreign gods to come to Rome. The wide range of altars and inscriptions found along the Rhine shows that the people were worshipping Roman deities together with Germanic and Celtic deities. Roman statues of gods also made it into Denmark, although whether the tribes adopted any aspects of Roman religion is unclear. Popular foreign cults also spread to Germania: statues of Isis have been found throughout the Roman-era Rhineland, from Cologne where she may have had a sanctuary, as far as Frisia and even Scandinavia (Turcan, *The Cults of the Roman Empire*, pp. 101-102). But Roman soldiers in Germania also raised altars to the *Genius Loci*, "spirit of the place," or in one case the *Præsides Huius Loci*, "Protectors of This Place," as a way of staying on good terms with whatever local spirit or wight might be in charge of a particular area (Saddington, "Roman Soldiers, Local Gods, and *Interpretatio Romana*," pp. 155-157). Even very localized Germanic holy powers were honored; there are many inscriptions from the Rhineland to beings with Germanic names that are otherwise completely unknown, such as *Sandraudiga* ("true abundance"), *Vagdavercustis* ("worker of mercy"), *Alateiva* ("fully divine"), the two *Ahueccaniae* ("prophetic spirits of the water"), and many more (see Simek, *Dictionary of Northern Mythology*, for a list). Some Germanic deities had sizable Roman-style temples that drew worshippers from a wide region, such as Nehalennia in the Netherlands (e.g. Hondius-Crone, *The Temple of Nehalennia*), and some of the Rhineland Matronae, triple goddesses honored under a bewildering variety of names (Simek, "Late Roman Iron Age Cult"; Shaw, pp. 41-47). These deities were honored with Roman rituals; their altars depict the same sorts of sacrifices that would have been rendered anywhere in the Empire.

However, the Romans tended to consider foreign deities as aspects of their own, and often used Roman names for other people's deities, a system that Tacitus called the *interpretatio Romana*. Inscriptions sometimes identify Germanic deities with Roman ones, as in the inscriptions to *Mercurius Cimbrianus*, "Mercury of the tribe of Cimbri" (Shaw, *Pagan Goddesses*, p. 38); the altar to *Mars*

Roman-style altar to the goddess Nehalennia from her temple near present-day Domburg, The Netherlands. Inscription reads *Deae Nehalenniae Ianuarinus Ambacthius pro se et suis v[otum] r[eddidit] l[ibens] m[erito]*, "To the Goddess Nehalennia, Ianuarinus Ambacthius has rendered his vow, freely and as deserved, for himself and his own." Janssen, *Romeinsche Beelden* (1845).

Statue of the Roman god Mars Ultor
(Mars the Avenger), whose cult was
founded by Emperor Augustus.
Tyberggård, Denmark. National
Museum of Denmark, CC BY-SA 2.0.

Thincsus, "Mars of the Assembly," raised by the Tungri; or the altar to *Mars Halamarđus*, combining the Roman name of Mars with a Germanic name that probably means "slayer of men," presumably a tribal war-god (Griebenberger, "Germanische Götternamen," pp. 388-389). When Tacitus said that the Germans worship Mercurius above all, he presumably meant a Germanic deity who had something to do with commerce, trickery, eloquence, travel, and/or conducting the souls of the dead. It's a reasonable guess that this refers to Odin, or *Wođanaz as his name would have been at the time. That said, the *interpretatio Romana* was not always consistent, and determining which Germanic deity is denoted by a Latin name is not always straightforward.

By the early 4th century, the Romans had adopted the seven-day planetary week, based on Hellenistic models and ultimately derived from Babylonian sources. Each day was ruled by one of the gods identified with a planet, and the Romans duly assigned their own corresponding deities: Sun-day, Moon-day, Mars'-day, Mercury's-day, Jupiter's-day, Venus'-day, and Saturn's-day (Zerubavel, *The Seven Day Circle*, pp. 12-20). When the day names were rendered into Germanic languages, the result was a fairly standardized *interpretatio germanica*: Sun-Day, Moon-Day, Tiw's-day, Wodan's-day, Thonar's-day, and Frija's-day. ("Saturday" never had a standard translation, perhaps because no Germanic god precisely fits the

Roman god Saturn.) It's not clear when the Germanic week-names were adopted. It was once thought that they appeared during the Roman period, but ironically, they may have been spread at a later time by the Christian Church, which generally took the position that the names of the old gods did not need to be feared because the old gods didn't exist (Shaw, "The Origins of the Theophoric Week").

Breaking Through

Germania did not remain static during the Roman Iron Age. It has often been assumed that northern tribes were constantly migrating southward in waves: the Gothic historian Jordanes called Scandinavia *vagina gentium*, "the womb of peoples." The truth seems to be that most of the Roman-era Germanic tribes were settled farmers, not especially given to nomadic wanderings. But the smaller tribes that Tacitus had described were beginning to gather into larger and more stable federations, such as the Alamanni ("all the folk") and the Franks. Improved agriculture and increasing trade meant that Germanic tribes had more food and money, which leaders could use to support full-time warriors. The weapons deposits from defeated armies reflect this process, even among tribes not in direct contact with the Romans. At Ejsbøl Mose, the gear of roughly two hundred men was sacrificed in a bog; all of them had thrusting and throwing spears, about sixty also had swords, and ten of these had horses (Heather, *Empire and Barbarians*, pp. 43-47). At Illerup, about three hundred men had shields with central bosses made of iron, forty had bronze bosses, and five had bosses overlaid with gold or silver (Ilkjær, *Illerup Ådal*, pp. 98-101). Both finds reflect, not mobs, but disciplined armies, with officers and commanders who exercised authority over the rank and file. By the mid-300s, some Germanic confederations could field armies of over 10,000 men, probably paying for them with a system of taxation (Heather, pp. 59-64).

Rome's policy was to ally with friendly tribes and use them to counter unfriendly ones. Friendly "barbarians" could be kept that way with rich gifts, annual subsidies, and favorable trade deals. In the late Empire, favored tribes could become *foederati*, receiving land to settle in exchange for taxes and a levy of men for the legions. Rome grew quite accustomed to filling its manpower needs and taxation quotas by settling migrants or defeated foes as *foederati* in underpopulated lands. More than one tribe ended up defending lands it had once raided. There were still periodic cross-border raids by tribes who were dissatisfied with their deal with the Romans, or who just saw their chance to grab some quick plunder. When the carrots didn't work, there was always the stick: the Roman army might burn the fields and villages of an unruly tribe, confiscating cattle, slaves, and conscripts, until their leaders promised to play nicely. Especially unruly tribes might find permanent garrisons on their land, or might be forced to move away from the border (Heather, *Empire and Barbarians*, pp. 81-90; Barbero, *The Day of the Barbarians*, pp. 13-16). A more serious problem was that *foederati* near the border, whose leaders had grown rich from trade and subsidies, were likely to find themselves invaded by tribes from farther away who wanted their own piece of the action (Heather, *Empire and Barbarians*, pp. 137-142).

In 166, the *limes* failed to hold: the Langobardi broke through the Roman borders in Venetia. Although they were soon repulsed, their neighbors the Marcomanni and Quadi soon crossed the border and besieged the city of Aquileia. After several years of fighting, the Emperor Marcus Aurelius finally drove them back—but at about the same time, he had to deal with the Costobocci and the Bastarnae, who may or may not have been Germanic-speaking, and who were ravaging from present-day Romania southward all the way to Greece. The stoic Romans managed to close the frontier again, with the help of allied troops from as far away as Denmark (Storgaard, "Cosmopolitan Aristocrats," pp. 115-118)—but it was not an easy victory.

Roman troops burning the huts of the Marcomanni, depicted on the column of Marcus Aurelius. Bartoli and Bellori, *Columna Antoniniana. . .* (1672).

The Marcomannic Wars exposed a persistent strategic weakness for Rome: the need to shift troops to put down a revolt, a civil war, or an invasion in one part of the Empire. This created weaknesses elsewhere on the frontier, which tribes hungry for glory (or just plain hungry) could exploit. At times, the Roman frontier resembled a continent-spanning game of Whack-A-Mole. The whacking was heaviest during the so-called Crisis of the Third Century, beginning in the year 235, when Rome suffered through a combination of economic depression, political instability, peasant revolts, civil wars, plagues, and invasions. At its height, the Empire briefly split into three. Wherever troops were pulled off the frontier to deal with conflict or support a claimant to the Imperial title, tribes broke through the *limes*. Belgium, Gaul, Upper Germany, Italy, Greece, and Thrace (present-day Bulgaria, more or less) were all invaded. It wasn't until 275 that the Romans had secured most of their old borders, and Dacia (present-day Romania) had to be abandoned for the time being. The emperor Diocletian finally managed to stabilize the government, but he had to fight the invading Alamanni again in 286.

Musset comments that, "In the end the brutal energy of Diocletian succeeded, after a generation of disasters, in keeping the Germans out of the Empire. But they had weighed up both its wealth and its weakness, and were not likely to forget either" (*The Germanic Invasions*, p. 11). And they didn't. During the Roman civil war of 350-353, when troops were pulled from the Rhine frontier, the Franks and Alamanni saw their chance and invaded Gaul. They were driven back at Argentoratum (Strasbourg) in 357—but when the victorious Emperor Julian decided to invade Persia, he took troops from the border again, and the Alamanni invaded again, forcing Julian's successor Valentinian to fight them again in 368 at Solicinium (somewhere in southwest Germany). And so it went on.

Contributors:

1st edition: Kveldúlfr Gundarsson.

2nd edition: New material by Ben Waggoner.

3rd edition: Reorganization and new material by Ben Waggoner.

Die for pressing designs into sheet metal, depicting a helmeted warrior who appears to be dancing (and who has had one eye deliberately damaged) followed by a warrior wearing a beast mask. Torslunda, Öland, Sweden. Swedish Historical Museum 618349. CC BY-SA 2.5.

CHAPTER FIVE

The Migration and Vendel Ages

350-792 CE

With the Migration Age, the Germanic peoples took their place in the mainstream of European history. By the end of this period, the wandering tribes had established realms in the dismembered Roman Empire, which would become the European nations of today. Why did they move, and how did they settle into their new lands?

Anglo-Saxon disc brooch, 7th century. Faversham, Kent. Metropolitan Museum of Art. Public domain.

End of an Empire

The Migration Age (ca. 350-550 CE) begins with the Roman Empire still holding strong, and ends with the western Empire divided into several realms ruled by tribal confederations that had migrated into the Empire's lands, settled down, and adopted Roman institutions to some extent. The history of this time is confusing; reputable sources are thin, and it gets hard to keep track of who was who. Nevertheless, this is an important time for our spiritual traditions, because many of our heroic legends are set against this backdrop. The Migration Age is the time of Sigurd the Volsung and Beowulf and Hrólfr kraki and King Arthur. The historical persons and events behind these legends, if they even existed, have left almost no reliable historical evidence. But no matter: they continue to inspire tellers of tales, down to the present day. This is the time of serpent-patterned swords and swine-crested helms, ring-giving rulers and rich hoards of gold, tragic betrayals and trusty heroes. (And also, awesome alliteration.)

Many historians over the past five hundred years have seen the Migration Age as a destructive invasion of ignorant, savage "barbarians." The truth is more complex. The "invaders" generally didn't want to destroy the Roman Empire. In fact, the trade benefits and subsidies that the Romans gave tribes on their border were one major inducement to migration in the first place (Heather, *Empire and Barbarians*, pp. 134-142). Some tribes needed land to settle in safety, and were willing to pay Roman taxes, follow Roman laws, and serve in the Roman legions in exchange. For their part, the Romans needed people to work the land, pay taxes, and defend the long borders. The newcomers often had sanction from the Empire to settle where they did; there were even been instances when one Roman faction covertly encouraged a tribe to migrate into the Empire, in order to cause problems for a rival (Goffart, *Barbarian Tides*, p. 79). Often the tribes were happy to maintain Roman administration and adopt the Latin language: this is why no one in Spain still speaks Suebian, Visigothic, or Vandalic, no one in France speaks Burgundian or Franconian, and no one in Italy speaks Langobardic. The Visigothic king Athaulf, who had fought beside Alaric when he invaded Italy, allegedly said that "he, at first, was ardently eager to blot out the Roman name and to make the entire Roman Empire that of the Goths alone. . . [but later] he chose to seek for himself the glory of completely restoring and increasing the glory of the Roman name by the forces of the Goths, and to be held by posterity as the author of the restoration of Rome, since he had been unable to be its transformer" (Orosius, *Seven Books of History* VII.43; transl. Deferrari, pp. 361-362). While these may not be his exact words, there is no reason to doubt that they reflect the actual mood of the time.

As we mentioned in the previous chapter, there had been trade, travel, and intermarriage across the Roman frontier for centuries. Ever since the Edict of Caracalla in 212 CE, full Roman citizenship had been available to all free men and women in the Empire, not just natives of Italy. Now that citizenship no longer depended on ethnicity, many people of Germanic heritage became citizens. Most of the battles of this time between "Roman" and "barbarian" armies had "barbarians" fighting on both sides. In fact, by this time, most of the Roman officer corps, including some of Rome's greatest generals, were descended from Germanic-speaking tribes (Todd, *The Early Germans*, pp. 59-61), and Roman armies had adopted some Germanic weaponry, such as round shields (Coulston, "Late Roman Military Equipment Culture," pp. 475-477). On the other side of the border, tribes on the move often picked up members along the way; the Gothic hosts, for example, came to include other Germanic tribespeople (such as Vandals, Heruli, and Saxons), Slavs, Romans, Indo-Iranian people (such as Alans and Sarmatians), and non-Indo-European speakers such as Finns, Huns, and even a few Jews (Wolfram, *History of the Goths*, pp. 5-8, 300-302). It would take a few centuries for anything like modern nationalities to appear.

Enter the Huns

The Migration Age may be said to begin with the arrival of the Huns, a nomadic people from the central Asian steppes. The Huns' original homeland and language are still uncertain. They may or may not be the same as the people known as the Xiongnu in Chinese histories, who lived on the central Asian steppes until the 1st century CE (Thompson, *The Huns*, p. 1). Around the year 370, the Huns crossed the Volga River and moved into eastern Europe. In 375, they devastated the Ostrogothic kingdom north of the Black Sea.

The Goths were forced to move. Despite some previous incursions into Roman territory, they had had treaties with Rome for fifty years, providing soldiers in exchange for shipments of grain. They were allegedly so friendly to Rome that the Greek orator Libanius claimed that the Goths "treated our emperor as if he were theirs" (quoted in Barbero, *The Day of the Barbarians*, p. 23). In 376, refugees from a Gothic tribal group known as the Tervingi asked to settle in the Empire as *foederati*. The Eastern Emperor Valens granted them permission to cross the Danube and receive food aid and land for settlement. Unfortunately, the Roman officials in charge bungled the relief effort, stole the relief supplies, and mistreated the Goths.[12] Pushed to the limit, the outraged Goths rose in rebellion and pillaged the province of Thrace for two years. Valens himself led an army against them, but his nephew Gratian, the Western Emperor, was dealing with an invasion of Alamanni and couldn't spare many troops to assist. On August 9, 378, the Goths decisively defeated the Romans near the city of Adrianopolis (now Edirne, in European Turkey). Valens and many of his officers were killed, and the military strength of the Eastern Empire was seriously compromised (Barbero, pp. 43-112). Valens's successor Theodosius made a truce with the

---

12. Ammianus claims that Roman officials would trade dogs to starving Goth families in exchange for their children; *History* XXXI.4.11, transl. Rolfe, vol. 3, pp. 406-407.

Goths, who would retain their identity and much of their autonomy for the next few centuries. In fact, to replenish the troops killed at Adrianopolis, Roman leaders increasingly had to hire entire bands of Goths and other "barbarians" as mercenaries. Even as the Roman Empire was trying to maintain its integrity against the "barbarians," it was coming to depend on them more and more (Barbero, pp. 130-141).

Gothic hostility broke out again in the next generation. The Gothic leader Alaric had started his career as a mercenary in Roman service and risen to command all Gothic mercenaries. He had allied with Theodosius and fought alongside Roman troops against the Franks at the Battle of Frigidus in 394. Allegedly feeling poorly rewarded after the battle, in which he'd lost 10,000 men, Alaric switched sides and marched on Constantinople, turned towards Greece, and pillaged until he was bought off by getting the job of top military commander in Illyricum (corresponding to the former Yu-

Captured idols of the Goths, carried by camels in a triumphal Roman procession, as depicted on the now-destroyed Column of Arcadius in Constantinople, commemorating a Roman victory in the year 400. Each idol supposedly consisted of a tree-trunk, fitted with a carved head, and dressed in fine clothing. Menestrier, *Columna Theodosiana. . .*, 1765.

goslavia, more or less). When this seemed insufficient, he headed for Italy, where Roman forces, commanded by the half-Vandal general Stilicho, fended him off. But when the incompetent Emperor Honorius committed two blunders—having Stilicho executed, and massacring the families of Goths in the Roman army, which drove them to desert to Alaric—Alaric blockaded Rome in 408.[13] Alaric was bought off with a rich ransom and 40,000 freed Gothic slaves, but he returned in 410 and sacked Rome. He died soon after, but under the command of his brother-in-law Athaulf, the Visigoths moved on to southern Gaul and Spain. A dynasty of Visigothic kings would rule much of Spain until the Arab invasions of the 700s (Heather, *Empire and Barbarians*, pp. 191-202).

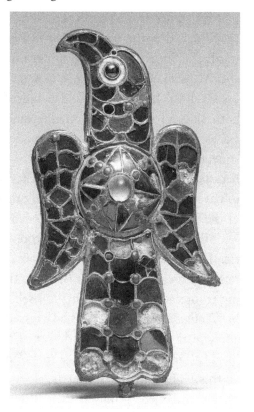

Gothic eagle brooch. Walters Art Museum, Baltimore, Maryland. Public Domain.

Stilicho had pulled troops from the Rhine frontier to defend against Alaric—*and* against a host of Goths under Radagaisus, which had entered Italy in 405/6. Stilicho defeated Radagaisus and incorporated 12,000 of his men into his own army, but the Rhine frontier was left open to a group of Vandals, Suebi, and Alans that crossed the Rhine at Mogontiacum (Mainz) on December 31, 406. Why they migrated is unclear; the Huns may have driven them from their homelands along the Danube, or they may have been survivors of Radagaisus's forces looking for another way in (Drinkwater, "The Usurpers," p. 273). The cumulative effect of all these invasions was to cut Roman troop numbers in the west in half; something like eighty regiments were lost (Heather, *Empire and Barbarians*, p. 175). The migrants

---

13. Warned that he would face massive resistance, Alaric allegedly replied, "The thicker the hay, the easier the mowing!"

met resistance from Franks who were loyal to Rome, but pressed on until they reached Spain, which they ruled until the Visigoths came in 420. Afterwards the Suebi still held on to a realm in northwest Spain, and the Vandals and Alans maintained a realm in southern Spain (Goffart, *Barbarian Tides*, pp. 73-108). In 429, the Vandals moved into north Africa. Now controlling both sides of the western Mediterranean, including some of the Empire's richest farmland, they sacked Rome in 455, after knocking down the city's aqueducts to encourage surrender.[14] This is how the tribal name "Vandal" became a by-word for wanton destruction, although the Vandals don't seem to have been more destructive than other tribes, by the rather low standards of the time.

Stilicho had also withdrawn troops from Britain to defend against Alaric. The remaining Roman troops in Britain chose a new commander and raised him as their emperor (Constantine III), and he took the best remaining troops across the Channel himself. Constantine's forces fought the Suebi, Vandals, and Alans that had crossed the Rhine, and held on to Gaul for a few years, but after several defeats, Constantine was captured and executed in 411. (Drinkwater, "The Usurpers," pp. 271-287, gives a good overview of all this.) The tribe of Burgunds, along with some Alans, promptly chose an aristocrat named Jovinus as their Emperor. Jovinus promptly used his questionable authority to grant the Burgunds a kingdom as *foederati* on the western side of the Rhine, centered on Borbetomagus (Worms). Jovinus himself would be captured and executed in 413, but the Burgundian kingdom lasted until 437, when Huns in Roman service destroyed it (Drinkwater, pp. 288-290). The Burgunds' name still survives near their first kingdom, in the Burgundy or Bourgogne region of France, but the Burgund survivors re-established a new kingdom to the south, in what is now the Savoy region of France. This second kingdom lasted until 534, when it was absorbed by the Franks.

The Romans in Britain had already built a line of coastal forts to defend against Saxon pirates, known as the *litus Saxonicum*, the "Saxon Shore" (Heather, *Empire and Barbarians*, pp. 285-286). Unfortunately, Constantine III's expedition had stripped Britain of troops for its own defense. In 411, the emperor Honorius responded to a British appeal for help by stating that they would have to fend for themselves. Solid historical facts become scarce

---

14. Which, of course, is why the pump don't work.

here; most of the histories of Britain for this time were written centuries after the events happened. But legend has it that Britain was attacked from the north by the Picts. The British king Vortigern allegedly asked for help from the Angles, Saxons, and Jutes, peoples from the North Sea coast of present-day Denmark and north Germany, who

Aerial view of Burgh Castle, a Roman fort along the "Saxon Shore," near preset-day Great Yarmouth, Norfolk, East Anglia, England. The fort is 205 meters (673 feet) wide. Photo by John D. Fielding, Wikimedia Commons, CC BY 2.0.

first came to Britain in the year 449, according to the *Anglo-Saxon Chronicle* (transl. Swanton, pp. 12-13). Other sources, and archaeological evidence, add Frisians and Rhineland Franks to the list of newcomers. Led by two kings named Hengist and Horsa ("stallion" and "horse"), the newcomers defeated the Picts and were awarded land—but more came, and claimed more territory, fighting for over a hundred years until most of Britain was in their hands, except for Wales, Cornwall, and northern Scotland (Bede, *Ecclesiastical History* I.15-16, transl. Sherley-Price, pp. 62-64). According to the 6th century chronicler Gildas, a Romano-British leader, Ambrosius Aurelianus, successfully resisted the Angles and Saxons for a time, defeating them in battle at Badon Hill (*De excidio Brittaniae* 25-26, transl. Giles, pp. 22-23). A latter history attributed to the Welsh monk Nennius gives the name of the British commander at Badon Hill as Arthur (*Historia Brittonum* 50, transl. Giles, pp. 28-29). While there is virtually no solid documentation of what really happened, this is the origin of the legend of King Arthur.

The old view that the Anglo-Saxons came in a mass migration that wiped out the Romano-British is now not thought to be true. There remains debate over whether large numbers of Anglo-Saxons migrated to Britain, or whether a relatively small Anglo-Saxon elite assumed rulership over a mostly unchanged Romano-British people, known as *elite transfer* (a.k.a. the "Three Men in A Boat Theory;" see Heather, *Empire and Barbarians*, pp. 266-268). New evidence from ancient and modern DNA suggests the truth was somewhere in between; there was neither a genocidal replacement of the

British by huge Anglo-Saxon hordes, nor a tiny Anglo-Saxon elite ruling a Romano-British population. The modern population of eastern England collectively derives about 40% of its ancestry from Anglo-Saxon migrants—who, unsurprisingly, show genetic links with today's Dutch and Danish populations. But there was intermarriage between migrants and natives at a very early date, and some of the social elites of the early Anglo-Saxon period were culturally Anglo-Saxon, but genetically closer to the earlier British (Schiffels et al., "Iron Age and Anglo-Saxon Genomes"). This is confirmed by early legal codes and genealogies that mention rulers and nobles with Celtic names (Heather, p. 275).

A second branch of the Gothic peoples, the Ostrogoths, would also invade Italy. The last few Western Emperors had been puppets appointed by Germanic military leaders. In 476, a Germanic commander, Odoacer, deposed the last Western Roman Emperor, a nonentity named Romulus Augustulus. Odoacer ruled Italy as its king, theoretically in the name of the Eastern Emperor. But the relationship soured, and in 488, following the usual tactic of playing barbarian factions off against each other, the Eastern Emperor Zeno commissioned the Ostrogothic king Theodoric to recapture Italy. By 493, Theodoric had claimed all of Italy and killed Odoacer. Ruling from the city of Ravenna, always in the name of the Eastern Emperor, his reign was remembered as a good one; by 511, his realm included most of Spain, southern France, and north Africa, either under his direct rule or under liege kings. Theodoric was also noted for maintaining Roman institutions, rebuilding Roman cities, and sponsoring learning and scholarship (Burns, *History of the Ostrogoths*, pp. 64-87).

Mausoleum of Theodoric in Ravenna, Italy. Photo by Paolo Monti, BEIC Library, courtesy of Wikimedia Commons. CC BY-SA 4.0.

Unfortunately, after Theodoric died in 526, his successors were unable to hold their realm against the new Emperor Justinian's desire to reconquer Italy. After twenty years of war, the Eastern Roman Empire regained Italy in 552 or 553, killing the last Ostrogothic king Teias at the Battle of Mons Lactarius (Burns, *History of the Ostrogoths*, pp. 214-215). The surviving Ostrogoths stayed in Italy and submitted to Byzantine rule. But Italy had been severely weakened and de-populated, and there wasn't much resistance to yet another migration. The Langobards, who had supposedly come from Scandinavia in the distant past, were living in Pannonia (present-day western Hungary). Allegedly invited by the disgruntled Byzantine general Narses, the Langobards and some Saxon allies marched into Italy in 586. The Langobards occupied north and cen-tral Italy, with the last northern Italian city, Pavia, falling to them in 572. Despite Frankish and Byzantine incursions, they would hold this realm until Charlemagne conquered it in 774 (Christie, *The Lombards*, pp. 58-79).

The Ostrogothic kingdom had tried to maintain Roman government, but its collapse essentially marked the end of the Western Roman state. One person who tried to preserve Roman institutions was Theodoric's personal secretary Cassiodorus. A devout Christian, he turned his country estate into a monastery after retiring from public life in 544. He advocated maintaining much of the old Roman educational curriculum as a support to Christian theology; he assembled a sizable library, and he encouraged the copying and binding of manuscripts (*Institutiones* 27-31, transl. Halporn and Vessey, pp. 158-166). As Heathens, we may not especially care for his religion—but without the intellectual traditions that he and others encouraged, especially the tradition of copying manuscripts, we would know far less than we do about the world of our forebears.

The Nibelungs: Legend and History

In 437, Roman troops with Hunnish auxiliaries attacked the kingdom of the Burgunds and destroyed it, killing their king Gundahari. This was probably done at the instigation of the Roman general Aetius, as a way of handling a barbarian kingdom that was growing too powerful for comfort. But the story was transformed as it was told and retold, growing into the great tale of the downfall of the Burgundian royal house, the Nibelungs. In legend, Attila the Hun lured the Burgundians to his hall and tried to kill them there to win their gold. After a desperate battle, Gunther and his kinsman Hagen were taken prisoner and tortured, but died without giving up the location of their gold. It fell to Gunther's sister Gudrun to take a terrible vengeance on Attila. The treasure of Gunther and Hagen was none other than the Rhinegold, taken by the gods from the Rhine, hoarded by the dragon Fafnir, and won by the mightiest of heroes, Sigurd Fafnir's Bane, who joined the Nibelungs and married Gudrun but was treacherously slain for his treasure.

The best-known versions of are the Old Norse *Vǫlsunga saga*; the Volsung poems in the *Poetic Edda*; the Norse *Þiðreks saga*, a translation of a lost German text; and the Middle High German *Nibelungenlied*. All of these (and more) were sources for Richard Wagner's operatic cycle *Der Ring des Nibelungen*. Parts of the story are also told or alluded to in the Old English poems *Beowulf* and *Waldere*, and there are even depictions of the legend on artworks such as the church doors from Hylestad, Norway, and several runestones and carvings from Britain and Scandinavia. Historically, the tale is inaccurate. Attila was still very young when the Huns destroyed the Burgundians; Theodoric, in legend the greatest hero in Attila's band, had not been born in 437; and the Norse version of the story then brings Gudrun's sons to the court of Jǫrmunrekr,

Sigurd killing the dragon Fafnir, as carved on the Hylestad stave church doors in the late 12th century. Kunsthistorisk Museum, University of Oslo, CC BY-SA 4.0

the same as the Ostrogothic king Ermanaric who died in 375. Sigurd / Siegfried and Brynhild / Brünnhilde *may* have been based on the Frankish King Sigibert, who did marry a Visigothic princess named Brunichildis and who was murdered in 575, but if this is the case, then Sigibert has been inserted into events that took place a century before he was born (Gentry et al., *The Nibelungen Tradition*, p. 26). Nor do the different versions agree with each other. To give one example out of many: in *Vǫlsunga saga*, Sigurd's father is fostered at the court of King Hjalprek of Denmark because his father has died in battle—but in the *Nibelungenlied*, his counterpart Siegfried is the beloved son of the prince of Xanten, who is very much alive. All of this matters little. Whoever Sigurd was, whether or not he existed at all, he became the most celebrated hero in all of Germanic literature. Sigmund speaks of his unborn son Sigurd in *Vǫlsunga saga* 11: *hans nafn mun uppi, meðan verǫldin stendr*—"his name will be remembered as long as the world lasts"—and this has certainly proven to be true.

Legends also grew up around Theodoric, told in a cycle of Middle German poems (where Theodoric has become *Dietrich*), as well as in *Þiðreks saga* and a few Old English poems such as *Deor* and *Waldere*. In legend, he became Attila's greatest warrior, fighting alongside him against the Nibelungs. He is with Attila because he has been exiled from his own rightful kingdom, centered on Verona in Italy, by his wicked uncle Ermanrich (a substitute for the historical Odoacer). Eventually he returns and wins it back. Another set of Middle German heroic poems depicts Dietrich's encounters with various giants and dwarves. In Christian lore, he was the son of the Devil, who could spit fire and was carried off to Hell alive on his own horse. In some folk tales, he leads the Wild Hunt.

Change of Faith: Conquest and Conversion

At the end of the fifth century, Theodoric and his Ostrogoths held Italy; the Anglo-Saxons ruled most of England; the Visigoths were still migrating through France to Spain; the Vandals were settled in Northern Africa; and the Franks had claimed most of modern France, although the Burgundians held their kingdom in the southeast. By this time, these peoples were familiar with Christianity. In fact, many had already adopted it. Constantine I had officially permitted Christianity in 313, and even before that date it had spread through the Empire. Christians captured by the Goths spread their faith among them, as did missionaries during times when the Goths were at peace with Rome. The most famous missionary, Ulfila ("Little Wolf"), devised an alphabet for the Gothic language, and he and his associates trans-

Line from the *Codex Argenteus*, by far the largest surviving manuscript in Gothic,
using the modified Greek alphabet that Ulfilas devised. The line is from Matthew 6:15
and reads *iþ jabai ni afletiþ mannam*, "if you do not forgive men." Facsimile
from Bosworth, *The Gothic and Anglo-Saxon Gospels*, 1874.

lated the Bible into Gothic. Most of his translation is lost, but most of the
Gospels and a fragment of the Old Testament survive—the only significant
surviving text in any East Germanic language. Christian Goths had suffered some persecution from pagan Goths in 348, when Ulfila was driven
into exile, and again in 367-378. But once the Goths had settled within
the Empire, between 382 and 395, most of them converted to Christianity
(Thompson, *The Visigoths in the Time of Ulfilas*, pp. 106-107). Christianity
had been proclaimed the state religion of the Empire in 380, and while
paganism was not yet outlawed, barbarians with their eyes on a military or
civil career would have found it advantageous to convert. This process of migration, partial integration into Roman society through fighting and negoti-
ation, and conversion, seems to have been the model for all those Germanic
tribes who settled in Roman lands (Thompson, pp. 128-129).

Still, the new religion wasn't universally accepted. Alaric himself had
outwardly adopted Arian Christianity, but he supposedly retained belief in
the old gods as well: the historian Claudian reports Alaric as having said,
"The gods, too, urge me on. Not for me are dreams or birds, but the clear
cry uttered openly from the sacred grove: 'Away with delay, Alaric; boldly
cross the Italian Alps this year and thou shalt reach the city'" (*Gothic War*
544-547; transl. Platnauer, vol. 2, pp. 164-165). The Gothic pre-Christian
religion was eventually abandoned, but Heathen elements, such as the wearing of torcs and arm-rings by priests, survived in Visigothic Christianity.

It's significant that what the Goths and other tribes converted to was the
Arian sect of Christianity. Propounded by the priest Arius, Arianism holds
that Jesus Christ did not always exist—he is not *coeternal* with God the Father, but was created in time. Therefore, the Son is subordinate to God the
Father, and there is no Holy Trinity of three equal Persons. The reason this
matters for us is that Arianism was condemned as a heresy by Christian sects
that believed in a Trinity. It was these Trinitarian sects—called Athanasian,

after the theologian Athanasius, or Nicene, after the Council of Nicaea that formulated this creed—that eventually gained the upper hand politically. The Arians were tolerant of dissenting faiths: Theodoric (or at least Cassiodorus writing in his name) wrote in a letter to the Jewish community of Genoa that "We cannot order a religion, because no one is forced to believe against his will" (Cassiodorus, *Letters* II.27; transl. Hodgkin, p. 186). Theodoric's son Theodahad (or Cassiodorus again) wrote to Justinian that "For seeing that the Deity suffers [permits] many religions, we should not seek to impose one on all our subjects. He who tries to do otherwise flies in the face of the Divine commands" (Cassiodorus, *Letters* X.25; transl. Hodgkin, p. 437). The Athanasians were not so tolerant: they forced the Arians, who by this time included other Germanic tribes such as the Vandals and Langobards, to adopt Athanasian Christianity, which to this day remains "orthodoxy" for the great majority of Christians. This is, in part, why we have so few texts in the Gothic language, and virtually nothing in Langobardic or Vandalic: whatever might have been written down was at risk of being destroyed as heretical.

England

The picture was a bit different in Britain. There had been Christians in Britain since the first century, and much of the population was Christian when the Angles and Saxons arrived. However, the vestiges of the Roman military and society were much weaker, and the invaders, coming from a homeland that had never been part of the Empire, had no reason to associate the acceptance of Roman ways with the acquisition of large-scale power. British Christianity was pushed into Wales, Cornwall, and Ireland, and the Heathen ways of the newcomers stayed strong for another few generations. The Anglo-Saxons maintained trade and cultural ties to Jutland and Frisia, and artifacts like the Sutton Hoo treasures indicate very close ties between the East Anglian dynasty and the kings of Sweden. Relatively little was written about Anglo-Saxon Heathen belief, but it seems to have resembled both the traditions of the continental North Sea Germans and the Scandinavian traditions of the Vendel Age.

As soon as they arrived, the Anglo-Saxons found distinctive places to worship their gods and goddesses and feel their might. God-names compounded with -*leah* (grove or clearing in a grove) and -*feld* (field) imply that the Anglo-Saxons worshipped in sacred groves and fields, as their kin on the Continent did. Such names range from *Tislea* "Tiw's grove" to *Thunresfelda* "Thunor's field" and *Thunresleah* "Thunor's grove" (modern Thursley). Hilltops were also dedicated to worship, such as Tishoe, "Tiw's spur of land". Names like *Wodnes hlæw* (modern Wenslow) and *Thunores hlæw* (modern Thunderlow) suggest that some burial mounds (*hlæw*) were linked with gods, although names like *Scuccan hlæwe* "goblin's mound" (modern Shucklow) and *Dracan hlæw* "dragon's mound" (modern Drakelow) hint that monsters might also live in mounds (Semple, "A Fear of the Past," pp. 112-118). A few places were named for elves, giants, or monsters, and these tend to be fissures, caves, pools, bogs, and ruins, such as the now-lost *Grendeles pyt*; *Þyrs pytt* "giant's pit"; or Nikerpoll, "pool of the *nicor*," the water-monster (Semple, "In The Open Air," pp. 24-33). A number of places are named for a *hearg*, "harrow," an outdoor sacred place. Many of these *hearg* sites stood on hills, such as Harrow-on-the-Hill in Middlesex and Harrow Hill in Sussex. Excavation has revealed that these sites were recognized as special for thousands of years, with evidence of ritual enclosures, offerings, and sanctuaries. The Anglo-Saxons recognized the importance of places and landscapes that previous peoples had hallowed in their own ways, and in some cases they continued worshipping there, building square enclosures on or around old mounds, for example. When Christianity put an end to the old burial practices, many mounds became execution grounds and burial grounds for criminals (Semple, "A Fear of the Past," pp. 116-121; "Defining the OE *hearg*," pp. 371-385).

Evidence for Anglo-Saxon temples, in the sense of roofed buildings dedicated to worship, is harder to come by. Bede (673-735) mentions Heathen temples and shrines in his *Ecclesiastical History of the English People* (e.g. II.13, transl. Sherley-Price, p. 130), but these probably encompassed open-air enclosures as well as roofed buildings. The best candidate for a temple building so far appears to be at Yeavering, in northern Northumbria, which was rebuilt several times over hundreds of years. Yeavering included cemeteries, open-air constructions such as free-standing posts, and buildings. Building D2 at Yeavering is suspected to have been a temple; it lacked occupational debris (i.e. the waste that an ordinary household produced from everyday activity) and stood by a pit filled with regular deposits of ox-bones, including skulls. The free-standing posts around the site may have been god-figures, like the *ermula cruda* ("crude pillars") described by Aldhelm around the year 680 as pagan worship sites. A few place names like the lost *Thurstaple* in Kent (Thunor's pillar) also point to sacred pillars and god-poles (Hope-Taylor, *Yeavering*, pp. 276-282; Semple, pp. 40-41).

The Christian church began to push for conversion of the English in the early seventh century. Missionaries usually targeted kings and nobles, and when a king converted and his retainers followed suit, the realm might be said to have "become Christian." Political power played a large role in the decision to convert: on the one hand, a king who accepted baptism became the "godson" of the king who sponsored him, and might be expected to be subordinate to his new "father." On the other hand, a king who accepted Christianity might expect military, trade, and financial aid from other Christian kings. In any case, building the infrastructure of organizational Christianity—churches, monasteries, etc.—took longer, and getting everyone in the realm to adopt Christian beliefs and practices took longer still (Winroth, *The Conversion of Scandinavia*, pp. 103-104).

The first target for the missionaries was Æthelberht, king of Kent; his queen was a Frankish Christian, and his realm had considerable trade and cultural contacts with the Frankish kingdom. Pope Gregory sent a mission to Æthelberht in 596, led by a monk named Augustine. Æthelberht did not convert immediately, but showed tolerance and hospitality, saying:

> Your words and promises are fair indeed; but they are new and uncertain, and I cannot accept them and abandon the age-old beliefs that I have held together with the whole English nation. But since you have traveled far, and I can see you are sincere in your desire to impart to us what you believe to be true and excellent, we will not harm you. We will receive you hospitably and take care to supply you with all that you need; nor will we forbid you to preach and win any people you can to your religion (Bede, *Ecclesiastical History* I.25; transl. Sherley-Price, pp. 75-76).

Pope Gregory later sent more priests, including Mellitus, to whom he also sent a famous letter, instructing him to tear down pagan idols but not temples. Temples were to be reconsecrated as churches, and pagan feast days were to be made into Christian feast days; animals that would have been sacrificed to the gods and goddesses could still be killed and eaten for food at Christian holy days (Bede, *Ecclesiastical History* I.30; transl. Sherley-Price, pp. 92-93). Æthelberht formally converted around the year 600, and used his influence to encourage the conversion of Kings Sæberht of Essex and Rædwald of East Anglia (the most likely identity of the ruler buried in Mound 1 at Sutton Hoo). Still, it took another generation or two for the rulers to embrace Christianity completely; Rædwald raised a Christian altar alongside the harrows of his tribal gods, to the great irritation of the Christian priests (Bede, *Ecclesiastical History*, II.xv; transl. Sherley-Price, pp. 132-133).

Missionary efforts moved to the powerful kingdom of Northumbria, whose king Edwin had married the daughter of King Æthelberht of Kent (*Ecclesiastical History* II.9, p. 118). Bede tells a famous story at this point: as Edwin and his counselors were debating the merits of the new faith, a swallow flew through the hall, and one of the counselors compared man's life to the swallow: a brief passage through light and warmth, between two great unknowns. From a Heathen point of view, the most interesting part of Bede's story is the tale of Coifi the priest, who adopted the new religion and deliberately desecrated his own sanctuary by riding up on a stallion and throwing a spear into it—both of which were prohibited actions for priests (II.13, transl. Sherley-Price, pp. 129-131). This may suggest that the temple was a frithgarth where weapons could not be brought, similar to Ingimund's temple in *Vatnsdæla saga* 17. On the other hand, some Scandinavian graves had a spear cast into them, or were struck with another weapon, just before they were sealed, and the act of casting a spear over a living enemy to dedicate him to Odin is known from the Eddas and sagas (e.g. *Vǫluspá* 24). Coifi's act may have been similar: not desecration but consecration, a way of ritually "shutting down" his holy stead, closing it off from the human world and committing it to the gods (Semple, "In The Open Air," p. 31, Price, *The Viking Way*, pp. 95, 102).

The last English ruler to hold out against Christianity was Penda of Mercia. Penda was notably tolerant:

> King Penda himself did not forbid the preaching of the Faith to any even of his own Mercians who wished to listen; but he hated and despised any whom he knew to be insincere in their practice of Christianity once

they had accepted it, and said that any who despised the commandments of the God in whom they professed to believe were themselves despicable wretches (*Ecclesiastical History*, III.21; transl. Sherley-Price, pp. 177-178).

Penda died in 659 in battle against King Oswiu or Oswy of Bernicia, a devout Christian who dedicated his daughter to perpetual virginity in the service of his god, in thanks for the victory. She was less than a year old at the time (*Ecclesiastical History* III.24, transl. Sherley-Price, p. 184).

The Continent

In 486 at the Battle of Soissons, the Salian Franks under their ruler Clovis (ca. 466–511; Germanic name probably *Hlodoweg) defeated the last remaining part of Gaul that nominally maintained allegiance to Rome. In a series of campaigns that followed, Clovis extended his rule over much of present-day France, pushing the Visigoths into Spain, claiming the northern Alamannic lands to the Rhine and beyond, and absorbing the Rhineland Franks into his own kingdom by killing their kings[15] (James, *The Franks*, pp. 79-91). One of these battles was allegedly the reason for Clovis's conversion to Christianity. Urged to convert by his wife Clotilde, a Burgundian princess who was already an Athanasian Christian, Clovis allegedly promised to convert when he saw his forces being killed in a battle against the Alamanni. When Clovis won this battle—the Battle of Tolbiac in 496—he followed through on his promise. As usual among the Germanic-speaking tribes, the ruler was also a religious leader, and if he changed his religion, most of his people would be obliged to follow. So the Franks nominally became Christians—although, on the one hand, some Franks seem to have adopted Christianity at an earlier date, and on the other hand, folk customs with a distinctly pagan flavor continued for many years after the "official" conversion (James, pp. 121-129). A century later, some Franks near Noyon threatened St. Eligius when they'd had quite enough of his preaching: "Although you are always bothering us, you will never uproot our customs, but

---

15. Clovis secured his hold on power by murdering his kinsmen. The chronicler Gregory of Tours mentions that towards the end of his life, Clovis lamented his lack of kin—not because he grieved for them, but because he'd run out of people to kill. See *History of the Franks* II.42, transl. Thorpe, p. 158.

we will go on with our rites as we have always done, and we will go on doing so always and forever" (*Vita s. Eligii*, transl. James, p. 125).

It was through Frankish influence that much of the conversion across the Rhine took place. Frankish rulers encouraged Irish and Anglo-Saxon missionaries, since the spread of Christianity facilitated the social and administrative unification of Northern Europe under Frankish rule. At the end of the seventh century, the conversion process began to expand towards the North Sea, where the Frankish conquest and the Christianization of the Frisians went hand in hand (Geary, *Before France and Germany*, p. 215).

S. VVLFRANNVS

RADBODVS

Radbod of Frisia, turning away from baptism at the last moment. Hamconius, *Frisia* (1620).

The Northumbrian priest Willibrord, backed by the Franks, attempted to convert Frisia, but met stern resistance from their king Radbod (Alcuin, *Life of Willibrord*, transl. Talbot, *The Anglo-Saxon Missionaries*, pp. 9-11). Radbod is best known for his decision to reject conversion, while standing on the brink of the baptismal font, on the grounds that "he could not leave the company of his ancestors, the Frisian leaders, to reside in that celestial kingdom with a puny pack of paupers." See *Vita Wulframi*, transl. Chisholm, *Grove and Gallows*, p. 61.) Willibrord's companion Winfrid, better known by his Latin name Boniface, began his missionary career in Frisia, and then shifted eastwards, founding churches and monasteries in Hesse, Thuringia, and as far east as Salzburg. He was canonized by the Roman Catholic Church for, among other things, his eager destruction of pagan holy places, notably the "Oak of Jupiter" (presumably Donar or Thunor) at a place called Gaesmere (possibly present-day Geismar near Fritzlar, although this is not certain; Willibald, *Life of Boniface*, transl. Talbot, *The Anglo-Saxon Missionaries*, pp. 62-64).

The Saxons to the east remained unconverted; while some of their nobles were sympathetic to Christianity, the non-noble Saxons saw it as a threat to the balance of power. Saxons killed two English missionaries around 695 (Bede, *Ecclesiastical History* 5.10, transl. Sherley-Price, pp. 280-282), and nearly killed the English missionary Lebuin (*Vita Lebuini*, transl. Talbot, pp. 230-233). But there had been periodic outbreaks of hostility across the border between the Franks and Saxons, and as the Merovingian dynasty was ending, the new Frankish rulers began pushing eastwards. Charle-

Top: Boniface chopping down the sacred oak. Shea, *Pictorial Lives of the Saints* (1922). Bottom: Boniface martyred by the Frisians. *Fulda Sacramentarium*, 11th century.

magne (748-814) embarked on nearly continuous wars against the Saxons. In 772, he destroyed the Saxon religious center, the Irminsul ("Great Pillar"), and in 776 he carried out a forced mass baptism in the Lippe River near Paderborn. Yet every baptism was followed by a new revolt, many of which were led by the Saxon noble Widukind. Charlemagne's measures grew increasingly harsh. After his victory at Verden in 782, Charlemagne massacred 4500 prisoners and imposed harsh laws on the survivors; his *Capitulatio de partibus Saxoniae* mandated death for any Saxon who refused baptism, and stiff fines for any who practiced Heathen rites (Dutton, *Carolingian Civilization*, pp. 59-60). This was still not enough to pacify the Saxons. Widukind himself was allegedly baptized in 785, and was paid off afterwards with lavish gifts. But the non-noble classes of the Saxons found Frankish rule and Christian demands intolerable. Alcuin, the Anglo-Saxon

The baptism of Widukind, as depicted by the 19th-century German artist
Alfred Rethel on a fresco (now destroyed) for the Aachen City Hall.
Ponten, *Alfred Rethel* (1911).

scholar at Charlemagne's court, pointed out that "If the light yoke and sweet
burden of Christ were to be preached to the most obstinate people of the
Saxons with as much determination as the payment of tithes has been exact-
ed, or as the force of the legal decree has been applied for faults of the most
trifling sorts imaginable, perhaps they would not be averse to their baptismal
vows" (quoted in Goldberg, "Popular Revolt," p. 478). Saxon rebellions kept
breaking out until 804, when Charlemagne deported all Saxons who lived
north of the Elbe River, giving their lands to his Slavic allies (Goldberg, pp.
475-477). Even then, Christians complained about the difficulty of getting
the Saxon lower classes to abandon their pagan ways. These Saxon lower
classes revolted one last time against their Christian overlords in 841, the
Stellinga revolt, asserting both their old legal freedoms and their old religion
(Goldberg, pp. 479-480). As Charlemagne's biographer Einhard reported,
"No war ever undertaken by the Frankish people was more prolonged, more
full of atrocities or more demanding of effort" (*Vita Karoli Magni* 7, transl.
Thorpe, *Two Lives of Charlemagne*, p. 61).

Scandinavia and the Vendel Age

While Scandinavia had been on the fringes of the Roman world, contact with Rome had influenced everything from political organization to

artistic styles. Great Scandinavian treasures from this time that give some insight into religion include the pair of solid gold horns, decorated with enigmatic figures, found at Gallehus. Unfortunately, the Gallehus horns were stolen and melted down in the 1800s, although detailed drawings remain. But testimony to the incredible skill of Scandinavian goldsmiths

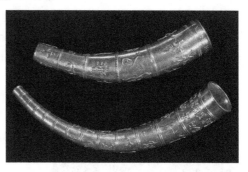

Replicas of the Gallehus horns. National Museum of Denmark, CC BY-SA 2.0.

remains in the form of five great gold collars dated to around 500 CE, each made of four to seven rings decorated with wirework and filigree. Too large and stiff for a human to wear comfortably, these collars may have been made for a carved wooden god or goddess image (Andersson and Jansson, *Treasures of Early Sweden*, p. 56). It is speculative but tempting to see these collars as models for Freyja's necklace Brísingamen. They might well have been thought of as worth four nights of a goddess's love.

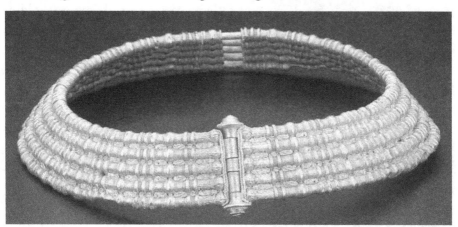

Five-ringed golden collar from Färjestad, Öland, Sweden.
Swedish Historical Museum 108870, CC BY 2.5.

By around 500 CE, rune carving had spread all over Scandinavia; most of our surviving runic inscriptions in the Elder Futhark date from this period. Runes also appear on the stamped gold pendants which are known today as *bracteates*, which Scandinavians began to make around the year 450

Roman solidus of Libius Severus (ruled 461-465 CE). Norra Sandby, Öland, Sweden. Swedish Historical Museum 110746, CC BY 2.5.

Early bracteate. Swedish Historical Museum 109759, CC BY 2.5.

Late bracteate. Swedish Historical Museum 110578, CC BY 2.5.

CE. The earliest bracteates are copies of Roman coins and medallions; in fact, actual Roman coins circulated in Scandinavia and were sometimes mounted and worn as pendants, in the same way that bracteates were. Later bracteates show a wider range of designs, and some bear rune inscriptions, ranging from complete futharks to short words such as **alu** or **laukaz**, probably for magical purposes. Many of the bracteate-images can be identified as gods or other religious figures. A horse and rider (often represented by only a head), frequently accompanied by a bird or birds, may represent Odin. Several show three humanoid figures, with the middle figure showing a branch protruding from his midsection; these probably depict the death of Balder. Others have a female figure holding spinning or weaving equipment, probably Frigg. Some show a man fighting beasts, or a man with his hand in a beast's mouth, possibly Tyr. Other types of bracteate show single animals, or animal *triskeles*, spiral designs made up of three serpents or other animals. In some of these, the animals are so tangled that it becomes hard to distinguish them, and this foreshadows the dominant artistic style of the Scandinavian Migration and Iron Ages: animal bodies, often merging into each other or interlaced in exceptionally complex and visually striking ways. Humans and animals often blend in this art, whether it's the bracteates that show birds emerging from a human head; brooches shaped like ravens or birds

142

of prey with human faces staring out, like the brooches from Besjebakken and Skørping in Denmark; the Åker buckle from Norway, in which a man's legs turn into boar's heads; or thousands more examples. Art like this may show gods and goddesses shapeshifting, or otherwise working through the forms of birds or animals. Alternately, it may show human *fylgjur*, parts of the soul that were said to take on animal shape (Hedeager, *Iron Age Myth and Materiality*, pp. 61-85).

A second type of artwork was also made from thin gold between 500 and 800 CE: *guldgubber* (meaning something like "golden old fellows"). These were either outline humanoid or animal shapes cut from sheet gold, or rectangular plaques pressed on a mold, much like the bracteates. Many of the pressed *guldgubber* show either one human figure, or a couple facing each other and embracing. These have been interpreted as depictions of Frey and Gerd; alternately, they may be tokens of marriages and other contracts. Most of these have been found at "magnate estate" sites; the site at Sorte Muld on Bornholm has yielded over 2500 of them. Some were deposited as offerings in the post-holes of buildings. Others may have been on public display, perhaps glued onto the posts. Unlike bracteates, guldgubbers were rarely worn as jewelry (Ratke, "Guldgubber").

Guldgubber showing a couple embracing. Helgö, Sweden. Swedish Historical Museum 110379, CC BY 2.5 SE.

The Fimbulwinter

Beginning in the year 536, Scandinavia was struck by several years of unusually cold temperatures. In fact, climate data from tree rings shows that the entire Northern Hemisphere was affected. The probable cause was massive amounts of volcanic ash and acid droplets, blasted into the stratosphere by two huge eruptions in 535-6 and 540 (Toohey et al., "Climatic and

Societal Impacts," pp. 1-2). Multiple historians in the Mediterranean and even China recorded strange mists that blocked sunlight and brought cold weather and crop failures (Stothers and Rampino, "Volcanic Eruptions," pp. 6362-6363; Arjava, "Mystery Cloud," pp. 78-83). The Byzantine historian Procopius wrote that "the sun gave forth its light without brightness, like the moon, during this whole year, and it seemed exceedingly like the sun in eclipse, or the beams it shed were not clear nor such as it is accustomed to shed. And from the time when this thing happened men were free neither from war nor pestilence nor any other thing leading to death" (*History of the Wars* IV.xiv.5-6, transl. Dewing, vol. 2, pp. 328-329).[16] At about the same time, an epidemic was ravaging southern Europe, known as the Plague of Justinian; it is known to have reached Germany in the 540s, although whether it reached Scandinavia isn't clear.

Whatever the cause, European society was dramatically disrupted. For example, there is chemical evidence, from traces of pollution in glacial ice, that silver mining and smelting essentially stopped in western Europe for a hundred years—which points to severe economic change, since silver was used for coinage (Loveluck et al., "Alpine Ice-Core Evidence," pp. 1575-1582). In Scandinavia, all signs point to agricultural collapse. Farms and villages and burial grounds were abandoned, including sites that had been occupied for a thousand years. Fossil pollen shows that land all over Scandinavia reverted from cultivated fields to wilderness, while abandoned boat houses and a lack of imported goods point to the collapse of maritime trade. In Uppland, Sweden, the number of occupied sites fell by as much as 75 percent, and it would take four to seven generations for society to return to prior levels of activity. It's been suggested that this event is the origin of the myth of the Fimbulvetr, the Fimbulwinter, three summerless years that will precede Ragnarǫkr (Gräslund and Price, "Twilight of the Gods?," pp. 431-437; but see Nordvig and Riede, "Are There Echoes of the AD 536 Event in the Viking Ragnarok Myth?" for a critique of this idea).

---

16. Historically well-documented volcanic eruptions have been known to cause colder gobal temperatures, from Laki in 1783 to Tambora in 1815 and Pinatubo in 1992. The culprit for the cold spell beginning in 536 might be the volcano Ilopango in Nicaragua (Toohey et al., "Climatic and Societal Impacts"), but Iceland has also been suggested as a culprit (Loveluck et al., "Alpine Ice-Core Evidence," p. 1575).

Environmental changes brought religious changes. The last vestiges of the old Bronze Age solar cult seem to have come to an end (Andrén, *Tracing Old Norse Cosmology*, p. 161-166). Large amounts of gold, including many ritually important objects, were sacrificed at this time across Scandinavia, possibly in a desperate attempt to restore the sun's light (Axboe, "The Year 536," pp. 186-188). The catastrophe also brought sweeping social change. When a catastrophe wipes out part of a population, it may enrich the survivors, who can take over abandoned land and resources step in to fill political vacuums. This seems to have happened in Scandinavia: elites were able to claim more land and exert more power over the survivors (Löwenborg, "An Iron Age Shock Doctrine," pp. 19-24). Religious activity around this time shifted from "places of power" in the landscape, to the halls of rulers. Weapons and gear of defeated armies stopped being deposited in sacrificial bogs. This may have been because wars were becoming rarer, as tribes confederated into larger proto-nations—but other bog sacrifices also stopped, whether humans, deity images, treasures, or other offerings. Instead, offerings began to be made in or near halls—sometimes left on stone altars or burned in fire pits, sometimes placed in the post-holes of great halls. For centuries, rulers continued to build halls where lesser folk would come to worship and give offerings. The pattern persisted even after the halls became churches (Fabech, "Organizing the Landscape," pp. 38-40). War booty was probably given by the ruler to his subordinates to ensure their loyalty, a practice mentioned several times in *Beowulf*. Funeral practices shifted from burials with rich grave goods to cremations with few goods, which probably reflects centralized authorities controlling the flow of wealth. The building of forts and defensive walls slowed down at the same time; this probably reflects a shift from constant intertribal fighting to higher authority keeping people in line (Näsman, "Ethnogenesis," pp. 5-6).

Beginning before the catastrophe but especially in its aftermath, we see the development of what archaeologists call *magnate estates*: unusually large, centrally located estates, with large halls in highly visible locations near major travel routes, sizable burial grounds, evidence for luxury crafts such as goldsmithing, and evidence of ports, markets, and imported trade goods. These estates were also focus points for religious ritual: we find offerings left in the post-holes of great halls, stone piles used as altars, and in a few cases even separate temples. Place names at these sites still preserve evidence of ritual activities that must have taken place there. For example, the regions surrounding a few magnate estates in Sweden include places named Göteve ("gods' sanctuary"), Torslunda ("Thor's grove"), Friggeråker ("Frigg's field"), and so on (Fabech, "Organising the Landscape," pp. 40-41).

Stamped human figure cut from sheet gold, from Gudme. National Museum of Denmark, CC BY-SA 2.5.

The oldest of these magnate estates is Gudme, on the Danish island of Fyn, which was active between about 200 and 600 CE. The largest hall was almost 50 meters (165 ft) long and covered about 500 m² (5380 ft²), with roof posts massive enough to support two stories. The site has yielded over 10 kg (22 lbs.) of gold, much of it scrap gold that was probably meant to be recycled; it is rich in Roman artifacts and includes trade goods from as far away as Anatolia (present-day Turkey). Excavations of the nearby port area revealed traces of goldsmithing, blacksmithing, carpentry, antler carving, and shipbuilding, along with more Roman goods such as glass beads and pottery. Gudme was also a site where offerings were made; its very name (ON *Goðheim*, "gods' home") suggests that it was an important religious center (Price, *Ancient Scandinavia*, pp. 266-270). In fact, Gudme in its prime would have matched the Eddic depiction of Asgard so well, with its great hall and wells and abundant gold, that it may have been deliberately built as an earthly reflection of Asgard (Hedeager, *Iron Age Myth and Materiality*, pp. 158-162).

Other magnate estates were founded later. Uppåkra, near Lund in Sweden, reached its height around 400 CE. Along with traces of large farms and halls, long-distance trade, and high-status crafts, Uppåkra included a small but sturdy two-story building, where a bronze beaker and glass bowl had been buried and other offerings had been deposited in the post-holes. This is probably a temple (Larson, "The Iron Age Ritual Building"; Price, *Ancient Scandinavia*, pp. 271-276). Tissø in Denmark became an active estate in the

6th century and would remain active until the 11th century. In the pre-Viking Age, it featured a great hall built around 550 CE (burned and replaced by a new great hall around 700 CE, for reasons unknown), ritual offerings deposited in a nearby lake, and evidence for trade and craft activities such as bronze casting and blacksmithing. It is significant that Tissø means "Tyr's Island" (Jørgensen, "Gudme and Tissø," pp. 277-282). Lejre,

Digital reconstruction of the appearance of the Uppåkrå temple. Sven Rosborn, Wikimedia Commons, CC BY-SA 2.5.

on the island of Zealand not far from the present-day town of Roskilde, was another estate: the great halls, built and rebuilt in the 500s, measured up to 50 meters in length, and a "ship-setting" of stones enclosed a cremation grave from the mid-7th century. In legends and medieval chronicles, Lejre is connected with the Scyldingas or Skjǫldungar dynasty of legendary Denmark, the royal family that included Hrothgar in *Beowulf* and Hrólfr in *Hrólfs saga kraka*. We can confirm, at least, that a great hall stood at Lejre close to the time frame when *Beowulf* is set, even if we can't prove that it was called Heorot (Christensen, "Lejre Beyond the Legend").

Gamla Uppsala probably began as a magnate estate, and there was once a great hall there, although its history is less well-known because later buildings are still standing on top of the old site. Prominent burial mounds close to settlements appear in the aftermath of the climate catastrophe, perhaps because the elites who claimed land needed to make visual statements of ownership—and this is true at Uppsala, where the large burial mounds have been dated to between 550 and 650 CE (Löwenborg, "An Iron Age Shock Doctrine," pp. 16-22). Uppsala became the heart of a powerful kingdom, trading furs and slaves with the realms to the east—a trade which would continue through the Viking Age. The famous boat graves from Vendel, Valsgärde, and Ultuna reveal the great wealth available to the elite; the Vendel site gave its name to the Vendel Age of Scandinavian prehistory (550-800 CE). Uppsala would remain an important center through the Viking Age.

Helmet from Grave XIV, Vendel, Sweden.
Swedish Historical Museum 120458,
CC BY 2.5.

Written sources mention a temple built there, whose remains may now be underneath the present-day church (Price, *Ancient Scandinavia*, pp. 271-276).

This shift in social organization parallels what was happening in Europe in general. Smaller tribes were coalescing into larger ones, and strong rulers were gaining power and using it. Descended from the gods, and counseled by their ancestors in their burial mounds, kings wielded power not only by the sword, but based on their unique relationship to their ancestors, including their divine ancestors. The Swedish ruling family of Ynglingar descended from Yngvi-Freyr; the Danish Skjǫldungar, whose best-known king was Hrólfr kraki, were descended from the hero Skjǫld and the goddess Gefjon; the Jarls of Hlaðir in northern Norway reckoned their decent from Odin and Skadi; and most of the Anglo-Saxon kingdoms' ruling families traced their origins to Woden.

Beowulf

Anyone who has taken high school English literature has heard of *Beowulf*, known from a single manuscript written around 1000 CE but based on much older material. Although the hero of the poem is a Geat from present-day western Sweden, and the first half of the poem is set on the Danish island of Zealand, *Beowulf* is unquestionably the greatest surviving piece of literature in Old English. As a young man, Beowulf saves the Danish king Hrothgar and his men from the nocturnal murders of the monster Grendel, by wrestling with the monster and ripping his arm off. When Grendel's mother avenges her son, Beowulf kills her in her lair at the bottom of a monster-infested pool. Returning home to his people and later assuming the kingship, Beowulf as an old man slays a dragon that was laying waste to his people's land, giving his life in the process.

The manuscript that we have was written by a Christian, and while scholars have never been able to agree on exactly how Christian the poem is, the consensus is that Christianity is so tightly woven into the fabric of the poem that it cannot be separated from the older traditions that are also present, even though the poem never specifically mentions Jesus, the cross, or any details of Christian doctrine (Fulk et al., *Klaeber's Beowulf,* pp.

Reconstruction of the Sutton Hoo helmet, Britsh Museum. Photo by Mark Ramsay, Wikimedia Commons, CC BY 2.0.

lxvii-lxxix). That said, while the poem espouses Christian morality, it transmits older heroic ideals that, perhaps, transcend specific religions. As he is dying, Beowulf boasts of his accomplishments as a ruler (lines 2732-2743):

Ic ðās lēode hēold	I ruled this people
fīftig wintra; næs sē folccyning	For fifty winters; there is no folk-king,
ymbesittendra ǣnig ðāra	Not one among my neighbors,
þē mec gūðwinum grētan dorste,	Who dared confront me with war-friends
egesan ðēon. Ic on earde bād	To threaten terror. On earth, I awaited
mǣlgesceafta; hēold mīn tela,	My appointed fate, held my realm rightly,
ne sōhte searonīðas nē mē swōr fela	Never attempted treachery, nor swore
āða on unriht. Ic ðæs ealles mæg	Many false oaths. Hurt unto death,
feorhbennum sēoc gefēan habban	I may take comfort in all of this,
forðām mē wītan ne ðearf waldend	Since the Ruler of Men has no cause to
fīra	reproach me
morðorbealo māga þonne mīn sceaceð	For kinslaying, when my life
līf of līce.	Departs from the body.

One event in *Beowulf* is confirmed in an independent source: King Hygelac's attack on the Frankish territories of Frisia, and his death there around 520, is told by Gregory of Tours in his *History of the Franks* (III.2, transl. Thorpe, pp. 163-164). This would make Beowulf a contemporary of Hrólfr kraki (who appears as Hrothulf in the poem) and the Yngling kings Angantyr (Ongentheow), Óttarr vendelkráki (Ohthere), and Hrólfr's adversary Aðils (Eadgils), whose deeds are preserved in the Norse *Hrólfs saga kraka*. Hrothgar (*Hróarr* in Old Norse, *Ro* or *Roas* in Latin) is said in other accounts to have ruled from Lejre, and as mentioned above, we have evidence of great halls built at Lejre close to the time when the poem is set (Niles, "Was There a Legend of Lejre?," pp. 256-265). *Beowulf* mentions Heathen worship close to halls (*æt hærgtrafum*, "at pavilions," line 175) and war booty kept by the victors and shared out, not deposited in bogs like the weapons-sacrifices of earlier centuries (2032-2038). This corresponds to a major change in ritual known to have happened around 500 CE, as mentioned above (Fabech, "Organising the Landscape," pp. 38-40). Since Grendel and his mother live in a bog and have accumulated a great hoard of treasure, the poem may reflect social tensions over this change; some have even identified Grendel's mother with the bog-dwelling earth goddess who once received offerings and who, by the time the legend took the form we now have, was seen as a villain (Battaglia, "The Germanic Earth Goddess," pp. 420-440). Whatever the case, *Beowulf* seems to preserve some knowledge of Migration Age Scandinavian practices.

Beowulf begins with the ship-burial of the legendary Scyld Scefing, whose body is sent out onto the waves with all his treasures. It ends with Beowulf being cremated amid his weapons and the dragon's gold, before his remains are laid in a great barrow on a headland, as a landmark for seafarers to look for "when the ships drive from afar over dark-misted flood." For a long time, it was thought that these descriptions were influenced by Viking Age burial customs, and thus mean that the poem was relatively late. This was changed by the excavations at Sutton Hoo in Suffolk, England. First excavated in 1938-1939, and re-excavated in 1965 and 1986-1992, Sutton Hoo included no fewer than seventeen burial mounds. Some of them had been looted, but Mound 1, dated to the early 630s, contained a man buried in a ship with spectacular grave-goods that had not been disturbed. One of the last Heathen kings of England—possibly though not certainly Rædwald of East

The Migration Age

Anglia—had been laid in his death-ship, surrounded by his weapons and wealth like Scyld Scefing. Even though his ship was buried rather than sent out to sea, it now seems that *Beowulf* has preserved some memory of Heathen burial customs. (See Carver, *The Sutton Hoo Story*, for an excellent account of the Sutton Hoo burial and its excavations.)

Excavation of the ship in Mound 1 at Sutton Hoo, 1939. Wikimedia Commons, Public Domain.

The Sutton Hoo burial is very much like the burials in the mounds at Vendel and Valsgärde in Sweden. Both included ship-burials, which are not found elsewhere at this time. Both contain helmets adorned with gold and *Pressbleche*—sheet metal plates embossed with designs showing warriors—and both contain shields with applied metal figures. The similarity in workmanship and artistic style suggest close cultural connections. Although the king buried at Sutton Hoo may have heard of Christianity, because he was buried with two silver baptismal ladles from Egypt, the folk who buried him so richly may have been making a deliberate point about their community with the Heathenry of the Swedes, at the same time that the kings of Kent just to the south had converted to Christianity and were trading with the Franks. The mounds at Uppsala—and several of the Sutton Hoo mounds, although not Mound 1—contained cremated human remains buried with treasures, so the description of Beowulf's burial is accurate for the time and setting of the poem.

Contributors:

1st edition: Kveldúlfr Gundarsson.

2nd edition: New material by Ben Waggoner.

3rd edition: Reorganization and new material by Ben Waggoner.

Ship from the Oseberg burial.
Kulturhistorisk Museum, University of Oslo. CC BY-SA 4.0.

CHAPTER SIX

The Viking Age

792–1066

*To many, "Northern tradition"
means "the religion of the Vikings."
As we have seen, that is a long way
from the whole truth, but the Viking
Age nevertheless plays a special part in
the memory and rebirth of the Elder
Troth. Museum exhibits, blockbuster
TV dramas, and documentaries on
the History Channel have gone far to
replace the image of the bloodthirsty
Viking in a horned helmet with a
more balanced view—but as Heathens, we need to know more.*

Gjermundbu helmet. Kunsthistorisk
Museum, University of Oslo.
CC BY-SA 4.0.

The Vikings are Coming!

The word *víking*," literally "person from the bay," means "raider" or "pirate." Please note that "Viking" is not an ethnic signifier; it's an occupation.
Many Norsemen never were Vikings, or were Vikings for a season or two
and then settled down—and not all Vikings were necessarily of Scandinavian
ancestry. All the same, the raiders gave their name to the "Viking Age,"
when bands of Heathen raiders swept down on Christian Europe, looting
and pillaging, as terrified monks prayed *a furore Normannorum libera nos
Domine*—"from the fury of the Norsemen, free us, o Lord!"[17] The Viking
Age is often said to have begun with the raid on the Christian monastery of
Lindisfarne, off the coast of England, in 792 or early 793 (there are various
readings of the *Anglo-Saxon Chronicle's* dates). That said, two recently discovered ship burials on the Estonian island of Saaremaa, dated to about 750,
bear the remains of twenty-eight men who all died violently. This shows

---

17. There's no contemporary source for the most famous form of that quote, but the sentiment was certainly sincere and widespread.

that the Vikings were going a-viking in the eastern Baltic for decades before they first turned their attention to western Europe (Peets et al, "Archaeological Investigations").

But why did the Norsemen begin spreading from their homes in the first place? Historians and archaeologists continue to debate this, but in all likelihood, a combination of factors touched off Viking expansion. Certainly ship-building technology had something to do with it. Ships had been used to carry bands of fighting men since at least the fourth century, the age of the mass sacrifice of boats and weapons at Nydam, Denmark, and ships had carried sizable numbers of Angles and Saxons across the North Sea to England. But by the Viking Age, the Viking ship had become one of the most advanced technologies in Europe. The recovery of sunken and buried Viking ships, notably the five ships recovered from the bottom of Roskilde Fjord at Skuldelev, Denmark, shows that shipwrights built both fast, slender warships (*langskipar*) and slower but more capacious trading ships (*knarrar*). While the slender, swift, dragon-prowed warships are perhaps the most iconic Viking ships, trading ships were no less important. Modern replicas, such as the ships built at the Roskilde Ship Museum using authentic boat-building techniques, have shown that these are remarkably seaworthy craft, light and strong, able to be hauled onto a beach or even portaged overland when necessary (Forte et al., *Viking Empires*, pp. 134-168).

Ships made both raiding and trading possible, and thanks to them, new sources of wealth began streaming into Scandinavia at the start of the Viking Age. A hoard of silver coins from the Islamic Caliphate, found at the Norse settlement of Staraja Ladoga in Russia and deposited after the year 786, was the first known measure of what became a great flood of silver into Scandinavia. This in turn may have touched off serious competition: kings and jarls needed money, both to maintain their reputation and to reward their hosts of fighting men. Young men, in turn, needed wealth in order to get married and purchase land—especially because there seems to have been a demographic surplus of young men, possibly because of female infanticide. All these factors working together may explain why the dragon-prowed ships made their fateful sailing to Lindisfarne (Barrett, "What Caused the Viking Age?").

Havhingsten fra Glendalough, the "Sea Stallion from Glendalough," lowering sail
outside Ramsgate Harbour. This is a modern replica of the Skuldelev 2 ship,
a probable warship, built in Ireland in 1042 and sunk in Roskilde Fjord in 1070.
Photo by Smudge 9000, Wikimedia Commons, CC BY 2.0.

A Brief Digression: Horned Helmets

It has to be said: There is no evidence that the historical Vikings wore
horned helmets in battle. Helmets of any kind are rare archaeological finds,
but no horned helmet has ever been found from the Iron Age or Viking
Age in a Germanic context. A horned helmet would have been a liability in
actual combat, adding unnecessary weight and giving an enemy something
to grab. Thus although plastic horned helmets are featured in Scandinavian
gift shops, old Viking movies, and the Minnesota Vikings football team
logo, they are fiction.

That said, it is true that bronze horned helms were worn in the Bronze
Age in Denmark, probably in ritual: horned figures are not rare in rock art,
and two bronze horned helmets turned up at Vaksjø. Archeologists have also
found several Viking Age male figurines—from Kungsängen and Uppåkra,
Sweden; Ribe, Denmark; Staraja Ladoga, Russia; and Levide, Gotland—
wearing what appear to be horned helmets at first glance. Depictions of
men in horned helmets also appear on artworks like the Finglesham golden
buckle from Anglo-Saxon England, the tapestries from the Oseberg ship;
and, from the Vendel Age, one of the dies from Torslunda, Sweden.

In more stylized artworks, such as the Oseberg tapestries, the helmets do appear horned. However, a close look at the more detailed figures reveals that the horns end in bird heads, as is especially clear on the heads from Ribe and Staraja Ladoga. Even some the more stylized artworks often depict the "horns" with forked tips, whereas on some of the more detailed figures, such as the dancing warriors on the Sutton Hoo helmet, the "horns" appear to have eyes and even feathers. These images probably represent either Odin or a human warrior ritually identified as Odin; the "horns" may be Odin's ravens (his thought and memory) coming forth from his head (Price, *The Viking Way*, pp. 320-323), or they might show the god sending his spirit forth in bird form, as he is said to do in *Ynglinga saga* 7. In fact, several of these "horned" figures were made with two eyes and then had one eye deliberately damaged, making it virtually certain that they depict Odin (Price and Mortimer, "An Eye for Odin," pp. 524-525; Pentz, "Viking Art," pp. 22-24). Many bracteates from the earlier Migration Age show a male humanoid figure with a high sweeping hairdo ending in the head and body of a bird, giving the impression that the bird is emerging from his head. Often there is a second bird close by, shown complete. If these figures represent Odin, as seems likely, they would confirm the idea that Odin was depicted with birds emerging from his head.

Head-shaped pendant from Ribe. National Museum of Denmark, CC BY-SA 2.0.

Slayers, Settlers, Merchants

Viking raids repeatedly hit western Europe in the ninth century. Viking ships sailed up the rivers of France: a band under the command of a leader named Reginheri sacked Paris in 845. (Reginheri is often assumed to be the inspiration for the semi-mythical Ragnar Loðbrók.) Viking raids were feared as far south as Spain, where Seville was raided in 844, according to the historian Ibn Hayyan (transl. Lunde and Stone, *Ibn Fadlān and the Land of Darkness*, pp. 105-109). In Ireland, where only small settlements had been known before, the Vikings built fortified bases

Breacteate showing a bitd emerging from the head. Skåne, Sweden. Haigh, "Notes in Illustration of the Runic Monuments of Kent" (1872).

known as *longphorts* (*longphuirt*, in Irish): Dublin, Cork, Limerick, Waterford, and Wicklow all began their lives as longphorts in the 840s. Meanwhile, a Swedish group known as the Rus (probably from the Norse word for "rowing," *róðr*, filtered through a Finnic language) or Varangians (from Norse *væringjar*, "sworn confederates"; Russian *Varjagi*) were trekking east and south down the Volga River. The *Russian Primary Chronicle* claims that the Varangians imposed tribute on the tribes of the region, who rose up and drove them away, but found that they could not get along with each other and invited the Rus back to bring order to the sprawling and unruly lands (transl. Cross and Sherbowitz-Wetzor, pp. 59-60). We well may be skeptical of how freely any such "invitation" might have been given, but whatever the case, by the mid- to late 800s, there were Norse rulers at Novgorod (*Holmgarðr*) and Kiev. In time, the realm of Russia took its name from the Rus, although they themselves called it *Garðariki*, "realm of towns." In 860 they besieged Constantinople, or *Miklagarðr* ("Great City") as they called it, but by the end of the century, some of them were taking service in the Varangian Guard, the Emperor's personal guard. Coming from a distant land, they had no conflicting loyalties to any of the rival factions at court that made "byzantine" a synonym for "complicated and devious."

Other bands of Norsemen explored even further east to *Serkland*, the Norse name for the lands of the Islamic Caliphate. In 913 and 943, Viking bands raided on the Caspian Sea (transl. Lunde and Stone, *Ibn Fadlan*, pp. 144-152). In 921, a band of Rus encountered the Arab diplomat Ibn Fadlan on the Volga River, in the present-day Russian republic of Tatarstan; his account of them is a precious source of information on the Norse in the east (transl. Lunde and Stone, pp. 45-55). Another ill-fated Viking expedition, led by one Yngvar, may have penetrated all the way to present-day Georgia and Azerbaijan around the year 1040. A set of runestones in Sweden records that many of Yngvar's men "fell in the east," and there is a saga telling of their voyage, although it is so full of wild legendary elements that it is hard to be sure just how far they got (*Yngvars saga viðfǫrla* in Waggoner, *Sagas of Imagination*, pp. 317-344).

Lindisfarne was only the first Viking raid on Britain, which had a number of rich and poorly defended churches and monasteries that made tempting targets. The semi-legendary Ragnar Lodbrok allegedly raided England in 865, in the reign of King Ælle of Northumbria, although the sources for exactly what happened are not clear and reliable. But Britain also had good farmland, and Viking warriors began to only to raid, but to claim land. In 866, a large force under unified command—supposedly led by the sons of Ragnar—invaded England with the intent to take and hold land, known in English chronicles as the Great Heathen Army. A second Viking host invaded in 870. After ten years, most of England was under Scandinavian control. The kingdom of Wessex, under the able leadership of King Alfred, was the only Anglo-Saxon kingdom that held out against the Danes. In 878 Alfred defeated the Danes at the Battle of Edington, securing the independence of Wessex, forcing their leader Guthrum and his folk to accept baptism, and fixing the boundaries of the area where they would be allowed to settle, a realm in northeastern England called the Danelaw.

Ynglinga saga tells how Haraldr, the king of Agder and several other small kingdoms in Norway, spent ten years at war to unite all of Norway under his own rule. Legend has it that he achieved this in the year 872 with his victory over the remaining independent kings at the Battle of Hafrsfjord. He had taken an oath not to cut his hair until he had won all of Norway;

after the battle, he was able to exchange his old nickname of Haraldr lúfa ("Matted Hair") for Haraldr hárfagri ("Fair Hair; Beautiful Hair"). Some scholars have questioned whether the actual process of Norwegian unification was so straightforward and brief. But legend has it that many prominent Norwegians found Haraldr's rule oppressive, and looked for places to settle out of his reach. Norsefolk settled on Orkney and Shetland and staked claims on northern Scotland as far south as Moray. (This is why nearly the northernmost part of Scotland is still called *Sutherland*; if you're sailing from Norway, it *is* the "southern land.") Rounding Scotland, they settled the Hebrides, the Isle of Man, and the Galloway region, where a mixed Gaelic and Norse population called the *Gall-Gaedhil* seems to have grown up beginning around 900 (Forte et al., *Viking Empires*, pp. 93-96). Others moved to Iceland soon after its discovery around 870.[18] Many of them came to Iceland by way of the Hebrides, where Scandinavian men often acquired wives or concubines: genetic analyses of modern Icelanders show that about 20-25% of the male founders of the Icelandic population, and about 70% of the female founders, were Gaelic in origin (Agnar Helgason et al., "mtDNA and the Origin of the Icelanders"; Agnar Helgason et al., "Estimating Scandinavian and Gaelic Ancestry"). This is consistent with analyses of DNA from the remains of Viking-era Icelanders (Sigríður Sunna Ebenesersdóttir et al., "Ancient Genomes from Iceland," pp. 1029-1030) and with genealogies in *Landnámabók*.

The name *Iceland* might sound unattractive—it was named when explorer Flóki Vilgerðarsson saw a lot of floating sea ice, according to *Landnámabók* (S5/H5). The interior of the island is barren and uninhabitable, covered by glaciers and lava fields, with volcanoes that periodically erupt. Yet the Gulf Stream kept the climate relatively mild, and fish abounded in both the rivers and the surrounding sea. The ring of land along the coast bore good pastureland and forests of scrub birches. The earliest histories, *Íslendingabók* and *Landnámabók*, tell the story of the settlement, while many of the "sagas of Icelanders" tell how the founders of important families came to Iceland. Gods or ancestors often guided them: Flóki Vilgerðarsson bless-

---

18. According to *Landnámabók*, there were a few ascetic Irish monks (*Papar*) on Iceland when the Norse arrived. While there were certainly *Papar* on Orkney, Shetland, the Faroes, and the Hebrides, scholars now question whether the *Papar* made it all the way to Iceland; currently, there is no unambiguous archaeological evidence that they were there.

ed (*blótaði*) three ravens while still in Norway and set them free on his voyage to show him land (*Landnámabók* H5); Thorolf Mosturskeggi threw his house-pillars overboard (carved with the image of Thor) and settled where they came ashore (*Eyrbyggja saga* 4); and Egill's father Skalla-Grímr dropped the coffin of his father Kveldúlfr, who had died while on the voyage, into the sea and settled where it drifted ashore (*Egils saga* 27).

Figure of Buddha from northeast India. Maximum width about 6 cm. Helgö, Uppland, Sweden. Swedish History Museum 108115, CC BY 2.5 SE.

While the Vikings are perhaps most famous for raiding, fighting, and exploring, they were also merchants, trading goods all the way from northernmost Norway and Ireland to north Africa and central Asia. Trading depots like Kaupang in Norway were originally occupied only in summers, but some grew into sizable towns, such as Hedeby in northern Germany and Birka in Sweden. Exotic items came north, tokens of the wealth and power of those who could own them—such as the peacocks in the Gokstad ship (Dobat, "Viking Stranger-Kings," pp. 192-194); a piece of silk from Birka that can be traced to China itself (Vedeler, *Silk for the Vikings*, pp. 35, fig. 16); seashells and shell beads from the Red Sea, found in female graves at several sites (Thedéen, "Immortal Maidens," pp. 106-111); and a bronze Buddha from northeast India, an Irish bishop's staff, and a Coptic christening ladle from Egypt, all of which ended up in Helgö, Sweden just a short time before the Viking Age proper (Lundström, "Helgö," pp. 24-31). Slightly less rare but still exotic goods included wine, swords, glassware, and pottery from Germany; crystal and carnelian from eastern Europe; and silks, spices, and glass from Byzantium and beyond (Winroth, *The Conversion of Scandinavia*, pp. 76-84). Hundreds of hoards of silver coins from the Islamic Caliphate, found all along the trade routes to Byzantium, attest to the sheer volume and richness of the eastern trade. The largest hoard, discovered in 1999 on the island of Gotland, contained over

14,300 coins and 486 arm rings, as well as jewelry, ingots, and hack-silver, silver objects broken up and traded by weight (Östergren, "The Spillings Hoard," pp. 323-330). Scandinavian traders earned such wealth by exporting amber, walrus ivory, furs, swords, honey, wax, and slaves to Byzantium and the Caliphate, as Islamic sources attest (Lunde and Stone, *Ibn Fadlan and the Land of Darkness*, pp. 112, 126, 169-170, 175, etc.). Over shorter distances, Scandinavians traded grain, wool, cloth, metal, and soapstone.

Silver dirhem of Caliph Al-Muqtadir, dated to 903 CE. Kannikegærdet, Bornholm, Denmark. National Museum of Denmark, CC BY-SA 2.0.

By the tenth century, the former raiders were forming more stable realms. Migration continued both eastward into Russia and westward to the British Isles and Iceland. In 911-2, the king of France, affectionately known as Charles the Simple, gave the whole province of Normandy to the Northmen from whom it gets its name. Their leader, Hrólfr Ragnvaldsson, also known as Rollo, swore fealty to the king and became Normandy's overlord. Meanwhile, in England, the Norse rulers in the British Isles were fighting each other, and the English saw their chance: Æthelstan took York from the Norse in 927, and defeated a host of Scots, Irish, and Norse at the Battle of Brunanburh in 937 (where Egil Skallagrimsson fought on the English side, as is told in his saga). Æthelstan thus became the first king of a united England, although after his death in 939 the Vikings took York again. Danish raids resumed in 997, and Æthelred the Unready (or, better translated, "the Ill-Advised") ordered a massacre of Danes in 1002. In revenge, Harald Bluetooth's son Svein tjúguskegg, known as Sweyn Forkbeard in English, began serious attacks on England. He, and his younger son Knútr (Canute in English sources), briefly ruled all of Britain, Denmark, and Norway, although Knútr's empire fell apart upon his death in 1035.

Greenland was discovered by Eiríkr inn rauði (Eric the Red) in 982, and settlement there began a few years later.[19] On a trip to Greenland in 985, Bjarni Herjólfsson was blown off course by a storm and became probably the first European to see mainland North America. Leifr Eiríksson set out to explore the new land; he sailed from Greenland to Helluland ("rock slab land," probably Baffin Island), to Markland ("forest land," probably Labrador), and then to Vinland ("grape land"). His settlement in Vinland, Leifsbuðir ("Leifr's booths") at a site that the Norse called Straumfjord ("fjord of currents"), lasted from 1000 to 1005. Leifr's kinsman by marriage Thorfinn Karlsefni made another voyage in 1009, settling for a while at a site called Hóp ("tidal pool"). But settlement proved unsustainable; the Norse were too far from their allies and surrounded by potentially hostile native people, called *skrælingjar* in the sagas.

The attempts to settle Vinland are described in two sagas which are not entirely consistent with each other, *Eiriks saga rauða* and *Grænlendinga saga*. These were considered dubious for many years, until excavations in the 1960s by Helge and Anne Stine Ingstad, at L'Anse aux Meadows in northern Newfoundland, provided solid evidence for Norse settlement. The house foundations at the site are typical of Scandinavian houses, and while the occupants did not leave many objects behind, excavation unearthed slag from iron working, an iron ship rivet, a soapstone spindle-whorl, a ring-headed bronze pin, and fragments of flintlike fire-striking stone that chemically match sources in both Iceland and Greenland (Wallace, "The Viking Settlement," pp. 208-224). The site was almost certainly a base for explorations farther south; the Ingstads found remains of butternuts and butternut wood (*Juglans cinerea*, a walnut relative), and these don't grow north of New Brunswick. Claims have been made that Thorfinn sailed as far south as Long Island, but perhaps a more realistic location for Hóp might be the areas around Chaleur Bay and Miramichi, New Brunswick, which seem to match *Grænlendinga saga*'s description of the region around Hóp (Wallace, "An Archaeologist's Interpretation," pp. 229-230). At this writing there is no conclusive archaeological evidence for other Scandinavian settlements in the New World, but investigations are still ongoing.

---

19. Eiríkr gave it that name to try to encourage people to settle there, but it wasn't a lie. The parts of Greenland that the Norse settled, on the southern and southwestern coasts, were not covered in ice and had plenty of grass-covered land for pasture.

Rune-carved slate found in a cairn on the island of Kingittorsuaq, Greenland, recording the visit of three hunters. At about 73°N latitude, this is the northernmost rune inscription and the only authenticated one from North America. The final six characters are unusual and their meaning is unknown. National Museum of Denmark, CC BY-SA 2.0.

Even without permanent settlements, the Greenland Norse occasionally sailed to Labrador to harvest timber. Some artifacts found at Native sites in Labrador and on Baffin Island suggest occasional trade or exchange with the Greenland Norse (Sutherland, "The Norse and Native North Americans," pp. 240-242). They may have exchanged more than artifacts; thousands of living Icelanders bear DNA sequence markers that most closely resemble sequences found in Native North American populations. Exactly when these genetic markers entered the Icelandic population is not certain, but it must have happened before about 1740, probably centuries before that date (Sigríður Sunna Ebenesersdóttir et al., "A New Subclade of mtDNA"). *Eiríks saga* mentions that the Norse captured a Native boy and girl in Labrador, baptized them, taught them to speak Norse, and brought them back with them. While the genetic evidence can't be dated firmly enough to confirm this specific episode, it seems very likely that a female with Native ancestry reached Iceland and left descendants at some time in the late Viking or Medieval periods.

Viking Religion

In one sense, there is no such thing as "Viking religion." Families and regions seem to have followed their own traditions, which might resemble others on a general level, but probably differed in detail. Analysis of Viking

Age place names suggests that Freyr was worshipped around Uppsala and on the Oslofjord, while Tyr was worshipped in Denmark but not elsewhere (Brink, "How Unified was the Old Norse Religion?," pp. 109-125). Thor seems to have been known almost everywhere in the Norse world: the Norse rulers of Ireland, for instance, were called the "tribe of Thor" (Turville-Petre, *Myth and Religion,* p. 94). Both saga accounts and place names suggest that Thor was the most honored god in Iceland, with Freyr and Njord also worshipped there. Odin, as the patron of poets and especially the god of battle, is prominent in skaldic poetry, but other lines of evidence, such as place names and personal names, suggest that he was not the most popular god in most areas. Skaldic influence also seems to have led to the formulation of Odin's hall as a warriors' afterlife; people who were not part of a warband had different concepts of an afterlife (Gunnell, "How High was the High One?," pp. 105-114).

Silver Thor's Hammer pendant from Skåne, Sweden. Swedish History Museum 106659, CC BY 2.5 SE.

The Hammer of Thor is by far the most common Viking Age mythological symbol. It is depicted on at least two runestones, but its most widespread use is as pendants. Pendant Hammers range from exquisite works of art in silver filigree such as the magnificent hammer from Skåne with its eagle's head and staring eyes, to much plainer hammers of bronze, iron, and stone. It was also customary in Sweden to place multiple iron Hammers and other symbols on iron rings; these were buried with the dead and may or may not have been worn in life (Gräslund, "Thor's Hammers," pp. 190-191). It's often said that Hammer pendants became popular as a response to the Christian habit of wearing crosses. Some recent scholars have questioned this conclusion (Nordeide, "Thor's Hammer in Norway," pp. 218-222). However, a Danish soapstone block for jewelry casting includes molds for both hammers and crosses.

Soapstone mold for casting
crosses and Thor's hammers.
Trendgaarden, Denmark.
National Museum of Denmark,
CC BY-SA 2.0.

Evidently the smith was happy to accommodate different tastes (Roesdahl and Wilson, *From Viking to Crusader*, p. 191).

The oldest surviving texts that recount Heathen myths in any detail are the poems of the Viking Age. These fall into two basic classes, "eddic" and "skaldic." While eddic poetry is relatively straightforward, skaldic poetry used far more complex forms and meters, and required more background knowledge to comprehend, than any European poetry of that time. Yet if we can believe the sagas, the best skalds had dozens of long skaldic poems memorized, like Stuf Thordarson, who once recited thirty (or possibly sixty; accounts vary) of the shorter praise-poems (*flokkar*), and swore that that wasn't half of the *flokkur* he knew, and that he knew half again as many long praise-poems (*drápur*; see ÍF V, p. 285). Great skalds could also improvise complicated verses on command, like Thjodolf in *Sneglu-Halla þáttr* 3 (ÍF IX, pp. 267-268). Medieval Icelandic antiquarians such as Snorri Sturluson considered the poems to be reliable sources of information—since any tampering with the wording would have wrecked the meter. They preserved, explained, and commented on these poems long after the Viking Age was over. This is why most folk learn about the Germanic gods and goddesses by their Old Norse names, against the background of Viking Age culture: our richest hoard of mythological texts dates from this time and place.

The Conversion of the North

As was discussed in the section on the conversion of England, the conversion of Scandinavia was a multifaceted matter. A king might decide to adopt Christianity, for reasons that had at least as much to do with politics as with personal faith. Building the organizational Church and getting its message to everyone took much longer, and there is evidence of Heathen practices and "mixed faith" persisting for centuries after the "official" date of conversion.

Some Scandinavians had encountered Christianity as far back as the Migration Age, and Charlemagne sent a missionary to Denmark as early as 823. The deposed Danish king Harald Klak adopted Christianity in 826 at the court of Charlemagne's son Louis the Pious, in exchange for Frankish support in winning back his throne, but he never regained power in Denmark. The Frankish bishop Ansgar, who also preached in Sweden, founded churches in the trading towns of Hedeby and Ribe; the Arab traveler al-Tartushi mentions a church at Hedeby still in existence in 965 (Winroth, *The Conversion of the North*, pp. 105-112). However, Denmark did not "officially" convert until King Harald adopted Christianity in 965, as he proclaimed on the Jelling runestone. Accounts differ as to how this happened. According to Adam of Bremen, Harald was forcibly converted by Otto I, the Holy Roman Emperor (*History of the Archbishops of Hamburg-Bremen* II.iii; transl. Tschan, pp. 55-57), but Adam is suspected of having made up the story (Winroth, *The Conversion of Scandinavia*, p. 113). According to *Heimskringla*, Harald accepted Christianity after witnessing the emperor's bishop Poppo miraculously carry glowing hot iron without getting burned (*Óláfs saga Tryggvasonar* 27). Whatever happened, Harald built a church between the burial mounds that he had raised at Jelling for his father Gorm and mother Thyre. He is thought to have dug up his father's burial mound, which he had built as a pagan gesture in 958, and moved most of his remains into the church—evidently an attempt at post-mortem baptism (Pedersen, "The Jelling Monuments," pp. 303-304; Winroth, pp. 112-115).

Crucifixion scene on the Jelling Stone. National Museum of Denmark, CC BY-SA 2.0.

Harald's conversion did not lead to immediate peace between Denmark and the Holy Roman Empire: hostilities continued, and Otto II defeated the Danes in 974. Harald responded to the threat by reinforcing the Danevirke, the earthen wall and palisade on his southern border. At five strategic locations, he also built great ring-forts: perfectly circular, divided into quarters, and containing timber houses laid out in groups of four. When Otto II died in 983, the threat receded, and the ring-forts were abandoned (Roesdahl and Sindbæk, "Introduction," pp. 13-16). Incidentally, a woman was buried at the ring-fort at Fyrkat (built around 980), with rich and unusual grave goods, including silver amulets, white lead cosmetics, henbane seeds (an anesthetic and hallucinogen), a pot of ointment, and a metal staff. It is strongly suspected that she was a seeress in life, perhaps Harald's close advisor, right up to the adoption of Christianity or even a bit afterwards (Pentz et al., "Kong Haralds Vølve"). Two Thor's Hammer amulets were found at the Aggersborg ring fort in northern Jutland, as well as a miniature sickle and a miniature shield that were probably amulets. Evidently not all of Harald's loyal subjects were Christians (Pedersen et al., "Dress Accessories," pp. 288-289, figs. 6.113, 6.114).

Harald held power in Norway from 970 to his death in 986, but even before he claimed the Norwe-

Aerial view of the Trelleborg fortress, near Slagelse, Denmark, built duringthe reign of Harald Bluetooth (d. 986). National Museum of Denmark, CC BY-SA 2.0

Pendant from the Fyrkat grave. National Museum of Denmark, CC BY-SA 2.0

gian throne, Christianity began making inroads in Norway. King Hakon the Good converted during a stay in England at the court of his foster-father King Athelstan (894–939). When he returned home, his choice proved unpopular, and his friend Sigurðr jarl of Hlaðir persuaded him to return to the old ways. After he died in 961, Eyvindr Skáldaspillir praised him for upholding the old ways (*Hákonarmál* 18, ed. Finnur Jónsson, *Skjaldedigtning* vol. B1, p. 59):

Þá þat kyndisk, hvé sá konungr hafði	It was made known then, how that king had
vel of þyrmt véum,	Respected the holy places well,
es Hákon báðu heilan koma	When all the ruling and reigning powers
ráð ǫll ok regin.	Bid Hakon be welcome.

Hakon was killed in battle against the sons of Eirík Blood-Axe; although Hakon's forces won the battle, rule passed to Eirik's son Harald Greycloak. He and his brothers only ruled with support from Harald Bluetooth, and as Christians, they destroyed the holy places (causing bad weather and famine, according to Eyvindr skáldaspillir). However, Hakon the son of Sigurðr jarl, a liegeman of Harald Bluetooth, organized an ambush and killed Harald; he ruled as Harald's vassal at first, but eventually threw off his allegiance and ruled independently. Harald had forced Hakon to be baptized and sent him back to Norway with priests, but Hakon ditched the priests and held to his Heathen troth. The skald Einar Skálaglamm describes his rule as a return of prosperity in *Vellekla* 15 ("Scarcity of Gold"; ed. Marold, p. 303):

Nú grœr jǫrð sem áðan;	Now the Earth grows green as before;
aptr geirbrúar hapta	The wealth-diminisher [ruler] lets
auðrýrir lætr ôru	The messengers of the spear-bridge
óhryggva vé byggva.	[warriors]
	Inhabit the gods' sanctuary without sorrow.

Unfortunately, Hakon was killed by another descendant of Harald Fairhair, Olaf Tryggvason, who had adopted Christianity as part of a peace agreement to get him to stop pillaging England (Winroth, *The Conversion of Scandinavia*, pp. 115-116). Olaf may not have been a very devout Christian—Adam of Bremen reports rumors that he never was one, and mentions that he was so devoted to taking omens from birds that he was nicknamed Craccaben, "Crow Bone" (*Krákabein* in Norse; *History of the Archbishops* II.xl, transl. Tschan, p. 82). But whatever his personal convictions might have been, Olaf found Christianity politically expedient as a tool for gaining and keeping power. According to his saga in *Heimskringla,* his missionary methods included bribery, followed by torture if the bribery failed. For example, Olaf tried to convert the chieftain Eyvindr Kinnrifi with flattery and offers of gifts; when Eyvindr remained resolute, Olaf resorted to threats, and finally tortured him by setting a brazier of glowing coals on his belly, which burst from the heat (*Óláfs saga Tryggvasonar* 76). It's hard to know how much of this violence was motivated purely by power politics and how much might have come from sincere devotion. What seems clear is that such methods won Olaf no friends. The magnates of the kingdom revolted, and Olaf died by the hands of his enemies in the naval Battle of Svold, in 1000 CE. Queen Sigríðr storráða (often translated "Sigrid the Haughty" but perhaps better rendered as "Sigrid the Strong-Willed") organized the alliance that brought

Sigrid tells Olaf, who has just slapped her, that "this may well be thy death!" Artwork by Hans Egedius, *Kongesagaer* (1899).

Olaf down. She herself is well remembered for Olaf Tryggvason's courtship of her; she refused to convert to Christianity, but offered to allow him to retain his own faith. His response was to strike her in the face and call her a "heathen bitch," which brought their courtship, and ultimately his kingship, to rather sharp ends.

Olaf had sent missionaries to Iceland, who had managed to convert some prominent Icelanders while facing resistance by others. By the year 1000, the Heathen and Christian factions in Iceland were each declaring the other side "out of law," meaning that legal agreements and contracts by people on one side would not be considered binding on people on the other side. Quite apart from this threat to stability, Iceland's dependence on trade with Norway gave Olaf leverage, as did the fact that Olaf was holding sons of leading Icelandic families as hostages. It was decided that all folk should live under one faith and one law, and Thorgeir the Lawspeaker—the person whose duty was to recite the laws at the Althing—would choose which it was to be. Thorgeir covered himself with his cloak and lay still for a day and a night, a ritual which hints at some form of seeking visions or communication with the gods (Jón Hnefill Aðalsteinsson, *Under the Cloak*, pp. 103-123). When he came forth again, he decreed that Iceland would become Christian, but that certain Heathen practices, including the eating of horsemeat and the exposure of deformed infants, could be practiced in private. Thorgeir's decision (or inspiration) to pursue a relatively gentle conversion, with temporary accommodations for Heathen practice, protected Icelanders against possible reprisals from Olaf, while creating conditions that allowed the old myths and stories to be remembered and preserved.

After Olaf Tryggvason was killed, Norway was briefly ruled by liegemen of King Svein of Denmark. They were driven out by Olaf Haraldsson, who during his lifetime was called (although probably not to his face) Óláfr inn digri, literally "Olaf the Fat," but also connoting "Proud," "Puffed-Up," or "Full of Himself". The new Olaf supposedly shared the old Olaf's zeal for forcible conversion as a political tool:

> He investigated how people were keeping Christianity, and where he found shortcomings, he taught them the right way. He took it so much to heart, if there were any people who were not willing to give up Heathenry, that he drove some out of the country. Some he had maimed in the hands or feet, or had their eyes put out; some he had hanged or cut down, but he left no one unpunished who wasn't willing to serve God (*Óláfs saga helga* 73; ÍF 27, p. 101).

However, he managed to alienate even his Christian subjects. When the Danish king Knútr invaded Norway, he won the country without any bloodshed. Olaf fled, and when he tried to return, he faced massive resistance:

> They summoned all the people, thanes and thralls. . . and they had such a great host that no one had ever seen such a great host assembled in all

Norway. . . . there were many landowners and a great many powerful farmers, but the bulk of it was made up of cottagers and laborers. . . The host was strongly urged on to fury against the king (*Óláfs saga helga* 216, ÍF 27 p. 320).

Olaf was slain at the battle of Stiklarstaðir in 1030, and declared a saint in 1031.

Organized Heathen worship survived longest in Sweden. Since Sweden's trade links and cultural contacts tended to lie to the east, they were under less pressure to convert. As early as 829, the Frankish king Louis the Pious sent the missionary Ansgar to Sweden at the invitation of King Bjorn. Ansgar and his successors preached in Sweden for decades afterwards, and also evangelized in Denmark and northern Germany. Ansgar's success was rather mixed, and new waves of missionaries had to be sent, but the church persisted after Ansgar's death (Rimbert, *Vita Ansgari*, chs. 9-12, 17-20; transl. Robinson, *Ansgar*, pp. 48-73; Adam of Bremen, *History of the Archbishops* I.xv-xxxiv, transl. Tschan, pp. 21-35; see Winroth, *The Conversion of Scandinavia*, pp. 105-112). Sources for what happened next are sparse,

Olaf is killed at Stiklarstaðir, as depicted in *Flateyjarbók*. Stofnun Árna Magnússonar, Reykjavík.

Crucifix from grave 660, Birka, Sweden. 10th century. Swedish Historical Museum 108914. CC BY 2.5.

although some later Swedish kings seem to have been Christian. According to a story preserved at the end of *Hervarar saga* and also in *Heimskringla*, King Olaf Skotkonung adopted Christianity at about the same time as Olaf Tryggvason in Norway, but he proved unpopular. After he was force to abdicate, Christianity was neglected. A later king, Ingi, adopted Christianity again, but he was driven away by the assembly, who took Ingi's brother-in-law Svein as their new king because he was willing to sacrifice to the old gods. Known as Blót-Svein, he ruled for only three years before Ingi returned and killed him. Ingi imposed Christianity for good around 1100 (Tolkien, *The Saga of Heidrek the Wise*, pp. 61-63).

The Last Viking

The Viking Age is sometimes said to have come to its "official end" with the death of "the last Viking," Haraldr *hardráði* ("harsh counsel" or

Harald Godwinsson's death, depicted in the Bayeux Tapestry. The words read HAROLD INTERFECTUS EST, "Harold Is Killed." Opinions vary as to whether Harold is the man on the left seemingly trying to pull an arrow out of his eye, or the man on the right being ridden down by a Norman on horseback. Photo by Myrabella, Wikimedia Commons, Public Domain.

"harsh rule"; known in Old English as *Harald Hardrada*) at the Battle of Stamford Bridge in England, on September 25, 1066—the last attempt by a Norse ruler to conquer another land.[20] Haraldr himself, who had previously served in the Varangian Guard in Byzantium (among other adventures) was known as a cunning strategist as well as a mighty warrior. Unfortunately, no sooner had the English king Harold Godwinson defeated Haraldr hardráði than he was called to march his weary army back south to Pevensey, where William the Bastard, the Viking-descended but French-speaking and assimilated Norman duke, had just

---

20. The story goes that the English offered to grant Haraldr land in England—specifically, six feet of land, or a bit more since he was a tall man.

landed with his own forces. On October 14, 1066, Harold Godwinson fell in the resulting battle at the nearby town of Hastings. William the Bastard became better known as "William the Conqueror," and the Normans imposed their own feudal system and language upon the Anglo-Saxons. Resistance to William's rule led to aggressive reprisals in northern England in the winter of 1069-1070, the "Harrying of the North"; William's men burned crops, causing terrible famines. Legends grew up about a leader of the English resistance, known as Hereward the Wake (e.g. Swanton, "The Deeds of Hereward" pp. 28-99); but by 1076, William had effective control of the entire country, redistributing lands to loyal lords, and building castles and churches throughout England as part of a strategy for maintaining control.

After the death of Haraldr hardráði, his descendants continued to rule, but Norway came to be split by a growing civil conflict between two factions, each of which had its own candidates for the throne: the more aristocratic Baglers and the less aristocratic Birkebeiners. Hakon Hakonarsson (Hakon IV), supported by the Birkebeiners, managed to reunite and stabilize the country by about 1240. That accomplished, he turned his attention westward; by playing the Icelandic chieftains against each other, he was eventually able to incorporate Iceland into the Norwegian kingdom in 1262. Then it was time to reassert his claims on Scotland and the Hebrides, where the Norse jarls of Orkney were increasingly coming into conflict with the growing kingdom of Scotland (Forte et al., *Viking Empires*, pp. 293-296). Hakon sailed with a fleet to western Scotland to assert his claims. On October 2, 1263, his forces fought the Scots at the Battle of Largs; it was more or less a draw, but Hakon needed a decisive win and didn't get one. He withdrew to Orkney, intending to carry on with the fight next year, but he died that winter. In 1266, Norway formally gave up its claims to Man and the Hebrides, although Orkney and Shetland remained nominally under Scandinavian control until 1472 (Forte et al., pp. 256-264).

Edred Thorsson once wrote that Germania was "the last to fall" (*A Book of Troth*, p. 12), the last pagan land to adopt Christianity. That's not true. Even after the Scandinavian countries had adopted Christianity, their Finnic, Slavic and Baltic neighbors to the east remained pagan. Inspired by the Pope's calls to spread the Christian faith (and by the desire to control rich resources and major trade routes, and by rivalry with the Eastern Orthodox Church), Scandinavian and German kings embarked on the so-called

Northern Crusades against their pagan neighbors. Some of the early "crusades" were scarcely different from Viking raids. Sweden allegedly crusaded against the Finns to the east as early as the 1150s; this seems to be more legend than fact, but by 1295 the entire Baltic coast of Finland was in Swedish hands (Christiansen, *The Northern Crusades*, pp. 113-122). German and Scandinavian forces moved against the pagan Balts and Slavs. In 1168, the army of King Valdemar I of Denmark destroyed the Slavic fortress and temple of Arkona on the island of Rügen, where he tore down an idol of the god Svantovit and forcibly baptized 1300 pagans (*Knýtlinga saga* 122; ÍF 35, pp. 304-306).

Beginning in 1229, the Teutonic Knights, an order of mostly German warrior-monks, began pushing into eastern Europe. By 1410, they had carved out their own theocratic state, the *Ordensland*, that stretched from present-day Poland all the way to Estonia (Christensen, pp. 82-92). Still, it was not until 1387 that the rulers of Lithuania formally adopted Christianity. Meanwhile, the Sámi people of northern Scandinavia maintained their traditional beliefs more or less undisturbed until serious conversion attempts got underway in the seventeenth and eighteenth centuries.

Contributors:

1st edition: Kveldúlfr Gundarsson.

2nd edition: New material by Ben Waggoner.

3rd edition: Reorganization and new material by Ben Waggoner.

Detail of the Stora Hamars stone, Gotland, Sweden.
Swedish Historical Museum 108206. CC BY 2.5.

CHAPTER SEVEN

Medieval to Modern

1150–1900

After the conversion to Christianity, the old ways were lost—or were they? Here is the story the history books won't tell you: the saga of beliefs which refused to die, although for a time they went underground, surviving in manuscripts and folktales until the time was right for Idunna's apples to make them live once more and inspire new generations of poets, artists, and thinkers.

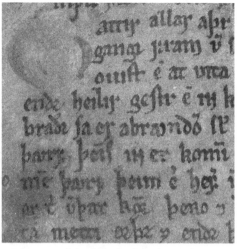

Opening of the *Hávamál* in the Codex Regius. The first two lines read **Gattir allar aþr gangi fram**, "Everyone should look around before he steps forward." Stofnun Árna Mágnussonar, Reykjavík.

Eddas and Sagas

Modern Heathens have rarely, if ever, claimed that their religion descends in an unbroken line of transmission from pre-Christian times. Nonetheless, in scattered folktales, charms, and folk customs, fragments of old belief did survive for centuries after the "official" Christianization of the Germanic lands. Rune-carved sticks excavated from the Bryggen district of Bergen, Norway, dating to about 1400, include magic spells invoking Odin; so do Icelandic books of magic from the 16th and 17th centuries. Norwegian folktales recorded in the 19th century mention the hammer-wielding "Tor Trollesbane"; south German folktales recorded at the same time tell of a girl named Fried who wept precious tears searching for her husband Woud. Swedish charms recorded in the 19th century called on Odin, Thor and Frigg; English folklore knew the standing stones called "Weyland's Smithy." Trolls, giants, and spirits of the wilderness were still seen and remembered; spirits of the house and farm still received offerings, and ancestors still watched over the lands they had once lived on. Tales of Heathen heroes were still told, albeit reworked to suit new tastes; the 13th-century German *Nibelungenlied* is a courtly retelling of the story of Sigurd the Volsung.

It was in Iceland, however, that the single largest body of lore on the pre-Christian religion was preserved. It's worth taking a closer look at why this happened.

Writing the Lore in Iceland

Whatever trauma Christianity might have inflicted on the old ways and on the souls of those who followed them, it gave Iceland one precious gift: manuscript culture. This included the Latin alphabet; the technologies of making ink and parchment and pens and bound books; and the general habit of writing books and consulting them. Christianity is a "religion of the book," and to practice it, Christians had to make and read books—not only the Bible, but biblical commentaries, theological treatises, lives of saints, books of sermons, texts on medicine and the calendar, and similar edifying literature. In its own way, this was an information revolution (Ross, *Cambridge Introduction to the Old Norse–Icelandic Saga*, pp. 43-47).

Manuscript culture was, of course, prevalent everywhere else in the Christian world. But it took a unique turn in Iceland, and the reason was that Iceland had neither a king, nor a formal church, until the year 1268. Before the conversion, as far as we can tell, local chieftains—the *goðar*—had built *hof* (temples) and charged fees, the *hoftollr*, for their upkeep.[21] The pattern continued after the conversion: *goðar* built churches on their land and kept the income from tithes and offerings. Men from powerful families claimed the right to appoint priests, and some were ordained as priests themselves—without giving up their old habits of fighting, playing power politics, and marrying wives and concubines. (Clerical celibacy never really took hold in Iceland.) Owning a church could be lucrative, and the institutional Church had no say in how the money was used. Bishops who tried to bring the Icelandic church into compliance with Rome were largely ignored: the Diocese of Skálholt attempted to wrest control of church income from the chieftains in 1179—a wrangle called the *Staðarmál*, the "estates affair"—

---

21. The word *goði* originally meant a pagan priest, but Icelandic *goðar* were also secular leaders. Both the word and the office persisted long after Christianity was adopted.

and lost. The institutional Church wouldn't gain control of church income until 1297 (Byock, *Medieval Iceland*, pp. 143-164).

By about 1200, six main families controlled most of the *goðorðar* ("chief-taincies; offices of *goðar*") in Iceland. Their leaders, the *stórgoðar* or "great chieftains," were jockeying for power. The resulting time of unrest, which sometimes broke out into open warfare, is called the Sturlung Age, after the powerful Sturlung clan. Meanwhile, King Hakon IV of Norway (1204-1263) had asserted his control over a united Norway by 1240, after a long period of civil strife. Hákon began playing the leading Icelandic families against each other, offering various factions his support in exchange for their promises to support him as king. In 1262, after years of fighting that left many of their best leaders dead, Iceland accepted Hakon's rule and his laws.

The reason this matters for us is that, until 1262, Iceland had a class of wealthy chieftains who were subject neither to a King, nor to the institutional Church. These chieftains used literacy as another tool for gaining and wielding power. Some sagas, for example, were written to support a chieftain's claim to a particular part of Iceland by showing that his ancestors had lived there from the earliest days. Others were written to promote solidarity in a district by giving the people a sense of shared history (Kristinsson, "Lords and Literature," pp. 1-17). Still other sagas could be used to show that Iceland, which uniquely in medieval Europe had no kings, had just as noble a heritage as any other country. These sagas presented a network of genealogies that connected Icelanders to legendary heroes, royal dynasties, and even the heroes of the Trojan War (Ross, "Development of Old Norse Textual Worlds," pp. 372-380). Especially after coming under the rule of the kingdom of Norway, Icelanders felt the need to show their kinship to Scandinavian kings and heroes—and also to demonstrate how their independent-minded ancestors dealt with kings who got too pushy. This seems to have been a touchy subject: an anonymous scribe wrote in a manuscript of *Landnámabók* that "Many people say that it is useless knowledge to write about the land-taking. But on the contrary, we think that we know how to answer foreigners when they accuse us of being descended from slaves or scoundrels, if we know our true ancestry with certainty" (ÍF I, p. cii; see Mitchell, *Heroic Sagas and Ballads*, pp. 121-126). Still other sagas were created to bring a touch of class to a rather rough and rugged society: Hakon IV of Norway sponsored the translation of "romances of chivalry," including tales of Charlemagne and Arthur's knights, both to bring his kingdom into line with Continental tastes and to instruct his retainers in the values of feudal chivalry. These soon found their way to Iceland, where they inspired the composition of original knightly romances. While Iceland never really had a knightly class of its own, such tales suited the tastes of royal officials and wealthy landowners (Barnes, "Romance in Iceland," pp. 267-270).

The result of all this was the creation, beginning before 1200 and continuing until about 1400 or so, of the largest body of non-Latin literature in medieval Europe: the *sagas*. "Icelanders' sagas" (*Íslendingasǫgur*) tell the stories of the founding families of Iceland. "Kings' sagas" (*konungasǫgur*), including those in *Heimskringla*, tell the lives and deeds of the Norse kings. "Sagas of elder times" (*fornaldarsǫgur*) are tales of the legendary past, such as *Vǫlsunga saga* and *Hrólfs saga kraka*. Less interesting to Heathens, but occasionally containing useful bits of information about the elder ways, are the "bishops' sagas" (*biskupasǫgur*), biographies of notable Icelandic churchmen; "holy men's sagas" (*heilagra manna sǫgur*), translations of saints' lives; "sagas of contemporary events" (*samtíðarsǫgur*), written about recent history; and "sagas of chivalry" (*riddarasǫgur*), translations of romances such as Arthurian legends, or original sagas composed in imitation of such romances. Still other sagas were translations of medieval histories, such as the *Trójumanna saga* about the Trojan War; *Rómverja saga* about the Roman Republic; and *Gyðinga saga* about the history of the Jews. (For examples of many of these saga types, the anthology *Sagas of Imagination*, published by the Troth, is a good place to start.)

The sagas often preserved traditional Norse poetry. In fact, some legendary sagas are thought to have originated as expanded prose commentaries on much older poems, growing up around the verses like a building around its scaffolding (Tulinius, *The Matter of the North*, pp. 57-63). Poetry was considered to be the most reliable source of historical information, partly because altering its words would destroy a poem's very tight rhyme and meter, and partly because it had always been the genre for recording heroic deeds in a memorable way. Snorri Sturluson wrote in his preface to *Heimskringla* that "we gathered most of our information from what we are told in those poems which were recited before the chieftains themselves, or their sons. We regard everything found in those poems about their expeditions and battles to be true. It is the habit of skalds to praise those who are in front of them most highly; but no one would dare to tell them about deeds which all who listened, including the chieftain himself, knew to be nothing but nonsense and lies. That would have been mockery, not praise" (ÍF 26, p. 5).

There has long been debate as to just how historically accurate the sagas are. The *konungasǫgur* that deal with later kings (or at least the lost sources of some of them) were actually composed by contemporary chroniclers, from roughly 1150 through about 1300. The "classical" sagas of Icelanders were probably composed around 1200, and continued to be written through about 1400, drawing on oral traditions passed down in Icelandic families, but influenced by other literary sources. Modern Icelanders have long argued over the extent to which the *Íslendingasǫgur* are historical. Americans might think of these sagas as similar to Western novels and films—set in a known historical time and place, based on real people (cowboys, miners, the Lakota tribe, the 7th Cavalry, etc.), and featuring at least some people who really existed (Jesse James, General Custer, Sitting Bull, etc.), but using this history to comment on contemporary society, with anything from careful historical accuracy to creative fantasy. The *fornaldarsǫgur* are a much more mixed bag. Some of them, the so-called "sagas of adventure," are complete fantasies, with plenty of Viking derring-do but no historical basis that we can see; even in the medieval period they were sometimes called *lygisǫgur*, "lying sagas." Even *fornaldarsǫgur* with a distant historical basis have often had plenty of mythic and fantastic elements added, sometimes from the old mythology and sometimes from the "sagas of chivalry" (Tulinius, *The Matter of the North*, pp. 60-63). Still, the basic stories of the older *fornaldarsǫgur* were surely part of Norse oral tradition in some form throughout the Viking Age, and some are known in other Germanic traditions, such as the Vǫlsungs, or the Danish royal family of Skjǫldungs in *Hrólfs saga kraka* (who appear as the Scyldings in *Beowulf*). But like the *Íslendingasǫgur*, the *fornaldarsǫgur* often make creative use of the past to comment on the present (Tulinius, pp. 65-69).

Medieval Icelanders generally took pride in their heroic ancestors, even when they were pagans. In some cases they may have gone out of their way to depict their ancestors as more ferocious than they actually were: for example, the accounts of the "blood-eagle" may have been based on a misunderstanding of skaldic poetry coupled with antiquarian enthusiasm for the savage Vikings (Frank, "Viking Atrocity and Skaldic Verse"). And while some Icelandic authors went out of their way to depict the old Heathen customs as wicked, foolish, and disgusting—notably the two monks who compiled *Flateyjarbók*—most seem to have been relatively sympathetic towards memories of Heathen gods and religion. Certainly poets didn't stop using kennings that referred to the old gods and myths. Sometimes the authors' fondness for the old ways can go overboard; in some cases they may have added sensationalized "Heathen customs" to give their sagas that certain archaic flavor. But the sagamen preserved a rich body of mythologic and legendary lore that, despite its many gaps, imaginative additions, and maddening contradictions, is unparalleled in Europe.

Ari Þórgilsson the Wise (1067-1148) was the first Icelandic historian; his account of the settlement of Iceland is now known as *Íslendingabók*. Ari may also have written or helped to write the first version of *Landnámabók*, a listing of 435 early settlers of Iceland, their ancestors and descendants, and the places where they settled. *Landnámabók* contains many short anecdotes that seem to have been "fleshed out" in later sagas. But Snorri Sturluson (1179–1241) is by far the best-known Icelandic scholar and historian. Snorri was twice elected Lawspeaker of Iceland (1215–1219 and 1222–1231), and as a major political figure and member of the powerful Sturlung family, he had to navigate a minefield of conflicts—between rival clans in Iceland, between factions in Norway, and between Iceland's independence and King Hakon's desire to rule it. His luck ran out in 1241, when his son-in-law Gizurr Þorvaldsson led an attack on his estate at Reykholt, and Snorri was dragged out of the house and killed.

Statue of Snorri Sturluson at Reykholt, Iceland, sculpted by Gustav Vigeland. Photo by Christian Bickel, Wikimedia Commons. Public Domain.

From our perspective, Snorri's historical role is overshadowed by his work as an author and historian. Concerned that the new generation of poets was forgetting the old myths, which were crucial for understanding the kennings and allusions in skaldic poetry, he wrote a textbook of Norse poetry, the *Edda* (often called the *Prose Edda* or *Snorri's Edda*). He included poems and verses by many skalds whose work would otherwise be lost, and to explain their poetic language, he retold the major Norse myths. We can't take his work uncritically; he was well educated in both Christian theology and in Classical mythology, and we can trace influences from both in the *Edda*. He also "smoothed out" various versions of the myths into a single story, and some aspects of his work, like depicting Odin as the ruler of the gods, may not reflect pre-Christian thought. Yet his work is one of our most precious sources for the old mythology. Snorri also compiled *Heimskringla*, a history of the kings of Norway containing both his own writing and earlier sagas that he had fleshed out; and he is suspected (though not proven) to have written *Egils saga Skallagrímssonar*. The tale of Snorri's own life is told in the near-contemporary *Sturlunga saga* (Whaley, "Snorri Sturluson," pp. 601-602).

By the late 1300s, intermarriage among the royal houses of Denmark, Norway, and Sweden meant that there were people who had plausible claims to more than one throne. Olaf Hakonarsson (1370-1387) was briefly king of both Denmark and Norway. The finest medieval manuscript from Iceland, the *Flateyjarbók*, may have been intended as a gift for him to instruct him in wise rulership, but he died before it was completed (Rowe, *The Development of Flateyjarbók*, pp. 22-27). After his death, his mother Margaret became regent of both kingdoms, got herself elected as regent of Sweden as well, and declared her great-nephew Eric of Pomerania as her heir. Thus began the Kalmar Union, a union of three independent kingdoms who just so happened to have the same king. Although theoretically an equal partner, Norway came to be dominated by Denmark, in part because Norway lost up to 60% of its population to the Black Death in 1348-1350. Iceland came under Danish control, and would not gain full independence until 1947. The new rulers paid little attention to their North Atlantic outposts; the Norse settlements in Greenland disappeared around 1500 for reasons that are still unclear, and King Christian I pawned Orkney and Shetland to Scot-

Odin, depicted in a manuscript of the Eddas dated 1765-6, SÁM 66. Stofnun Árna Magnússonar, Reykjavík.

land in 1468 and 1469, and never redeemed them (Gunnar Karlsson, *History of Iceland*, pp. 100-105). Colder global climates between 1300 and 1800 made farming, fishing, and trade more difficult in Iceland, and may have also contributed to the extinction of the Greenland settlements. Danish trade monopolies and general neglect strangled Iceland's economy, and periodic volcanic eruptions and epidemics caused hardships of their own—on top of all the difficulties one might expect to face when trying to make a living on a rocky sub-Arctic island (Gunnar Karlsson, pp. 138-192).

The heritage of sagas and poems was one thing that the Icelanders always clung to. As early as 1185 or so, Saxo Grammaticus had praised them for their diligent learning despite the poverty of their land: "They regard it as a real pleasure to discover and commemorate the achievements of every nation; in their judgment it is as elevating to discourse on the prowess of others as to display their own" (*History of the Danes*, Preface, transl Fisher, p. 5). Even in the worst times, Icelanders preserved and treasured their lore. The custom of copying manuscripts by hand, and even the composition of new sagas, didn't end until the early 20th century (Driscoll, *Unwashed Children of Eve*, pp. 1-12). Sagas and poems were recited to entertain families and keep spirits up during the long dark winter evenings, and children grew up learning from the old stories and acting them out in play (Jón Karl Helgason, "Continuity?," pp. 65-75). As the Icelandic poet Davíð Stefánsson wrote in 1930, in an ode ("Hátídaljóð") commemorating the 1000-year anniversary of the Althing:

því lifir þjóðin,	The people survived
að þraut ei ljóðin,	because the poetry did not die out,
átti fjöll fögur	they had fair mountains
og fornar sögur,	and sagas of old,
mælti á máli,	they spoke a language
sem er máttugra stáli. . .	stronger than steel. . .

The Renaissance of Northern Scholarship

The late 1400s and early 1500s saw three historical developments which would ultimately prove crucial for the revival of Heathenry. One was Gutenberg's invention of the printing press, which made it possible to disseminate information far more widely, accurately, and cheaply than before. Printing in turn fed the growth of Humanism, with its motto *ad fontes!*—"back to the sources!"—leading to a resurgence of interest in ancient authors. Finally, the Protestant Reformation, usually said to begin in 1517, ended in the breaking away of the state churches of England, Germany, and the Scandinavian countries from the Roman Catholic Church. This development may not seem relevant to Heathenry, and in fact in some ways it was detrimental: the Calvinist and Puritan movements suppressed a number of customs, such as Yule celebrations, that still preserved fragments of pre-Christian culture. Nonetheless, the Protestant Reformation spurred revivals of nationalist feeling and encouraged the study of national history. As the Lutheran reformer Phillip Melanchthon said, "It is an act of piety to study the achievements of one's own country" (Kelley, "*Tacitus Noster*," pp. 161-162). Reformation theology also emphasized the individual's personal relationship with God and ability to read the Bible—which led to translations of the Bible into contemporary languages, which in turn inspired the growth of literacy and literature.

All of these factors worked together in the rediscovery of Tacitus's *Germania*, which was discovered in the 1420s, first printed in 1472, and frequently reprinted throughout the next century. Not only did *Germania* spark Germans' interest in their own history, it contributed to a new sense of nationhood. Even before the Reformation, the image of the German nation maintaining its independence in the face of Rome, and praised by a Roman for its virtues, resonated deeply in the hearts of many. German scholars of

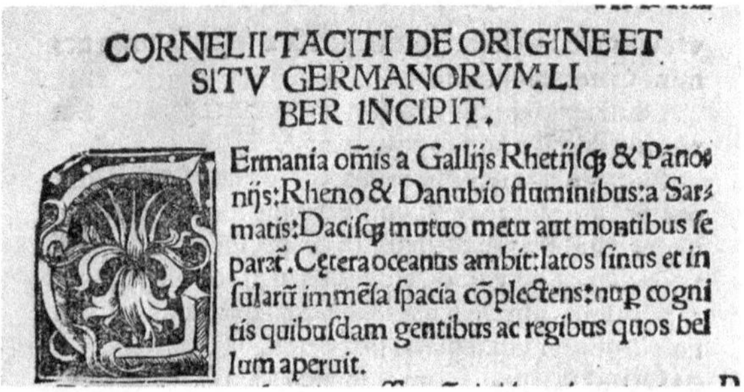
CORNELII TACITI DE ORIGINE ET
SITV GERMANORVM LI
BER INCIPIT.
Ermania om̃is a Gallijs Rhetijsq & Pãno
nijs: Rheno & Danubio fluminibus: a Sar
matis: Dacisq mutuo metu aut montibus se
parat̃. Cetera oceanus ambit: latos sinus et in
sularũ immẽsa spacia cõplectens: nup cogni
tis quibusdam gentibus ac regibus quos bel
lum aperuit.

One of the earliest printed editions of Tacitus's *Germania.* Nanni, *Berosvs Babilonicvs. . .* (1511)

the time affectionately spoke of *Tacitus noster,* "our Tacitus," and held up Tacitus's image of Germans as simple, brave, honest, freedom-loving folk, superior to the decadent legalism of Rome (Kelley, "*Tacitus Noster*," pp. 156-162). Sometimes the love for Tacitus went a bit overboard: for example, the humanist Aventinus claimed that Tuisto, ancestral father of all the Germans, had been Noah's favorite son and the first lawgiver among the Germans. He took Tacitus's description of ancient German worship and concluded that the Germans had always freely and naturally worshipped God in their hearts, under the open sky. Tacitus's plain statements that the Germans were polytheists who sacrificed humans seem not to have bothered him (Krebs, *A Most Dangerous Book*, pp. 114-122). More positively, Martin Opitz (1597–1639), the first major poet in the modern German language, cited Tacitus's description of ancient German songs to argue that the German language had been, and still was, fit for the most refined poetry (Krebs, pp. 141-148).

In England, Henry VIII's break with the Roman Catholic Church led him to close of the monasteries in 1536. The contents of many monastic and church libraries were destroyed or scattered. Over the next two centuries, private book collectors were able to save many books, including most of the surviving Anglo-Saxon manuscripts. Robert Cotton is the most noteworthy; his collection, now the heart and soul of the British Library, included both the only manuscript of *Beowulf* and the only manuscript of the "Old English Rune Poem," as well as historical writings such as the *Anglo-Saxon Chronicle*, Bede's histories, and many other treasures. Robert Harley and his son Edward, the Earls of Oxford, also assembled a noteworthy collection, now also in the British Library (Basbanes, *A Gentle Madness*, pp. 87-96, 107-109). As manuscripts accumulated, the Cottonian and Harleian libraries began to attract scholars. One of them, Humfrey Wanley, the Harley family librarian and one of the earliest authorities on Old English, transcribed a number of manuscripts relating to the runes, including the "Old English Rune Poem" (whose original manuscript was destroyed in a fire in 1731; Wanley's transcript is the only surviving text). He and other "antiquarians" of his day began to study and translate both English and Scandinavian rune inscriptions surviving in Britain. His studies essentially founded rune scholarship in England (Bennett, "The Beginnings of Runic Studies in England"). Wanley's cataloguing of manuscripts in the Cottonian, Harleian, and other libraries brought much lore to light. To give just one example, Wanley was the first person to notice the "Tract. . . written in Dano-Saxon poetry, and describing some wars between Beowulf a King of the Danes of ye family of the Scyldingi, and some of your Swedish Princes" (Wright, "Humfrey Wanley," p. 109).

Sweden in the sixteenth and seventeenth centuries was a rising European power; King Gustavus Adolphus (ruled 1611–1632), the "Lion of the North," intervened in the Thirty Years' War and won decisive battles that expanded its territories and its influence. At its height, the Swedish Empire controlled present-day Finland, Estonia, and parts of Norway, Denmark, Germany, and Russia, and even established a North American colony on the site of present-day Wilmington, Delaware. With this expansion came a surge of nationalist feeling. *Storgöticism*, "Great-Gothicism," identified the Swedes with the ancient Goths, who had originally come from Sweden (at least according to Jordanes and other ancient historians). As the first to settle Europe after Noah's Flood, the Goths of Sweden had given rise to all other Europeans—or so it was claimed. Johannes Magnus, the last Roman Catholic Archbishop of Uppsala, published *Historia de Omnibus Gothorum Sueonumque Regibus* (*History of All Kings of the Goths and Swedes*) in 1554. Here he traced the history of Sweden

Johannes Magnus's "Gothic Alphabet." According to Johannes Magnus, runes were the oldest script in the world, invented before or just after the Biblical Flood; they were carved on stones beginning in the reign of the fifth Swedish king Siggo. *Historia de omnibus Gothorum Sueonumque regibus* (1558).

Olaus Magnus's depiction of (left to right) Frigg, Thor, and Odin, the old gods of the Goths. *Historia de Gentibus Septentrionalibus* (1555).

back to Noah's son Magog the founder of the Goths and first of their 230 kings, drawing on a mixture of ancient sources and exceptionally creative speculation. He used his history to comment on the turbulent politics of his time, taking potshots at the Danes and at Lutherans (Roberts, *Gustavus Adolphus*, vol. 1, pp. 508-515; Johannesson, *The Renaissance of the Goths*, pp. 73-91). Johannes's brother, Olaus Magnus, was appointed Archbishop after his brother's death, but never served in Sweden. In exile in Rome, Olaus published *Historia de gentibus septentrionalibus* (*History of the Northern Peoples*) in 1555. This encyclopedic account of Scandinavia introduced Europe to everything from skis to reindeer to runestones to legends of the old gods. Again, it had a political meaning; it was intended to assert Sweden's priority and greatness, and also to show its noble audience the best way to govern (Johannesson, pp. 187-206).

The ancient Goths were taken quite seriously in Sweden, even after the Reformation. Like the Swedes themselves, the Goths had conquered many lands and triumphed against the might of Rome. King Gustavus Adolphus dressed for his coronation as the legendary Gothic king Berig (King, *Finding Atlantis*, pp. 34-37). Johannes Bureus (1568–1652), Sweden's national antiquarian and librarian, began a systematic program of studying Sweden's runestones, documenting 663 stones, some of which have since been lost and are known to us only through his drawings. Bureus developed a mystical interpretation of the runes, the *Adulruna*, which blended Norse paganism with the Kabbala and Hermeticism. Despite the eclectic nature of his work,

Johannes Bureus's notes on the "Adelrunæ" from a 1612 manuscript, *Antiquitates Scanzianae* (Scandinavian Antiquities). The runes at the top are interpreted as the word *fader*, "father." Below, the three "adelrunæ" are interpreted as "Father, Son, and Holy Spirit." Kunglinga Biblioteket, Stockholm. Public Domain.

Bureus recognized the power and relevance of the old Gods (Roberts, *Gustavus Adolphus*, vol. 1, pp. 517-515; Karlsson, "Kabbalah in Sweden," pp. 88-91).

Another Swede, Olof Rudbeck (1630–1702), claimed that Swedish was the oldest language in the world, and Sweden was in fact the site of Atlantis, with its founder Atlas identified with Atli from the Volsung legend (King, *Finding Atlantis*, pp. 138-155). This may sound like the work of a crank, but Rudbeck was a brilliant scholar in many fields—among other things, he discovered the lymphatic system, composed music, and designed buildings for Uppsala University. When an Icelander named Jonas Rugman brought a trunkful of saga manuscripts to Uppsala, Rudbeck studied them intensively

Johannes Bureus's Adulruna symbol, from his 1612 manuscript *Antiquitates Scanzianae* (Scandinavian Antiquities). All fifteen of Bureus's runes can be assembled into this diagram. Kunglinga Biblioteket, Stockholm. Public Domain.

and brought them to the attention of scholars (King, pp. 37-39). Rudbeck also carried out careful excavations and descriptions of archaeological sites

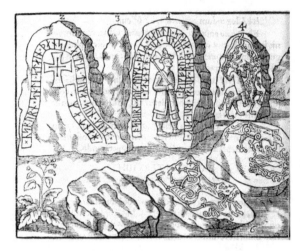

Ole Worm's drawing of the runestones at Hunnestad, Skåne, Sweden (part of Denmark at the time). Most of these stones were destroyed in the 1780s, and are known only from his description. *Danicorum Monumenta* (1643)

and artifacts (King, pp. 55-59). By the standards of scholarship at his time and place, Rudbeck's belief in a Swedish Atlantis was overenthusiastic, but not unreasonable.

Denmark was not far behind Sweden; the rival countries were frequently at war, and there was something of a competition to see whether Denmark or Sweden had the most glorious heritage (Hafstein, "Bodies of Knowledge," p. 17). The Danish scholar Ole Worm (1588-1644) eagerly collected information about Denmark's past. In 1622, he convinced the Danish government to send out an order to Danish priests, requesting details on ancient sites, monuments, and customs and traditions in their regions. Worm was especially interested in runes, and he sent out artists to draw runestones as accurately as possible; in 1643, he published *Danicorum Monumentorum* (*Monuments of the Danes*), the first systematic work on rune inscriptions (Hafstein, pp. 14-16). Worm's Icelandic colleague, Arngrimr Jónsson, found a manuscript of Snorri Sturluson's *Edda* in 1628 and passed it on to him. In 1643, Icelandic bishop Brynjólfur Sveinsson acquired a manuscript of poems which he gave to King Frederick III; now called the *Codex Regius* ("Royal Book"), this is the main manuscript from which most of the poems of the *Poetic Edda* are derived, although a few were added from other manuscripts.[22]

---

22. Bishop Brynjólfr is the one who called this collection of poems the *Poetic Edda* as a counterpart to Snorri's *Edda*; the *Codex Regius* itself does not use the word. He attributed the book to Sæmundr the Wise, an actual 12th-centuty Icelandic priest and scholar, who appears in Icelandic folktales as a great wizard who could control the Devil with black

But the greatest collector of old lore was Árni Magnússon (1663-1730), an Iceland-born scholar at the Danish court, who visited his homeland on official missions in the early 1700s and used the opportunity to collect every manuscript he could beg, buy, or borrow for copying. Despite losses in the Copenhagen fire of 1728, his collection, now known as the Arnamagnaean collection and divided between institutes in Denmark and Iceland, remains a priceless archive (Gunnar Karlsson, *History of Iceland*, pp. 258-260).

Árni Magnússon, known in Latin as Arnas Magnaeus. Wkimedia Commons, Public Domain.

Worm and Bureus may be considered the founders of systematic runic studies. Rising interest in the Scandinavian past was also shown by the collection and publication of Danish folk ballads, beginning in 1591 and continuing into the 1600s (Rossel, *Scandinavian Ballads*, p. 4). Seventeenth- and eighteenth-century crown decrees in both Sweden and Denmark (which at the time included present-day Norway) required clergymen and officials to gather historical information, including legends, tales, and ballads.

The Lutheran Church also began earnest missionary work among the Sámi peoples of northern Scandinavia, a remote region which had hitherto been neglected (Roberts, *Gustavus Adolphus*, vol. 1, pp. 425-426). Although the Church and the Scandinavian states tried to repress Sámi traditional religions, some of the missionaries left documentation of the indigenous religion, as did visiting scientists and explorers. The Sámi tradition is historically different from the Norse, but the two are known to have influenced each other: the Sámi were widely regarded by Viking-era Scandinavians as skilled in magic, and "Lapp sorcerors" and "Finnish sorcerors" (actually Sámi) appear in several sagas and in folktales. The influence went the other way as well: Sámi groups in Norway and Sweden grafted the traits of several Norse gods onto their own, and continued to honor them for centuries after

---

magic. While the historical Sæmundr almost certainly had nothing to do with the manuscript, the *Poetic Edda* was often called "Sæmundr's Edda."

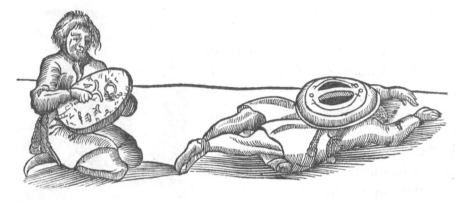

Two Saami *noiadi*, one drumming and one in a trance. Schefferus, *Lapponia* (1673).

the Christianization of the Norse people. Þórr Karl, "Old Man Thor," was borrowed into the Sámi language as the hammer-wielding, troll-bashing Hora Galles, while the Sámi in Norway and parts of Sweden invoked Veraldar Oinen, "man of the world," a figure very much like Freyr and even represented by phallic idols (Karsten, *Religion of the Samek*, pp. 24-26, 47-49). By the 1800s, scholars were beginning to apply these Sámi traditions to the study of Norse religion.

The Thirty Years' War

Many of the developments we've discussed ultimately stem from the Protestant Reformation. Unfortunately, so did the Thirty Years' War between 1618 and 1648, one of the most destructive wars in European history. Originally a war between Protestant and Catholic states within the Holy Roman Empire, it eventually dragged in most of the European powers. When it was over, something close to 50% of the population of the German states had died from war, famine, and disease.

One of the end results of the war was that the Netherlands finally gained their independence from the Hapsburg rulers of Spain. Tacitus's *Germania* had described the warlike Germanic tribe of the Batavi, and his *Histories* recounted the Batavian revolt against Rome in CE 69-70. The Dutch were happy to claim the Batavi as forebears, creating a foundational myth that helped to unify the seven provinces of the Netherlands. As one Dutch historian wrote in 1685, "War is often necessary for the support of liberty, and the ancient Batavii were lovers of one and the other" (Gonzales Sanchez,

"Deconstructing Myths," pp. 89-94). The Frisians, whose land became one of the seven United Provinces of the Netherlands, rediscovered their ancient pagan King Radbod and made him part of a great dynasty stretching back into heroic legend (Nijdam and Knottnerus, "Redbad," pp. 101-105).

The other result of the Thirty Years' War that would be important for modern Heathenry was the continued persecution of German nonconforming sects, notably Anabaptist sects such as the Amish and Mennonites. Facing economic ruin and repeated outbreaks of war as well as religious persecution, many Germans looked for an escape. In 1683, Francis Daniel Pastorius founded Germantown, Pennsylvania, the nucleus of the Pennsylvania German community. The customs and folklore brought by the immigrants that followed him would blossom into "Pennsylvania Dutch" culture. Their rich folk religious and magical traditions would give rise to *Braucherei* (healing), *Hexerei* (folk magic), and eventually the Urglaawe tradition in modern Heathenry. In Urglaawe, the goddess Holle is considered the protectress of the immigrant Germans, who guided them to their new home and ensured the survival of their culture (Schreiwer, *First Book of Urglaawe Myths*, pp. 1-6).

The Romantic Revival

Germany

In the late eighteenth and early nineteenth centuries, European scholars turned towards a new approach to history, philosophy, and the arts: Romanticism. Romanticism is a multifaceted phenomenon that developed differently in different countries, and it's hard to sum up in a short space. Very briefly, it can be said to include: emphasis on the individual's unique identity and spiritual development; guidance by intuition and emotion over reason; appreciation for untamed nature; freedom from "classical" rules of behavior and aesthetics; and the belief in an idealized past, with the spirit of an entire people as the natural source of its highest artistic expression.

In Germany, the Romantic revival of interest in the heroic past began as early as the 1750s, when Johann Jakob Bodmer published a series of medieval German poems and epics, including the first complete edition of the *Nibelungenlied*. This inspired a circle of late 18th century poets, sometimes called "the Bards," to break away from French-inspired models and imitate the ancient Germanic bards in spirit (Greenway, *The Golden Horns*, pp. 125-136; Williamson, *The Longing for Myth*, p. 75). The best known, Friedrich Gottlieb Klopstock (1724-1803), wrote odes and dramas in honor of Arminius and the German gods, alongside his perfectly pious Christian hymns and poems:

Wodan! unbeleidigt von uns,
Fielen sie bei deinen Altären uns an!
Wodan! unbeleidigt von uns,
Erhoben sie ihr Beil gegen dein freies
Volk!

Weit halle dein Schild! dein
Schlachtruf töne,
Wie das Weltmeer an dem Felsen-
gestade!
Furchtbar schwebe dein Adler und
schreie nach Blut und trinke Blut!
Und die Thale des heiligen Hains
decke weißes Gebein!

Wodan! Without provocation from us,
They fell upon us, beside your altars!
Wodan! Without provocation from us,
They raised their axe against your free folk!

Far may your shield ring! May your battle cry resound
Like the World Sea against the rocky shore!
May your eagle soar, bringing terror, and scream for blood and drink blood!
And may bleached bones cover the valley of the holy grove!

—*Hermanns Schlacht* [Herman's Battle], scene 2 (1769)
Sämmtliche Werke, vol. 6, p. 50

But the most influential German Romantic was philosopher and theologian Johann Gottfried Herder (1744-1803). Herder's political philosophy begins with the observation that humans are naturally social organisms, bound to each other by bonds of kinship, friendship, and shared culture and language. Human governments began as extensions of these natural bonds. When governments arose that imposed leaders unnaturally, such as hereditary monarchy and despotism, the result was misery. The best social organization is that which arises naturally and organically:

the most natural state is, therefore, *one* nation [*Volk*], an extended family with one national character. . . . For a nation is as natural a plant as a family, only with more branches. Nothing, therefore, is more manifestly contrary to the purposes of political government than the unnatural enlargement of states, the wild mixing of various races and nationalities under one sceptre. . . . Such states are but patched-up contraptions, appropriately called state-*machines*, for they are wholly devoid of inner life, and their component parts are connected through mechanical contrivances instead of bonds of sentiment (*Ideas for a Philosophy of History* IX.iv; transl. Barnard, *J. G. Herder*, p. 324).

The German word *Volk* is not easy to translate; it has meanings that go beyond the usual meanings of the English cognate "folk." A *Volk* is more than a group of people: what unites a *Volk* is a transcendental, "natural" essence that all members of the *Volk* share, carried in their innermost selves as a spring of personal inspiration and group unity (Mosse, *The Crisis of German Ideology*, p. 4). To Herder, the natural bond that defined and inspired the German *Volk* was their common language and culture. Language, in particular, was the best expression of the true essence of a *Volk*, its *Volksgeist* or "folk soul" (Arvidsson, *Aryan Idols*, p. 26). The best government for a *Volk* was that which expressed and safeguarded the *Volk*'s own essence, its own unique nature and identity. This took on increasing urgency during the Napoleonic Wars, when Napoleon's armies conquered most of the German states and brought the Holy Roman Empire to an end. Even though Napoleon's regime only lasted a few years, it left many Germans longing for national unity. As Herder's follower, the philosopher Johann Gottlieb Fichte (1762–1814), wrote in his "Thirteenth Address to the German Nation":

. . . the first, original, and truly natural boundaries of the State are beyond doubt their internal boundaries. Those who speak the same language are joined to each other by a multitude of invisible bonds by nature herself, long before any human art begins; they understand each other and have the power of continuing to make themselves understood more and more clearly; they belong together and are by nature one and an inseparable whole. Such a whole, if it wishes to absorb and mingle with itself any other people of different descent and language, cannot do so without itself becoming confused, in the beginning at any rate, and violently disturbing the even progress of its culture. (transl. Jones and Turnbull, pp. 223-224)

Herder has been called a "proto-Nazi," but this is not quite fair. A *Volk*, for Herder, was united by shared language and culture, not by race. Herder did not believe that any one *Volk* was better than another; each was simply different: "The negro has as much right to consider the white man a degenerate, a born albino freak, as when the white man considers him a beast, a black animal. . . . The negro, the [Native] American, the Mongol has gifts, talents, preformed dispositions that the European does not have. Perhaps the sum is equal—only in different proportions and combinations" (*Letters for the Advancement of Humanity* no. 116, transl. Forster, *Philosophical Writings*, pp. 394-395). He believed that the greatest development of a *Volk* would be possible under liberal democracy, with freedom of speech and the press. And although he recognized the wide spectrum of human diversity, he did not recognize the existence of separate human races: "In short, there are neither four or five races, nor exclusive varieties, on this earth. Complexions run into each other; forms follow the genetic character; and *in toto* they are, in the final analysis, but different shades of the same great picture which extends through all ages and all parts of the earth" (*Ideas for a Philosophy of History* VII.i; transl. Barnard, *J. G. Herder*, p. 284). Herder also favored women's rights, opposed anti-Semitism, and even more strongly opposed colonialism and slavery. Although a devout Christian and an ordained minister, he recognized the harm done by enforcing Christianity on conquered peoples:

Even Christianity, as soon as it had effect on foreign peoples in the form of a state machine, oppressed them terribly; in the case of several it so mutilated their own distinctive character that not even one and a half millennia have been able to set it right. Would we not wish, for example, that the spirits of the northern peoples, of the Germans, of the Gaels, the Slavs, and so forth, might have developed without disturbance and purely out of themselves? . . . .

Let the land be named to which Europeans have come without having sinned against defenseless, trusting humanity, perhaps for all aeons
to come, through injurious acts, through unjust wars, greed, deceit, op-
pression, through diseases and harmful gifts! Our part of the world must
be called, not the wise, but the *presumptuous, pushing, tricking* part of the
earth; it has not cultivated but has destroyed the shoots of peoples' own
cultures wherever and however it could.

—*Letters for the Advancement of Humanity* no. 114, transl. Forster,
Philosophical Writings, pp. 381-382)

Unfortunately, many of those who were inspired by Herder's concept
of the *Volk* would forget the more humane aspects of his thought. Herder's
fellow philosopher Immanuel Kant argued in the 1780s that humans all
descended from a common ancestor, but differing climate conditions had
permanently altered them, with Europeans the least "degenerate" and Native
Americans the most "degenerate." Kant did change his mind in the 1790s and
adopt much more egalitarian views (Kleingeld, "Kant's Second Thoughts"),
but his earlier views were supported by J. F. Blumenbach (1752–1840), who
collected and measured skulls from around the world in an attempt to prove
that Europeans were the original human race, from which all others had
degenerated (Kitson, "Politics," pp. 680-685). Although he himself did not
believe that any race was intellectually inferior, this belief seems to have been
overlooked by later ideologues.[23]

Romantic nationalism inspired people to look beyond the Bible, Greece,
and Rome for their historical roots and modern sense of identity. The German Romantics didn't necessarily want to revive their old religion and actually worship the old gods—many of them were perfectly pious Lutherans
or Roman Catholics. What they wanted was to draw on the old myths as
a source of artistic and spiritual inspiration, just as the Greek and Roman
myths had been drawn on since the Renaissance. This inspired the philosopher Friedrich Schlegel among others; although he was skeptical of the
value of "the Nordic-barbaric mythology of the ancient Germans and Scan-

---

23. Blumenbach, by the way, felt that the people of the Caucasus Mountains came the
closest to the ideal standard of humanity. It is thanks to him that "Caucasian" came to be
used as a term for light-skinned Europeans.

dinavians" (quoted in Williamson, *The Longing for Myth*, p. 67), he called
for the reawakening of all the old mythologies of the world to create a new
fountainhead of artistic expression: "to accelerate the genesis of the new
mythology, the other mythologies must also be reawakened according to
the measure of their profundity, their beauty, and their form" (*Dialogue on
Poetry*, transl. Behler and Struc, pp. 86-87). As one correspondent wrote in
1818, "For the holy and everything that has its roots in it, the German has
nothing to do but turn to the *Edda*" (quoted in Williamson, p. 102).

Where ancient texts might be lacking, Romantics turned to the common people, who they thought might have preserved the ancient ways in
their songs and stories. Herder was one of the first to collect and publish
folksongs; his 1773 collection was called *Stimmen der Völker in ihren Lie-
dern*, "Voices of the Peoples in their Songs." But the most famous German
collectors of folklore were the brothers Grimm, Jacob (1785–1863) and Wilhelm (1786–1859), who collected their famous "fairy tales" (*Kinder- und
Hausmärchen*, "Tales for Children and Home") between 1806 and 1812.
Contrary to popular belief, the Grimm brothers did not publish their tales
to amuse children; they were serious scholars of linguistics. Jacob Grimm
worked out the sound relationship between Germanic and other Indo-European languages, which he published in 1819 in his *Deutsche Grammatik*.
Unusually for scholars of the time, Grimm refused to restrict his studies to
"proper" language; he realized that the rustic dialects of uneducated peasants
could be valuable for reconstructing a language's history. The same was true
of the tales that these peasants told (Shippey, "A Revolution Reconsidered,"
pp. 6-9).

The Grimms and other scholars continued to publish and study old texts,
including the Grimms' edition of the *Poetic Edda* in 1815, and Wilhelm's
1829 edition of medieval German heroic ballads. They also began compiling
a huge dictionary of the German language (which would not be completed
until 1961). All their work came together in Jacob Grimm's massive distilla-
tion of language, lore, and literature: *Deutsche Mythologie*, first published in
1835, and known in English as *Teutonic Mythology*. This was Grimm's grand
effort to reconstruct what he felt had once been a coherent pan-German-
ic mythological system, by piecing together every fragment that he could
find, and applying the same comparative methods to reconstruct what was
missing that he had applied so successfully to languages. As he wrote: "Our

mythology. . . . has been taken away forever. I turn to the sources that remain of it, which are partly written artifacts and partly the ever-flowing river of living custom and legend. The former can reach high, but they show themselves broken and torn, while present-day popular traditions hang on threads that connect them directly with antiquity" (*Deutsche Mythologie*, Preface; transl. Williamson, *The Longing for Myth*, p. 102). Grimm's attempt to reconstruct a single grand Germanic mythology now looks entirely too optimistic; myths and practices simply vary too much across space, and change too much over time, to

Jakob Grimm (1785-1863). Photo by Franz Hanfstængel. Wikimedia Commons, Public Domain.

form a single unified "mythos" (Shippey, "A Revolution Reconsidered," pp. 9-25). Nonetheless, he inspired other folklore collectors, notably Andreas Faye, Jørgen Moe and P. Christian Asbjørnsen in Norway; A. A. Afzelius in Sweden; Elias Lönnrot in Finland; Sven Grundtvig in Denmark; Jón Árnasson in Iceland; and Cecil Sharp and F. J. Child in Britain (Kvideland and Sehmsdorf, "Nordic Folklore Studies Today," pp. 4-5).

Grimm's work also inspired later scholars such as James Frazer and Max Müller in their attempts to reconstruct the origins and development of the world's myths and religions. Many of the conclusions of the early mythologists and folklorists are now discredited or disputed by today's academics—such as Max Müller's belief that all mythology and religion had begun as metaphors for the sun's course across the sky (Müller, "On the Philosophy of Mythology," pp. 156-161; Arvidsson, *Aryan Idols*, pp. 74-90); Eduard Gerhard's claim that all ancient goddesses were aspects of a Great Mother Goddess; Johann Bachofen's idea that the earliest societies had been matriarchies, which only later evolved the refined higher spirituality needed for proper patriarchy (Arvidsson, pp. 99-102); James Frazer's belief that all cultures had revered a dying and resurrected god of vegetation; or the widespread assumption that rural folk practices preserved pagan religion more or less intact (Hutton, *Triumph of the Moon*, pp. 32-42, 111-131). A more sinister development was the tendency to view Indo-Europeans as fundamentally different from the other main branch of "white people," the Semites. Some scholars of the time saw the Indo-Europeans as uniquely capable of rationality, abstract thought, freedom, and enlightenment, unlike the Semitic peoples (Arvidsson, pp. 91-123).

At the same time, archaeology was beginning to develop as a scientific discipline in its own right, rather than a gentlemanly form of looting. More and more of the physical evidence of the Anglo-Saxons, continental Germans, and Scandinavians was discovered, studied, and placed in a chronological context in the later part of the 19th century. John Kemble in England, Conrad Engelhardt and J. J. A. Worsaae in Denmark, and Wilhelm and Ludwig Lindenschmidt in Germany are just a few of those who contributed to a relative archaeological timescale, which made it possible to date finds with increasing precision and work out how cultures had changed with time (Todd, *The Early Germans*, pp. 262-264). Engelhardt is especially noteworthy for pioneering the systematic excavation of Iron Age bog deposits in south Denmark between 1858 and 1865, notably the famous deposits at

Thorsbjerg, Nydam, Kragehul, and Vimose (Wiell, "Denmark's Big Find Pioneer," pp. 66-83).

Finally, the Romantic interest in old legends and myths found artistic expression. By far the most famous artist to draw on the old mythology was Richard Wagner (1813-1883). Almost all of Wagner's mature operas draw on heroic German legends, from *Tannhäuser* (1845) to *Parsifal* (1882). His only mature opera that doesn't, *Der Meistersinger von Nürnberg*, ends with a passionate exhortation in favor of art as an expression of the German *Volk*: *zerging' in Dunst / das heil'ge röm'sche Reich, / uns bliebe gleich / die heil'ge deutsche Kunst!*

Richard Wagner as Wotan, with his valkyries carrying exhausted opera lovers to Walhall. Grand-Carteret, *Richard Wagner en Caricatures* (1892).

198

"Even if the Holy Roman Empire were to collapse into dust, holy German art would still remain for us!" But his greatest work, and one of the greatest presentations of Germanic mythology, was *Der Ring des Nibelungen,* a cycle of four operas, begun in 1848 and not performed in its entirety until 1876. Lasting about sixteen hours in all, and including some of the most demanding music for singers and orchestra alike, the *Ring* is what Wagner called a *Gesamtkunstwerk* or "complete artwork": one that synthesizes music, drama, movement, and visual arts into the service of one great purpose.

Wagner had called himself *der deutscheste aller Deutschen,* "the most German of all Germans," and saw his work in almost religious terms, as a sacred expression of the German spirit (Spotts, *Bayreuth,* p. 77). He himself was inspired in part by Grimm's *Teutonic Mythology,* which he remembered first reading in 1843:

. . . I was enchained by a wondrous magic. The baldest legend spoke to me of its ancient home, and soon my whole imagination thrilled with images; long-lost forms for which I had sought so eagerly shaped themselves ever more and more clearly into realities that lived again. There rose up soon before my mind a whole world of figures, which revealed themselves as so strangely plastic and primitive, that, when I saw them clearly before me and heard their voices in my heart, I could not account for the almost tangible familiarity and assurance of their demeanour. The effect they produced upon the inner state of my soul I can only describe as an entire rebirth. Just as we feel a tender joy over a child's first bright smile of recognition, so now my own eyes flashed with rapture as I saw a world, revealed, as it were, by miracle, in which I had hitherto moved blindly as the babe in its mother's womb. (*My Life,* vol. 1, p. 314)

To create the *Ring* cycle, Wagner read deeply in the Eddas, sagas and medieval German legends, but he did not present them "as written." Like many storytellers before and since, he used the old myths creatively, to put forth his own ideas on life, politics, and philosophy. His depictions of the gods do not always match the ancient sources, or come across as reverent; for example, Fricka (Frigg) is presented as a shrew who berates Wotan for his marital infidelity and utter disregard for decency.[24] Heathen opera fans

---

24. This tells you everything you need to know about Wagner's first marriage.

should probably read both *Vǫlsunga saga* and *Nibelungenlied* before watching the *Ring* cycle, since Wagner altered their plot considerably for his own artistic reasons. More troubling is the fact that Wagner was blatantly, obsessively anti-Semitic, a trait which got worse in his later life thanks to his friendship with Arthur de Gobineau (see chapter 2),[25] and much of his personal life was a shambles, due—in part—to his boundless egotism and spendthrift financial habits. But however flawed he was as a human being, Wagner was also a brilliant composer, whose operas transformed classical music and inspired millions of devotees, including not a few Heathens.

Carl Emil Döpler, the costume designer for the first production of the *Ring*, did as much as anyone to create the "Viking look": horned and winged helmets, metal lingerie for the valkyries, and so on. Döpler visited museums around Germany and Denmark to study archaeological finds before creating his costume designs, and productions of the *Ring* followed them scrupulously for decades (Spotts, *Bayreuth*, pp. 57-58). Many aspects of his reconstructions, notably the horned and winged helmets, are now known to be historically inaccurate. That said, they have proved oddly persistent. . . .

Mathilde Dennery as Brünnhilde in Wagner's *Ring*, ca. 1906. Public Domain. Courtesy of Archive.org.

---

25. To be fair, anti-Semitism was widespread across the political spectrum, and Wagner's views, though repugnant, were not unusual for the time. He was also warmly friendly with several Jewish musicians. The man could be maddeningly contradictory. See Magee, *The Tristan Chord*; Callow, *Being Wagner*; and Williamson, *The Longing for Myth*, pp. 203-210, for accounts of his life and thought. How much anti-Semitism actually made it into Wagner's work is debated by music historians; some of his characters, like Alberich and Mime in the *Ring*, are suspected to be based on Jewish stereotypes.

Scandinavia

The Romantic impulse quickly spread to Scandinavia, where many artists and poets argued for adopting Norse deities and myths alongside, or
even in place of, the Greek and Roman deities and myths that had inspired
so much older literature. Inspired by Klopstock, the Danish poet Johannes
Ewald presented his first drama based on mythic themes, *Rolf Krage*, in
1770, while his fellow poet Adam Oehlenschläger (1779-1850) retold Norse
legends in odes, epics, and dramas, beginning in 1803 (Gerven, "Is Nordic
Mythology Nordic or National?," pp. 52-55).[26] Oehlenschläger inspired Ni-
kolaj F. S. Grundtvig (1783-1872), a Lutheran clergyman and author who
was well read in the Icelandic sagas, and who was also a pioneer in the study
of Old English literature. Grundtvig tried to synthesize a philosophy from
Norse mythology, and used the old myths to inspire nationalist feeling in
his native Denmark, in his *Nordens Mytologi* and in later works (Greenway,
The Golden Horns, pp. 161-166; Schulz, "Crossing the Borders," pp. 220-
223). He also inspired the founding of folk high schools (*Folkehøjskole*),
institutions for lifelong learning that would teach arts, national traditions,
and useful skills to members of all social classes. Also worth mentioning
is Jacob Langebek (1702–1775), the Danish national archivist who tried
to collect and publish every text on the medieval history of Denmark. His
successor as archivist, the Icelander Grímur Jónsson Thorkelin (1752–1829)
traveled to England and transcribed the manuscript of *Beowulf* (Shippey,
"Introduction," pp. 3-6).

Oehlenschläger's writings found an audience in Sweden, where a literary
club called the Gotiska Förbund ("Gothic Society") combined an interest
in ancient Norse literature and culture with the desire for national reform.
Founded in 1811, the Gotiska Förbund published a literary magazine called
Iduna, which presented poems and stories on Norse themes. There was
considerable debate over whether and how the Norse gods could be used
in literature and fine art, in the ways that the Greek and Roman gods had
been used for centuries. Poets like Per Henrik Ling, Erik Gustaf Geijer, and
Erik Johan Stagnelius drew on the ancient myths and tales in their poetry

---

26. Oehlenschläger wrote the words to the Danish national anthem, and thanks to him,
   millions of Danes have sung *det hedder gamle Denmark og det er Frejas sal*—"It is called
   old Denmark, and it is Freyja's hall!"

and plays (Benson, *The Old Norse Element*, pp. 124-143; Gerven, "Is Nordic Mythology Nordic or National?," pp. 55-61).

Sen, I gudar!	See, you gods!
Jag är för gammal	I'm too old
för nya läran	for this new creed
om vite Kristus—	of the White-Christ—
vill ej till himlen,	I don't want to go to heaven,
till andra gudar	to other gods
och sankt Peter,	and Saint Peter,
som jag ej känner.	whom I do not know.
Döpter är jag	I've been baptized
i rödan blod	in the red blood
av fiender slagna	of slain enemies,
och föraktar	and I despise
att helgas av vatten.	being sanctified by water.

—Erik Gustaf Geijer, "Den Siste Kämpen" ("The Last Warrior"), 1811. *Samlade Skrifter*, part 1, vol. 3, pp. 193-194

The Götiska Forbund soon came to be led by the most famous Swedish poet of the 19th century, Esaias Tegnér (1782-1846), a professor of classics at Lund University (Benson, *The Old Norse Element*, pp. 182-184). By far Tegnér's most famous work was *Frithiofs saga*, a retelling of the Old Norse *Friðþjófs saga*. First published in its entirety in 1825, *Frithiofs saga* consists of twenty-four cantos, each one in a different poetic form. Praised by international figures such as Goethe, who loved its *alte, kraftige, gigantischbarbarische Dichtart* ("old, mighty, gigantic-barbaric verse style"), *Frithiofs saga* was translated into every European language, including twenty-two times into English. It inspired composers to set its romantic love story to music.[27] It inspired Kaiser Wilhelm II of Germany to raise a giant statue of the hero Fridthjof overlooking the Sognefjord in Norway, where the saga is

---

27. Probably the best was the Swedish composer Elfrida Andrée's 1898 opera *Fritiofs saga*, first performed in its entirety only in 2019. A suite of its music has been recorded (Sterling CDS1016-2). Heathens who like classical music should definitely give it a listen.

set. What's ironic is that *Friðþjófs saga* is not a typical Icelandic saga; in fact, it seems to be a Norse re-telling of an Arabic story (Kalinké, *Bridal-Quest Romance*, pp. 109-123). Still, Tegnér's portrayal of the hero and his love interest charmed readers for decades. Much of the popular conception of Vikings as noble, honorable, brave, and free ultimately derives from Tegnér's poem (Waggoner, *Sagas of Fridthjof the Bold*, pp. xv-xxv).

Scandinavian painters and sculptors also drew inspiration from Germanic mythology. Early nineteenth-century depictions of the Norse gods are often based on the familiar depictions of the gods in Greek and Roman art, which means that many of them

Monument to Fridthjof, Vangsnes, Norway. Photo by Ssolbergj, Wikimedia Commons. CC BY-SA 3.0.

wear much less clothing than one might expect for a cold climate. Later depictions drew on archaeological finds for a somewhat more historically informed look. The Danish sculptor Hermann Ernst Freund, the Swedish

Drawing of a detail from *Ragnarokfrisen* (Ragnarok Frieze) by Hermann Ernst Freund (1857), showing Thor fighting the Midgard Serpent. Müller, *Nordens Billedkunst* (1906).

sculptor Bengt Fogelberg, the Swedish artist Mårten Eskil Winge, and the Norwegian painter Peter Nicolai Arbo are just a few of the artists who created compelling works based on Norse myths. And by the mid-19th century, Scandinavian composers were tapping into their native mythology, folklore, and folk music: Norwegian composer Edvard Grieg drew on his country's rich folklore and folk music in his own work, as well as beginning the opera *Olav Trygvason*. The opera would have portrayed Norway's conversion to Christianity, but Grieg had a falling-out with the librettist and only managed to complete the first act, depicting a Heathen religious ceremony with magnificent music. The Danish composer J. P. E. Hartman wrote music for Oehlenschläger's plays on Nordic themes, as well as *Vǫlvens Spådom*, a musical setting of passages from *Vǫluspá* that is well worth hearing.

Two other figures from Scandinavian literary history should be mentioned here for their influence on American Heathenry. Viktor Rydberg (1828-1895) rose from poverty to become one of Sweden's best novelists and poets; his poem "Tomten" ("The Tomte" or "The Gnome") remains a favorite at Christmas. He later turned to the study of religion, publishing works on Christian theology, before embarking on an extensive study of Norse mythology, published as two volumes of *Undersökningar i germanisk mythologi* ("Researches in Germanic Mythology," 1886 and 1889; translated under the title *Teutonic Mythology*), followed by a popular school textbook, *Fädernas gudasaga* ("Our Fathers' God-Saga"), in 1887. Rydberg insisted on the deep Indo-European roots of the recorded myths, opposing the views of scholars like Sophus Bugge, who saw the myths as medieval creations based more on Christian mythology than on what the ancient Germanic peoples actually thought. In this, Rydberg was basically correct, although there are still features of the myths as told by people like Snorri Sturluson where we have to reckon with some influence from Christian learning. However, Rydberg placed the original homeland of the Indo-European speakers in north-central Europe (*Teutonic Mythology*, pp. 14-18).

The other striking feature of Rydberg's work is his assembly of the myths into a single grand, coherent storyline, often using obscure references and fragments as a sort of glue, and often creating equivalence between characters with different names and features. Rydberg saw himself as reconstructing a story that took shape in the Neolithic, in the home of the Proto-Indo-Europeans, which he identified as southern Scandinavia. The greatest hero of this monomyth is Svipdag, known from the late Eddic poem *Svipdagsmál* (divided into *Grógaldr* and *Fjǫlsvinnsmál* in many editions), but equated by Rydberg, on the basis of shared elements in their stories, with Freyja's husband Óðr in the Eddas and the heroes Otharus, Hotherus, and Erik the Eloquent in Saxo Grammticus's *History of the Danes* (*Teutonic Mythology*, pp. 507-548) Most scholars would argue that Rydberg's work is excessively speculative, using superficial similarities to link tales that may have no connection with each other. Many would go farther and point out that the Norse myths that we have never formed one single master narrative; what has come down to us is a scattered sample of stories that varied over space and time. H. R. E. Davidson, for example, has pointed out that "Such approaches arise from an assumption that the mythology was once complete and rational, so that it would prove satisfactory to a modern observer. . . . However we are dealing here with many different levels of belief, and also with confused traditions, which may have been worked on by earlier antiquarians long before modern scholars began their reconstructions" (*Myths and Symbols*, p. 197). That said, some modern Heathens find Rydberg's theories inspiring and have adopted them as part of their own theology.

The second figure lived and worked some time after the Romantic Era was over. Although trained as a linguist, Vilhelm Grønbech (1873-1938) became a professor of comparative religion at the University of Copenhagen. He wrote major works on Indian and European mysticism, ancient Greek culture, and Christian theology; he also wrote novels and poems. Within Heathenry, however, he is best known for his first major book, *Vor Folkeætt i Oldtiden* ("Our Ancestors in Ancient Times"), published in 1909–1912, and published in English translation in 1932, with some new material by Grønbech himself, as *The Culture of the Teutons*. Here he presented a rich and complex worldview that the ancient Germanic peoples supposedly held, based on his extensive reading in the sagas. Grønbech had a remarkable gift for presenting worldviews "from the inside," in such detail and with such sympathy that he seemed to be writing from the viewpoint of one who shared that worldview, even when this was not the case. He attempted to uncover the unspoken assumptions at the core of metaphysical worldviews by carefully analyzing the meanings of important words used within that worldview (Mitchell, *Vilhelm Grønbech*, pp. 14-16); for example, his discussion of *frith* is based on a thorough overview of how the word is used in the sagas.

There isn't space in this volume to offer a detailed, point-by-point critique of *Culture of the Teutons*. Future volumes of *Our Troth* will have occasion to discuss instances where Grønbech's thought is not truly consistent with the lore that we have. Critics have pointed out that Grønbech's work is based primarily on the Icelandic sagas; although these are by far the largest body of texts in any older Germanic language, they are still relatively late and influenced by Christianity, and they are not necessarily accurate representations of pre-Christian worldviews; in fact, there may be no single worldview that all the "Teutons" may be said to have shared, given that their cultures varied through time and across space (Mitchell, *Vilhelm Grønbech*, pp. 34-35). It is also worth pointing out Grønbech's vision of ancient Teuton-hood did inspire romantic nationalist scholars in early 20th century Germany (Schnurbein, *Norse Revival*, pp. 262-263; Mees, *Science of the Swastika*, pp. 86, 122-123). With all that said: despite the fact that Grønbech was not primarily a scholar of Germanic culture, his work has had a huge impact on modern American Heathenry. Many Heathens have found *The Culture of the Teutons* compelling (including the author of the first edition of this book) and will recommend it enthusiastically as a masterful guide to how our Heathen forebears truly saw the world. Modern Heathen concepts of frith and luck; of the soul as a collection of multiple parts; of the world as an enclosure (*innangarðr*) surrounded by a hostile and chaotic Outside (*útgarðr*)—all of these concepts loom large in modern Heathenry and all of them were taken in their present form from Grønbech's *Culture of the Teutons*. Grønbech's biographer has said that "he can create a self-sufficient reality within the covers of a book" (Mitchell, *Vilhelm Grønbech*, p. 13), and it seems that he has done so in Heathenry.

Britain

Romanticism in Britain also brought new interest in national history, in folk traditions, and in pre-Christian pagan religions, in part as a reaction to the rapid changes taking place in traditional life during the Industrial Revolution. Much of this interest was expressed in poems and stories praising the Greek and Roman deities, who had always been studied in the classical school curriculum (Hutton, *Triumph of the Moon*, pp. 15-31). Romantic authors also sought inspiration on Britain's legendary past, especially in the legends of King Arthur (as in Tennyson's *Idylls of the King*). Not every Romantic author or poet was enthralled with the Vikings and Anglo-Saxons; some disdained the old tales of "a Runic savage. . . boozing ale out of the skull of an enemy in Odin's hall" (quoted in O'Donoghue, *From Asgard to Valhalla*, p. 118). But some sought out the old myths for their sense of what was called "the Sublime"—their capacity to inspire awe and terror, something that many Romantics avidly sought in their work.

George Hickes's printing of the Old English Rune Poem.
Linguarum vetterum septentrionalium thesaurus (1703).

This interest had roots well before the Romantic era, going back to 1703, when George Hickes had published *Linguarum vetterum septentrionalium thesaurus* ("A Treasury of the Old Northern Tongue"), the first guide to Old Norse language and literature available in England, which also covered the grammar of the Old English and Gothic languages (Wawn, *The Vikings and the Victorians*, pp. 19-23). In 1770, Rev. Thomas Percy published both *Five Pieces of Runic Poetry*, his translations of important poems from the sagas, and *Northern Antiquities,* his translation of works by Paul-Henri Mallet, a Swiss professor at the University of Copenhagen who had learned Old Norse (Wawn, pp. 24-30; Greenway, *The Golden Horns*, pp 88-89). Even before Percy's work was published, the poet Thomas Gray wrote "The Descent of Odin," a retelling of the Eddic poem *Baldrs draumar*; and "The Fatal Sisters," based on Percy's translation of *Darraðarljóð* from *Egils saga Skallagrímssonar*:

Now the storm begins to lower,
(Haste, the loom of Hell prepare.)
Iron-sleet of arrowy shower
Hurtles in the darken'd air.

Glitt'ring lances are the loom,
Where the dusky warp we strain,
Weaving many a soldier's doom,
Orkney's woe, and Randver's bane.
     —*The Works of Thomas Gray*, vol. 1, p. 71

In 1797, Amos Cottle published the first English translation of the *Poetic Edda,* albeit working from a Latin translation of the original. Unfortunately, it wasn't a very good translation, although it did inspire other authors to explore the myths of the North (O'Donoghue, *From Asgard to Valhalla,* pp. 110-119).

More inspiration for this shift in tastes came from Sir Walter Scott, author of immensely popular historical novels. His novel *The Pirate* (1822) is set in Shetland and Orkney; although the action takes place around 1700, the novel is loaded with references to Viking legends surviving in the islands. The islands' wise-woman, Norna of the Fitful Head, claims to have made pacts with the ancient powers:

I learned to visit each lonely barrow—each lofty cairn—to tell its appropriate tale, and to soothe with rhymes in his praise the spirit of the stern warrior who dwelt within. I knew where the sacrifices were made of yore to Thor and to Odin, on what stones the blood of the victims flowed—where stood the dark-browed priest—where the crested chiefs, who consulted the will of the idol—where the more distant crowd of inferior worshippers, who looked on in awe or in terror. The places most shunned by the timid peasants had no terrors for me; I dared walk in the fairy circle, and sleep by the magic spring. (vol. 2, p. 133)

Scott's epic poem *Rokeby* is set during the English Civil War, but Scott took a few lines to recount the ancient history of its northern English setting, when the Vikings had named the land for their gods, especially a valley still known as Thorsgill (Canto IV, part 1, pp. 137-138):

> Beneath the shade the Northmen came,
> Fixed on each vale a Runic name,
> Reared high their altars' rugged stone,
> And gave their Gods the land they won.
> Then, Balder, one bleak garth was thine,
> And one sweet brooklet's silver line,
> And Woden's Croft did title gain,
> From the stern Father of the Slain;
> But to the Monarch of the Mace,
> That held in fight the foremost place,
> To Odin's son, and Sifia's spouse,
> Near Startforth high they paid their vows,
> Remembered Thor's victorious fame,
> And gave the dell the Thunderer's name.

Yet another author who inspired interest in the ancient Norse past was the essayist and historian Thomas Carlyle, whose 1841 lectures *On Heroes, Hero-Worship and the Heroic in History* stayed popular for a century. Though Carlyle sometimes wrote condescendingly of Norse religion, he nonetheless praised its power:

> The essence of the Scandinavian, as indeed of all Pagan Mythologies, we found to be recognition of the divineness of Nature; sincere communion of man with the mysterious invisible Powers visibly seen at work in the world round him. This, I should say, is more sincerely done in the Scandinavian than in any Mythology I know. Sincerity is the great characteristic of it. Superior sincerity (far superior) consoles us for the total want of old Grecian grace. Sincerity, I think, is better than grace. I believe that these old Northmen were looking into Nature with open eye and soul: most earnest, honest; childlike, and yet manlike; with a great-hearted simplicity and depth and freshness, in a true, loving, admiring, unfearing way. A right valiant, true old race of men. (pp. 48-49)

Scott and Carlyle helped inspire a network of scholarly enthusiasts for the Old Norse ways. Samuel Laing published his translation of *Heimskringla* in 1844—only the second Norse saga ever translated into English (Wawn, *The Vikings and the Victorians*, pp. 91-116). George W. Dasent, a journalist, diplomat, and professor, translated the *Prose Edda* (which he dedicated to Carlyle), several sagas, and a collection of Scandinavian folktales (Wawn, pp. 142-158). His popular translation of *Njáls saga* inspired readers to tour Iceland and make pilgrimages to important sites in the saga (Wawn, pp. 166-171). A friend said of Dasent that "Though a sincerely religious man, still I cannot help suspecting that in his heart of hearts he looked upon Christianity as a somewhat *parvenu* [newcomer] creed, and deemed that Thor, Odin, Freyja, etc., were the proper objects of worship" (Dasent, *Popular Tales*, p. xxxi). George Stephens, a British expatriate in Copenhagen, compiled every rune inscription he could find, from runestones to bracteates and coins, in his *Old Northern Runic Monuments of Scandinavia and England* (1866-7); while his translations were often incorrect, his work was indispensable for later scholars. The Anglo-Saxons weren't forgotten either. John Mitchell Kemble (1807–1857), a student of the brothers Grimm, published the first complete Modern English translation of *Beowulf* in 1837, and went on to publish editions and translations of more Old English texts, historical studies of Anglo-Saxon England, and (posthumously) one of the first overviews of Anglo-Saxon period archaeology (Stanley, *Imagining the Anglo-Saxon Past*, pp. 29-33). Benjamin Thorpe (1782–1870) also published and translated Old English writings, as well as publishing a translation of the *Poetic Edda* in 1866.

Some of these British scholars had lived in Scandinavia for a time and were able to study with leading authorities; for example, George Dasent spent five years in Stockholm as secretary to the British envoy, where he met Jacob Grimm among others. Other British scholars collaborated with Icelanders living in Britain. One of the greatest was Guðbrandur Vígfusson, who, at Dasent's urging, finished the monumental dictionary begun by deceased clergyman Richard Cleasby. Their *Icelandic-English Dictionary* has aided countless scholars ever since its completion in 1874 (Wawn, *The Vikings and the Victorians*, pp. 343-346). Guðbrandur also collaborated on the first complete collection of skaldic poetry, *Corpus Poeticum Boreale*, published in 1883 (although the English translations are notoriously inaccurate).

Another Icelander, Eiríkr Magnússon, collaborated with William Morris (1834-1896) on several saga translations. Morris was not only a translator, but a prolific poet and novelist, as well as an artist, designer, fine book printer, and labor activist. He not only collaborated with Eiríkr on translating *Vǫlsunga saga,* but retold it twice: as a prose novel, *The House of the Wolfings,* and as an epic poem, *The Story of Sigurd the Volsung*:

> "All hail, O Day and thy Sons, and thy
>   kin of the coloured things!
> Hail, following Night, and thy Daugh-
>   ter that leadeth thy wavering wings!
> Look down with unangry eyes on us
>   today alive,
> And give us the hearts victorious, and
>   the gain for which we strive!
> All hail, ye Lords of God-home, and ye
>   Queens of the House of Gold!
> Hail, thou dear Earth that bearest, and
>   thou Wealth of field and fold!
> Give us, your noble children, the glory
>   of wisdom and speech,
> And the hearts and the hands of heal-
>   ing, and the mouths and hands
>   that teach!"

—"How Sigurd Awoke Brynhild," *The Story of Sigurd the Volsung,* Book II. *Collected Works of William Morris,* vol. 12, p. 124

Cartoon by Edward Burne-Jones for a stained glass window by William Morris & Co., depicting Gudrid Thorbjarnardóttir. One of nine windows depicting Norse gods and scenes from the Vinland sagas, originally installed in the Vineland Estate in Newport, Rhode Island. Bell, *Sir Edward Burne-Jones: A Record and Review* (1910).

Still other Victorian writers celebrated the glories of the north: Matthew Arnold's long poem "Balder Dead" retells a Norse myth, while Algernon Swinburne's "Her-

tha" is a powerful invocation spoken by the German Earth goddess. The artists Edward Burne-Jones and Arthur Rackham created art based on myths,
legends, and folktales, including Norse mythology. Rackham was especially
noted for his illustrations of Wagner's *Ring* cycle.

Besides their ability to inspire "the Sublime," Old Norse myths and sagas had another attraction for Victorian authors. British enthusiasts for the
Vikings recalled the days when the Norse ruled much of Britain. The Vikings were not only genetic ancestors of many Britons, but had left traces in
British culture. As enterprising traders and conquerors who ruled the waves,
they were considered to be forerunners of the British Empire and good
models for 19th century Britons. Adventure novelist Robert M. Ballentyne
spoke for many at the conclusion of his 1869 children's novel *Erling the Bold*:

> Yes, there is perhaps more of Norse blood in your veins than you wot
> of, reader, whether you be English or Scotch, for those sturdy sea-rovers
> invaded our lands from north, south, east, and west many a time in days
> gone by, and held it in possession for centuries at a time, leaving a last-
> ing and beneficial impress on our customs and characters. We have good
> reason to regard their memory with respect and gratitude, despite their
> faults and sins, for much of what is good and true in our laws and social
> customs, much of what is manly and vigorous in the British Constitu-
> tion, and much of our intense love of freedom and fair-play, is due to
> the pith, pluck, enterprise, and sense of justice that dwelt in the breasts
> of the rugged old Sea-kings of Norway! (p. 437)

The United States

Interest in the Vikings surged in the United States with the awareness
that Leifr Eiríksson and his band had allegedly discovered North America
(which would be confirmed by archaeological discoveries in Newfoundland,
but not until the 1960s). The Danish scholar Carl Christian Rafn published
Antiquitates Americanae in 1837, which included the "Vinland sagas" and
other Norse texts, with Danish and Latin translations. His book caught
the eye of Eben Norton Horsford, a Harvard chemistry professor who had
become wealthy from his invention of modern baking powder. Horsford
grew obsessed with the idea that the Norse had discovered America, and

he began finding evidence, everywhere he looked, that his own town of Cambridge, Massachusetts had once been the great Viking citadel of Norumbega, founded by Leifr Eiríksson himself. He and his fellow enthusiasts reinterpreted everything from colonial-period stone buildings to Native American petroglyphs as evidence for Viking settlement, putting up plaques and monuments on every spot that he felt was a Viking site. No archaeologist today takes his claims seriously, and almost all of the "Viking evidence" found in what is now the United States is either a hoax, or misinterpreted (Wallace and Fitzhugh, "Stumbles and Pitfalls," pp. 374-380).[28] But in 1887, Horsford underwrote the bronze statue of Leif Erikson that still stands on Commonwealth Avenue in Boston (Goudsward, *Ancient Stone Sites*, pp. 29-32).

Horsford's neighbor, the poet Henry Wadsworth Longfellow (1807-1882), celebrated the Vikings in his poem "The Skeleton in Armor," about a skeleton which had been excavated in 1832 at Fall River, Massachusetts, buried in what looked like bronze armor.[29] Longfellow imagined the

Leif Erikson statue by Anne Whitney, Boston, Massachusetts. Photo by Rob Larson, Wikimedia Commons, CC BY 2.0.

---

28. The only Norse artifact found in the US that is widely accepted as genuine is the silver penny of Olaf Kyrre (1065-1080) found in 1957 at the Goddard site near Brooklin, Maine. However, it probably got there through trade networks, which extended as far as Labrador—not from Norsemen directly visiting Maine (Cox, "A Norse Penny from Maine," pp. 206-207).
29. The skeleton was almost certainly a 16th century Native American, buried with ornaments made from a brass kettle acquired through trade with Europeans. Unfortunately, the skeleton was destroyed in a fire in 1843, although the brass ornaments were sent to the National Museum of Denmark and are allegedly still there. See Goudsward, *Ancient Stone Sites*, pp. 22-25; Wallace and Fitzhugh, "Stumbles and Pitfalls," pp. 377-378.

Illustration from Longfellow's
"The Skeleton in Armor" (1877)

dead man commanding him to tell his story: he was a bold Viking who had eloped with a king's daughter and escaped to the New World.

"I was a Viking old!
My deeds, though manifold,
No Skald in song has told,
No Saga taught thee!
Take heed, that in thy verse
Thou dost the tale rehearse,
Else dread a dead man's curse;
For this I sought thee."
        —*The Poems of Henry Wadsworth Longfellow*, p. 431

Drawing on Samuel Laing's translation of *Heimskringla*, Longfellow retold Olaf Tryggvason's life in 1863 as part of *Tales of a Wayside Inn*, a long narrative poem composed of shorter poems in contrasting forms. The work was probably inspired by Esaias Tegnér's *Frithiofs saga*.[30]

I am the God Thor,
I am the War God,
I am the Thunderer!
Here in my Northland,
My fastness and fortress,
Reign I forever!

Here amid icebergs
Rule I the nations;
This is my hammer,
Miölner the mighty;
Giants and sorcerers
Cannot withstand it!

---

30. *Tales of a Wayside Inn* is best known for containing a poem on a different subject: "Listen, my children, and you shall hear / Of the midnight ride of Paul Revere. . ."

—"The Challenge of Thor," from "The Musician's Tale," *Tales of a Wayside Inn. The Poems of Henry Wadsworth Longfellow*, p. 300

Longfellow's fellow poet and professor James Russell Lowell (1819-1891) depicted the Vikings in "The Voyage to Vinland." In this poem, as the Vikings sight Vinland for the first time, the seeress Gudrida speaks a prophecy of Vinland's future, in which Lowell's American readers could recognize their own nation:

Here men shall grow up
Strong from self-helping;
Eyes for the present
Bring they as eagles',
Blind to the Past.

They shall make over
Creed, law, and custom;
Driving-men, doughty
Builders of empire,
Builders of men. . . .
—*Poetical Works of James Russell Lowell*, vol. 4, pp. 230-232

Americans saw the Vikings in the same way that they liked to see themselves: practical, enterprising, sturdy, freedom-loving people who sought out new lands where they might win wealth through honest work and trade.

The idea of Vikings in New World especially resonated with Scandinavian immigrants to the United States, because they could claim to be, not intruders, but ancestors of America—and not only "spiritual ancestors," whose Viking traditions of democracy and freedom had inspired English and American liberty, but physical discoverers of America as well. Rasmus B. Anderson (1846–1936), the first professor of Scandinavian studies in the US (at the University of Wisconsin), brought Rafn's work to the mainstream with his 1874 book *America Not Discovered by Columbus*, in which he wrote:

Yes, the Norsemen were truly a great people! Their spirit found its way into the Magna Charta of England and into the Declaration of Independence in America. The spirit of the Vikings still survives in the bosoms of Englishmen, Americans and Norsemen, extending their commerce, taking bold positions against tyranny, and producing wonderful internal improvements in these countries (p. 40).

He was joined by the diplomat and jurist Aaron Goodrich (1807-1887), who wrote how, during the intellectual darkness of the Middle Ages,

a people flourished in the extreme north, with whom enterprise and freedom were neither dead nor stagnant, who possessed scientific knowledge and applied the same to practical purposes; a people simple, fearless and energetic, republicans in practice if not in name, with whom chieftains were the fathers and protectors of their followers, sharing their perils and respecting their rights; a pagan people indeed, worshipers of Odin and Thor, believers in the joys of Walhalla, yet doers of deeds so noble as to be worthy [of] the most enlightened Christian: such were the Northmen; such their simple records, which bear every impress of truth, prove them to have been. . . . they were the worthy pioneers of European settlement on our shores; a hardy race counting on their own labor to develop the natural resources of the lands they discovered. (*A History*, pp. 69-70)

The Kensington Runestone.
Flom, "The Kensington Rune Stone" (1910)

It was probably this desire to truly belong to America that inspired the carving of the Kensington Runestone. This stone slab, found in 1898 on a farm near Kensington, Minnesota, was allegedly carved by Norse explorers who reached Minnesota in 1362. It was almost certainly carved by a 19th century Norwegian immigrant, but its authenticity was relentlessly touted by people like Hjalmar Holand, who spent fifty years writing a small flood of books and articles, promoting the stone as evidence that Scandinavians were the true discoverers of America[31] (Krueger, *Myths of the Runestone*, pp. 15-25). A few other "Viking runestones" have turned up elsewhere in America, notably the Heavener Runestone in Oklahoma. Few archaeologists take them seriously, but they do attest to the eagerness of some Americans to graft the Norsemen into their own history—an eagerness that would show up again in the controversy over Kennewick Man, discussed in Chapter 9.[32]

Rasmus Anderson advocated for designating October 9 as Leif Erikson Day, which Wisconsin first declared a state holiday in 1925. Between 1905 and 1907, Anderson took advantage of American interest in the Vikings by publishing fine editions of sagas and other Old Norse texts in translation, under the imprint of the Norrœna Society. At the same time, Ottilie A. Liljencrantz, the daughter of a Swedish immigrant, was writing popular novels about the Vikings, some of them set in Horsford's Norumbega. Her 1902 novel *The Thrall of Leif the Lucky* became the basis for one of the first Viking epic movies, *The Viking* of 1928 (which was also the first feature-length movie filmed entirely in Technicolor).

Unfortunately, some of the motivation for glorifying Leifr Eiríksson was sectarian and nativist. The late 19th century saw waves of immigration of Irish, Italians, and Poles into the cities of the United States. Prejudice grew against both the immigrants and their Roman Catholic faith, as the descendants of earlier English and German immigrants feared that the newcomers were "taking over."[33] In her 1891 book *The Icelandic Discoverers of America, or, Honor to whom Honor is Due*, Marie A. Brown argued that, because Christopher Columbus's claims on the New World had been supported by

---

31. One legacy of Holand's efforts was the name of Minnesota's professional American football team; "Minnesota Vikings" was intended "to represent the venturesome people who first populated the state" (Cullum, "Cullum's Column," *Minneapolis Morning Tribune*, August 6, 1960). Another was the raising of "Big Ole," a huge statue of a Viking holding a shield with the words "Birthplace of America," outside the town of Alexandria, Minnesota. Of course, even if the Kensington Runestone is genuine, it was carved 300 years *after* the end of the Viking era. . .

32. The Kensington Runestone itself is considered a forgery by almost everyone; see Wallace and Fitzhugh, "Stumbles and Pitfalls," pp. 380-384, for an overview of the case for forgery. Anthropologist Alice Kehoe isn't convinced; her book *The Kensington Runestone* is not so quick to dismiss it.

33. This was neither the first nor the last time that the descendants of previous immigrants to the United States would throw a ring-tailed conniption fit over newer arrivals.

the Pope, honoring Columbus would "gratify the covetousness of the Mother Church by turning the American republic over to it, as its spiritual and temporal property" (p. 10). Americans should recognize the Norse discovery, because Americans still bore "the principles of freedom the Norsemen infused into English blood and which found their fullest expression in the American colonists, leading them to declare independence" (p. 20). Meanwhile, Columbus had not only allegedly stolen knowledge of the New World from Icelandic manuscripts; he'd been greedy for looted wealth and slaves, as opposed to the Vikings' love of honest toil and free trade.[34] Columbus embodied the "Romish power" whose only aim was "the eradication of that principle and love of freedom that rendered all of Northern blood dangerous to the Church" (p. 52). Thus the Vikings could be invoked as authentically American symbols, superior to the sneaky un-American forces that wanted to destroy freedom. This attitude mirrors some of the nativist rhetoric that would later come from the folkish Asatru movement in America.

By the turn of the century, Norse mythology had gained such wide cultural recognition that it was recommended for grade school curricula. According to a popular educational theory of the time, the development of a child's mind paralleled the evolution of humanity, which meant that ancient mythologies were especially appropriate for younger grades (Gould, *Ontogeny and Phylogeny*, pp. 135-155). Textbook publishers promptly released a small flood of retellings of the Norse myths, adapted for children and copiously illustrated, with titles like *Asgard Stories* and *Tales from the Far North* and *Legends of Norselands*. One of them advised teachers to

> let [their students] carve out Viking ships, hang an Ygdrasil of their own with the world-symbols, build a house about a Branstock, map out for themselves an Asgard and Midgard and Utgard. As soon as they begin to *play the myths* their examination might be counted as passed. Let them act the Thor stories with all the strut of giants and bang of hammer that their Norse instincts may crave (and that the teacher's nerves can bear). . . . if this reading-course leaves the children full of questions, grieved for Balder, proud of Tyr, angry with Loke; if they quarrel as to which shall

---

34. The idea that the Vikings were averse to looting and slavery is one of the funnier claims in this book.

go one-eyed for Odin; if they cannot see a summer cloud without thinking of Skidbladner, that is success (Mabie, *Norse Stories,* pp. 260-261).

Contributors:

1st edition: Kveldúlfr Gundarsson.

2nd edition: New material by Ben Waggoner.

3rd edition: Reorganization and new material by Ben Waggoner. Thanks to Michaela Macha for checking the German translations.

93

Then the gods said, "Thor, you
must dress like Freyja. You will
have to play you are the bride."
Thor said, "I won't do it. You
will all laugh at me. I won't dress
up like a girl."
They said, "Well, that is the only
way we can get the hammer back."
Thor said, "I do not like to dress
like a girl, but I will do it." Then
they dressed Thor up like Freyja.
They put on Freyja's dress, necklace and vail, and braided his hair.
Loki said, "I will dress up too,
and be your servant."
They got into Thor's goat wagon
and went to the Giants' home.

94 THOR AND LOKI APPROACH THE HOUSE OF THE GIANTS.

Retelling for children of the myth of Thor's recovering his Hammer from Thrym.
Smythe, *A Primary Reader* (1896)

Procession of women in reconstructed Bronze Age dress, from what is billed as "the first Harvest Festival in the Third Reich," held in Ost-Prignitz, Brandenburg, Germany, on September 10, 1933. The swastika is patterened on rock art from Tösse in southern Sweden. Lechler, *Vom Hakenkreuz* (1934).

CHAPTER EIGHT

Germanic Religion and the Nazis

1871–1945

In the late 19ᵗʰ century, interest in German society surged in renewal movements to transform modern life. Many looked to the ancient past and the religion of their ancestors, as a path to national unity and renewal. Unfortunately, this took a very dark turn, with consequences that still haunt the world. As unpleasant as it

"Schwertwache" (Sword Vigil). Illustration by Hugo Höppener ("Fidus") for Ferdinand Avenarius, *Balladenbuch* (1912).

may be, we as Heathens cannot avoid facing how the old ways were twisted into support for vile crimes against humanity—and how some folk today refuse to let go of their poisoned legacy.

Life Reform

Although Germany had existed for centuries as a region with a shared language and culture, for most of its history it had been divided into a patchwork of assorted realms under the overall rule of the Holy Roman Empire. These ranged from major powers like Prussia and Bavaria, to princedoms the size of a postage stamp. An attempt by liberals to unify Germany as a nation-state in 1848 failed when the conservative nobility refused to give up its privileges, but under a more conservative political regime led by Prussia, full unification finally happened in 1871. The new country rapidly transformed into an economic powerhouse: the cities swelled as people migrated in search of work, colonies were planted in Africa and the Pacific, scientific discoveries led the world, and technological innovations boosted the economy. Yet there was a backlash against the combination of technological progress and social conservatism that typified German society of the time. Some Germans were disappointed and frustrated that unification failed to solve all

221

of the country's problems, and in fact created new challenges (Mosse, *The Crisis of German Ideology*, pp. 1-4). Many felt that their newly industrialized, capitalist, rational society was destroying the nation's character and causing spiritual poverty (Treitel, *A Science for the Soul*, pp. 17-19). Others felt that "irrational" areas like astrology and parapsychology could point the way towards a new science that transcended base materialism (Staudenmaier, "Esoteric Alternatives," pp. 24-26).

Cover of the magazine *Theosophische Kultur* (1915), drawn by Hugo Höppener (Fidus). Wikimedia Commons, CC BY-SA 3.0.

One of the results was a new appreciation for mysticism. Astrology, Kabbala, Eastern religions, parapsychology, and spiritualism exploded in popularity. New spiritual movements ranged from Mazdaznan, a quasi-Zoroastrian faith involving vegetarianism and breathing exercises; to Monism, which held that matter and spirit were one and the same; to Theosophy, which claimed that all religions were derived from an ancient "Secret Doctrine" revealed by superior beings known as the Ascended Masters (Staudenmaier, "Esoteric Alternatives," pp. 26-30). Vegetarianism, organic farming, nudism, physical fitness, alternative medicine, communal living, and similar back-to-nature movements, collectively referred to as *Lebensreform* or "life reform," also became increasingly popular (Jeffries, "*Lebensreform*," pp. 93-101). So did the closely intertwined *Jugendbewegung* ("youth movement"), whose best-known aspect was the *Wandervogel* ("wandering bird") movement that advocated frequent hikes and rambles through nature, singing folk songs and reconnecting with the German land (Treitel, *A Science for the Soul*, pp. 154-161; Kennedy, *Children of the Sun*, pp. 69-124). Well-off Germans could

German nudists exercising with dumbbells at a *Lichtluftbad*, "light and air bath."
Ungewitter, *Die Nacktheit* (1906).

sample the simple life of nudism, meditation, and vegetarian cuisine at resorts and
intentional communities, such as Monte
Verità in Ascona, Switzerland. The most
devoted proponents of *Lebensreform*, called
the *Naturmenschen* ("Nature Men"), took
up radically simple lifestyles, letting their
hair grow, sleeping outdoors, and growing
their own food, or wandering on foot and
spreading their ideas. Incidentally, several
proponents of *Lebensreform* immigrated to
the United States around the turn of the
20th century. Some introduced schools of
alternative medicine, such as naturopathy;
others opened the first health food stores
in the United States. One group of long-
haired *Naturmenschen* moved to the southern California desert and became known
as the Nature Boys. The Nature Boys
and their American disciples lasted long
enough to inspire the hippie movement in
the 1960s (Kennedy, pp. 125-181).[35]

California Showing 'Em How to Live on $5 a Week and Be Happy in Big Cities

William Pester, born in Germany in
1885, one of the most famous "Nature Boys" of the California desert.
Oakland Tribune, July 27, 1919.

---

35. The song "Nature Boy," written by eden ahbez, an American disciple of *Lebensreform*,
went on to become Nat King Cole's first chart hit in 1948 (Kennedy, *Children of the Sun*,
pp. 167-177).

Loki, Odin, and Balder. Illustration by Hugo Höppener ("Fidus")
for Eduard Stucken, *Balladen* (1898).

German Religion

There was more to the story than Buddhism and nudism. *Lebensreform*, new religious movements, and occultism drew people from across the political spectrum, but they took a certain turn in politically conservative circles. A political movement called Progressive Reaction felt that the key to national unity was not capitalism, socialism, or industrialization, but a spiritual awakening of the German *Volk* that would revive their shared higher values and spiritual communion under the banner of a strong leader (Hermand, *Old Dreams*, pp. 41-49). While Herder had pointed to language and culture as the unifying essence of the *Volk*, this essence was increasingly defined as racial and genetic. As *völkisch* leader Ernst Hunkel exhorted his readers in 1914, "we are of holy German descent, of the blood from which will grow the salvation of the world" (quoted in Puschner, "One People," p. 12). Though threatened by degeneration caused by foreign influence, this *Volksgeist* ("folk-soul") or *Volkstum* ("folk-dom") still lived in folk traditions,

"Nibelungen." Illustration by Hugo Höppener ("Fidus")
from *Aus der Germanenbibel* (1920)

and it could be revived—as long as it could be kept pure and uncontaminated (Puschner, "One People," pp. 11-14). This was the time in which Carl Jung formulated his theory of the collective unconscious: the idea that people still carry the myths and symbols of their ancestors on an unconscious level, which can be tapped into in dreams, visions, and some mental illnesses. Jungian psychology drew on *völkisch* and other mystical ideas in circulation at the time, and influenced them in return (Noll, *The Aryan Christ*, pp. 98-119). Jung remains influential today in folkish Heathen circles—although his ideas are far more complex than the few paragraphs from his essay "Wotan" that folkish Heathens are fond of quoting, and he came to adopt ideas that contradict his earlier folkish beliefs (Dohe, *Jung's Wandering Archetype*, pp. 210-239).

Conservative scholars and politicians appealed once again to Tacitus, who had famously claimed that the Germans were the true natives of their land, the only people who still lived where they always had lived, unmixed with any immigrants (*Germania* 2, 4, pp. 130-131, 134-137). Just as Tacitus's German folk had always been "like no one but itself," the German people had to revive their unique *Volkstum*, their *Germanentum* ("Germanic-dom")—and defend it, if necessary (Krebs, *A Most Dangerous Book*, pp. 203-207). In the mid-1870s, one Hermann von Pfister-Schwaighausen coined the word *völkisch* as a Germanic substitute for Latin-derived *national*. By about 1900, under the influence of racists like Houston Stewart Chamberlain (1855–1927; incidentally, Richard Wagner's son-in-law), the word was coming to mean an ideology that saw the German *Volk* as not only unique, but superior. *Völkisch* ideologues might differ on many issues, but they were opposed to anything that might weaken or defile the German *Volkstum*, a list that usually included Jews, Slavs, the Roman Catholic Church, and trans-national political movements (Puschner, "The Notions *Völkisch* and Nordic," pp. 21-38).

For the *völkisch* thinkers, the way to make Germany great again was to nurture the *Volksgeist*, and one way to do that was to return to the spiritual ways that were already innate in the German *Volk* and thus somehow more "natural" and "authentic." The linguist Paul de Lagarde (1827–1891) had already called for Germans to put aside their division into Protestants and Catholics and seek the innate spirituality that united them. Although nominally Christian, Lagarde saw Christian dogma as stifling the living, dynamic, natural divine revelation that each *Volk* received from God. Unfortunately, he identified this stifling dogma with the Jews, whose nature, he felt, was completely irreconcilable with the true German *Volk* (Mosse, *The Crisis of German Ideology*, pp. 31-38). Lagarde exhorted Germans "to do everything appropriate to prepare the way for a national religion and to prepare the nation to accept that religion, which. . . must be a religion for Germany alone, if it is to be the soul of Germany" (quoted in Gossman, *Brownshirt Princess*, p. 31). Many heard what he said.

Opinions were divided as to exactly what this "innately German religion" was. For the *Deutsche Christen* or "German Christians," the natural German religion was a form of Christianity, purged of its Jewish elements (*Entjudung*, "de-Judafication"), and continuing the work of the Protestant Reformation through a newer Reformation. The conservative Austrian politician Georg von Schönerer had written in 1870: *Ohne Juda, ohne Rom, / Wird erbaut Germanias Dom*, "Without Judah, without Rome, / shall Germania's cathedral be built" (Mees, *The Science of the Swastika*, pp. 11, 25). Now, the *Deutsche Christen* saw Jesus as an "Aryan warrior." Far from being Jewish, their Jesus had fought valiantly against the Jews, actively battling for the transformation of this world, rather than yearning for the next one. Christian scholars even published revisions of the New Testament that deleted all positive references to Judaism (Heschel, *Aryan Jesus*, pp. 106-113; Puschner, "One People," pp. 21-23).

The *Deutsche Christen* often looked to medieval Christian mystics such as Meister Eckhard, who had stressed experiencing God as living within one's own heart. Another faction, the *Gottgläubige* or "God Believers," did not identify as Christian but believed in one God who was innate in the individual heart and soul and could be experienced without need for salvation from an outside source. For many, this same God was innate in the German *Volk* and could not be shared by anyone else. As the *deutschgläubige* ("German Believer") writer Ernst Hunkel wrote, "German religion is the religion innate in German people" (transl. Puschner, "One People," p. 26). In 1925, General Erich Ludendorff and his wife Mathilde founded the *Tannenbergbund*, which rejected Christianity and stressed Germans' sacred duty to manifest their inner God: "The German sees the soul itself permeated by God. . . . The God within you makes it your holy duty to accomplish self-creation" (quoted in Douglass, *God Among the Germans*, pp. 52-53). In 1933, Wilhelm Hauer founded the *Deutsche Glaubensbewegung*, the "Germanic Faith Movement," which rejected Christianity as unnatural for Germans. Hauer's God lived within the soul of every German, within the German *Volk*, and within German history, speaking through the "Ideal Will of the nation" (transl. Scott-Craig and Davies, *Germany's New Religion*, pp. 52-60).

But for some, a truly German religion meant going farther back into the past and returning to pagan religion. As the *völkisch* author Ernst Wachler wrote in 1901: "After all, the belief appropriate for our people once existed in a wonderful form. It is not dead, just buried; is it not possible to uncover the soil whence it sprang? Let us try to find a way into the world of our fairy-tales and myths, to the lost shrine of our Volk" (transl. Puschner, "One People," p. 24).

"Lichtgebet" (Prayer to the Light), the most famous design by the artist Fidus; he made multiple versions of this motif in several media. This one appeared in Henckell, *Aus meinen Gedichten* (1902).

LIEBIG COMPANYS FLEISCH EXTRACT.

Odin, das Oberhaupt der nordischen Götter.

One of six trading cards depicting Norse myths, packaged with Liebig's Extract of Meat (1894).

By the early 1900s, Germanic mythology was quite culturally familiar in Germany: middle-class Germans could buy Aegir cars, Fafnir motorcycles, Wotan stoves, Thor lightbulbs, Sleipnir cigarettes, Iduna home medical devices, and Edda chocolate bars. If they bought Liebig's Extract of Meat, their children could collect and trade cards with scenes of Norse myths or Migration Age heroes, among other themes (Zernack, "Old Norse–Icelandic Literature," pp. 166-168). Less consumerist and more conservative members of the growing counterculture, like the *völkisch* philosopher and publisher Eugen Diederich and his "Sera Circle," invoked the Sun and celebrated solstice rites in sacred groves (Mosse, *The Crisis of German Ideology*, pp. 57-61). Artists such as Ludwig Fahrenkrog, Karl Wilhelm Diefenbach, and especially Diefenbach's pupil Fidus (Hugo Höppener, 1868–1948) depicted fit, handsome nudes in beautiful natural settings, celebrating pagan-ish rituals, tilling the soil, or just frolicking.[36] A few visionaries planned or actually founded communes where a more perfect Germanic lifestyle could flourish on German soil. Probably the most extreme was Mittgart, planned by Willibald Hentschel in 1901 although never actually put into practice. Here, one hundred carefully selected "pure Aryan men" would devote themselves to farming, training for war,

---

36. Fidus was a lifelong Theosophist, and much of his work reflects his interest in Theosophy. As the Nazis rose to power, his work became increasingly nationalist, but it was never acceptable to the Party, which suppressed it in 1937 (Introvigne, "Fidus," pp. 218-240). He and his peers developed an artistic style known as *Jugendstil* or "Youth Style," the German version of Art Nouveau. Fidus's *Jugendstil* was rediscovered by psychedelic artists in the 1960s and inspired many album covers and rock concert posters. Another German who was popular in 1960s American culture was the author Hermann Hesse, who had briefly been a disciple of *Lebensreform* prophet Gusto Gräser. Hesse's experiences with *Lebensreform* would resurface in his books, notably *Siddhartha* and *The Journey to the East*.

and impregnating one thousand carefully
selected "pure Aryan women" to regenerate
the race (Mosse, pp. 108-125; Hermand,
Old Dreams, pp. 54-55). This would pave
the way for the return of the old gods:
Hentschel's 1901 novel *Varuna* envisioned
Wotan's return in rapturous purple prose:

He looks upon us not from temples or
the costly shrines of altars, nor from
the cross. For he is truly risen. He
wanders through clearings, through
forests, on paths, waves, and billows.
With a measured tread he strides behind the furrowing plow. He is there
where men are tested in battle and in
peril, where flags flutter and hearts beat
with greater courage. He finds pleasure
in hard and calloused hands and does
not turn his back when sweat flows
from the brow. He esteems all the wars

Portrait of the young artist Hugo
Höppener ("Fidus") with his mentor,
the artist and *Lebensreform* advocate
Karl Wilhelm Diefenbach (1851-
1913), on Diefenbach's commune
at Höllriegelskreuth, near Munich.
Spohr, *Fidus* (1902).

of man. His gaze rests musingly on the games of blond-haired children,
the prelude of future deeds. He loves tall, broad-hipped women more
than men could ever love them. He murmurs to them of future heroes.
Gently he leads those who wish to beget. . . (quoted in Hermand, *Old
Dreams*, p. 55)

In 1903, Ernst Wachler founded the open-air Bergtheater in the Harz
Mountains, on a plateau known as the *Hexentanzplatz* or "Witches' Dance
Floor;" it was a site for theatrical productions, but in 1912 his group held
the first public ritual dedicated to Wotan (Puschner, "One People," pp. 24-
25; Wolff, "Ludwig Fahrenkrog," pp. 225-228). In 1911, Otto Sigfrid Re-
uter (1876-1945) established the Deutscher Orden (German Order), which
encompassed pagan worship (Schnurbein, *Norse Revival*, pp. 38-41). At
about the same time, the artist Ludwig Fahrenkrog (1867–1952) was calling
for a pagan revival and writing mythic dramas that were staged at Wachler's

Illustration by Ludwig Fahrenkrog
for his play, *Baldur* (1908).

Bergtheater. By 1912, he had founded what would become the Germanische Glaubensgemeinschaft (GGG), or "Germanic Belief Society" (Wolff, "Ludwig Fahrenkrog," pp. 224-225).

Fahrenkrog's theology was not especially polytheistic, however. Much like the *Deutsche Glaubensbewegung*, he stressed the individual's direct experience of the Divine within, removing the need for any source of salvation outside the self. He summarized his creed in three principles: "1. *Gott in uns*, 2. *Das sittliche Gesetz in uns, und* 3. *die Selbsterlösung*": "God in us, the moral law in us, and self-redemption" (*Das Deutsche Buch*, p. 46). The *Bekentniss* (Catechism) that he wrote for the GGG never mentioned the old gods at all, and quoted Goethe, Kant, the Christian mystic Meister Eckhard, and *völkisch* authors such as Paul de Lagarde. His theology recognized a universal spirit, but not a polytheistic diversity (*Das Deutsche Buch*, pp. 31-33):

1. *Wir bekennen uns zu der Kraft des Geistes und des Lebens, die das All durchdringt und uns.*
2. *Und erkennen im All eine formbildende Kraft des Lebens, welche die Mannigfaltigkeit aller Erscheinungen bedingt, und anerkennen daher auch alle Sondererscheinungen in ihrer Naturnotwendigkeit als Offenbarungen der Kraft des Lebens. . . .*
5. *Mithin glauben wir und wissen, daß eine Religion der Germanen nur aus Germanen geboren werden kann.*

Vignette from *Das Deutsche Buch*, Ludwig Fahrenkrog's book
for initiates into the Germanische Glaubens-Gemeinschaft (1923).

6. *Religion is uns das reine, weltbejahende tat- und erkenntnisfrohe Ber-
   hältnis der Seele zum Geist des Alls und zu seinen Erscheinungs- und
   Offenbarungsformen.*

1. We commit ourselves to the power of the spirit and the life that per-
   meates the universe, and us.
2. And we recognize a creative power of life in the universe, which determines the diversity of all phenomena, and therefore we also recognize all exceptional phenomena in their natural necessity as reve-
   lations of the power of life. . . .
5. Therefore we believe and know that a religion of the Germans can
   only be born from Germans.
6. Religion is for us the pure, world-affirming relationship, that glories
   in deeds and in understanding, of the soul to the Spirit of the Universe and to its forms of manifestation and revelation.

German Racial Mysticism

One of the schools of thought that was popular in Germany at this
time was Theosophy. Theosophy was founded in 1875 in New York by
the Russian medium Helena Blavatsky, who claimed to channel mysterious
messages from highly evolved beings called the Mahatmas. Their messages
inspired Blavatsky to create an all-encompassing system of thought that
drew on all the world's spiritual traditions, including both Western mysti-

cism and Eastern religions. Theosophy aimed to lead humanity through its foreordained progression through seven stages in its evolutionary progress: the seven "root races," each divided into seven sub-races. The first five "root races" had been the now-vanished Polarians and Hyperboreans, followed by the Lemurians, the Atlanteans, and the Aryans; the next two "root races" were only just beginning to appear in Asia and South America. Each "root race" was destined to give rise to a higher race that would inherit the good qualities of its predecessor, as all human souls successively reincarnated through existences in every race (Jinarājadāsa, *First Principles*, pp. 46-61). Although Blavatsky clearly stated that the Aryan "root race" included people of all skin colors—and although any given human soul would incarnate in every race over millions of years—the doctrine lent itself remarkably well to racist interpretations. Incidentally, Blavatsky prominently incorporated the Indian symbol of the swastika into the emblem of Theosophy. Together with the discovery of swastikas at the archaeological site of Troy, as well as in old Scandinavian and German artifacts, this popularized the swastika as a "Pan-Aryan" symbol (Mees, *Science of the Swastika*, pp. 57-60).

"Orthodox" Theosophy was popular in Germany in its own right (until 1937 when the Nazis suppressed it). However, it inspired ethnonationalist offshoots that drew on what was claimed to be the ancient wisdom of the Germanic ancestors, instead of the ancient wisdom of India. Ariosophy or Theozoology was developed by ex-Catholic priest Jörg Lanz, often known as "von Liebensfels."[37] Lanz put forth his ideas—a weird mix of Theosophy, mystical Christianity, and Norse religion—in his journal *Ostara*. For Lanz, the cosmic life-force found its highest expression in the blond, light-skinned "Aryans," the *Gottermenschen* or "God-men," who were locked in an endless eugenic struggle against the dark-skinned rabble of "sodomistic apes" and "human monkeys," fit only for enslavement (Hermand, *Old Dreams*, pp. 51-58; Goodrick-Clarke, *The Occult Roots of Naziism*, pp. 164-165). Guido List,[38] a popular author of novels and plays about the Germanic past, developed Armanism, based on the secret knowledge of an "Ario-German" aris-

---

37. Lanz claimed kinship with the aristocratic family of von Liebensfels. Whether or not he actually had the right to use the name is unclear; see Goodrick-Clarke, *The Occult Roots of Nazism*, pp. 106-107.

38. Guido List is frequently referred to as Guido von List. Like Lanz, List claimed noble descent and added the aristocratic "von" to his name beginning in 1903. Whether he actually had noble family connections is questionable.

tocratic society, the *Armanen*. Temporarily blinded while recovering from a cataract operation in 1902, List had visions and claimed to have tapped into ancestral memories of the Armanen. Probably List's best-known contribution is the eighteen-rune futhark that, he claimed, was used by the Armanen priesthood, with complex symbolism attached to every rune, in a system that was more than a little similar to Qabalah. The syllables containing each rune, known as *kala*, could be used to break down spoken words and reveal their secret meanings (Goodrick-Clarke, *The Occult Roots of Naziism*, pp. 66-69).

List and his followers traced the esoteric knowledge of the Aryan race and its Armanen priesthood down through the centuries, finding runes encoded everywhere from German heraldry, to medieval masons' marks, to the timber designs (*Fachwerk*) on medieval half-timbered houses, and even in the shapes of traditional baked goods (Mees, *The Science of the Swastika*, pp. 60-62). Enthusiasts founded the Guido von List Society in 1908, largely funded by the industrialist Friedrich Wannieck and dedicated to publishing and distributing List's ideas. List himself did not develop a system of runic practice, but his followers did: Friedrich Bernhard Marby developed a system of *Runengymnastik* (rune gymnastics), while Siegfried Kummer refined Marby's system of

The Old City Hall at Dillenburg, from Philipp Stauff's book *Runenhauser* (1913). According to Stauff, the upper story bears a row of S-runes (*sol* or *sigi* in the Armanen system), and beneath the central windows is a pair of L-runes (*laf* in the Armanen system).

poses into *Runenyoga* (rune yoga), which included both static poses and rune dances. Kummer also developed rune *mudras* (hand gestures), in which the hands assumed the shape of a rune letter. List and his followers also devised rune *mantras*: chants intended to direct the runes' powers. They saw the

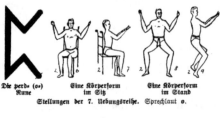

runes as energy fields permeating the cosmos, which the properly attuned (and genetically pure) practitioner could tap into, shape, and send out (Goodrick-Clarke, *The Occult Roots of Naziism*, pp. 154-163). There was even an attempt to found a utopian community dedicated to List's ideas; between 1919 and 1924, initiates could visit or live at "Breidhablik," near Danzig on the Baltic coast, and join the "supernational Aryan union," min-

Friedrich Bernhard Marby's *Runenyoga* postures for *perthro*. *Die Rosengärten und das Ewige Land der Rasse* (1935).

gling List's teachings with the usual nudism and vegetarianism (Mosse, *The Crisis of German Ideology*, p. 120). Many of these practices would eventually find their way into Neopagan rune magic, especially through the books of Edred Thorsson; the rune postures and chants that he presents in his book *Futhark*, for example, are directly borrowed from Kummer and Marby,

Cover of Guido List's fokish "catechism," *Der Unbesiegbare* (*The Invincible*), 1898

although adapted to the 24-rune Elder Futhark (Schnurbein, *Norse Revival*, pp. 41-42).

Rise of the Nazis

How did God create people?

Just as God made the plants and animals of many different species from the very beginning, He also created us humans, according to His wise will, in several kinds of tribes, from which the different *Völker* originated.

What is a Volk?

Every larger union of people, which has its own language, writing and history, and is unique in sense, custom and way of thinking, is called a *Volk*.

Why did God create the different Völker?

So that life is preserved.

What is life?

Life is a battle and the prize of the battle is life. . . .

God loves and protects hard-working, courageous *Völker* who keep faith and justice in a holy way, and rewards them with goodness and freedom. As a reward, he sends them great men, who lead them to power, greatness and wealth. . . .

God turns away from lazy, cowardly, envious and selfish *Völker*, and punishes them with bondage and annihilation.

—Guido List, *Der Unbesiegbare* (The Invincible), 1898

In the aftermath of Germany's defeat in World War I, and the political clashes that followed, many Germans felt that Germany had been humiliated and was in dire need of national renewal. For some, this included spiritual renewal through a return to *Völkisch* traditions. Unfortunately, this search for renewal "cross-fertilized" with Christian hatred for the Jews—a medieval tradition, but one that had been especially fanned by Martin Luther, who penned venomous attacks on the Jews. Anti-Semitism would have been unfathomable to pre-Christian Heathen tribes; even after Christianization, texts like the Norse *Gyðinga saga* and the Anglo-Saxon *Judith* retell stories from Jewish history in a favorable light, with no hint that

"Germania 1915", sometimes called "Germania Aufbebende"—"Germany Arising and Shaking With Rage," more or less— by Hugo Höppener ("Fidus"). Illustration for *Bühne und Welt*, vol. 17, November 1915. Digitized by Staats- und Universitätsbibliothek Hamburg, CC BY-SA 4.0.

Illustration by Fidus from *Die Schönheit*,
vol. 16 (1919/20). The caption reads:
"If you expect rising peoples like the
Germans to have to bear with religious politics, in just the same way they will
need a political, i.e. folkish religion."

the writers had any reason to see
the Jews as inherently wicked. But
the removal of all legal restrictions
on Jews in the German Empire in
1871 created a counter-reaction by
those who had long seen even assimilated Jews as an alien people.

Völkisch ideology was also fueled by the eugenics movement.
Considered quite respectable
and popular in the United States
around the turn of the century,
eugenics was an attempt to apply
biological evolution and genetics to
improve humanity through selec-
tive breeding, encouraging those
deemed "fit" to have children, and
discouraging the "unfit" from re-
producing by any means necessary
(Micklos and Carlson, "Engineering American Society"). The toxic
combination of *völkisch* nationalism, anti-Semitism, and eugenics
created a deadly mixture of ideology and imagery. This helped to
fuel the rise of the Nazi regime,
which in turn led to the indescrib-
able suffering and murder of millions of Jews, Slavs, Roma, and so many
others. It also did terrible harm to the very Germanic religion and culture
that the Nazis claimed to uphold.

The Nazi Occult

Sensationalist authors like Trevor Ravenscroft, Louis Pauwels, and
Jacques Bergier have claimed that Nazism was permeated by the occult.
This makes for entertaining books, video games, and movies about Indiana

Jones. It also tends to distract from the thoroughly mundane, un-occult, un-mystical means that the Nazis used to perpetrate unimaginable horror. It's somehow reassuring to imagine that the Nazis were controlling, or controlled by, mysterious dark forces. It is harder to cope with the fact that the Nazis were mostly people like ourselves—and that we have the same potential as they did to create horrors on a massive scale, without needing occult help.

The truth seems to be that mysticism, like political pan-Germanism and anti-Semitism, was very much "in the air" across the political spectrum of early 20th century Germany. There were a number of societies in early 20th century Germany that mingled reactionary politics with *völkisch* and occultist imagery: aside from List's and Lanz's groups, there were the Nordungen, the Werdandi League, the Mittgart League, and the Walsung Order, to name just a few (Hermand, *Old Dreams*, p. 44). Several early Nazis were members of such groups, or at least had been influenced by the messages these groups were putting out. Probably the best known was the Thule-Gesellschaft, an ally and to some extent a cover for a larger secret lodge known as the Germanen-Orden, led by a charlatan named Rudolf Glauer, who took the name Baron Rudolf von Sebottendorf. In 1918 he founded a special interest group within the Thule-Gesellschaft, the Politischer Arbeiterzirkel (Political Workers' Circle), which in turn founded the Deutsche Arbeiterpartei (German Workers' Party), which attracted many people outside the Thule-Gesellschaft. This was the group that Adolf Hitler joined and later renamed the *Nationalsozialistische Deutsche Arbeiterpartei* (NSDAP), or Nazi Party for short (Phelps, "'Before Hitler Came',"pp. 256-258).

Emblem of the Thule-Gesellschaft. Wikimedia Commons, Public Domain.

However, few prominent Nazis had anything like a serious commitment to occultism or paganism of any sort—and those who did tended to be disavowed by the Party as it gained power. There's no evidence that the

Deutsche Arbeiterpartei itself was ever especially concerned with anything occultic. Sebottendorf published a book in 1933, *Bevor Hitler kam* (*Before Hitler Came*), claiming that his Thule Society essentially founded the Nazi Party; however, the Party suppressed the book, and Sebottendorf moved to Turkey and disappeared (Phelps, "'Before Hitler Came'," p. 245). Alfred Rosenberg, who wrote *The Myth of the Twentieth Century* as a long exposition of Nazi philosophy, is sometimes claimed as a pagan, having written things like "The longing to give the Nordic race soul its form as a German church under the sign of the Volksmythos, that is for me the greatest task of our century" (quoted in Williamson, *The Longing for Myth*, p. 291). But in the third edition, he complained that his critics had gotten his ideas all wrong:

> What was overlooked was the great reverence for the founder of Christianity expressed in the work. . . . Overlooked was the fact that I presented Wotanism as a *dead* religious form. . . and instead I was falsely accused in the most unscrupulous fashion of advocating a return to the "pagan cult of Wotan" (quoted in Rabinbach and Gilman, *The Third Reich Reader*, p. 124).

Wilhelm Hauer, founder of the *Deutsche Glaubensbewegung*, was also alleged to be a pagan, but he complained about earlier pagan movements who had, he thought, taken things too literally:

> . . . several of the earlier societies attempted to restore to a place of honor the heritage of ancient Teutonic and Nordic religion, and they often did it in a very romantic, even fantastic, manner. But such attempts are merely the accompanying phenomena which arise in the case of all great movements; they are mere caricatures of the real thing, and one is not entitled to judge the whole movement by them. We have no intention of awakening the old gods to life; we know perfectly well that they will never emerge from their twilight, and that each new age must mold its own religious norms. If we mention here and there the old Teutonic deities, they serve only as symbols, just as the classical deities have been used as symbols in art and poetry since the Renaissance; and the reason is the same in both cases: they express ideals which we feel to be essen-

tially akin to us. . . . But we should have to regard prayers to Wotan, or hymns and sacrifices to Thor, as a parody of German Faith. (transl. Scott-Craig and Davies, *Germany's New Religion*, pp. 34-35)

It also should be noted that most Germans who were serious pagans and occultists blended their practices with a lot of other traditions that had little or nothing to do with what ancient Heathens actually did. As we have seen, many of the advocates for reviving "the ancient German religion" were calling for a variety of monotheistic deism or pantheism, not polytheism as such. Ideas about German prehistory spread with almost no regard for logic or evidence. Guido List, for instance, claimed that after the Christian suppression of the Armanen priesthood, its ideas were transmitted by esoteric groups such as the Rosicrucians, Templars, kabbalists, and Freemasons— which gave him license to draw on all of them in constructing his Armanen Orden (Goodrick-Clark, *The Occult Roots of Nazism*, pp. 33-90). The same could be said of Rudolf John Gorsleben, who combined esoteric runology with astrology, Theosophy, and the "Krist-religion" of ancient Atlantis (Goodrick-Clark, pp. 153-163).

While the Nazis sometimes found it tactically useful to treat the older *völkisch* leaders as allies, Hitler himself was scornful of attempts to revive German paganism (Puschner, "One People," pp. 7-8). In one conversation he complained that "there is such a lot of nonsense talked about the cult of Wotan and the spirit of the Edda. . . . These idiotic windbags have no idea what their spouting causes" (Steigmann-Gall, *The Holy Reich*, pp. 142-143). In another, he stated, "It seems to me that nothing would be more foolish than to re-establish the worship of Wotan. Our old mythology ceased to be viable when Christianity implanted itself. Nothing dies unless it is moribund. . . . A movement like ours mustn't let itself be drawn into metaphysical digressions. It must stick to the spirit of exact science. It's not the Party's function to be a counterfeit for religion" (*Hitler's Secret Conversations* no. 39, p. 51). In *Mein Kampf* (ch. 12, p. 361), Hitler poured out further scorn on pagan revivalists:

The characteristic thing about these people is that they rave about old Germanic heroism, about dim prehistory, stone axes, spear and shield, but in reality are the greatest cowards imaginable. For the same people who brandish scholarly imitations of old German tin swords, and wear a dressed bearskin with bull's horns over their bearded heads, preach for the present nothing but spiritual weapons, and run away as fast as they can from every Communist blackjack. . . . I came to know these people too well not to feel the profoundest disgust at their miserable play-acting.

And in a speech to his cabinet on January 30, 1934, Hitler listed the enemies of the Nazi regime, and included "that little group of *völkisch* ideologists who believe that it is only possible to make the nation happy by eradicating the experiences and consequences of two thousand years of history to start out on new trails, clad, so to speak, in their 'bearskins'" (ed. Domarus, *Hitler: Speeches and Proclamations*, vol. I, p. 421).

The only organization within the Nazi state where "pagans" had any real influence was the SS Ahnenerbe ("Ancestral Heritage"), a think tank founded by Heinrich Himmler, commander of the SS (*Schutzstaffel*, "Protection Squadron") and chief architect of the Holocaust. Himmler did go in for Germanic *völkisch* mysticism, and saw his SS as a new chivalric order. The Ahnenerbe's task was to provide indoctrination for SS men in the greatness of their ancestors, as well as to produce academically respectable propaganda supporting Nazi racial policy. The Ahnenerbe's cofounder and first director, the lay scholar Hermann Wirth (1885-1981), envisioned a highly advanced Nordic Aryan race, originating in the lost Arctic realm of Atlantis many thousands of years ago. These people had worshipped a great World-Spirit who revealed himself through the cosmic order, especially through the cycle of the seasons (Douglass, *God Among the Germans*, pp. 55-58). Wirth believed that the traditional symbols used by the Germanic peoples, from folk art to rune letters, but especially the Bronze Age petroglyphs of Norway and Sweden, encoded the knowledge of this ancient sun-cult. If they could be decoded, they would lead to spiritual and physical renewal of the German *Volk* (Pringle, *The Master Plan*, pp. 58-75; Junginger, "Nordic Ideology," pp. 49-51; Löw, "The Great God's Oldest Runes," pp. 112-118, 123-127).[39]

Himmler himself made some stabs at creating pagan-inspired rituals for the SS, with input from occultist Karl Maria Wiligut, a former Imperial

---

39. So enthusiastic was Wirth about Scandinavian rock art that he permanently damaged several panels while making plaster casts (Pringle, *The Master Plan*, p. 69).

Austrian army officer who claimed to be in psychic contact with his ancient noble ancestors, the Adler-Wiligoten family. It was Wiligut who designed the SS *Totenkopf* ("Death's Head") ring, using runes from a futhark of his own devising. Heavily influenced by a mishmash of Theosophy, ceremonial magic, Eastern mysticism, and other notions, Wiligut called his monotheistic faith "Irmin-Kristianity" and claimed that it had been founded 12,500 years ago when the martyred prophet Baldur-Chrestos proclaimed the true worship of "Krist." Wiligut claimed that the "Wotanism" of Guido List was actually a false faith that had usurped Irminism (Goodrick-Clarke, *Black Sun*, pp. 217-225; Steigmann-Gall, *The Holy Reich*, pp. 86-113, 129-132). On Wiligut's advice, Himmler renovated the 17th-century castle at Wewelsburg to be a ritual center for the SS. To create his vision of the SS as a "chivalric order," he drew on the historical Teutonic Knights, and on medieval legends of Lohengrin, Parsifal, and the Holy Grail, at least as much as he did on Germanic paganism. In fact, Jörg Lanz von Liebensfels had already tried to renovate an old castle at Werffenstein to be a völkisch "grail castle" in 1908, and in the 1930s the Nazis built or renovated several *Ordensburgen*, "knightly order castles," as training centers for the elite, so the idea of a castle for a modern "knightly order" was not unique to Himmler (Goodrick-Clark, pp. 125-126; Hermand, *Old Dreams*, pp. 239-245).

Himmler's circle of crank scholars and occultists continues to inspire certain *völkisch* pagans with their spooky aura. What is often overlooked is that they never had much real power in the Nazi apparatus. Hitler himself had nothing but contempt for Himmler's interests:

> What nonsense! Here we have at last reached an age that has left all mysticism behind, and now he wants to start that all over again. We might just as well have stayed in the church. At least it had tradition. . . . Isn't it enough that the Romans were erecting great buildings when our forefathers were still living in mud huts; now Himmler is starting to dig up these villages of mud huts and enthusing over every potsherd and stone axe he finds. All we prove by that is that we were still throwing stone hatchets and crouching around open fires when Greece and Rome had already reached the highest stage of culture. We really should do our best to keep quiet about this past. (Speer, *Inside the Third Reich*, pp. 94-95)

After publishing a fraudulent historical document called the *Oera Linda Book*, Wirth was replaced as director of the Ahnenerbe in 1937 by a formally trained academic (and observant Protestant), Walther Wüst. Wüst was able to get more funding for the Ahnenerbe, but he also shifted its focus to more orthodox scholarship (Link and Hare, "Pseudoscience Reconsidered," pp. 115-116). Wirth resigned in 1938, and Wiligut was "allowed" to retire in 1939, once word got out that he'd been committed to a mental hospital from 1924 to 1927. When the war broke out, the Ahnenerbe shifted focus to scientific and medical research—including horrific experiments on concentration camp inmates—and cultural studies were sidelined (Junginger, "Nordic Ideology," pp. 51-55).

The Nazi movement was very good at tapping into the energy of disaffected people who were looking for national renewal. At times, they did this using ancient symbols which had been popularized by earlier *völkisch* movements, most notably the swastika, but also the sunwheel and certain rune-letters. However, what ultimately guided the Nazi regime was the *Führerprinzip*, the "Führer principle"—absolute obedience to one's leaders, who in turn were absolutely obedient to theirs, with Adolf Hitler at the top of the hierarchy and accountable to no one and nothing but his own will. Every aspect of life, including religion, culture, and scholarship, had to be brought into alignment with Nazi doctrine. The term for this was *Gleichschaltung*, "coordination"—the placement of every aspect of society in the unquestioning service of the Nazi state. This applied to Germanic religion and history: their primary value was as convenient tools for propaganda.

To give just one example of how *Gleichschaltung* worked: Before the Nazi regime came to power, the influential and highly nationalist archaeologist Gustaf Kossinna (1858–1931) had claimed that archaeological cultures (i.e. regions with distinctive styles of artifacts over certain timeframes) correlated perfectly with ethnic groups. He used this to support his claim that the Germans were identical with the ancient Indo-Europeans, and that they had always lived in northern Europe, where they had developed the highest culture in the world (Klejn, "Gustaf Kossinna," pp. 318-324). Using Kossinna's belief that material culture always corresponded perfectly with ethnic identity, any finds of artifacts that looked "Germanic" could be used to support German territorial claims (Arnold, "The Past as Propaganda," pp. 121-125). This included the Ukraine and Crimea; since the Goths had once lived there, Germany had the right to claim them for the pure "Aryan race." Discussing his plans to turn the Ukraine and Crimea into a great Germanic colony, Hitler actually said, "In any case, my demands are not exorbitant. I'm only interested, when all is said, in territories where Germans have lived before" (*Hitler's Secret Conversations*, no. 29, p. 30). And this is why SS Ahnenerbe agents entered Crimea just behind the front lines. As the Crimean Jews were being slaughtered, the Ahnenerbe looted Crimean museums and archaeological sites in search of the treasures of the lost Gothic empire—not because they held mystic powers, like the Ark of the Covenant in *Raiders of the Lost Ark*, but because they could be used to legitimize Nazi territorial claims (Pringle, *The Master Plan*, pp. 211-226).

Suppression of the Occult

In the end, the "paganists" never became a dominant force in Nazi circles, for two simple reasons: there were too few of them, and they were split into small squabbling factions. Whatever they may have thought about ancient Germanic gods and heroes, about ninety-five percent of all Germans remained registered members of the Protestant and Catholic churches, before, during, and after the war (Heschel, *Aryan Jesus*, p. 14). Favoring the paganist movement would have been a liability to the Nazis. Hitler himself admitted that "for the political leader the religious doctrines and institutions of his people must always remain inviolable; or else he has no right to be in politics" (*Mein Kampf*, p. 116). Indeed, the Nazis were far more successful in appealing to Christians: several German Protestant dioceses formed the German Evangelical Church, or Protestant Reich Church, which formally allied with the Nazi state. Dissenters, who formed the Confessing Church, opposed state interference in church affairs but did not necessarily disagree with Nazi ideology, although some did try to resist (Steigmann-Gall, *The Holy Reich*, pp. 155-189). Some Nazi

Deutsche Christen, "German Christians," celebrating Luther Day in Berlin in 1933. Bundesarchiv, Bild 102-15234, CC-BY-SA 3.0.

leaders were openly anti-religious, and Hitler privately thought that Christianity was on the verge of collapse (e.g. *Hitler's Secret Conversations* no. 39, pp. 48-52), but in public, he and his followers were quite willing to ally themselves with the Christian supermajority and appeal to Christian values. The party's official platform, the "Twenty-Five Points" of 1920, promised religious freedom but advocated "Positive Christianity," meaning Christianity stripped of its Jewish elements (Steigmann-Gall, *The Holy Reich*, pp. 13-15). Hitler was happy to depict himself as "acting in accordance with the will of the Almighty Creator: by defending myself against the Jew, I am fighting for the work of the Lord" (*Mein Kampf*, ch. 2, p. 65). He appealed to Catholics and Protestants to put aside their differences and unite behind his program to "actually fulfill God's will, and not let God's word be desecrated" (ch. 11, p. 562).

In fact, after gaining power, the Nazis suppressed pagan and occultist groups, even those with *völkisch* leanings. Hitler made his intentions very clear in a speech on September 6, 1938:

> For the National Socialist Movement is not a cult movement; rather, it is a völkisch and political philosophy which grew out of considerations of an exclusively racist [*rassischen*] nature. This philosophy does not advocate mystic cults, but rather aims to cultivate and lead a Volk determined by its blood. . . . Hence the National Socialist Movement will not tolerate subversion by occult mystics in search of an afterlife. They are not National Socialists but something different, and in any event, they represent something that has nothing to do with us.
>
> —ed. Domarus, *Hitler: Speeches and Proclamations*, vol. II, p. 1146

Hitler's words were soon backed by deeds. Friedrich Bernhard Marby was imprisoned between 1937 and 1945. Siegfried Kummer vanished during the war, and his fate is still unknown. In 1936 the GGG was forbidden to meet. Ludwig Fahrenkrog survived the war, but his art and writings were suppressed, and GGG leader Ernst Wachler may have died in a concentration camp in 1944 or 1945 (Wolff, "Ludwig Fahrenkrog," pp. 237-238). The end came in 1941, when Rudolf Hess made his unauthorized flight to Britain to negotiate for peace. Attributing Hess's action to his affinity for the occult, the Nazi Party banned all public displays of an occultist or "supernatural" nature. On June 4, the Gestapo was ordered to take action against "secret doctrines and fringe sciences." After the ban, the military continued to test a few occultists for potential military applications (as the US did during the Cold War). For example, the Navy experimented with clairvoyance and pendulum dowsing to find convoys and submarines, but abandoned the tests when it was clear that they had failed (Schelleinger et al., "Pragmatic Occultism," pp. 157-166), and "scientific" astrologers whose work might have propaganda value were allowed to continue plying their trade under close supervision (Kurlander, "Hitler's Supernatural Sciences," pp. 133-138). But for all intents and purposes, organized esotericism was dead (Steigmann-Gall, *The Holy Reich*, pp. 232-233).

The Nazi Legacy

Despite the facts that the Nazi movement was not "pagan" at all, and that the ancient lore does not promote anything like "white supremacy," the pre-Christian imagery that the Nazis used became closely associated with their ideology. There are, unfortunately, Nazi-sympathetic and white supremacist Heathens today who claim to honor the old gods. Their continued misuse of our holy symbols drives away good people who are drawn to Heathenry, and others who could work with us on shared goals, but who do not wish to associate with Nazis. We can no longer use one of our ancient holy signs, the swastika, and we have to be careful about using others, such as some of the runes, because this might give people the idea that we might be sympathetic to the Nazis.[40] The taint is one with which all Heathens have to deal sooner or later.

Another lingering effect of Nazism is the fact that some of the academic experts that Heathens draw on were Nazi or other Fascist sympathizers, at least for parts of their careers. There were certainly crackpots who had supporters in the Ahnenerbe, and some of their ideas still find a hearing on the lunatic fringe, such as the "Black Sun," the mystic power source for the "Aryan race" (Goodrick-Clarke, *Black Sun*, pp. 128-150). The fraud-

---

40. At this writing (2020), the Troth's official policy is not to use the swastika at all, for any purpose—the taint on it is felt to be too great for the foreseeable future. We cannot enforce this except at Troth-sponsored events, but we urge all Heathens to avoid using the swastika, and all our symbols, in any way that would give the appearance of endorsing Nazi or white supremacist ideology.

ulent *Oera Linda Book*, which Hermann Wirth promoted so eagerly that
he embarrassed the Ahnenerbe and lost his job, also continues to circulate
among a few groups not noted for critical thinking skills. But there were
also respected scholars who put their minds at the service of the Nazis.
Some of them were never called to account for their actions, and went on
to long academic careers. Jan de Vries, for example, wrote the classic reference work *Altgermanische Religionsgeschichte* and several other landmarks in
Germanic studies. Unfortunately, he collaborated with the Nazis after their
invasion of the Netherlands; among other things, he wrote a children's book
in 1942, *Onze Voorouders*, to teach Dutch children respect for their German brethren. Otto Höfler's 1934 doctoral thesis, *Kultische Geheimbünde der
Germanen*, became a favorite of Himmler's for its enthusiastic discussion of
cultic warrior bands; Himmler got him a professorship at the University of
Munich, and after the war he ended up as a professor in Vienna, continuing
to write and publish. Both de Vries and Höfler influenced Georges Dumézil,
who was decidedly not sympathetic to the Germans, but who was affiliated
with the right-wing Action Française movement in the 1930s (Lincoln, *Theorizing Myth*, pp. 121-137). Herbert Jankuhn directed the excavations at the
Viking-era site of Hedeby under the sponsorship of the Ahnenerbe, wrote a
popular account of the site from a very ethnonationalist point of view (Link
and Hare, "Pseudoscience Reconsidered," pp. 116-123), and directed the
Ahnenerbe's looting of the Crimea. He went on to become Germany's most
respected archaeologist after the war. A number of other former Ahnenerbe
scholars managed to conceal their past and ended up in comfortable positions (Pringle, *The Master Plan*, pp. 299-325). This does not mean that
their scholarly work is automatically wrong, or that people who make use
of it are Nazi sympathizers. *Altgermanische Religionsgeschichte*, for example,
remains a masterful synthesis of Germanic religion, and it's not generally
considered to be excessively ideologically biased. Jankuhn's academic writing
on Hedeby generally avoided biased language and is considered a masterful
work. Neither the authors of this book, nor the Troth as a whole, have any
desire to try to mandate what sources a Heathen may and may not read;
we're not in the business of creating a Heathen *Index Librorum Prohibito-
rum*. But it never hurts to read scholarship from this time especially criti-
cally and carefully.

Rising from the Ruins

The war ended with Germany devastated and divided. The old pagan groups were dispersed, but a few tried to rebuild. Ludwig Fahrenkrog lived until 1952, and his GGG carried on after his death until the 1960s. A former SS member, Wilhelm Kusserow, founded a *völkisch* religious organization in 1952, the *Artgemeinschaft* ("Community of Our Kind," more or less). A similar group, the *Goden-Orden*, was founded in 1957. The Guido von List Society also reformed after the war, while eclectic occultist Karl Spiesberger (1904–1992) published books on the Armanen runes, trying to remove the old ideology that had tainted them. Most of these groups remained small and obscure, but their ideas would go on to influence the New Right movements of France and Germany in the 1960s and 1970s, which are still influential in folkish Heathenry (Schnurbein, *Norse Revival*, pp. 48-50).

In the English-speaking world, Norse mythology was largely spared the negative reaction to Germanic mythology, probably because the Scandinavian countries had either been neutral or occupied in the war, and the Nazis had never had much popular support in Scandinavia. Ironically, Germanic mythology and legend re-entered the cultural mainstream in the English-speaking world through the work of a devout Christian and avowed anti-Nazi: Professor J. R. R. Tolkien, author of *The Hobbit* and *The Lord of the Rings*. Tolkien wrote that he had "set myself a task. . . being precisely to restore to the English an epic tradition and present them with a mythology of their own" (*The Letters of J. R. R. Tolkien*, p. 180). Deeply learned in both Anglo-Saxon and Norse literature and linguistics, he drew on his scholarship in creating his world. Just to give a few examples: his dwarf-names come straight out of *Vǫluspá*, as does the name of Gandalf ("wand-alf" or "magical alf"), who himself bears more than a little resemblance to Odin wandering the world in pursuit of knowledge. Bilbo's theft of the cup from Smaug's hoard is a straight steal from *Beowulf*; Aragorn's ancestral sword, broken at his father's death and reforged when it is time for him to win his rightful place, is borrowed from the sword of the Vǫlsungs. Tolkien's prose and poetic style also drew on Old Norse and Old English literature. To give just one example, the lament of the Rohirrim, "Where now the horse and the rider? Where is the horn that was blowing?" (*The Two Towers*, p. 112) is based on lines from the Old English poem *The Wanderer*: *Hwær cwom*

247

mearg? Hwær cwom mago? Hwær cwom maþþumgyfa? "Where has the horse gone? Where has the hero gone? Where has the treasure-giver gone?" (lines 92-96, ed. Krapp and Dobbie, *The Exeter Book*, p. 136).

Although Tolkien was not the first writer of fantasy literature, his writing inspired and continues to inspire epic fantasy literature that draws on mythological themes. His friend C. S. Lewis had been captivated by the feeling of "Northernness" early in life, before his conversion to Christianity (Lewis, *Surprised by Joy*, pp. 17, 73), and even afterwards, he drew on Norse mythology together with Greek and Roman mythology in his Narnia series of books (although his Norse figures tend to be villains). Other writers kept up the tradition of portraying Vikings as heroic. Edison Marshall's 1951 novel *The Viking* retold material from the sagas of Ragnar Lodbrok; it was in turn adapted into the 1958 film *The Vikings*, starring Kirk Douglas and Tony Curtis, and famous among Heathens today for the line "Hail Ragnar! Hail Ragnar's beard!" Movies like *Prince Valiant* (1954) and *The Long Ships* (1964) and *The Norseman* (1978) kept the heroic Viking image alive, with varying degrees of historical accuracy. And two dates loom especially large in history for all who love the old ways of the North: 1962, when The Mighty Thor made his comic book debut; and 1970, when "Immigrant Song" was released as the first single from *Led Zeppelin III*.

Today, in 2020, Norse gods and Viking heroes can be found everywhere from children's books to Japanese anime to contemporary poetry (O'Donoghue, *From Asgard to Valhalla*, pp. 181-199). The hit TV series *Vikings* has been the most obvious manifestation, but nods to Viking and Scandinavian culture have turned up everywhere, from children's movies like *How to Train Your Dragon* and *Frozen*; to blockbusters like *The Lord of the Rings*; to popular magazines such as *National Geographic*. New archaeological discoveries and fresh scholarship are changing the ways in which we think of the Germanic-speaking peoples and their myths, and reaching new audiences through channels that range from podcasts and online videos, to documentary films and major museum exhibitions. A small flood of mass-market books on Norse mythology and history has followed, from retellings of the myths to lavishly illustrated coffee-table books of Viking artworks. And the old lore is available as never before. In 1984, the old AFA had to launch a letter-writing campaign to get Lee Hollander's translation of the *Poetic Edda* back into print (see *The Runestone* no. 50, pp. 12-13, and no. 52, inside back cover)—but since 2000, three new translations of the complete *Poetic Edda* have been published, older translations have been reprinted, and several translations in the public domain are available on the Internet. New translations of the sagas are also available in modern English, as old ones have been reprinted or put on-line. It's a good time to be a Heathen. . .

Contributors:

1st edition: Kveldúlfr Gundarsson.

2nd edition: New material by Ben Waggoner.

3rd edition: Reorganization and new material by Ben Waggoner.

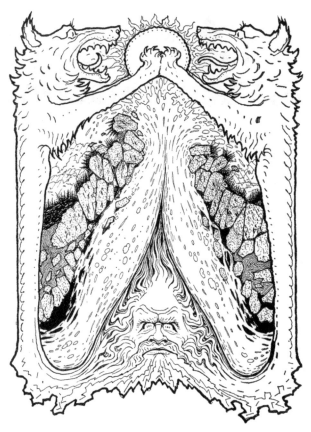

Fidus, "Gotterdammerung."
Illustration for Eduard Stucken, *Balladen* (1898).

Outdoor harrow (altar) at Trothmoot 2018.
Photo by Ben Waggoner.

CHAPTER NINE

The Heathen Rebirth

1931–onwards!

The Troth banner flies over Trothmoot 2019. Photo by Ben Waggoner.

It has taken years for the modern Heathen movement to grow back from the Nazi devastation, and the past history of hatred still manifests today and has to be confronted. Yet through the labor of thousands of people whose love for the old ways gave them the strength for great efforts, Heathenry has rebuilt and is continuing to rebuild itself. Our ways are rooted deeply in old traditions, and yet are able to meet the spiritual needs of humanity in today's world.

The pre-war attempts to revive Germanic religion had been tainted almost beyond repair by ideologies that the Nazis would successfully tap into, and all too many who call themselves Ásatrú or Heathens or Odinists continue to promote their ideology to this day. As this chapter will show, some of the modern Heathen revival's roots lie in dark places indeed. It is not our intent to smear anyone, or to go muckraking for shock value. That said, it does us no good to pretend that the unsavory parts of our past never happened, or are no longer relevant. Heathens speak of *wyrd* and *ørlǫg*—the manifold ways in which past deeds work their way into the present. We, of all people, need to understand that we are not exempt from *ørlǫg*—what has been laid down by past actions.

Despite its origins, and despite setbacks, modern Heathenry has become a growing and thriving religious movement. Some Heathen groups, including the Troth, are actively working to shed remaining influences from the dark corners of our past, and take our place as a vibrant movement that does not need hate, bigotry, white supremacy, or racial exclusion in order to flourish.

The Founders

A. Rud Mills

Alexander Rud Mills (1885-1964), an Australian lawyer who wrote under the pen name of Tasman Forth, became enamored both with Fascism and with the idea of Odinism as the natural religion for "the British Race." He toured Europe from 1931 to 1934. In Germany, he met Nazi leaders, including Adolf Hitler (who was, however, not especially interested in his ideas) and Erich Ludendorff and his wife, founders of the *Tannenbergbund*. Mills was also influenced by the Armanism of Guido List. In England, he met leading fascists, attended meetings of Oswald Mosley's British Union of Fascists, and apparently tried to found a group called the Moot of the Anglekin Body (Bird, *Nazi Dreamtime*, pp. 19-20, 30-31, 116-117). Back in Australia, Mills began producing a series of books expounding his own unique take on the elder religion, beginning with his 1933 book of poems *Hael! Odin!* In Melbourne, he founded the Anglekin Body, also known as the Anglecyn Church of Odin. Allegedly, his Thursday night ceremonies at his home on the outskirts of Melbourne drew as many as 120 people. His book of liturgies and hymns, *The First Guide Book to the Anglecyn Church of Odin*, was published in 1936 (Winter, *The Australia First Movement*, pp. 39-41; Bird, 116-117).

A. Rud Mills

A. Rud Mills in 1943. National Library of Australia, **https://trove. nla.gov.au/version/193453956** Public domain.

Mills's Odinist religion was quite different from what modern Ásatrú would later become. Like the Germanic Faith movements in Germany, Mills's Odinism was nearly monotheistic: Odin was essentially synonymous with the One God, being "that of the Great One which man can know" (*The Odinist Religion*, p. 117). Odin was also the name of a mortal man, also known as George, Sigge, Zag-Dar, or

Adam-Thor, who was "hallowed as the greatest and the most beloved of all messengers of the Great One" (*The Odinist Religion*, pp. 31-35; *First Guide Book*, pp. 17, 61). The other Norse deities are not mentioned as often, but Mills saw "the Thor" as a personification of Odin's active strength, while "the Baldur" was a sort of divine image in all humanity: "All children born upon the earth are children of the All-Father, and the Baldur is in each of us" (*The Odinist Religion*, p. 160). Mills neatly solved the academic question of whether Freyja and Frigg might be the same: his Odin was married to "Freyga," a maternal figure. Mills also made frequent references to angels. An important aspect of his theology was the idea that God had assigned each person a natural position in life with its own duties and obligations. This he called the "Gard in God," and every man's purpose was to work faithfully at his Gard in God, as a small part of the great whole.

Mills's understanding of historical Scandinavian and Anglo-Saxon culture was rather fanciful by scholarly standards. His Odinist liturgy was heavily based on the Anglican Christian order of worship: *The First Guide Book* includes "Morning Service," "Communion," and "Evensong," as well as rites for fast days ("Vigils and Days for Partial Abstinence") and a list of ten "Commandments," six of which are identical to six of the biblical Ten Commandments (p. 63). Written in rather flowery language in imitation of the Anglican Book of Common Prayer, the *First Guide Book* includes "scripture" readings and feast days dedicated to the *Eddas* and *Beowulf*—but also to Shakespeare, Newton, Nelson, and other English worthies, as well as to the traditional patron saints (or "chief elements") of the four British nations: George (England), Andrew (Scotland), David (Wales), and Brian (Ireland) (pp. 13-14, 48-49). He wrote a number of Odinist hymns; the main difference between his hymns and Christian hymns is that his hymns end by singing, not "A-men," but "Wo-tan." His liturgy also showed more than a little Masonic influence; the initiation ceremony for new members reads like a cross between the Sacrament of Baptism from the *Book of Common Prayer* and the initiation of an Entered Apprentice Mason (*First Guide Book*, pp. 76-78; see Winter, *The Australia First Movement*, p. 44; Bird, *Nazi Dreamtime*, p. 123).

This dependence on Christian models is perhaps understandable for a man who is founding a religious movement from scratch, given the limited scholarship available to him at the time. But less forgivably, Mills's writings

reveal an obsession with the Jews, whom he blames for essentially everything wrong with the world, including Christianity: "Under Christianity
with its cloak of sanctity, the Jews and the usurer have their feet upon our
neck" (*The Odinist Religion*, p. 29); "Till our people see it, the Jews have
got us enslaved, spiritually and otherwise, till we, devitalised, decay and die"
(p. 246); "the Jews, generally speaking, recognise the degradation and dis-
integration of the peoples under Christian culture, and by its direction and
otherwise, have hopes of ruling over such people (and over all the world's
peoples if Christianity be spread over the world). . . Jews try to hasten the
process by using the many powers in their control" (*First Guide Book*, p. 34).
One belief that would pass to folkish Heathenry was Mills's insistence that
genetics determines spirituality, and that following a "foreign" religion was
the root cause of social malaise: "Our own racial ideals and traditions (not
those of another) are our best guide to health and national strength" (*The
Odinist Religion*, p. 7). Another was the importance of banning interracial
marriage: "Odinists do not marry persons racially distant from them. They
understand the dangers of mongrelism and the mating of opposites" (*The
Odinist Religion*, p. 54).

Mills's political position is unmistakable: he was also publishing outright Nazi propaganda, including two issues of a paper called the *National
Socialist* in 1936 and 1937, which bore a swastika on the masthead.[41] He per-
sonally sent a copy of *The Odinist Religion* to Hitler, and he worked closely
with Australian Fascist leaders (Winter, *Dreaming of a National Socialist
Australia*, pp. 42-47; Bird, *Nazi Dreamtime*, pp. 88-92, 116-119). In March
1942, Mills was detained under harsh conditions by the wartime Australian
government along with members of the isolationist Australia First discussion group, which he had joined in 1941 (Bird, *Nazi Dreamtime*, pp. 257).
Whether his detention was legally justifiable is still debated by Australian
historians. Some have called it an illegal infringement of civil rights. Others
point to the threat of Japanese invasion as justification for the measure—
some of the Australia First circle were advocating cooperation with Japan,
although Mills himself seems not to have done this (Bird, *Nazi Dreamtime*,
pp. 316-320). In any case, Mills was released in December 1942, with no
criminal charges filed. His Anglecyn Church of Odin seems to have dis-

41. The front page of one issue is reproduced in Bird, *Nazi Dreamtime*.

solved, although some members allegedly continued to practice in secret (Osred, *Odinism*, pp. 189-191).

After the war, Mills tried and failed to win restitution for his imprisonment. He allegedly tried to re-establish his church in the 1950s as the First Church of Odin, but it was not successful (Gardell, *Gods of the Blood*, p. 167). He self-published his last work on Odinism, a booklet called *The Call of Our Ancient Nordic Religion*, in 1957, and died in obscurity in 1964 (Osred, *Odinism*, p. 194).

Else Christensen and Prison Odinism

In Denmark before World War II, Else Ochsner Christensen (1913-2005) had been active in the syndicalist movement, a labor movement relying on general strikes and direct action to give power to workers. Her husband Aage Alexander Christensen (1904-1971) was a Strasserite—a worker-centered, anti-capitalist version of National Socialism, often at odds with Nazi orthodoxy.[42] When Nazi Germany occupied Denmark in 1943, both were detained, and Alex was imprisoned for six months. In the aftermath of the Second World War, they emigrated, first to England (on their sailboat), and then in 1951, to Canada, where they settled in Toronto. Else made contact with far-right activists, including James K. Warner, an American Nazi organizer who had been inspired by A. Rud Mills's writings and served for a time as high priest of a mystical white supremacist religion called the Odinist Religion and Nordic Faith Movement (Turner, *Power on the Right*, p. 113). Disillusioned with Odinism as a religion for national socialists, Warner gave her his Odinist materials, including A. Rud Mills's *The Call of Our Ancient Nordic Religion*. She corresponded with Mills's widow for a time, and was inspired to found the Odinist Fellowship, also known as the Odinist Movement, in 1969 (Gardell, *Gods of the Blood*, p. 166; Sannhet, "An Interview with Else Christensen," pp. 10-20). In August 1971, after Alex's death, Else published the first issue of her new newsletter, *The Odinist*. For a few years, she also published a second periodical, *The Sunwheel*. As early as the second

---

42. Strasserites were sometimes called "beefsteak Nazis"—brown on the outside (referring to the brown shirt worn by the Nazi *Sturmabteilung*, the "storm troopers") and red on the inside (the color used by the Communist movement). Otto Strasser, one of the brothers who founded the movement, was killed in 1934 in Hitler's purge of his rivals known as the Night of the Long Knives.

Typical copy of *The Odinist* from 1986.

issue of *The Odinist*, she was citing Mills's "Gard in God" concept (p. 9). However, early issues more frequently quoted far-right political theorists, notably Francis Parker Yockey, whose book *Imperium* remains influential on the far right.

Christensen stayed based in Toronto until late 1978, when she moved to Crystal River, Florida.[43] By the early 1980s, she had started a prison outreach ministry and was able to get Odinism recognized as a legitimate religion by the Florida prison system. The system also recognized her as a licensed vendor, which allowed her to sell materials to prisoners. However, in 1993, she was arrested for drug smuggling. Many of her followers regarded her arrest as a politically motivated frame-up, but she herself claimed only that unscrupulous dealers had tricked her into serving as an unwitting drug mule (Gardell, *Gods of the Blood*, p. 176; Sannhet, "Interview with Else Christensen," p. 30). After five years in prison, she was deported to Canada, where she lived on Vancouver Island, publishing a new newsletter called *Midgard Pages*, until her death in May 2005.

Christensen was and is a controversial figure in Heathenry. She had a strong influence on many Ásatrúar in the early days, who affectionately remember her as "the Folk Mother." Some persons who knew her late in her life have described her as somewhat "folkish" but not racist, and before her death she had allegedly stepped back from promoting political stances, preferring to emphasize the cultural aspects of Odinism. On the other hand, her past connections to National Socialist and other radical far-right groups are matters of record, and her writings contain some blatant racial separatist

---

43. Some have mistakenly claimed that her Odinist Fellowship was always based in Florida. But all early issues of *The Odinist* bear a Toronto mailing address. She announced the move in *The Odinist* no. 36, p. 10.

and anti-Semitic rhetoric. She made it clear that she was cloaking a racial agenda in religious guise: "I don't think that anybody mistook my opinions from what we wrote in *The Odinist*, but nobody could put a finger on what we said, because we said it in a way that it couldn't be clamped down at. . . . Everybody knows that the Jews rule the whole damned world, so you cannot fight their combined power. You need to watch your step" (quoted in Gardell, p. 171). Sometimes it wasn't hard to put a finger on it: she wrote that "The struggle unfolding before our eyes is the age-old fight between opposite, racially-conditioned inner values, reflecting the endless conflict of race vs race, people vs people, nation vs nation: a conflict between alien Asiatic credos (in all their various forms) and Western Aryan tribalism with its ideals of personal responsibility and folk identity" (*An Introduction to Odinism*, p. 2) She made it clear that these "alien Asiatic credos" included both Judaism and "its illegitimate Christian offspring"; the Jews had stolen most of their religious concepts from older pagan religions, but "grafted their own peculiar effusions" (p. 3). Marxism, "the secular gospel of Judeo-Christianity," came in for similar condemnation (p. 5). Material from *The Odinist* was sometimes reprinted in the white supremacist journal *Liberty Bell*, which published rather peppery correspondence debating whether Odinism, Christian Identity (Christianity but with the white race as God's Chosen People), or Creativity (a sort of white supremacist pantheism) was the best religion for white nationalists ("A Reply to a Reply / Letters to the Editor," pp. 42-52).

Christensen admitted that when she founded the Odinist Fellowship, she was an agnostic, making a "rational decision" to test Mills's ideas. Later she came to believe in gods as elements within the human mind: "the subconscious elements of Urd, which we have given mythological names such as Odin, Thor, Frey, or Baldur" (Sannhet, "Interview with Else Christensen," p. 11). She advised Odinists to form study groups and hold meetings, but rarely did she mention rituals or write about Norse religion as such, stating that rituals and rune lore were valid parts of Odinism but that she herself was "simply not able to deal with them" (Sannhet, p. 23). *The Odinist* tended to espouse the view that the Gods were symbolic of the forces of nature: "We conceive of Gods as being the force throughout the universe which controls gravity, rotates the planets and makes the stars shine in accordance with natural law" ("God Concept," *The Odinist* no. 91, p. 3). Her 1980 booklet *Introduction to Odinism*, and the Giallerhorn Book Service that she operated through the 1980s, listed some books on Norse mythology, but far more books on political and social issues from anarchist, right-wing, and racist viewpoints. Early issues of *The Odinist* contained some articles on Viking-era culture, but very little information about how to practice Odinism as a religion; most of the content was political, social, and cultural commentary from a far-right perspective. For example, one issue (no. 27) was dedicated almost entirely to denouncing abstract art as "one of innumerable tools. . . to de-personalize the identity of the Western Soul!" Another (no. 35) gushed with praise for *Star Wars* as a brilliant display of "Aryan Myth, which transmits Aryan heroic dynamism, Aryan mysticism and Aryan theotechnics." Issues in the late 1980s contained lengthy installments of a history of "Aryan" civilization from ancient Sumeria onward. There wasn't much Odin in this Odinism.

While Christensen was at least not actively calling for violence, not everyone shared her restraint. In 1983, David Lane (1938-2007) became a founding member of a white supremacist terrorist group, The Order, whose ultimate aim was to overthrow the US government in a racial war. After a crime spree that included armed robberies, counterfeiting, and the murder of a suspected informer, Lane drove the getaway car for the murder of Denver radio talk show host Alan Berg, on June 18, 1984. Lane was convicted and sentenced to 190 years in prison, where he died in 2007. While in prison, Lane turned from Christian Identity to racist Odinism. He, his wife Katja, and fellow white supremacist Ron McVan founded Wotansvolk, dedicated to what Lane preferred to call Wotanism. (Lane interpreted Wotan as a "backronym" for Will Of The Aryan Nation.) Lane and McVan co-authored the book *Temple of Wotan* in 1995, laying out the beliefs and rituals of Wotansvolk. While Wotansvolk was not the only racist Odinist movement, the Federal Bureau of Prisons and most state prison systems recognized it as a valid religion and a licensed vendor, giving it considerable reach (Gardell, *Gods of the Blood*, pp. 217-220). Although the organization itself came apart in the early 2000s, its books are still in print, and Wotansvolk kindreds remain active in prisons and in the outside world. Lane and Wotansvolk remain an inspiration to other explicitly racist groups and individuals that use Norse religion. Lane is perhaps best known for coining the motto known as the "Fourteen Words": "we must secure the existence of our people and a future for White children." The number 14, often combined with 88—a numerical cipher for the letters HH (Heil Hitler), and also for Lane's "88 Precepts" of Wotanism—has become a widespread symbol in far-right circles, even in groups that don't espouse any pagan religion (Michael, "David Lane and the Fourteen Words," pp. 43-61).

John Yeowell and the Odinic Rite

Leslie William Yeowell, better known as John (1918-2010), described himself as "a bit of a drifter" in his teenage years (Parker, *Inside the Foreign Legion*, p. 93). His drifting had included membership in the British Union of Fascists (BUF), including a time as a bodyguard to BUF leader Oswald Moseley, followed by service in the anti-Communist Irish Brigade in the Spanish Civil War. Joining the French Foreign Legion in 1938, he fought the Germans alongside British forces at Narvik, Norway, in 1940 (Parker, pp. 93-116). After France surrendered and the Allies evacuated Norway, he transferred to the British Army, where he fought in India and Burma in special operations units (Chindits) behind the Japanese lines. After the war, he took a job with the Ministry of Agriculture (Parker, pp. 117-118).

In the late 1950s—possibly after another tour of duty in the Foreign Legion, although documentation seems to be lacking—Yeowell made contact with John Gibbs-Bailey, another former BUF member who allegedly had been involved in small, independent Odinist groups about which little is known (Heimgest, "Time to Honour an Unsung Hero," pp. 3-4). Several scholars have suggested that Gibbs-Bailey might have been part of A. Rud Mills's group in London (Schnurbein, *Norse Revival*, p. 57; White, "Northern Gods," p. 251). However, Yeowell claimed not to have heard of Mills, mentioning instead a few people who'd been inspired by a 1930 book by Laurence Waddell called *The British Edda*, an eccentric mashup of Arthurian legend with Norse, Celtic, and Sumerian mythology (*Odinism Today* no. 5; quoted in Sannhet, "Interview with Else Christensen," p. 10). Yeowell also came across copies of *The Odinist* and corresponded with Else Christensen, who sent him the names of her three subscribers in England. The five men formed the London Odinist Committee for the Restoration of the Odinic Rite in April 1973 (Yeowell, quoted in Sannhet, p. 10). Yeowell became the first leader and spokesman, taking the name Stubba, while Gibbs-Bailey, who was in poor health at the time, adopted the name Hoskuld and worked behind the scenes as treasurer (Heimgest, "Time to Honour an Unsung Hero," p. 4).

The Committee began publishing its own newsletter, *Raven Banner*, and establishing local groups, known at the time as *gemoots*. One of Gibbs-Bailey's small, obscure Odinist groups had developed statements of ethics, the Eight Virtues and the Eight Charges. At Yeowell's suggestion, one entry was added to each list, producing the Nine Noble Virtues that are commonly invoked in Ásatrú, and the less well-known Nine Charges (Heimgest, "Time to Honour an Unsung Hero," p. 3). The group established contact with Steve McNallen's Viking Brotherhood and advertised in *The Runestone*—in fact, John Yeowell was slated to perform McNallen's first wedding in 1975, although unforeseen circumstances kept him from attending ("Norse Notes," *The Runestone*, vol. 4, no. 1, pp. 2-3). The Odinist Committee briefly disbanded, but reorganized in 1980, shortening their name to "the Odinic Rite." Several smaller groups merged with the Rite: an esoteric group called the Frey Hof, which had been founded in the 1960s, joined in 1980, together with a group called Saxnot or SaxNot. Yet another group, the Heimdal League, joined in the mid-80s. In 1988 the OR gained Registered Charity status in Britain, the first polytheistic religious organization to do so (IRMIN, *Interview with a Gothi*, pp. 13-14; Osred, "A Multi-Faceted Life," pp. 104-107).

At least one other organization existed in Britain in the early 1970s: the Anglo-Saxon Church of Woden, which put out a newsletter called *Valkyrie*. The copy in this author's possession [BW] consists mostly of diatribes against liberalism and Communism, although it also contains an excerpt from A. Rud Mills's writings. John Yeowell referred to the group as "incredibly pathetic" (*Odinism Today* #5, January 1992; quoted in Sannhet, "An Interview with Else Christensen," p. 10). The group seems to have dissolved in the mid-1970s. Probably more important in the overall scheme of things in the UK was the Norse Film and Pageant Society, a group of Viking re-enactors and craftsmen, which also sold and rented historical gear and props to stage and movie companies. Founded in 1971 and led by Peter Seymour, the Society used reenactment events to spread knowledge of Odinism. An elite group within the Society, known as the Odin Guard, apparently practiced Heathen worship. Seymour left the Society in 1977 and founded a rival group; he attended the first Althing in the US ("Althing–1980," *The Rune-stone* no. 33, p. 4) and served as a "foreign correspondent" for *The Runestone*, keeping Americans abreast of Odinism in the UK (e.g. *The Runestone* no. 25). The Society still exists; now known as The Vikings, it is one of the larg-est re-enactment societies in Britain, although to the author's knowledge [BW] it does not formally sponsor pagan worship.

In 1989, Yeowell stepped down as Director of the Court of Gothar (DCG; the formal title of the Odinic Rite's leader), and former Heimdal League member Heimgest (Jeffrey Holley) became Director (IRMIN, *Interview with a Gothi*, pp. 12-14; Stinar, "The Odinic Rite Speaks," p. 3). The Odinic Rite split in 1991. For a while there were two groups using the name "Odinic Rite," which were distinguished by their monomarks (mail forwarding names): the Odinic Rite (Runic), led by Heimgest; and the Odinic Rite (Edda), led by Ingvar (Ralph Harrison), which kept the original OR's legal status of Registered Charity. John Yeowell allied with the Odinic Rite (Edda) for several years, but later returned to the Odinic Rite (Runic) (Harvey, "Heathenism," pp. 54-57). The Odinic Rite (Edda) changed its name in 1998 to the Odinist Fellowship—not to be confused with Else Christensen's original Odinist Fellowship—and remains active in Britain. In 2014, the Fellowship acquired and refurbished a historic building in the town of Newark-on-Trent to serve as a temple (Odinist Fellowship, "Newark Odinist Temple"). The Odinic Rite (Runic) kept its original name, and as of 2019 is still under the leadership of Heimgest. It has established official branches in North America (the Odinic Rite Vinland) and several European countries. Some of these are now independent. The Odinic Rite Deutschland was founded in 1994, but moved away from the Odinic Rite in theology and practice, and formally severed the last ties to the Odinic Rite in 2006. Now the Verein für Germanisches Heidentum, it eschews the right-wing political slant that the Odinic Rite tends to espouse, but retains some folkish ideas ("Geschichte," **https://www.vfgh.de/der-vfgh/geschichte/** ; Schnurbein, *Norse Revival*, pp. 75-76, 134-136). The Odinic Rite of Aus-tralia was founded independently by a group of students at the University of Melbourne in the early 1970s. Remembering A. Rud Mills's legal troubles, they got the Attorney General of Australia to issue a ruling that it was legal for them to form a polytheist organization. They soon made contact with the Odinic Rite in England. Today, the Odinic Rite of Australia is a separate organization for legal purposes, but is "in full communion" with the larger Rite (Osred, "A Multi-Faceted Life," pp. 108-109).

Stephen McNallen and the Asatru Free Assembly

Inspired by fantasy literature and movies—especially Edison Marshall's novel *The Viking*—and disenchanted with the Roman Catholic Church of his upbringing, Stephen McNallen, a student and ROTC cadet at Midwestern University in Wichita Falls, Texas, began worshipping Odin privately in 1968. Seeking like-minded folk, he founded the Viking Brotherhood and began publishing a journal, *The Runestone*, in the spring of 1972, "dedicated to the revival of that religion as epitomized during the Viking Age, and to the revival of the values of courage, freedom, and personal independence which are associated with it." (vol. 1, no. 1, p. 2). That year, the Viking Brotherhood gained tax-exempt status from the IRS, the first formal government recognition of any Germanic religious group in the US.

The early Viking Brotherhood was small—the first issue of *The Runestone* consisted of eleven copies (McNallen, *Ásatrú*, p. 62). Early issues contained little information on how to practice the Norse religion; they were dedicated mostly to aspects of Viking culture and history, and to praising individual freedom as opposed to collectivism and conformity. The religion espoused in early issues of *The Runestone* essentially amounted to being brave, daring, free, and anti-collectivist. While it endorsed ecological awareness, it eschewed mysticism as well as Christianity. Prayer and devotion were not encouraged: "I wonder what sort of person it takes to demean their god by worshipping him, thus making him into nothing more than a keeper of slaves" (*The Runestone*, vol. 2, no. 2, p. 5). It was also extremely male-centered, with little mention of goddesses except for the valkyries. In the third issue (Fall 1972), McNallen admitted to a correspondent that "we have not yet devised the necessary rituals for formalized meetings, though we have some of these in the works. It is not terribly pressing at the moment because we are 1) small and 2) very scattered. There just aren't enough of us in any one place to conduct rituals." He added that "Though women have a definite place with us, ours is basically a warrior religion, one based on self-assertion, courage, and other attributes generally considered masculine. As a result, our female goddesses. . . are de-emphasized" (p. 10).

McNallen had long been a political conservative: as a college student, he had served as acting chair of Midwestern University's chapter of the conservative student group Young Americans for Freedom ("GOP Begins Youth Drive"). His early writing in *The Runestone* was known to express dissatisfaction with politically liberal policies such as affirmative action. However, he was not originally concerned with race: he stated in the very first issue of *The Runestone* that "Being a Viking is not a matter of race or nationality, it is a matter of the mind and the heart" (pp. 7-8). In the third issue, responding to a Wiccan correspondent who wondered whether Celtic and Norse religionists could be friendly today, he stated that "Following the Norse religion is wholly apart from race or national origin" (p. 10). But in the pages of the fourth issue (vol. 1, no. 4, p. 12), McNallen announced that he'd made contact with another group of followers of the Norse gods, based in Toronto. That was Else Christensen's Odinist Fellowship. McNallen himself has reminisced that 1974 was when he began to leave his "universalist" views behind (*Ásatrú*, pp. 62-63; see also Gardell, *Gods of the Blood*, pp. 259-260), and the content of *The Runestone* bears this out.

It's worth looking at the larger context. The late 1960s and early 1970s were the time when many groups were trying to break out of the social pigeonholes where they had been placed. The Stonewall Riots in 1969 had galvanized the campaign for gay rights; Native American activists had occupied Alcatraz between 1969 and 1971, and Wounded Knee in 1973; Cesar Chávez had been leading labor actions within the Chicano Movement, notably the Salad Bowl strike of 1970–71; and the Black Power movement was in full swing, with the Black Panther Party reaching its peak membership in 1970. "Second wave" feminism was on the move, with landmarks such as passage of Title IX in 1972 and the *Roe vs. Wade* ruling in 1973. At the same time, new religious movements outside of the mainstream were suddenly turning up all over America, ranging from the Jesus Movement (often known as "Jesus freaks"), the Unification Church (the "Moonies"), and the Children of God (now called "The Family"), to Buddhist and Hindu-inspired movements such as ISKCON (the "Hare Krishnas") and Transcendental Meditation. Pagan, New Age, and occult groups were also going public, and the media was taking notice: *Time* magazine's cover story for June 19, 1972 was "The Occult: A Substitute Faith," covering everything from Anton LaVey's Church of Satan to Neopagan groups such as Aidan

Kelly's NROOGD. Books like Sybil Leek's *Diary of a Witch* (1968) and *The Complete Art of Witchcraft* (1971), Lady Sheba's *Book of Shadows* (1971), and somewhat later, Hans Holzer's *Pagans and Witches* (1978) and the first edition of Margot Adler's *Drawing Down the Moon* (1979), were the first to disseminate information about Neopagan religion into the mainstream.

Early Ásatrú in America stood at the intersection of these trends. In some ways it was inspired by the new social and religious movements, while in other respects it was a reaction against them, similar to the reaction that fueled the rise of the New Christian Right at the same time (Calico, *Being Viking*, pp. 3-4). McNallen opposed some of these new movements, writing statements like "The gay revolution has become more or less accepted. The family as a viable unit has been crippled" (*The Runestone*, vol. 4, no. 1, pp. 9-10). The Moral Majority would have agreed. On the other hand, he

STEPHEN A. McNALLEN, ODINIST
wears Thor's hammer amulet

Stephen McNallen. "Latter-Day Norse Folk Plan a Sacrifice Here." *Berkeley Gazette*, March 11, 1977, p. 10.

was inspired by others, writing favorably in later years of the American Indian Movement and Native author Vine Deloria, for example. And while he would denounce "Eastern culture, with its anti-egoic philosophy" (*The Runestone*, no. 17, p. 9) and aspects of the New Age movement (vol. 3, no. 4, pp. 3-4), his own movement would end up drawing on Wicca as it took shape.

McNallen managed to keep publishing *The Runestone* while serving as a US Army officer, qualifying as an Airborne Ranger and serving in Germany. Once he had resigned his commission and moved back to California (first to Berkeley, then to Turlock, and later into the Sierra Nevada), the Viking Brotherhood began meeting regularly and developing a more organized structure. On March 20, 1977, the Berkeley group held the first public ritual to Odin, which was covered in the local press (*The Runestone*, no. 19, p. 3; Jernigan, "Latter-Day Norse Folk"). That fall, the

Viking Brotherhood began the process of changing its name to the Ásatrú Free Assembly, or AFA (*The Runestone*, no. 21, p. 2). Beginning with *The Runestone* 24 in 1978, the AFA began to publish a ritual calendar, including many holidays that are still widely observed. They also began paying more attention to the goddesses and the Vanir. Much of this new ritual structure looked a lot like Wicca, notably the Eightfold Wheel of the Year. By 1979, the AFA was changing its organizational structure from loose local groups known as *skeppslags* (Old Norse for "ship's crew") to tighter and more activist groups called *kindreds*. That year, the AFA held its first annual Althing in Lafayette, California. As of that summer, the AFA's records allegedly showed 500 members (Flowers, "Revival," p. 285 n15).

McNallen's own worldview had been shifting from libertarian idealism towards white nationalism. In the early 1980s, he established several specialist groups and guilds within the AFA. One of these was the Committee on Odinist Social Concerns (COSC), which proposed to tackle "the lack of ethnic identity among people of Northern European descent and the evils which spring from this lack of basic tribalism—the loss of our culture, the defamation of our history, and reverse discrimination (called 'affirmative action' by the bureaucrats). We believe that Ásatrú is an expression of the soul of our people, and that the future of our ancestral faith is intimately connected with the future of our people as a cultural and biological group" ("Hyperborea," *The Runestone* 31, p. 13). McNallen's often-republished article "Metagenetics" (*The Runestone* 34, pp. 4-6; published in 1980, not 1985 as some sources state) made it clear that spirituality was a function of biological ancestry. For McNallen, Ásatrú was only for people of northern European descent.

The Ásatrú Free Assembly broke up in 1987; the last known issue of *The Runestone* came out in January, and Althing 8 was canceled. The immediate cause of the breakup was the unmanageable workload: McNallen and his wife were regularly spending up to sixty hours a week on AFA work, on top of their day jobs. Attempts to ask the AFA for some compensation for their time were rebuffed (McNallen, *Asatru*, p. 64). An attempt to spin off the AFA's publishing arm into a for-profit business called Nineworlds Publications, which might have generated some income for McNallen (and enabled him to advocate political positions without jeopardizing the AFA's nonprofit status), seems to have gone nowhere ("Editorial," *The Runestone* no. 60, p.

1). There was a final attempt to divide up the AFA workload among a committee of core members calling themselves the Southern Heathen Leadership Conference (a spoof of the Southern Christian Leadership Conference, the civil rights organization led by Dr. Martin Luther King Jr.) This was not enough to save the AFA (Kaplan, "Reconstruction," pp. 204-205). By November 1987, McNallen made it known that he was retiring the name "Ásatrú Free Assembly" and did not wish to be contacted (Edred Thorsson, *History of the Rune-Gild*, p. 111).

There had always been a fault line under the surface of the AFA: tension between members who were primarily interested in Norse culture and religion, and members with a white nationalist or even neo-Nazi political agenda. Although McNallen himself has denied that this tension was the cause of the breakup, the effort to manage it had clearly taken its toll. McNallen later reminisced that "people sniped at us because we weren't racial enough—or because we were TOO racial!" (Ward, "A Founding Father," p. 20)

McNallen had long attacked Nazis as just another variety of collectivist, the antithesis of the freedom-loving Vikings (e.g. *The Runestone*, vol. 3, no. 1, 1974, pp. 8-10). In 1979, he had denounced a San Francisco neo-Nazi group that was holding meetings under the name of "The Odinist Society," insisting that "our movement does *not* consider itself allied with National Socialism." He added, however, that "We realize and sympathise with the legitimate frustrations of white men who are concerned for their kind and their culture. These concerns are fully justified. It is a tragedy that these men are driven to radical groups such as the NSWWP simply because there is no well-known, responsible organization working for white ethnic awareness and identity" (*The Runestone* 25, 1979, pp. 13-14). There was an inherent contradiction here. The AFA was trying to assert that it was not based on racist fear and hatred. At the same time, it was stoking fear that traditionalist northern Europeans were in imminent danger of extinction, with activist Ásatrú as their only salvation from genocide—a fear that tended to fuel the very racism that the AFA claimed it was opposing.

McNallen's rant in the Fall 1975 issue of *The Runestone* ("Editorially Speaking," vol. 4, no. 1, pp. 9-10) is typical of his political writing around this time. Minus the Heathen deities, it reads like the more excitable writings being put out by the John Birch Society or the Worldwide Church of God at the time:

> We are tottering on the edge of catastrophe, on the very brink of disaster and so very few people give a damn. The gay revolution has become more or less accepted. The family as a viable unit has been crippled. Drug usage has become an integral part of our society. Bureaucracy grows; freedom shrinks. The domains of our culture are whittled away and our enemies stand on the ancient breeding grounds of our peoples. On every front, we're taking a licking. . . .
>
> Dammit! Unless something is done, we as a culture have had it! Nature doesn't forgive losers, she allows their enemies to kill them. If we are to survive, we must fight tooth and nail, without hesitations or half measures. Thinking about it won't help. Talking about it does little. I for one am sick and tired of the weakness and indecision which has so far characterized our efforts. What have you done for your beliefs lately? We need fighters! There's a hell of a lot to be done! . . . .
>
> We do not have forever. In fact, we may have very little time at all. Indications are that we are in a crucial stage where we stand to lose all if we do not fight. Perhaps, allegorically (or not so allegorically!) Ragnarok is at hand. Those of us who are loyal to Odin, Thor, and Frey see our duty and will not submit to the forces of the enemy who surrounds us.

One example of the fine line that the AFA had been trying to walk: A correspondent in *The Runestone* 39 (Spring 1982), who had attended the 1981 Yule gathering, complained that "perhaps half, or perhaps less, of the crowd were card carrying members of the KKK or the American Nazis," and raised the question "is Odinism a religion of hate?. . . Is there room for the politics of hate in Ásatrú?" (pp. 17-18). McNallen assured the letter-writer that "not more than a couple" of those at the gathering were Klansmen or Nazis, and avowed that "Odinism does not and will not preach hatred of other races" (pp. 18-19). This might have been more convincing if an ad for *The Turner Diaries* had not appeared on the inside back cover of the very same issue. The AFA was attempting to have its mead and drink it too, as it were. Yet for some, McNallen's attempts at moderation weren't enough. Several outright white supremacists and neo-Nazis who left the AFA at

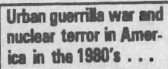

Ad for *The Turner Diaries,* as it appeared in *The Runestone* no. 39 (Spring 1982) and in several other issues around that time.

this time went on to found openly racist Odinist organizations (Goodrick-Clarke, *Black Sun*, pp. 262-269; Gardell, *Gods of the Blood*, pp. 177-178, 182-183).[44]

In the wake of the collapse of the AFA, Mike "Valgard" Murray of the Arizona Kindred founded the Ásatrú Alliance in 1986, a loosely-organized group of member kindreds. Inheriting the resources of the defunct AFA, the A.A. expanded its journal, *Vor Trú* ("Our Faith"), which the Arizona Kindred had begun publishing in 1977. The A.A. also took responsibility for the annual Althings. Unlike the AFA (and the Troth), the A.A. was and still is an alliance of kindreds; individuals cannot become members of the A.A. directly, but must join an A.A. affiliated kindred. Murray himself had a rather interesting past: he had been involved with the American Nazi Party in the 1960s, before joining Else Christensen's Odinist Fellowship and eventually serving as its vice president (Kaplan, *Radical Religion*, p. 20). He had also been a spokesman for the outlaw motorcycle gang Iron Cross MC—which had a history of issuing statements like "The Iron Cross is comprised of WHITE fighters who have the courage of our ancient Teutonic and Viking ancestors—Men who will not permit degeneration in any form of our White race or culture by any scum sucking filth. . . . WE, MEN OF THE IRON CROSS, shall lead our White brothers

---

44. First published in 1978, *The Turner Diaries* describes a violent race war between the US government and a white supremacist group called The Organization, culminating in the creation of a whites-only state armed with nuclear weapons, which carries out national and then global genocide of all non-whites, Jews, and liberals. Written under a pseudonym by William Luther Pierce, leader of the neo-Nazi National Alliance, the book inspired David Lane's terrorist group The Order, the 1995 Oklahoma City bombers, and several less famous criminals.

to final, brutal and blood-soaked victory!" (Carpenter, "A Warning"; see also Turner, *Power on the Right*, p. 93). However, the A.A. mostly dodged the controversy that had bedeviled the AFA by stating that members were free to adopt any political position that they chose, but the organization itself would not take political stands (Kaplan, pp. 20-21). There was still friction between racist and antiracist contingents in the A.A., notably at Althing 9 in 1989 (Kaplan, pp. 87-91). By 1995, the A.A. had written into their by-laws the declaration that "Ásatrú is the ethnic religion of the indigenous Northern European peoples."

Garman Lord and Theodish Belief

A movement that would have a powerful impact on Heathenry in the US, far out of proportion to its size, was Theodish Belief.[45] Unlike the AFA, which had concentrated on the Viking Age, Theodish Belief was originally focused on Anglo-Saxon lore, beliefs, and social structures. Theodish Belief aimed to use ancient texts and modern scholarship to reconstruct not merely the basics of pre-Christian religious practice, but a "retro-heathen" mindset explicitly based on life and thought in pre-Christian tribal societies. Theodish groups developed the concept of *thew*—customary norms of behavior within a society, encompassing everything from moral premises and religious mandates to table manners. They tried to create modern equivalents of the social structures of the ancient tribes from which they drew inspiration, with a system of ranks (*arrungs*) held together by *hold-oaths* between people of different ranks. Rather controversially, this included the rank of *thrall* ("slave") for provisional members—who could earn their freedom and rise through the ranks, once they had proven that they truly understood thew.

Thomas Germain began his religious career in Watertown, New York, practicing Wicca in the Algard tradition under the craft name of Merlin Solomon. He founded an advisory committee called the Witan (OE "council of advisors"), which morphed into the American Society for Astro-Psychical Research (or Amerisyche for short), which in its turn came to sponsor a Wiccan coven, the Coven Witan (Holzer, *Witches*, pp. 149-150; McQueen, *A Short History*, pp. 7-9). After both Amerisyche and the Coven Witan had broken up, Merlin invoked and was visited by the deities Woden and

---

45. From Old English *þeodisc*, "of the tribe; of the people."

Classified ad for Amerisyche
in *Fate* magazine, March 1973

Frige, on July 4, 1976. He soon reformed the coven as the Witan Theod (from OE *þēod*, "tribe; nation"), adopting the new name of Garman Lord. Shortly thereafter, Ealdoræd Lord (then known as Sægæst) founded the Moody Hill Theod. After a period of inactivity, the Witan Theod resumed its work, gradually replacing most of its Wiccan traditions with research into historic Anglo-Saxon religious practices. In 1989, both theods formed an "umbrella" organization called the Winland Ríce[46] (realm) of Theodish Belief, with Garman Lord as its Æþeling. Garman's group within the Ríce came to be known as Gering Theod.[47] Moody Hill Theod left the Ríce in 1992, but Theodish Belief continued to grow, and in 1993 established its first offshoot, Wednesbury Leod[48] in Missouri, led by the twin brothers Berry and Terry Canote, better known as Swain and Eric Wodening (McQueen, pp. 11-18; Wodening, *Þéodisc Geléafa*, pp. 21-24). Garman Lord was raised on a shield, a ritual by which he assumed the office of sacral king, at Midsummer of 1995, the first Cyning (king) in modern Theodish history.

One of Garman Lord's earliest associates, Gert McQueen, went on to serve as an Elder and Redesman of the Troth, writing prolifically for the Troth's journal *Idunna*. She was also successful in lobbying the U.S. Army Chaplain's Corps to adopt guidelines for recognizing Heathenry in general and Theodish Belief in particular. The Wodening brothers also wrote prolifically for *Idunna* until Garman and Gerd began their own small publishing venture, Theod Press, which published their writings among many other books, booklets, and cassettes. A skilled graphic designer, Garman had published the journal *Vikingstaff* in the early 1980s; as Theodish Belief developed, he began to publish *Theod* magazine. Garman's book *The Way of the Heathen* outlined how to practice Theodish Belief without being part of a tribe in the Winland Ríce. Unfortunately, power struggles within the Troth

---

46. Pronounced with two syllables, like "ree-cheh," not like the word "rice."
47. *Gering* literally means "offspring of the year" or "offspring of the harvest" (from *ger*, "year, harvest," also the name of the Anglo-Saxon rune ᛡ). It was often translated as "Sprout of the Sprout."
48. From Old English *leōd*, "people."

contributed to the Winland Ríce ending formal ties with the Troth in 1995 (Wodening, *Þéodisc Geléafa*, p. 25).

Although it began with an Anglo-Saxon Heathen focus, Theodish Belief was never meant to be restricted to the ways of the Angles and Saxons in Britain. One Wiccan feature that was retained in Theodish Belief was the custom of lineage: "High Theodism" refers to those Theodish groups that began as fosterages within the Winland Ríce. Many of them focused on the ways of continental Germanic tribes. The Fresena Rike, led by Gerd Groenewold, was founded in 1994 and revived in 2005 as the Axenthof Thiad; it focused on Frisian thew. The Normannii Thiud was formed in 1997 by Dan Halloran, and Folcaha Thiod (later the Sahsisk Thiod), led by Êrmund Ethiling Lilley, came into fosterage in July 2002, focusing on the continental Saxons. The Guta Kuni (Gothic Kin) was founded by Ælfric Thegn in 2001, as a Hall within the Winland Ríce; and in February 2004, the Œðelland Cynn of the Jutes was formed by Daniel Flores and Rich Culver in Texas. The Theods that descend from fosterage by the Winland Ríce/ Gering Theod, or by one of its fostered groups, are collectively referred to as "High Theodish" (Wodening, *Þéodisc Geléafa*, pp. 25-28). Several "Greater Theodish" groups also appeared; these did not begin by fosterage under the Winland Ríce, but were inspired by Garman Lord's book *Way of the Heathen*, which expounds on the philosophy of Theodism. The books of Swain Wodening, notably *Hammer of the Gods*, were also influential in spreading information about Anglo-Saxon Heathen traditions as they might be practiced today. Still other groups were founded that were not Theodish at all, but nonetheless focused on Anglo-Saxon or continental German Heathenry. The Irminen Gesellschaft, promoting a specifically German variety of Heathenry, drew a great deal of its principles from Theodish Belief.

After some controversy within the Theodish community in 1996, Swain Wodening and Winifred Hodge left the Winland Ríce to establish a more democratic alternative, Þæt Angelseaxisce Ealdriht ("The Anglo-Saxon Ancient Rights"). The Ealdriht was the largest Anglo-Saxon-focused organization in the Heathen community, until it was dissolved in November 2004 to facilitate the growth of regional tribal communities, most notably the Miercinga Ríce, centered in Texas and the Midwest, and the Néoweanglia Þéod under Brian Smith, which spanned the Northeast (Wodening, *Þéodisc Geléafa*, pp. 28-29). In June 2006, Swain Wodening stepped down as Æþeling of the Miercinga Ríce; his wife Teresa became the Miercinga Ríce's Æþelinga, the first woman to lead a Theod.

At this writing, organized Theodish Belief still exists, but it has withdrawn somewhat from an active role in the wider Heathen community. Garman Lord stepped down from kingship in 2005, although the Winland Ríce resumed public activity in 2019. Dan Halloran, leader of the Normannii Thiud within the Ríce, was elected a New York City Councilman in 2009, the highest-ranking elected official from the Heathen community (as of this writing). However, he was arrested for allegedly taking bribes in 2013, convicted in 2014, and as of 2020 is serving a term in Federal prison (Vega, "10 Years in Prison"). Unfortunately, Theodish Belief received a lot of negative press upon his election, and again on his conviction—especially when pictures surfaced of Halloran wearing regalia and carrying out rituals, which looked bizarre to outsiders (e.g. Thrasher, "America's Top Heathen"). His conviction splintered the Normannii Thiud, which had been one of the largest and most active Theods. Some of the other older groups have dissolved or gone inactive—although others carry on, such as Hwítmersc or White Marsh Theod, and the Ealdríce Théodish Fellowship.

Nonetheless, Theodish Belief had an impact on American Heathenry far out of proportion to its numbers. Theodish Belief spread the awareness that Heathenry did not have to be limited to the Vikings—there was much gold to be mined from the lore and folklore of the Germanic-speaking peoples of continental Germany and England. These ancient ways were not simply Norse religion with slightly different god-names; they could be rebuilt and followed as traditions within greater Heathendom. Theodsmen set high standards for scholarship, some going so far as to compose poems and songs in ancient languages such as Gothic, Old English, and Old Frisian. Theodish Belief also had an immense impact on general Heathen ethics and behavior, especially as expressed in ritual. Its attempt to create a true "retro-Heathenry" that would reconstruct not just the outer forms of the ancient religion, but the mentality of the tribal society that practiced it, may seem quixotic, perhaps impossible, and arguably not all that desirable. Nonetheless, it inspired many Heathens to do some serious thinking about the metaphysics behind their practices. Many Heathen groups today, some of which have never identified as Theodish at all, draw on values, ethics, theology, and practices that ultimately originated in Theodish practice.

Sveinbjörn Beinteinsson and the Ásatrúarfélagið

The single most import-
ant founder of modern Ásatrú in
Iceland was the poet and farmer
Sveinbjörn Beinteinsson (1924–
1993). Sveinbjörn was very much
an Icelandic traditionalist: he lived
on a farm with no electricity, he
refused to drive a car or adopt most
farming machinery, and he was
both a masterful poet in his own
right and an expert on traditional
Icelandic poetry, notably the long
ballad-like poems known as *rímur*.
Although considered somewhat
eccentric, he was respected for his
lifestyle and his poetry—even re-
citing it at rock concerts, as seen
in the 1982 documentary *Rokk í
Reykjavík*. He strongly believed
in the land-spirits of Iceland, the
huldufolk, and felt their presence
all around him (Strmiska and Sigrvinsson, "Asatru," pp. 166-167;
Jónina K. Berg, "Sveinbjörn Bein-

Sveinbjörn Beinteinsson, founding
Allsherjargoði of the Ásatrúarfélagið. Photo
by Jónina K. Berg, Wikimedia Commons.

teinsson," pp. 263-268). In the winter of 1971, Sveinbjörn met with the
writer Dagur Þorleifsson and the actor and clothing store owner Jörmundur
Ingi Hansen, and decided to form a society to renew Icelandic paganism.
The Ásatrúarfélagið (Ásatrú Fellowship) began to take shape at a meeting
on April 20, 1972, with Sveinbjörn named as the first *Allsherjargoði* (chief
priest). On the summer solstice that year, the group held its first blót, at
Sveinbjörn's farm at Dragháls.

It's worth noting that Icelandic Ásatrú developed under very different
social conditions from American Ásatrú. In Iceland, the Eddas and sagas

were and are honored cultural treasures and a source of national pride.[49] Icelandic Ásatrú was not a matter of rediscovering a suppressed and nearly forgotten cultural heritage, but reviving the spiritual dimension of a cherished cultural heritage. Icelandic Ásatrú also evolved in a far more ethnically and culturally homogeneous society than American Ásatrú did. The tensions over ethnicity and race that were obvious from the early days of the AFA were not nearly as strong in Icelandic Ásatrú (Strmiska and Sigrvinsson, "Asatru," pp. 163-164).

The challenge that the Ásatrúarfélagið had to meet was state recognition. Unlike the United States, Iceland has an officially state-supported church, the Evangelical Lutheran Church of Iceland. While freedom of religion is guaranteed in the Icelandic constitution, the Lutheran Church was and still is supported by government funding, including a "tax for the congregation" (*sóknargjald*). The Ásatrúarfélagið sought official state recognition in Iceland, which would have entitled it to a share of the *sóknargjald*. Despite opposition from the Church, the Ásatrúarfélagið won recognition in May 1973, allowing it to perform legally binding ceremonies and collect a share of tax revenues. (After Sveinbjörn was dismissed by the Ministry of Religion after the first attempt to gain recognition, in December 1972, lightning struck nearby and knocked out the Ministry's electricity. Hail Thor! See Jónina K. Berg, "Sveinbjörn Beinteinsson," pp. 269-271.)

The Ásatrúarfélagið grew slowly during Sveinbjörn's time as Allsherjargoði, but began expanding under the leadership of Jörmundur Ingi Hansen after Sveinbjörn's death. Jörmundur was much better at dealing with the media, but his leadership was called into question, and he stepped down in 2002. He was first replaced by Jónina Kristin Berg as interim Allsherjargoði, and then in 2003 by noted composer Hilmar Örn Hilmarsson, who has led the Ásatrúarfélagið to the present day. Ironically, the Ásatrúarfélagið received a boost from the celebration of the 1000-year anniversary of Christianity in Iceland, which was held at Thingvellir at the same time that the Ásatrúarfélagið was holding its annual Þingið festival at the same place.

---

49. After years of debates and negotiations, in 1961 the Danish government agreed to return important Icelandic manuscripts to Iceland. The first two manuscripts, the *Codex Regius* and *Flateyjarbók*, arrived on a Danish Navy frigate, on April 21, 1971. Fifteen thousand people crowded Reykjavík harbor to witness the return, and almost everyone else in the country watched the event on television or listened to it on the radio. See Greenfield, *The Return of Cultural Treasures*, pp. 1-4, 10-46.

Denied the use of facilities built for the Christian celebration at Thingvellir, the Ásatrúarfélagið won a surprising amount of public sympathy, while the church looked mean-spirited (Strmiska and Sigrvinsson, "Asatru," pp. 167-173).

As of 2019, the Ásatrúarfélagið is the largest non-Christian religion in Iceland, with over 4000 members (out of a population of about 300,000), the. It acquired a burial ground in 1999, and at this writing, a temple is being constructed on Öskjuhlíð, a wooded hill inside Reykjavík. After various delays, construction is projected to be completed by the end of 2020.

The Growth of European Ásatrú

In mainland Europe, there were people trying to form Germanic pagan groups as early as the 1970s. Some of them were "foreign correspondents" for *The Runestone*; a woman named Helge Möller, for example, wrote that "I don't think there is much serious pagan activity going on here in Denmark or other parts of Scandinavia for that matter. . . . sorry to say no contact from the people I was looking for, the serious pagans of the Norse tradition. I'm sure they are out there somewhere, they must be." (*Runestone* #25, Fall 1978, p. 17) In Switzerland, a man named Jean-François Moyer lamented having to cease publishing his newsletter *Skuld* after four issues, because he felt that European Odinists "use it as a camouflage for political activities and make with it a substitute for the religion or a pseudo-spirituality." (*Runestone* #28, Summer 1979, p. 14)

It was not until the 1990s that organized national groups appeared in most Scandinavian countries—inspired to some degree by Iceland's Ásatrúarfélagið, but drawing on their own national traditions and folklore as well. Scandinavian groups that emphasize their national folk customs often identify not as Ásatrú, but as *Forn Sed* (in Swedish and Norwegian) or *Forn Siðr* (ON). This phrase, meaning "old customs" or "old way," is the term that is actually used in the sagas for the pre-Christian religion.

In Sweden, small groups appeared as early as 1975, but most disbanded or have left public view. Currently, the largest group in Sweden was founded in 1994 as the Sveriges Asatrosamfund (Swedish Asatru Assembly). After a period of reorganization in the early 2000s, the SAS grew steadily, gaining state recognition as a religious organization in 2007; in 2010 it changed its name to Samfundet Forn Sed Sverige (The Swedish Assembly for the Old Way). In 1996, Samfälligheten för Nordisk Sed (SNS; Community for the Nordic Way) formed as an association of kindreds, focusing more on Swedish national traditions (Gregorius, "Modern Heathenism in Sweden," pp. 64-71). Forn Siðr was founded in Denmark in 1999, and was recognized as an official religious organization by the Danish government in 2003, serving as an umbrella organization for local groups. A breakaway Danish group, Nordisk Tingsfællig (NTF), formed in 2010 with a more apolitical stance and a desire to create new forms of ritual (Amster, "It's Not Easy Being Apolitical," pp. 43-45). In Norway, a few small groups appeared and disappeared before Bifrost (later Åsatrufelleskapet Bifrost) was formally recognized by the Norwegian government in 1996, also as an "umbrella" organization for local groups. In 1998, Foreningen Forn Sed split from Bifrost. Norwegian Heathenry has had a lot to cope with; Bifrost was organizing right as Norway was gripped by its own version of the "Satanic Panic." It didn't help that the Norwegian black metal music scene embraced both Viking and Satanic imagery; Varg Vikernes of the band Mayhem had gained considerable notoriety by burning down historic churches, and then by murdering his bandmate Euronymous in 1993. To top it all off, in 1999, Vigrid was founded as a blatantly neo-Nazi organization that uses Norse myths and symbols; the group has been linked to violent acts. Åsatrufelleskapet Bifrost has tried to counter the bad publicity generated by groups like these, taking an explicitly antiracist stance (Asprem, "Heathens Up North," pp. 45-67).

In Britain, the Odinic Rite and Odinist Fellowship take no official political positions, but the membership of both groups tends to fall on the far right end of the spectrum. A third right-wing group, Woden's Folk, draws heavily on English (as opposed to Norse) cultural identity, inspiration from Wotansvolk in the US, and its founder's own personal vision, which allegedly bears a striking resemblance to BBC television programs from the 1980s. All three espouse folkish ideology, in which only those of northern European ancestry are capable of connecting with the old gods (White, "Northern Gods for Northern Folk," pp. 250-266). But there have been non-folkish groups in Britain ever since Pete Jennings founded Odinshof in 1985. Mike Robertson founded the Kith of Yggdrasil in 2002. More recently, the Facebook group Asatru UK began holding real-world meetups in 2013. As of 2019, Asatru UK is the largest inclusive Heathen group in the UK, and holds an annual meeting in York as well as other meetings elsewhere. The Kith of the Tree and Well, led by Philip Parkyn (who has also served for years as the Troth Steward for the UK), was founded in 2016.

In May 1983, Elisabeth Hooy-Schuur, a Dutch-born woman living in London who had been initiated into Gardnerian Wicca in 1980, had a personal crisis of faith and called on Odin. Receiving a powerful answer, she devoted herself entirely to him, took the name Freya Aswynn, and founded a temple. (Tanya Lurhmann's book *Persuasions of the Witch's Craft* depicts her at this time, easily recognizable under a pseudonym; see pp. 22-27, 329.) In 1986 she became Drightine of the Rune-Gild UK, stepping down in 1992 in the aftermath of the scandal over Edred Thorsson's Setian affiliation (see below). She went on to start an English affiliate to the Ring of Troth, the Ring of Troth UK (later the Ring of Troth Europe), which lasted until 2011. Her book *Leaves of Yggdrasil*, later reprinted as *Northern Mysteries and Magic*, has been a strong influence on the development of rune esoterica in modern Heathenry.

The formation of groups in Germany was a bit more fraught, because of the association in the minds of many between pagan religion and the Nazis. One of the first was a refounded Armanen-Orden, founded by Adolf and Sigrun Schiepfer, who had both been active in right-wing nationalist politics. In 1990, Sigrun founded ANSE, the *Arbeitsgemeinschaft Naturreligiöser Stammesverbände Europas* (Working Group of Nature-Religion Tribal Associations of Europe) as a networking group and "umbrella organization" for ethnicist neopaganism. One of the first attempts to found a Heathen group free of the taint of the past came in the autumn of 1982, when Géza von Neményi started gathering a group in West Berlin, which already had an active occult community. His group came to be called the Heidnische Gemeinschaft, and von Neményi went out of his way to disavow any support for racism, Nazi ideology, or extremism. In 1991, von Neményi refounded the Germanische Glaubensgemeinschaft (GGG), winning the legal right to use their name (Hegner, "Hot, Strange, Völkisch, Cosmopolitan," pp. 178-183; Schnurbein, *Norse Revival*, pp. 55-56). The Eldaring was founded in Germany in 2000 as a partner of the Troth; it is now an independent organization, but continues to uphold an inclusive vision for Heathenry. Other German inclusive organizations include the Asatru Ring Midgard, founded in 2004 by Michaela Macha and Michael Schütz, and Nornirs Ætt, founded in 2005. Rabenclan, founded in 1994, has served as an umbrella organization for anti-fascist pagans of all sorts (Gründer, "Neo-Pagan Traditions," pp. 269-270).

More and more countries are seeing the formation of Heathen groups. European non-folkish groups that have grown in the past twenty years or so include Het Rad (The Wheel) and De Negen Werelden (The Nine Worlds) in the Netherlands, Asatru Schweiz in Switzerland, and Asatru Ibérica in Spain. Every three years beginning in 2009, European groups have held the triennial International Asatru Summer Camp (IASC) for mutual collaboration, learning, and fun. In October 2017, the Troth co-sponsored the first Frith Forge meeting (which we hope will be the first in a long series of meetings), in partnership with the Verein für Germanisches Heidentum and joined by inclusive Heathen groups from Spain and Switzerland as well (Leigh-Hawkins, "Frith Forge," pp. 15-17). There is growing interest in Heathenry in Brazil at this writing, and the Troth has also worked with a thriving kindred in Costa Rica (Clare, "Jörð's Folk," *Idunna* #87, pp. 30-32).

A Tradition Takes Shape

The Forging of the Ring of Troth

One invited guest at the first AFA Althing in 1979 was Stephen E. Flowers, better known in Heathen circles as Edred Thorsson. A graduate student at the University of Texas at Austin, Thorsson had joined the AFA in 1978 and founded the Austin Kindred. At the Althing, he presented workshops on runic esoterica and received initiation as a goði. He and Mitchell Edwin Wade—a close colleague in Thorsson's religious and magical work, who unfortunately died in 1989—began developing a cycle of seasonal rituals, which would eventually be published in *A Book of Troth*. (Thorsson, *History of the Rune-Gild*, pp. 104-108) In 1980, he founded the Rune-Gild as an initiatory order for those dedicated to the study of runic magic. Initially, it had an "outer court," the Institute of Runic Studies, Ásatrú (IRSA), to teach the more "mundane" aspects of runes and prepare students for more esoteric studies (*The Runestone*, vol. 34, pp. 10-11, 15; Chisholm, "The Awakening of a Runemaster," pp. 84-86; Thorsson, *History of the Rune-Gild*, pp. 20-22, 198). Flowers received his MA in 1980, with a thesis on rebirth in the legend of Sigurd the Volsung; and his PhD in Germanic Studies in 1984 with a thesis called *Runes and Magic*, under the supervision of noted scholar Dr. Edgar Polomé. He taught for several years as a lecturer in the Departments of English and Germanic Languages at the University of Texas. Unfortunately, he was unable to gain a permanent academic position, and his lectureship at UT ended in 1989, although he taught at Austin Community College for ten more years.

The collapse of the AFA left a vacuum; no other national organization in the US was able to advocate for Ásatrú. One of its few potential rivals had been the agnostic and ethnocentric Runic Society, founded in 1974 by N. J. Templin of Milwaukee, whose primary activity was demanding that Denmark turn Greenland over to the Society to be an Odinist homeland.[50] Clearly this was a non-starter, and the Runic Society had folded around 1980, its dream of owning Greenland forever unfulfilled.

Feeling that someone had to pick up the fallen Raven Banner, Edred Thorsson and James Chisholm formally founded the Ring of Troth in a magical working on December 20, 1987, in Austin, Texas. The Ring of Troth was founded to be a non-racist organization dedicated to the promotion of the religion and culture of the Germanic peoples. Furthermore, the AFA had always been Stephen McNallen's "baby," and it had fallen apart when he stepped down. Mindful of the AFA's fate, Edred intended that the Ring of Troth should not "belong to" any single leader (*History of the Rune-Gild*, p. 118). The name was deliberately chosen to have the initials RoT. While critics of the organization have been known to point out that this spells "rot," what Edred had in mind was the Norse word *rót*, meaning "root": the roots of new growth for the old ways (Thorson, p. 126).

James Chisholm was the first Steersman of the Ring of Troth, and Edred Thorsson served as the first Drighten (an advisory, "elder statesman" role) and Warder of the Lore. The first issue of the Troth's new journal, *Idunna*, came out in early 1988. The founders were soon joined by Dianne Luark Ross, whose tireless work as the fledgling organization's secretary and publisher kept the organization alive. Those who were there have called her

---

50. When Queen Margrethe of Denmark toured the midwestern US in 1976, Templin harassed her with demands for Greenland until he was banned by her security detail. He was later quoted as saying "We're not one of those off the wall nutty organizations" (Kuyper, "Runic Society," p. 5).

"the Wendy to our Lost Boys" and "the heart and soul" of the early Ring of Troth, and in 1990 she was recognized as the Ring's Woman of the Year—an honor rarely given (Thorsson, "Drighten's Rede," p. 40; see also Thorsson, *History of the Rune-Gild*, p. 115; Lüsch-Schreiwer, "At the Tiller," pp. 1-3). They were also soon joined by a young Dallas resident, Stephan Grundy, better known in Heathen circles as Kveldúlfr Gundarsson. Thorsson's *A Book of Troth,* outlining his vision for the Ring of Troth and presenting basic lore and rituals, was published by Llewellyn in 1989—the first book from a commercial publisher to put forth Ásatrú as a living tradition (Thorsson, *History of the Rune-Gild*, pp. 111-114). In August 1991, Dianne turned *Idunna* over to Þórfinn Einarsson (Ed Van Cura), whose desktop publishing skills gave the journal a fresh new look; he was recognized as Man of the Year in March 1992.

The original organizational plan for the Ring of Troth, as laid out in Edred Thorson's *A Book of Troth*, was different from what it would later become. The members of the organization's governing body, originally called the Ring of High Rede, were appointed to nine-year terms. Elders (licensed clergy) were expected to have university degrees in Heathen-relevant fields (*A Book of Troth*, pp. 208-209). The expectation was that the Troth would build a cadre of highly trained clergy, who could set up temples (hofs) supported by donations, and work full-time as teachers, ritual leaders, and local administrators, much like the role of ordained clergy in mainstream Christian denominations (pp. 204-205). Edred envisioned that "there will arise a great and learned troop of wise and true folk, who will go forth into the world to rebuild that which has been lost" (p. 122). While this may be an admirable goal, in practice it was never feasible; there are few, if any, places in the US where Heathens are concentrated enough to support a full-time Elder from their collective resources. The Austin kindred did attempt to establish hofs in the area; unfortunately, they proved unsustainable (Thorsson, "Holy Steads," pp. 1-2; *History of the Rune-Gild*, pp. 118-119; Chisholm, "From Hearth to Hof," p. 41; "From the Helm," *Idunna* #12, p. 1).

As the organization grew beyond the small kindred in Austin, it was buffeted by several scandals. Edred Thorsson had briefly been a member of Anton LaVey's Church of Satan, and at the time, he and James Chisholm were members of the Temple of Set, a theistic Satanist organization founded by Michael Aquino, which had broken away from the Church of Satan.

This might not raise eyebrows today, and it was not even especially theologically strange: Setians don't worship Set, but revere him as a giver of intellect, inquiry, and enlightenment, and as such, he might be said to resemble Odin the eternal seeker and teacher of wisdom. But there had long been an anti-Satanic strain in American Ásatrú. Articles in *The Runestone*, for example, had denounced Satanism as nothing but an aberrant variety of Christianity, unacceptable to any self-respecting Ásatrúari (*The Runestone* 25, pp. 5-8; 26, pp. 10-13). Furthermore, the United States was gripped by the "Satanic Panic" in the late 1980s. Satanists were said to be recruiting innocent teenagers, planting backwards messages in rock music and occult rituals in Dungeons & Dragons™. Self-proclaimed "occult experts" were reaching an eager audience, and making a lot of money, by "exposing" alleged "Satanic cults" that ritually abused and murdered children. Michael Aquino's home was raided by the San Francisco Police Department in 1987 on suspicion of child sexual abuse, although in the end no charges were filed (Gardell, *Gods of the Blood*, p. 390 n20).

A former member of the Ring of Troth, Rob Meek (Ingvar Solve Ingvisson), who had briefly served as the Troth's Reeve (secretary; see "Announcements," *Idunna* #4, p. 35), found out about Thorson's Satanic associations. Meek, who was mentally unstable because of an inoperable brain tumor, denounced Thorsson, Chisholm, and the Ring of Troth to everyone he could, alleging that Satanists were trying to take over Ásatrú (Kaplan, *Radical Religion*, pp. 22-25).[51] In response, the Ásatrú Alliance adopted a position statement at Althing 9 in 1989, disavowing "any connection between Ásatrú and the 'prince of darkness' or any other alien deities." The Alliance stated that "In secretly associating himself with satanic organizations, and insinuating satanic teachings into his work, particularly in the Rune Gild, Edred has let us down" (quoted in Kaplan, "Reconstruction of the Ásatrú and Odinist Traditions," p. 218). The Odinic Rite adopted a similar statement: "Undisputably, any form of Setianism or Satanism is utterly alien to the spirit of Odinism and cannot be reconciled to the genuine restoration of the Germanic heathen faith" (*ORBriefing* 86, 21 Fallow 2239 [June 21, 1989]; reprinted in Thorsson, *History of the Rune-Gild*, pp. 224-225).

---

51. Meek was inspired by Geraldo Rivera's widely-watched TV special on Satanism, which aired on October 24, 1988. See Thorsson, *History of the Rune-Gild*, pp. 93-95, 116-121; Chisholm, "From the Helm," *Idunna* #13, p. 3.

The Ring of Troth was badly shaken again when Rob Meek murdered his wife, Anne Harrington, in February 1991. She was a dear friend of many in the Troth, as well as editor of the independent journal *Northways*. Her death was deeply mourned, and it cast a pall over the Ring of Troth, despite the fact that Meek had left the organization by the time he committed the murder. Under increasing pressure, Chisholm and Thorsson felt the need for new leadership and a fresh start. After several prospects turned down the job, James Chisholm was finally able to turn the Steersmanship over to Prudence Priest at Ostara of 1992. Edred Thorsson stepped down from his offices as Drighten and Warder of the Lore; Kveldúlfr Gundarsson took the office of Warder of the Lore and has remained in office ever since. A full nine-member High Rede was also appointed at this time (Kaplan, *Radical Religion*, pp. 26-29).

During Priest's term as Steerswoman, the Ring of Troth managed to shake off the scandals of its past and build a firmer foundation. By 1993, realizing that it would always be difficult to find people with the full qualifications for Eldership, the Troth adopted a second "rank" of clergy: Godmen or Godwomen could be ordained without the academic qualifications, although they still had to demonstrate an understanding of the lore. This has since become the Troth's primary clergy program: as of 2020, the title of Elder is awarded for long and outstanding service, but does not confer the status of ordained clergy. Also in 1993, Kveldúlfr proposed the creation of the Steward program of appointing regional representatives for outreach and networking ("Regional Organization of the Troth," *Idunna* 19, pp. 24-25), and this was adopted with modifications a year later. Meanwhile, while working on his doctoral dissertation at Cambridge University, Kveldúlfr proposed that the Troth publish a comprehensive book on all aspects of Heathenry, with contributions from as many Heathens as possible. This was *Our Troth*: Kveldúlfr edited the first edition and wrote a great deal of the content.[52] Publication was no easy task, but the heroic efforts of William H. West and Joel Radcliffe got *Our Troth* into print by the end of 1993 (West, "The Intriguing Account," pp. 37-38).

---

52. How he managed to pull this off in less than six months is something we're still trying to figure out. William West says that "Kveldúlfr's world goes on hold" ("The Intriguing Account," p. 37). The editors of the subsequent editions would agree.

A number of important books on runes and Heathen religion found commercial publishers in the early 1990s—most of them by scholars and leaders associated with the Troth. Although the pagan and New Age publisher Llewellyn is sometimes derided in Heathen circles for publishing excessively imaginative books, they did also publish Edred Thorsson's *A Book of Troth* and *Northern Magic*, Freya Aswynn's *Leaves of Yggdrasil* (lat-

The first edition (1993) and second edition (2005-6) of *Our Troth*.

er reissued as *Northern Mysteries and Magic*), and Kveldúlfr Gundarsson's *Teutonic Magic* and *Teutonic Religion*. These were the first books to make information about Ásatrú and Germanic magic available nationwide. In fact, Edred Thorsson briefly worked as a consulting editor for Llewellyn, and was able to get *Leaves of Yggdrasil* and *Teutonic Magic* published. Unfortunately, he found Llewellyn's corporate culture less than congenial, and was unable to counter the tide of poorly researched but popular mass-market books, which he now refers to as "occultizoid nincompoopery" (*History of the Rune-Gild*, pp. 39-51). Partly in response to this lack of understanding from the "establishment," Heathen authors began to publish through their own private presses, creating books and booklets that had a strong influence within the Heathen community, if not much recognition outside of it. Eric Wodening's *We Are Our Deeds* and Garman Lord's *The Way of the Heathen* were highlights of a sizable line of books and booklets from Theod Press, while Edred's Rúna-Raven Press published a number of works on religion, runes and esoterica by Edred, James Chisholm, and others.

At the same time, interest in another area of Norse magic, *seiðr*, was also growing. *Seiðr* is repeatedly described in the Norse sagas as a magical practice that can be used to foresee future events or affect other people's perceptions. The original tradition was lost centuries ago, but a number of individuals have tried to rebuild it based on descriptions in the sagas. The best-known is probably Diana L. Paxson, who was initially inspired by a visionary experience at a "core shamanism" workshop led by Michael Harner in August 1987. (Diana tells the story herself in her books *Trance-Portation*, pp. 95-96; and *Odin*, pp. xix-xxiii). Paxson soon moved beyond Harner's method to explore the primary Norse sources. She began developing the practice of oracular seiðr with her kindred Hrafnar and the working group Seiðhjallr, and continues to teach it in workshops throughout the U.S. and in Europe.[53] Oracular seiðr has now become an accepted aspect of Heathen practice, and several active groups of seiðr workers around the world are developing their own traditions.

By the mid-nineties, the Ring of Troth had grown to over three hundred members, who were increasingly interested in shaping the organization's future. Branches of the Ring of Troth had formed in Europe (now defunct) and Australia (which evolved into the independent Assembly of the Elder Troth). As early as 1992, Grendel Grettison (Al Billings) set up the first e-mail list for the Troth, known as "Trothline" ("Electronic Communications," p. 37). However, there were differences of opinion as to how the organization should be governed, and conflicts were growing between the Steerswoman Prudence Priest and other factions in the Troth. Þórfinn Einarson stepped down as *Idunna* editor in June 1994, after issue #23. Will West, who had published *Our Troth*, became the next editor, but he departed after two issues, and for a time there was no steady editor; a series of editors were appointed and then left or were dismissed. Accounts of what was happening at this time have something of a "he-said-she-said" air; suffice it to say that conflicts between strong-willed personalities were making it increasingly difficult to keep frith, and Priest's leadership style and decisions tended to generate strong reactions, especially among those who wanted a more democratic style of governance. (See Thorsson, *History of the Rune-Gild*, pp. 120-126; Garman Lord, "The Evolution of Theodish Belief"; McQueen, "Gert Remembers.") After the Rede passed a vote of no confidence, Prudence Priest resigned as Steerswoman on March 8, 1995, and went on to form her own organization, the American Vinland Association. On February 14, 1995, Edred Thorsson formally offered to step in and return the Troth to the form that he had originally intended, but he stipulated that the Rede had to vote to accept him unanimously. This did not happen, and Edred formally declared himself separated from the Troth on March 21. From then

---

53. An early version of Hrafnar's seiðr rite as it was done in late 1989 appears in Bainbridge, "A Seiðr Rite," *Idunna* no. 11, pp. 9-13.

on, he would concentrate on work with the Rune-Gild (Thorsson, pp. 230-234). Those who were there refer to this event as "the Glorious Revolution," a nod to the British Revolution of 1688 that saw James II deposed.

The Asatru Folk Assembly

After several years working as a middle school teacher and as a correspondent for *Soldier of Fortune* magazine, Steve McNallen "came out of retirement" and rebuilt the AFA in 1994. McNallen has claimed that he returned because "a corrupt faction was making inroads into the Germanic religious movement. . . which denied the innate connection of Germanic religion and Germanic people, saying in effect that ancestral heritage did not matter. This error could not be allowed to become dominant" (Ásatrú, pp. 65-66). In an interview from 1998, McNallen made it clear that this "corrupt faction" was the Troth (Ward, "Stephen McNallen," p. 21). He was disgusted with "liberals, affirmative-action Asatrúers, black goðar, and New Agers" (quoted in Gardell, *Gods of the Blood*, p. 261)—and the new AFA was now the Asatru *Folk* Assembly. In 1997 the new AFA, the A.A., and the Odinic Rite attempted to confederate in the International Asatru/Odinist Association (IAOA), but this only lasted a few years.

The second AFA is associated with a controversy that seems rather odd in retrospect. In 1996, a nearly complete 8300-year-old human skeleton was unearthed in Washington state, near the town of Kennewick. The skeleton, "Kennewick Man," was claimed by the local Native American tribes as an ancestor of theirs. Under the Native American Graves Protection and Repatriation Act (NAGPRA; 25 USC §3002), the tribes had the right to claim any remains that could be culturally or genetically linked to them, and treat them according to their customs. However, Kennewick Man's physical features did not seem typical of Native Americans, and anthropologists suspected that Kennewick Man might not be related to modern Native Americans, but rather to an unrelated group that had also migrated to North America. If true, this would give the tribes no legal right to the remains. The AFA made headlines when they jumped into the legal battle over custody of the bones, claiming that Kennewick Man was an ancient European and a follower of Ásatrú. Thus the bones rightfully belonged to them, as members of a modern "native European religion"—which could now be shown to be just as indigenous to America as the Native Americans were. In fact, because Kennewick Man showed signs of a violent death, McNallen thought that it might reopen the question of "who genocided who?" (quoted in Gardell, *Gods of the Blood*, p. 150). One could be forgiven for thinking that the whole thing was a publicity stunt; nonetheless, the AFA was allowed to carry out a Norse-style ritual over the bones (Lyke, "Pagans, Tribes, Scientists Battle"). The legal wrangle dragged on for nine years; McNallen later claimed that the Federal government "had white guilt and political correctness on their side; we were identifiably members of that nasty, genocidal, oppressive European race" (*Ásatrú*, p. 67). The AFA did not have enough resources to continue pursuing its case, and for several years it ceased to exist as a membership-based organization, although it maintained a Website.

In April 2005, the AFA resumed soliciting memberships. It has built its own network of clergy, "Folkbuilders," and affiliated kindreds. McNallen stepped down as *Allsherjargoði* in May 2016, turning the reins over to its board of directors, currently led by Matt Flavel. At this writing, he remains a vocal and influential spokesman for folkish Ásatrú. Unfortunately, the rhetoric coming from the AFA has increasingly been openly white nationalist, with considerable overlap between the AFA's messaging and the wider alt-right (Calico, *Being Viking*, pp. 206-211). McNallen remains active on the political right, and has become increasingly less veiled about his ideology. He has publicly endorsed the "Fourteen Words" of David Lane and made it clear that "I will fight for my race, primarily with words and ideas, but I will fight more literally if I have to" ("What Stephen McNallen Really Thinks About Race," *National Vanguard*, March 12, 2017). In a recent podcast (*Midgard Rising*, November 23, 2019, starting at 51:55), he made his position clear:

> *McNallen*: We fight not just for us, we fight not even for our immediate progeny, we fight not even for that civilization that we have built painstakingly over the centuries with all its up and downs and continued forces knocking it this way and that. Ultimately, we are at a point at which we are fighting for the physical existence of our people.
>
> *Interviewer*: Now, when you say "we," and "our people," do you mean white people, the white folk?

McNallen: Yeah. By whatever name. Us. Yeah. Our guys. Our side. It's OK to take our side, you know, as someone has said. Yeah, that's pretty much what I mean.

Interviewer: And do you— how integral do you think the gods are to our success, our native European gods?

McNallen: I think— I think that one of our best hopes of resolving this issue without horrible suffering and strife, or, if this suffering and strife is to come, to at least resolve it victoriously, is to awaken our people spiritually.

A postscript: In 2004, the scientists finally won legal permission to study Kennewick Man. . . . and DNA testing, and more thorough physical measurements, showed that he was, in fact, closely related to the modern Native peoples of the region where he was found. Kennewick Man had never been European at all (Rasmussen et al., "Ancestry and Affiliations"). In 2017, his remains were returned to the Columbia River tribes, who buried them according to their traditions in an undisclosed location.

The Troth Rises Again

Jeffrey Kaplan's 1997 book *Radical Religion in America* concluded a section on the history of the Troth with a pessimistic prediction:

The Troth, wracked by internal dissension and plagued by splits based more on personality than on substance, has begun to unravel. The always contentious email lists by which Troth members communicate has for years been a forum for the most divisive personal invective imaginable. The Troth's journal, *Idunna*, has seen editors brought in and then dismissed for instituting too critical an editorial policy. The Ring of Troth simply shows few signs of stabilizing. . . (p. 30)

The fact that you're reading this shows that Kaplan's prediction did not come true. Membership dropped after the reorganization, but William Bainbridge, the next Steersman, was able to get the Troth stabilized, although *Idunna* was published irregularly for a time. The eventual outcome of the Glorious Revolution was more responsive and representative governance. The Steersman or Steerswoman and most Rede members are now elected to three-year terms. New e-mail lists were established—this time, with moderators who were usually able to keep personal invective off the lists. By the beginning of 1997, Bainbridge was able to turn over *Idunna* publication duties to Diana Paxson "until we have found a volunteer with the requisite calling and abilities to take over as regular Shope" ("At The Tiller," p. 1). Fortunately for us all, Diana's "temporary" appointment has lasted for twenty-three years and ninety-three issues (and counting). With Lorrie Wood's able assistance with the intricacies of desktop publishing software, *Idunna* has increased in quality over time. Diana briefly served as Reckoner (treasurer) in 1998, and *also* served as Steerswoman after Bainbridge's term was over, from 2000 to 2002. After three years of editorial labor, Diana also edited and published the second edition of *Our Troth* as two volumes, in 2006 and 2007. The office of Shope was originally designated to handle all publications, but this became more than one person could easily handle. Ben Waggoner, who had done a large amount of work on the second edition of *Our Troth*, was appointed Shope at Trothmoot 2007, with Diana continuing as *Idunna* publisher, and, since 2008, as Clergy Coordinator.

The Troth in the mid-2000s saw itself as "a resource for heathenry," as Redesman and godman Rod Landreth put it. The Troth tried to pursue a "big-tent" policy in which both folkish and non-folkish members could find something of value. In 2006, the Troth added a Lore Program to give training in the more scholarly and academic aspects of Heathenry, filling part of the role of the dormant Elder program. Although the Troth had had a Steward for prison ministry since the early 2000s, the question of whether the Troth should engage in prison ministry was still sometimes debated; this ended with the establishment of the In-Reach Program in 2013, an attempt to counter the racism and white supremacy prevalent in prison Heathenry (Lüsch-Schreiwer, "The Troth 'In-Reach Program'," p. 32).

But Heathen organizations are not nearly as insulated from the wider society as, perhaps, they might like to think—and social tensions in the "outside world" tend to be mirrored inside organizations. As political polarization increased in American society, so it did within the Troth, and holding the "big tent" together grew increasingly difficult. There were several instances of both folkish and inclusive Heathens storming out of the Troth throughout the 2000s, albeit nothing as dramatic as the Glorious Revolution. Matters came to a head in 2016, when the Ásatrú Folk Assembly stated very clearly on social media that non-European and non-cisgender/heterosexual persons were not welcome in their organization. In response, 180 organizations in 20 different countries (as of this writing) signed Declaration 127—named for verse 127 of the *Hávamál*: *hvars þú bǫl kannt, kveð þú þér bǫlvi at, ok gefat þínum fjándum frið*, "wherever you recognize evil, call it evil, and give no peace to your enemies." Declaration 127 stated that its signers would no longer have anything to do with the AFA; the AFA was free to espouse bigotry, but they were on their own (http://declaration127.com). Groups like Heathens Against Hate and the Alliance for Inclusive Heathenry arose in an effort to counter the bigoted messaging coming from the AFA and their allies.

Independent Kindreds

This history may give the impression that the only important deeds were being done by the national or international organizations. Of course, that's not the whole story at all. The doings of the Troth, the AFA, and the other national groups are easier to trace for a historian, simply because they have produced more records of their existence and make more of them available. But there are hundreds of kindreds today, and perhaps thousands since the 1970s, that never affiliated with a national organization. Many have come and gone without leaving any documentation, aside from the memories of their former members, or perhaps a few yellowing copies of newsletters and meeting minutes that may never find their way to an archive. Yet in their own ways, they have contributed to weaving the wyrd of Heathenry today.

Some independent kindreds have grown large and accomplished much. Just to name a few: Raven Kindred was based in the northeastern US, and later bifurcated as it grew, into Raven Kindred North and Raven Kindred South. Raven Kindred North was one of the first Ásatrú organizations to have a significant WWW presence, and their pages, including the kindred ritual book *Ravenbók*, were an important online resource in the early days of the Web. Raven Kindred North remains one of the kindreds that puts on the annual East Coast Thing every August since 1999, a major gathering that draws attendees from all over the country. Northvegr, based in the Midwest, at one time hosted a huge online library of translated sagas and other texts useful to Heathens. In the 2000s, several regional associations of individuals and kindreds, some affiliated with a national organization and some not, joined together to host regional gatherings, such as Our Meadhall Moot in Missouri and Central States Moot in Oklahoma. Between 2009 and 2015, Jotun's Bane Kindred, based in Kansas City, held an annual regional gathering, Lightning Across The Plains, that drew upwards of 200 Heathens at its peak. Many of these are no longer held, but new kindreds and regional groups continue to sponsor gatherings and other outreach activities.

Several independent kindreds and other organizations, and even some highly motivated individuals, served the growing Heathen community in the 1980s and 1990s by publishing their own newsletters and magazines. Paralleling the self-published magazine ("zine") culture of the time, these ranged from plain photocopies to professional productions. David Bragwin James and Alice Karlsdóttir edited *Boreas*; Anne Hathaway edited *Northways*, as we mentioned; Eagles Reaches Kindred of Houston published *On Wings of Eagles*; and Prudence Priest and her group Freya's Folk (and later the American Vinland Association) began publishing *Yggdrasil* in 1984. In the 1990s Gamlinginn published *Ásatrú Update*; Raven Kindred of Ásatrú published *Ásatrú Today*; Lavrans Reimer-Møller published *Marklander*, which he kept going into the 21st century; and Icelander Þorsteinn Guðjónsson published the English-language Ásatrú journal *Huginn & Muninn*. Winifred Hodge Rose and her organization Frigga's Web published *Lína*. From mid-1991 through the end of 1993, Will von Dauster edited and published a beautifully made glossy

A selection of Heathen journals from the late 1980s and early 1990s.

magazine, *Mountain Thunder*, which he had to shut down when he could not maintain such a high-quality magazine at a low cost. There were others—*Ask & Embla, Berserkrgangr, Leidstjarna, Mjolnir, Nine Virtues News, Raven's Cry, Tru North* (published in Canada), and more. The guilds of the old AFA had newsletters and magazines of their own, some of which kept going after the AFA dissolved: *The Frothing Vat* for the Brewers' Guild, *Sleipnir* for the Aerospace Technology Guild, and so on. Websites and blogs now largely fill the niche that these journals once filled, and copies are all but impossible to find today. But they provided an important outlet for Heathen writing and networking in the pre-Internet era. Few lasted longer than a couple of years, but they and their creators deserve to be remembered with honor.

Wicca, Neopaganism, and Reconstructionism

In 1954, Gerald Gardner announced the existence of modern Wicca with his book *Witchcraft Today*. Depending on what sources you believe, he either revealed the existence of an unbroken initiatory lineage of witches who still practiced the ancient native religion of the British Isles, or made the whole thing up by cobbling together bits of ceremonial magick, pieces of folklore, academic speculations about ancient religion, and his own personal obsessions. (See Hutton, *Triumph of the Moon*, especially pp. 205-252, for a carefully researched if somewhat skeptical view.) Whatever its origins, early British Wicca was a fairly conservative and secretive movement, but it was transformed by its introduction into the United States in the 1970s. Witchcraft came to stand for women's empowerment and political and social liberation (Hutton, pp. 340-368).

While British Traditional Wicca in the Gardnerian lineage remains a living tradition, Wicca and Wiccan-inspired paganism in the US (collectively called Neopaganism for lack of a better word) have blossomed into a rainbow of sects, traditions, and groups, some drawing from historical cultures (Norse Wicca, Egyptian Wicca, etc.), and some borrowing unabashedly from many cultures at once ("eclectic" paganism). The explosion of popular-level books on Wicca, witchcraft, and paganism means that individuals can and do identify as Wiccans, witches, or pagans without finding a coven or affiliating with a lineage at all. In 2015, an estimated 0.3% of Americans identified as

"Pagan or Wiccan," which works out to nearly one million people (Pew Forum, "America's Changing Religious Landscape"). This number presumably includes Heathens and other traditions, but the great majority of this group is likely to be Wiccan or Wiccan-influenced.

It's difficult to discuss the Neopagan-Heathen relationship, because "Neopaganism" itself is so incredibly diverse that it can hardly be covered by a single word. An old-school Gardnerian Wiccan; a New Age "lightworker" who channels dolphin spirit guides from Atlantis; a radical Dianic feminist; and a teenager who's just bought a book of spells in the local chain bookstore may all identify as "Neopagan," while being as different from each other, in fundamental beliefs and outlook, as any one of them is from any given Heathen. All the same, many Heathens will insist loudly that Wicca and/or Neopaganism have nothing to do with Ásatrú or Heathenry, and that any Heathen whose practices resemble Wicca in the slightest detail is Doing It Wrong.

There are some sizable theological and cultural differences between the two camps. Traditional Wicca and its offshoots emphasize gender polarity, often seeing the world's deities as emanations of one God and one Goddess. Heathen deities are certainly gendered, but there is much less of an emphasis on gender balance. Many Heathens are "hard polytheists," honoring a number of gods and goddesses who are seen as separate, interacting individuals. Such folk might take offense at the common Neopagan assumption that "all the Gods are One God," which sometimes seems to carry the implication that what Heathens do and believe is no different from what Neopagans do. Magic plays a role in both Heathenry and Neopaganism, but Heathens are far less likely than Neopagans to make it central to their religious practices; Heathen blóts are generally held to honor and thank deities, not to "raise energy" or to alter the universe in accordance with the worshippers' wills. Less fairly, some Heathens hold a negative stereotype of Wicca as "fluffy"—frivolous, unable to handle the harsh realities of life, and lacking roots in real tradition or scholarship. "Eclectic" pagans have a reputation for borrowing cultural practices, such as rune divination, without always understanding their deeper significance for the communities where they developed, and some Neopagan authors have been sloppy in their research, or presented "lore" that has imaginative appeal but no factual basis whatsoever. This approach can come across as extremely disrespectful. Heathens who are accused of fitting this stereotype are often derided as "Wiccatrú," which is usually meant as an insult. (See the widely distributed essay by Devin Gillette and Lewis Stead, "The Hammer and the Pentagram," for an old but still relevant discussion.)

It is true that Neopagan attempts to use Germanic religion have sometimes not been received well. Mention of Ralph Blum's books on runes, or Ed Fitch's 1990 book *The Rites of Odin*, is guaranteed to make seasoned Heathens roll their eyes and wince. It might also be true—possibly—that the "pop Wicca" of authors like Silver Ravenwolf has inspired a certain number of people to identify as pagans without any serious commitment, or to mindlessly borrow deities and practices from multiple cultures without understanding what they're doing. That being said, the truth is that, as the largest and most active Neopagan tradition around, Wicca had a strong influence on Ásatrú in the 1970s and 1980s. A number of American Ásatrú traditions are demonstrably derived from Wiccan practice: the Hammer Rite, for example, is not documented anywhere in Norse lore, but is obviously a borrowing of Calling the Quarters in Wicca, itself a borrowing of the Golden Dawn's Lesser Banishing Ritual of the Pentagram. What has become the traditional Ásatrú ritual calendar, with its main holy feasts at the equinoxes, solstices, and cross-quarter days, also looks much more like Wicca's Eightfold Wheel of the Year than the historically documented holy days (although some feasts, such as Yule, are common to both). The AFA was even known to sanction skyclad rituals in its early days (see "The Ride with the Valkyries," *The Runestone* no. 39, p. 9). Many Heathens come to Heathenry after a period of time in Wicca or other Neopagan traditions; Theodish Belief, for example, began as a Wiccan apostasy. Some people continue to maintain their oaths and allegiances to Neopagan groups and deities long after they begin to identify as Heathen.

Wiccans and other Neopagans have also led the fight for religious freedom in many areas. For example, the editor [BW] knows the person who got paganism officially recognized by the US Air Force, at the cost of her own military career. Court battles have recognized Wicca as a valid religion under US law (e.g. *Dettmer v. Landon*, District Court of Virginia, 1985), and decisions like this can be cited in support of Heathens as well. Wiccans have also fought for the rights of prisoners to have religious items and texts, beginning in 1983 with David Marsh's lawsuit in Michigan. A 2007 lawsuit filed by Americans United for Separation of Church and State won the right for Wiccan military service members to have the pentacle on their government-furnished headstones—which in turn set a precedent for the approval of the Hammer of Thor in 2013, and for the current Veterans' Administration (US) policy of accepting any emblem of a deceased serviceperson's "sincerely held belief" for placement on a gravestone. Finally, Wiccan and Neopagan individuals, groups, and gatherings have often drawn the fire of Christian fundamentalists, while slowly increasing the perception in the US that non-mainstream religions are acceptable and not threatening. (The 1993 documentary *The March on Fort God* is worth watching as a case study.) Heathenry has benefited from all these efforts, whether we know it or not, and it is ungenerous and shabby to dismiss all Neopagans as "fluff bunnies" while we benefit from what their community has done.

The Troth itself expects its members to share "a defining personal loyalty to the Gods and Goddesses of the Northlands," but has never mandated any specific ways of expressing that loyalty. As a result, the Troth has always had members who identify as Wiccan or Neopagan, or who maintain affiliations with such groups. This has been known to cause some public relations problems for the organization, as well as internal tension. Heathenry is still trying to find a distinctive identity and voice in the greater culture, and part of any group's process of self-definition is the definition of what it is *not*—hence the rejection and hostility in some Heathen quarters for anything that smacks of Wicca. That need not and does not mean, however, that relationships between the two can never be frithful and fruitful. There are still differences between Wicca and Heathenry in theology and practice—but there is no shortage of issues where pagans of all persuasions can and should work together: issues of religious freedom and tolerance, prison ministry, and so on.

Beginning mostly in the 1990s, although in some cases drawing on the work of earlier visionaries, various seekers around the world founded a number of Reconstructionist religions, with the purpose of rebuilding one culture's pre-Christian religion as authentically as possible. These include the reconstructed religions of the ancient Greeks (Hellenismos, Dodekatheism), Egyptians (Kemeticism), Romans (Religio Romana), Balts (Romuva, Dievturiba), Slavs (Rodnovery), Celts (Senistrognata, Págánachd, Ildiachas), Finns (Suomenusko), Hungarians, Canaanites, Sumerians, Mongols, and

others. Some of these groups were inspired, in part, by the example of Ásatrú, which remains the oldest and the largest "recon" religion (although how
strictly reconstructionist Ásatrú / Heathenry is, can be, or should be, varies
among groups and is sometimes the topic of vigorous debate). Also worth
mentioning here is ADF, *Ár nDraíocht Féin* / A Druid Fellowship, a Neopagan Druid organization building on the religious traditions of the Indo-European-speaking peoples. Heathens and other Reconstructionists generally
share an appreciation for serious scholarship, and relations between them
are usually mutually respectful. Like Heathenry, however, some of these
Reconstructionist movements have sizable wings with strong links to ethnic
nationalism, racism, anti-Semitism, and similar ideologies (Saunders, "Of
Gods and Men," pp. 136-149).

The View from Today

In the wider world, Heathenry remains small, but new expressions of
Heathen troth continue to appear. One of the most dynamic is Urglaawe,
founded and led by the Troth's former Steersman Robert Lütsch-Schreiwer.
Urglaawe is Pennsylvania German for "ancient belief"; it is based on the
surviving folklore of the Palatinate Germans who emigrated to Pennsylvania
and maintained and developed their own unique culture, preserving their
own concepts of the old gods and spirits in their folklore.

When the first edition of this book was published in 1994, the World
Wide Web was barely beginning to grow. Most on-line communication
about Heathenry took place on BBS servers, or on USENET groups such as
alt.religion.asatru—which, as this author [BW] recalls, consisted of roughly
10% intelligent and informative posts and 90% cranky sociopolitical rants,
flamewars, and invective, ranging from merely irrelevant to downright de-
ranged. Getting a copy of *Our Troth* was difficult for anyone who wasn't
already a Troth member or didn't know where to look—and once the first
printing was sold out, no more were available.

When the second edition came out in 2006, the World Wide Web had
exploded in size, and most of the first edition of *Our Troth* had been placed
online. The second edition was published through print-on-demand, an
Internet-dependent technology that made it possible for *Our Troth* to be
distributed worldwide and stay in print indefinitely.

Now, in 2020, the Internet has further transformed the ways that humans interact with each other, with the explosion of social media. There are strong Heathen presences on Facebook, Instagram, Quora, and other platforms; hundreds of active Heathen blogs; dozens of podcasts; and a huge number of Websites, ranging from authoritative and scholarly to, shall we say, imaginative. Solitary folk can now find and communicate quickly with like-minded Heathens around the world, while kindreds who used to practice in isolation now make contact with others across the continent. Heathen scholars have access to texts which were once only available in larger academic libraries, and can make their own writings available quickly to a larger audience. Print-on-demand publishers now allow Heathen authors to produce and market so many books and e-books, including this one, that it is hard to keep up with them all.

On the negative side, however, since virtually anyone can put up a Web site, it can be hard to find reputable information on Heathenry (or anything else) in a swirling sea of misinformation, dodgy scholarship, plagiarism, commercial noise, and general weirdness. The same problems with misinformation, rumors, and "fake news" that bedevil online political discourse are problems in the Heathen sphere. Heathens are as prone as anyone else to get drawn into self-reinforcing "echo chambers" that amplify their own existing worldviews and prejudices, instead of challenging them constructively. And although the Internet is perhaps the most powerful tool that humanity has ever devised, ours is still very much a religion grounded in the natural world and in human contact. Building a sense of community among geographically scattered people has long been a challenge for Heathen groups. Some Heathens have held "online blóts" and similar rites (e.g. Lewis, "Online Rituals," *Idunna* #119). At this writing (May 2020), with the Covid-19 virus forcing the cancellation of meetups and gatherings, the challenge of trying to meet people's spiritual and social needs without in-person contact has become particularly pressing.

There is a constant problem with the hijacking of our myths and symbols by those with a racist political agenda, and it's gotten worse in recent years. Openly and covertly racist Heathens have used social media effectively as a tool for recruitment, solidarity, and dissemination of noxious ideas. Racists who may not identify specifically as Heathen have appropriated myths, themes, and symbols of Germanic religion for their own purposes.

Some have been inspired by these perversions of our lore to commit terrible crimes. The gunman who murdered Muslim worshipers in Christchurch, New Zealand in March 2019, wrote "I will see you in Valhalla" in his manifesto (Kirkpatrick, "Massacre Suspect Traveled World"); and a man who burned three historically black churches in Louisiana in April 2019 identified as Ásatrú and had set up altars to Odin and Hel (Capps, "Matthews Into Pagan Gods"; The Troth, "Louisiana Church Burnings"). Racism and white supremacy remain serious problems for Heathenry, and the anti-racist wing has not always kept up. Thus many good people who might otherwise be drawn to Heathenry, or who might work with Heathens on issues of common interest, are kept away because of our unfortunate association with racist ideology. The Troth has begun building alliances with inclusive organizations in Europe and developing ways to counter the threat of racist Heathenry. In 2017, the Troth co-sponsored the first Frith Forge conference in Germany, with representatives of inclusive groups from nine different countries (Leigh-Hawkins, "Frith Forge," pp. 15-17). The next Frith Forge was intended to take place in Canada in 2020; the coronavirus pandemic forced its cancellation as an in-person event (although at this writing it is scheduled to take place online), but further conferences are planned for the future.

The founder of the Troth, Edred Thorsson, stated that "The Troth will be satisfied with nothing less than the *re-establishment* of the Troth as the natural religion within this culture" (*A Book of Troth*, p. 122). His dream remains far distant, and it's not necessarily shared by all Heathens, many of whom would settle for freedom, tolerance, community, and better mead. Even in the service of these more modest goals, there's much work still to be done, both inside the Troth and in the wider world. Yet we've come a long way and overcome many setbacks. The Troth stands with those kindreds, associations, and individuals who are working to show the world that the old ways live again; that they do not entail white supremacy, racism, or fascist ideology; and that they can bring strength, comfort, and a sense of meaning to people today. With the help of the gods and goddesses, wights and ancestors, we work for it to grow and strengthen in years to come. As long as there are people whose hearts and minds are drawn to the old ways, the Troth will strive to be there for them.

Contributors:

1st edition: Kveldúlfr Gundarsson.

2nd edition: New material by Ben Waggoner. Thanks to the following individuals for providing information: Êrmund Alderman, Gerd Groenewold, Swain Wodening (history of Theodism); Heimgest DCG OR, Osred OR Australia (history of the Odinic Rite); Steve McNallen (history of the AFA).

3rd edition: Reorganization and new material by Ben Waggoner. Some material on Theodish Belief adapted from "Tribal Traditions" in *Our Troth* vol. 2 (2006). Thanks to Tim Adams, Dara Grey, Victoria Ravenswood, and Lauren Crow Thacker for helpful comments; Michaela Macha for information on Heathenry in Germany, and André Lundin Keidser for information on Heathenry in Sweden. Special thanks go to the National Library of Australia for providing copies of rare publications by A. R. Mills.

Memorial altar for Dianne Luark Ross, August 25, 2018.
Photo by Rob L. Schreiwer.

Bibliography

Note: Persons with Icelandic or Icelandic-style names are alphabetized by first name. Alphabetization follows hybrid rules. Icelandic long vowels (á, é, í, ó, ú) are treated as separate letters that come after their short counterparts. Icelandic ð comes after d, but þ comes after z. Scandinavian and German letters æ, å, ä, ø, ö, ü are treated as separate from a and o and come at the end of the alphabet; thus Byock comes *before* Bäckmann. The German digraph ß is alphabetized as "ss". Particles before a surname (*de, van, von*, etc.) are not considered part of the last name unless they are capitalized; Jan de Vries is alphabetized under V, but Angela Della Volpe is alphabetized under D.

All references to the Prose Edda, unless otherwise cited, are from: Snorri Sturluson (ed. Anthony Faulkes). *Edda. Vol. 1: Prologue and Gylfaginning. Vol. 2a: Skáldskaparmál: Introduction, Text, and Notes. Vol. 2b: Skáldskaparmál: Glossary and Index of Names*. London: Viking Society for Northern Research, 2005-2008.

All references to the *Poetic Edda*, unless otherwise cited, are to Jónas Kristjánsson and Vésteinn Ólason, eds. *Eddukvæði*. 2 vols. Reykjavík: Hið íslenzka fornritafélag, 2014.

All references to Icelandic sagas, unless otherwise specified, are taken from the Íslenzk Fornrit editions published by Hið íslenzka fornritafélag. When the Norse text is quoted directly, this is cited in the text as ÍF (Íslensk Fornrit) followed by volume and page numbers.

All references to *Beowulf*, unless otherwise specified, are taken from Fulk, R. D., Robert E. Bork and John D. Niles (eds.) *Klaeber's Beowulf*. 4th Edition. Toronto: University of Toronto Press, 2008.

All translations are by Ben Waggoner except as noted otherwise.

"A Reply to a Reply: Letters to the Editor." *Liberty Bell*, vol. 11, no. 11 (1984), pp. 42-52.

Adam of Bremen (Francis J. Tschan, ed.) *History of the Archbishops of Hamburg-Bremen*. New York: Columbia University Press, 2002.

Adovasio, J. M., Olga Soffer and Jake Page. *The Invisible Sex: Uncovering the True Roles of Women in Prehistory*. Walnut Creek, Ca.: Left Coast Books, 2007.

Agnar Helgason, Sigrún Sigurðardóttir, Jeffrey R. Gulcher, Ryk Ward, and Kári Stefánsson. "mtDNA and the Origin of the Icelanders: Deciphering Signals of

Recent Population History." *American Journal of Human Genetics*, vol. 66, no. 3 (2000), pp. 999-1016.

Agnar Helgason and nine others. "Estimating Scandinavian and Gaelic Ancestry in the Male Settlers of Iceland." *American Journal of Human Genetics*, vol. 67, no. 3 (2000), pp. 697-717.

Alaric Albertsson. *Travels through Middle Earth: The Path of a Saxon Pagan.* Woodbury, Minn.: Llewellyn, 2009.

Ammianus Marcellinus (John C. Rolfe, transl.) *History.* 3 vols. Loeb Classical Library. Cambridge, Mass.: Harvard University Press, 1939.

Amster, Matthew H. "It's Not Easy Being Apolitical: Reconstruction and Eclecticism in Danish Asatro." Kathryn Rountree, ed. *Contemporary Pagan and Native Faith Movements in Europe: Colonialist and Nationalist Impulses.* New York: Berghahn, 2015. Pp. 43-63.

Anderson, Rasmus B. *America Not Discovered by Columbus: A Historical Sketch of the Discovery of America by the Norsemen, in the Tenth Century.* Chicago: S. C. Griggs & Co., 1874.

Andersson, Aron, and Ingmar Jansson. *Treasures of Early Sweden.* Uppsala: Almqvist & Wiksell, 1984.

Andersson, Gunnar. "Among Trees, Stones, and Bones: The Sacred Grove at Lunda." Anders Andrén, Kristina Jennbert, and Catharina Raudvere, eds. *Old Norse Religion in Long-Term Perspectives: Origins, Changes, and Interactions.* Lund: Nordic Academic Press, 2006. Pp. 195-199.

Andrén, Anders. *Tracing Old Norse Cosmology: The World Tree, Middle Earth, and the Sun in Archaeological Perspectives.* Lund: Nordic Academic Press, 2014.

Anthony, David W. *The Horse, The Wheel, and Language: How Bronze-Age Riders from the Eurasian Steppes Shaped the Modern World.* Princeton, N.J.: Princeton University Press, 2007.

Anthony, David W. and Don Ringe. "The Indo-European Homeland from Linguistic and Archaeological Perspectives." *Annual Review of Linguistics*, vol. 1 (2015), pp. 199-219.

Arjava, Antti. "The Mystery Cloud of 536 AD in the Mediterranean Sources." *Dumbarton Oaks Papers*, vol. 59 (2005), pp. 73-94.

Arnold, Bettina. "The Past as Propaganda: Totalitarian Archaeology in Nazi Germany." Tim Murray and Christopher Evans, eds. *Histories of Archaeology: A*

Reader in the History of Archaeology. Oxford: Oxford University Press, 2008. Pp. 120-144.

Arvidsson, Stefan. *Aryan Idols: Indo-European Mythology as Ideology and Science.* Chicago: University of Chicago Press, 2006.

Asingh, Pauline. "The Magical Bog." Pauline Asingh and Niels Lynnerup, eds. *Grauballe Man: An Iron Age Bog Body Preserved.* Moesgaard: Moesgaard Museum / Jutland Archaeological Society, 2007. Pp. 274-289.

—. "The Bog People." Pauline Asingh and Niels Lynnerup, eds. *Grauballe Man: An Iron Age Bog Body Preserved.* Moesgaard: Moesgaard Museum / Jutland Archaeological Society, 2007. Pp. 290-315.

Asprem, Egil. "Heathens Up North: Politics, Polemics, and Contemporary Norse Paganism in Norway." *The Pomegranate,* vol. 10, no. 1 (2008), pp. 41-69.

Axboe, Morten. "Towards the Kingdom of Denmark." Tania Dickinson and David Griffiths, eds. *The Making of Kingdoms. Anglo-Saxon Studies in Archaeology and History,* vol. 10. Oxford: Oxford University Committee for Archaeology, 1999. Pp. 109-118.

Bailey, Douglass W. "The Figurines of Old Europe." David Anthony and Jennifer Y. Chi, eds. *The Lost World of Old Europe: The Danube Valley, 5000-3500 BC.* New York: Institute for the Study of the Ancient World / Princeton, N.J.: Princeton University Press, 2009. Pp. 112-127.

Bainbridge, William. "A Seiðr Rite." *Idunna,* vol. 3, no. 3, issue #11 (August 1991), pp. 9-13.

—. "At The Tiller." *Idunna,* no. 30 (Winter 1996-7), pp. 1-2.

Ballentyne, Robert M. *Erling the Bold: A Tale of the Norse Sea-Kings.* London: James Nisbet & Co., 1869.

Barbero, Alessandro (John Cullen, transl.). *The Day of the Barbarians: The Epic Battle That Began the Fall of the Roman Empire.* London: Atlantic Books, 2007.

Barnard, F. M. *J. G. Herder on Social and Political Culture.* Cambridge: Cambridge University Press, 1969.

Barnes, Geraldine R. "Romance in Iceland." Margaret Clunies Ross, ed. *Old Icelandic Literature and Society.* Cambridge: Cambridge University Press, 2000. Pp. 266-286.

Basbanes, Nicholas. *A Gentle Madness: Bibliophiles, Bibliomanes, and the Eternal Passion for Books.* New York: Henry Holt & Co., 1995.

Battaglia, Frank. "The Germanic Earth Goddess in *Beowulf*." *Mankind Quarterly*, vol. 31, no. 4 (1991) pp. 415-446.

Baumer, Christoph. *The History of Central Asia: The Age of the Steppe Warriors.* London: I. B. Tauris, 2012.

Bede (Leo Sherley-Price, transl.) *Ecclesiastical History of the English People.* London: Penguin Books, 1990.

Bennett, J. A. W. "The Beginnings of Runic Studies in England." *Saga-Book of the Viking Society for Northern Research*, vol. 13, no. 4 (1950-51), pp. 269-283.

Benson, Adolph Burnett. *The Old Norse Element in Swedish Romanticism.* New York: Columbia University Press, 1914.

Bird, David S. *Nazi Dreamtime: Australian Enthusiasts for Hitler's Germany.* London: Anthem, 2014.

Bjørn, Rasmus Gudmundsen. "Foreign Elements in the Proto-Indo-European Vocabulary: A Comparative Loanword Study." MS Thesis, University of Copenhagen, 2017.

Bogucki, Peter. "How Wealth Happened in Neolithic Central Europe." *Journal of World Prehistory*, vol. 24 (2011), pp. 107-115.

Boldsen, Jesper L. and Richard R. Paine. "The Evolution of Human Longevity from the Mesolithic to the Middle Ages: An Analysis Based on Skeletal Data." Bernard Jeune and James W. Vaupel, eds. *Exceptional Longevity: From Prehistory to the Present.* Odense: Odense University Press, 1995. **https://www.demogr.mpg.de/Papers/Books/Monograph2/start.htm** Accessed May 6, 2020.

Bradley, Richard. "Midsummer and Midwinter in the Rock Carvings of South Scandinavia." *Temenos*, vol. 44, no. 2 (2008), pp. 223-232.

Brady, Caroline. *The Legends of Ermanarik.* Berkeley: University of California Press, 1943.

Brink, Stefan. "How Uniform was the Old Norse Religion?" Judy Quinn, Kate Heslop, and Tarrin Wills, eds. *Learning and Understanding in the Old Norse World: Essays in Honour of Margaret Clunies Ross.* Turnhout: Brepols, 2007. Pp. 105-136.

Brown, Marie A. (Mrs. John B. Shipley). *The Icelandic Discoverers of America, or, Honor to whom Honor is Due.* New York: John B. Alden, 1891.

Burenhult, Göran. *Arkeologi i Sverige.* 2nd ed. 3 vols. Höganäs: Wiken, 1991.

Burl, Aubrey. *The Stone Circles of Britain, Ireland and Brittany.* New Haven and London: Yale University Press, 2000.

Burns, Thomas S. *A History of the Ostrogoths.* Bloomington: Indiana University Press, 2004.

Byock, Jesse. *Medieval Iceland: Society, Sagas, and Power.* Berkeley: University of California Press, 1988.

Calico, Jefferson F. *Being Viking: Heathenism in Contemporary America.* Sheffield: Equinox, 2018.

Callow, Simon. *Being Wagner: The Story of the Most Provocative Composer Who Ever Lived.* New York: Vintage, 2018.

Campbell, Lyle. *Historical Linguistics: An Introduction.* Edinburgh: Edinburgh University Press, 2013.

Capps, Andrew "Matthews into Pagan Gods, Metal Music." *Lafayette Daily Advertiser*, Lafayette, La. April 12, 2019. Pp. A1, A4.

Carlyle, Thomas. *On Heroes, Hero-Worship and the Heroic in History.* London: James Fraser, 1841.

Carpenter, George "Paranoid George." "A Warning to our Racial Enemies." *Statecraft*, vol. 3, no. 2 (May-June 1970), p. 9.

Carver, Martin. *The Sutton Hoo Story: Encounters with Early England.* Woodbridge: Boydell, 2017.

Cassiodorus (Thomas Hodgkin, transl.) *The Letters of Cassiodorus.* London: Henry Frowde, 1886.

— (James W. Halporn and Mark Vesey, transl.) *Institutions of Divine and Secular Learning; and On the Soul.* Liverpool: Liverpool University Press, 2004.

Cassius Dio (Earnest Cary, transl.) *Roman History.* 9 vols. Loeb Classical Library. Cambridge, Mass.: Harvard University Press, 1961.

Cauvin, Jacques (Trevor Watkins, transl.) *The Birth of the Gods and the Origins of Agriculture.* Cambridge: Cambridge University Press, 2007.

Chadwick, H. M. *The Cult of Othin.* London: C. J. Clay & Sons, 1899.

Chisholm, James. "From Hearth to Hof." *Idunna*, vol. 2, no. 4 / issue #8 (1990), p. 41.

—. "From the Helm." *Idunna*, vol. 3, no. 3 / issue #12 (1991), p. 1.

—. "At The Helm—On Fear and Hyperbole." *Idunna*, vol. 3, no. 4 / issue #13 (1991), pp. 2-3.

—. "The Awakening of a Runemaster: The Life of Edred Thorsson." In Thorsson, Edred. *Green Rûna—The Runemaster's Notebook: Shorter Works of Edred Thorsson, Vol. 1 (1978–1985)*. 2nd ed. Rûna-Raven Press, 1996. Pp. 81-89.

—. *Grove and Gallows: Greek and Latin Sources for Germanic Heathenism*. Smithville, Tex.: Rûna-Raven Press, 2002.

[Christensen, Else.] *An Introduction to Odinism*. Crystal River, Fla.: Giallerhorn Book Service, 1980.

Christensen, Tom. "Lejre Beyond the Legend—The Archaeological Evidence." *Siedlungs- und Küstenforschung im südlichen Nordseegebiet*, vol. 33 (2010), pp. 237-254.

Christiansen, Eric. *The Northern Crusades*. New ed. London: Penguin, 1997.

Christie, Neil. *The Lombards*. Oxford: Blackwell, 1995.

Clare, Victoria. "Jörð's Folk: Costa Rican Ásatrú." *Idunna*, no. 87 (Spring 2011), pp. 30-32.

Claudian (Maurice Platnauer, transl.) *Claudian*. 2 vols. Loeb Classical Library. Cambridge, Mass.: Harvard University Press, 1922.

Cleasby, Richard, and Gudbrand Vigfusson, *An Icelandic-English Dictionary*. Oxford: Oxford University Press, 1874.

Cline, Eric H. *1177 B.C.: The Year Civilization Collapsed*. Princeton: Princeton University Press, 2014.

Colaruso, John. *Nart Sagas from the Caucasus: Myths and Legends from the Circassians, Abazas, Abkhaz, and Ubykhs*. Princeton, N.J.: Princeton University Press, 2002.

Conard, Nicholas J. "A Female Figurine from the Basal Aurignacian of Hohle Fels Cave in Southwestern Germany." *Nature*, vol. 459, no. 7244 (2009), pp. 248-252.

Conard, Nicholas J., Marina Malina, and Susanne C. Münzel. "New Flutes Document the Earliest Musical Tradition in Southwestern Germany." *Nature*, vol. 460, no. 7256 (2009), pp. 737-740.

Coulston, J. C. N. "Late Roman Military Equipment Culture." Alexander Sarantis and Neil Christie (eds.) *War and Warfare in Late Antiquity: Current Perspectives*. Vol. 2. Leiden: Brill, 2013. Pp. 463-492.

Cox, Steven L. "A Norse Penny from Maine." William W. Fitzhugh and Elizabeth Ward, eds. *Vikings: The North Atlantic Saga.* Washington DC: Smithsonian Institution Press, 2000. Pp. 206-207.

Cross, Samuel Hazzard and Olgerd P. Sherbowitz-Wetzor (transl.) *The Russian Primary Chronicle: Laurentian Text.* Cambridge, Mass.: Mediaeval Academy of America, 1953.

Cullum, Dick. "Cullum's Column: 'Minnesota' is Designation of Pro Grid Team." *Minneapolis Morning Tribune*, August 6, 1960, p. 21.

Cunliffe, Barry. *The Ancient Celts.* Oxford: Oxford University Press, 1997.

—. *The Extraordinary Voyage of Pytheas the Greek.* New York: Penguin Putnam, 2003.

—. *Europe Between the Oceans: 9000 BC–AD 1000.* New Haven, Conn.: Yale University Press, 2008.

Curry, Andrew. "The Road Almost Taken." *Archaeology*, vol. 70, no. 2 (March/April 2017), pp. 33-37.

Damgaard, Peter de Barros, and 50 others. "The First Horse Herders and the Impact of Early Bronze Age Steppe Expansions into Asia." *Science*, vol. 360 (2018), eaar7711.

Dasent, George Webbe. *Popular Tales from the Norse.* New Edition. Edinburgh: David Douglas, 1912.

Davidson, H. R. E. *Myths and Symbols in Pagan Europe: Early Scandinavian and Celtic Religions.* Syracuse, N.Y.: Syracuse University Press, 1988.

Davið Steffánson. "Hátídaljóð, 930–1930." *Heimskringla* (Winnipeg), June 25, 1930, p. 1. **http://timarit.is/viewpageinit.jsp?issId=153307** Accessed May 27, 2019.

Della Volpe, Angela. "From the Hearth to the Creation of Boundaries." *Journal of Indo-European Studies*, vol. 18, no. 1-2 (1990), pp. 157-184.

Dexter, Miriam Robbins. "Reflections on the Goddess *Donu." *Mankind Quarterly*, vol. 31, nos. 1-2 (1990), pp. 45-57.

Diamond, Jared. *Guns, Germs and Steel: The Fates of Human Societies.* New York: W. W. Norton, 1997.

Dobat, Andres Siegfried. "Viking Stranger-Kings: The Foreign as a Source of Power in Viking Age Scandinavia, or, Why There Was a Peacock in the Gokstad Ship Burial?" *Early Medieval Europe*, vol. 23, no. 2 (2015), pp. 161-201.

Dobres, Marcia-Anne. "Venus Figurines." Brian M. Fagan, ed. *The Oxford Companion to Archaeology*. New York and Oxford: Oxford University Press, 1996. Pp. 740-741.

Dohe, Carrie B. *Jung's Wandering Archetype: Race and Religion in Analytical Psychology*. London and New York: Routledge, 2016.

Douglass, Paul F. *God Among the Germans*. Philadelphia: University of Pennsylvania Press, 1935.

Dowden, Ken. *European Paganism: The Realities of Cult from Antiquity to the Middle Ages*. London and New York: Routledge, 2000.

Dowson, Thomas A. and Martin Porr. "Special Objects—Special Creatures: Shamanistic Imagery and the Aurignacian Art of Southwestern Germany." Neil S. Price, ed. *The Archaeology of Shamanism*. London and New York: Routledge, 2001. Pp. 165-177.

Drinkwater, J. F. "The Usurpers Constantine III (407-411) and Jovinus (411-413)." *Brittania*, vol. 29 (1998), pp. 269-298.

Driscoll, Matthew. *The Unwashed Children of Eve: The Production, Dissemination and Reception on Popular Literature in Post-Reformation Iceland*. Enfield Lock: Hisarlik Press, 1997.

Dumézil, Georges. *Gods of the Ancient Northmen*. Berkeley: University of California Press, 1973.

—. "'Le Borgne' and 'Le Manchot': The State of the Problem." Gerald James Larson, ed. *Myth in European Antiquity*. Berkeley: University of California Press, 1974. Pp. 17-28.

Dutton, Paul Edward (ed.) *Carolingian Civilization: A Reader*. Peterborough, Ontario: Broadview Press, 1993.

Edred Thorsson. "Holy Steads in the Spring-Time of Our New Folk." *Idunna*, vol. 2, no. 4 / issue #8 (1990), pp. 1-2.

—. "Drighten's Rede." *Idunna*, vol. 2, no. 4 / issue #8 (1990), p. 40.

—. *A Book of Troth*. 1st ed. St. Paul, Minn.: Llewellyn, 1992.

—. *History of the Rune-Gild. The Reawakening of the Gild, 1980-2018*. North Augusta, S.C.: Arcana Europa, 2018.

Eisler, Riane. *The Chalice and the Blade: Our History, Our Future*. San Francisco: HarperSanFrancisco, 1987.

Eller, Cynthia. *The Myth of Matriarchal Prehistory: Why an Invented Past Won't Give Women a Future.* Boston: Beacon Press, 2000.

Eliade, Mircea (Willard R. Trask, transl.) *Shamanism: Archaic Techniques of Ecstasy.* 2nd ed. Princeton, N.J.: Princeton University Press, 2004.

Ellis, H. R. *The Road to Hel.* New York: Greenwood Press, 1968.

Enright, Michael J. *Lady with a Mead Cup: Ritual, Prophecy, and Lordship in the European Warband from La Tène to the Viking Age.* Dublin: Four Courts Press, 1996.

Eriksen, Berit Valentin. "Resource Exploitation, Subsistence Strategies, and Adaptiveness in Late Pleistocene-Early Holocene Northwest Europe." Lawrence Guy Straus, Berit Valentin Eriksen, Jon M. Erlandson, and David R. Yesner, eds. *Humans at the End of the Ice Age: The Archaeology of the Pleistocene-Holocene Transition.* New York and London: Plenum, 1996. Pp. 101-128.

Fabech, Charlotte. "Organizing the Landscape: A Matter of Production, Power, and Religion." Tania Dickinson and David Griffiths, eds. *The Making of Kingdoms. Anglo-Saxon Studies in Archaeology and History*, vol. 10. Oxford: Oxford University Committee for Archaeology, 1999. Pp. 37-48.

Fagan, Brian M. "Three-Age System." *The Oxford Companion to Archaeology.* New York and Oxford: Oxford University Press, 1996. Pp. 712-713.

Fahlander, Fredrik. "Messing with the Dead: Post-Depositional Manipulations of Burials and Bodies in the South Scandinavian Stone Age." *Documenta Praehistorica*, vol. 37 (2010), pp. 23-31.

Fahrenkrog, Ludwig. *Das Deutsche Buch.* 3rd ed. Leipzig: Wilhelm Hartung, 1923.

Fichte, Johann Gottlieb (R. F. Jones and G. H. Turnbull, transl.). *Addresses to the German Nation.* Chicago: Open Court, 1922.

Finnur Jónsson. *Den Norsk-Islandske Skjaldedigtning.* Copenhagen: Gyldendal, 1912-1915.

Flint, Valerie I. J. *The Rise of Magic in Early Medieval Europe.* Princeton, N.J.: Princeton University Press, 1991.

Flowers, Stephen E. "Revival of Germanic Religion in Contemporary Anglo-American Culture." *Mankind Quarterly*, vol. 21, no. 3 (1981), pp. 279-294.

Foote, P. G, and D. M. Wilson. *The Viking Achievement.* Revised ed. London: Sidgwick & Jackson, 1980.

Forte, Angelo, Richard Oram, and Frederik Pedersen. *Viking Empires*. Cambridge: Cambridge University Press, 2005.

Frank, Roberta. "Viking Atrocity and Skaldic Verse: The Rite of the Blood-Eagle." *English Historical Review*, vol. 99, no. 391 (1984), pp. 332-343.

Fulk, R. D., Robert E. Bork and John D. Niles (eds.) *Klaeber's Beowulf*. 4th Edition. Toronto: University of Toronto Press, 2008.Gantz, Jeffrey. *Early Irish Myths and Sagas*. London Penguin, 1981.

Gardell, Mattias. *Gods of the Blood: The Pagan Revival and White Separatism*. Durham, N.C.: Duke University Press, 2003.

Garman Lord. "The Evolution of Theodish Belief. Part 5: The World of Ásatrú." Gering Theod. **https://web.archive.org/web/20160422035629/http://www. gamall-steinn.org/Gering/Evol-pt5.htm** Accessed March 31, 2019.

Geary, Patrick J. *Before France and Germany: The Creation and Transformation of the Merovingian World*. Oxford: Oxford University Press, 1988.

Geijer, Erik Gustaf. *Samlade Skrifter*. 13 vols. Stockholm: P. A. Norstedt & Söner, 1849-1854.

Gejvall, Nils-Gustaf. "The Fisherman from Barum—Mother of Several Children! Palaeo-Anatomic Finds in the Skeleton from Bäckaskog." *Fornvännen*, vol. 65 (1970), pp. 281-289.

Gelling, Peter, and H. R. Ellis Davidson. *The Chariot of the Sun and Other Rites and Symbols of the Northern Bronze Age*. New York: Praeger, 1969.

Gentry, Francis G., Winder McConnell, Ulrich Müller, and Werner Wunderlich, eds. *The Nibelungen Tradition: An Encyclopedia*. New York: Routledge, 2002.

Geoffrey of Monmouth (Lewis Thorpe, transl.) *History of the Kings of Britain*. London: Penguin, 1966.

Gerven, Tim van. "Is Nordic Mythology Nordic or National, or Both? Competing National Appropriations of Nordic Mythology in Early Nineteenth-Century Scandinavia." Simon Halink, ed. *Northern Myths, Modern Identities: The Nationalisation of Northern Mythologies since 1800*. Leiden: Brill, 2019. Pp. 49-70.

Giles, J. A. (transl.) *The Works of Gildas and Nennius*. London: James Bohn, 1841.

Gillette, Devyn and Lewis Stead. "The Pentagram and the Hammer." **http://www. ravenkindred.com/wicatru.html** Accessed September 4, 2019.

Gimbutas, Marija. *The Slavs*. New York: Praeger, 1971.

—. *The Gods and Goddesses of Old Europe, 7000 to 3500 BC: Myths, Legends, and Cult Images*. Berkeley and Los Angeles: University of California Press, 1974.

—. *The Language of the Goddess: Unearthing the Hidden Symbols of Western Civilization*. San Francisco: Harper & Row, 1989.

Gløb, P.V. (Rupert Bruce-Mitford, transl.) *The Bog People: Iron-Age Man Preserved*. London: Faber, 1969.

—. (Joan Bulman, transl.) *The Mound People: Danish Bronze-Age Man Preserved*. Ithaca, N.Y.: Cornell University Press, 1974.

Gobineau, Arthur de (Adrian Collins, transl.). *The Inequality of Human Races*. New York: G. P. Putnam's Sons, 1915.

Goffart, Walter. *Barbarian Tides: The Migration Age and the Later Roman Empire*. Philadelphia: University of Pennsylvania Press, 2006.

Goldberg, Eric J. "Popular Revolt, Dynastic Politics, and Aristocratic Factionalism in the Early Middle Ages: The Saxon Stellinga Reconsidered." *Speculum*, vol. 70, no. 3 (1995), pp. 467-501.

Goldhahn, Joakim. "Bredarör on Kivik: A Monumental Cairn and the History of its Interpretation." *Antiquity*, vol. 83 (2009), pp. 359-371.

Gonzales Sanches, Sergio. "Deconstructing Myths, Constructing History. Dutch National Identity: Formulation and Evolution of the Batavian Myth." *Archaeological Review from Cambridge*, vol. 27, no. 2 (2012), pp. 85-110.

Goodrich, Aaron. *A History of the Character and Achievements of the So-Called Christopher Columbus*. New York: D. Appleton & Co., 1874.

Goodrick-Clarke, Nicholas. *The Occult Roots of Nazism: Secret Aryan Cults and their Influence on Nazi Ideology*. New York: New York University Press, 1992.

—. *Black Sun: Aryan Cults, Esoteric Nazism and the Politics of Identity*. New York: New York University Press, 2002.

"GOP Begins Youth Drive." *Wichita Falls Times*, Oct. 19, 1971, p. 9.

Gossman, Lionel. *Brownshirt Princess: A Study of the "Nazi Conscience."* Cambridge: OpenBook Publishers, 2009.

Goudsward, David. *Ancient Stone Sites of New England and the Debate Over Early European Exploration*. Jefferson, N.C.: McFarland & Co., 2006.

Gould, Stephen Jay. *Ontogeny and Phylogeny*. Cambridge, Mass.: Belknap Press, 1977.

Gray, Thomas. *The Works of Thomas Gray*. London: Pickering, 1836.

Gregorius, Fredrik. "Modern Heathenism in Sweden: A Case Study in the Creation of a Traditional Religion." Kathryn Rountree, ed. *Contemporary Pagan and Native Faith Movements in Europe: Colonialist and Nationalist Impulses.* New York: Berghahn, 2015. Pp. 64-85.

Gregory of Tours (Lewis Thorpe, transl.) *The History of the Franks.* London: Penguin, 1974.

Green, Miranda. *The Sun-Gods of Ancient Europe.* London: B.T. Batsford, 1991.

Greenfield, Jeanette. *The Return of Cultural Treasures.* Cambridge: Cambridge University Press, 1989.

Greenway, John L. *The Golden Horns: Mythic Imagination and the Nordic Past.* Athens, Ga.: University of Georgia Press, 1977.

Grendel Grettison (Al Billings). "Electronic Communications for Heathens." *Idunna*, no. 24 (September 1994), pp. 36-37.

Grienberger, Theodor von. "Germanischer Götternamen auf Rheinischer Inschriften." *Zeitschrift für Deutsches Altertum und Deutsche Literatur*, vol. 35 (1891), pp. 388-401.

Grimm, Jakob (James Steven Stallybrass, transl.) *Teutonic Mythology.* 4th ed. 4 vols. London: George Bell and Sons, 1883-1888.

Gräslund, Anne-Sofie. "Thor's Hammers, Pendant Crosses, and Other Amulets." Else Roesdahl and David M. Wilson, eds. *From Viking to Crusader.* New York: Rizzoli, 1992. Pp. 190-191.

Gräslund, Bo and Neil Price. "Twilight of the Gods? The 'Dust Veil Event' of AD 536 in Critical Perspective." *Antiquity*, vol. 86 (2012), pp. 428-443.

Grünberg, Judith M. "Mesolithic Burials—Rites, Symbols and Social Organisation of Early Postglacial Communities." Judith M. Grünberg, Bernhard Gramsch, Lars Larsson, Jörg Orschiedt, and Harald Meller, eds. *Mesolithic Burials— Rites, Symbols and Social Organisation of Early Postglacial Communities. International Conference, Halle (Saale), Germany, 18th–21st September 2013.* Halle: Landesmuseum für Vorgeschichte, 2016.

Gründer, René. "Neo-Pagan Traditions in the 21st Century: Re-inventing Polytheism in a Polyvalent World-Culture." Judith Schlehe and Evamaria Sandkühler, eds. *Religion, Tradition and the Popular: Transcultural Views From Asia and Europe.* Bielefeld: transcript Verlag, 2014. Pp. 261-281.

Gunnar Karlsson. *The History of Iceland.* Minneapolis: University of Minnesota Press, 2000.

Gunnell, Terry. "Pantheon? What Pantheon? Concepts of a Family of Gods in Pre-Christian Scandinavan Religions." *Scripta Islandica*, vol. 66 (2015), pp. 55-76.

—. "How High was the High One? The Roles of Óðinn and Þórr in Pre-Christian Icelandic Society." Stefan Brink and Lisa Collinson, eds. *Theorizing Old Norse Myth*. Turnhout: Brepols, 2018. Pp. 105-129.

Günther, Torsten, and 26 others. "Population Genomics of Mesolithic Scandinavia: Investigating Early Postglacial Migration Routes and High-Latitude Adaptation." *PLoS Biology*, vol. 16, no. 1 (2018): e2003703.

Haak, Wolfgang, and 9 others. "Ancient DNA, Strontium Isotopes, and Osteological Analyses Shed Light on Social and Kinship Organization of the Later Stone Age." *Proceedings of the National Academy of Sciences of the USA*, vol. 105, no. 477 (25 November 2008), pp. 18226-18231.

Haak, Wolfgang, and 38 others. "Massive Migration from the Steppe was a Source for Indo-European Languages in Europe." *Nature*, vol. 522 (11 June 2015), pp. 207-211.

Hafstein, Valdimar Tr. "Bodies of Knowledge: Ole Worm and Collecting in Late Renaissance Scandinavia." *Ethnologia Europaea*, vol. 33, no. 1 (2003), pp. 5-20.

Hakenbeck, Susanne E. "Genetics, Archaeology and the Far Right: An Holy Trinity." *World Archaeology*, vol. 51, no. 4 (2019): 517-527.

Harding, A. F. *European Societies in the Bronze Age*. Cambridge: Cambridge University Press, 2000.

Harild, Jens Andreas, David Earle Robinson, and Jesper Hudlebusch. "New Analyses of Grauballe Man's Gut Contents." Pauline Asingh and Niels Lynnerup, eds. *Grauballe Man: An Iron Age Bog Body Preserved*. Moesgaard: Moesgaard Museum / Jutland Archaeological Society, 2007. Pp. 154-187.

Harvey, Graham. "Heathenism: A North European Pagan Tradition." Graham Harvey and Charlotte Hardman, eds. *Paganism Today*. London: Thorsons, 1995. Pp. 49–64.

Hauer, Wilhelm, Karl Helm, and Karl Adam (T. S. K. Scott-Craig and R. E. Davies, transl.) *Germany's New Religion: The German Faith Movement*. New York: The Abingdon Press, 1937.

Heather, Peter J. *Empire and Barbarians: The Fall of Rome and the Birth of Europe*. Oxford: Oxford University Press, 2009.

Hedeager, Lotte. *Iron Age Myth and Materiality: An Archaeology of Scandinavia, AD 400–1000*. London: Routledge, 2011.

Hegner, Victoria. "Hot, Strange, Völkisch, Cosmopolitan: Native Faith and Neo-pagan Witchcraft in Berlin's Changing Urban Context." Kathryn Rountree, ed. *Contemporary Pagan and Native Faith Movements in Europe: Colonialist and Nationalist Impulses*. New York: Berghahn, 2015. Pp. 175-195.

Heimgest DCG. "Time to Honour an Unsung Hero." *ORBriefing*, no. 211 (Spring 2009), pp. 3-4. Also available at **http://www.odinic-rite.org/main/time-to-honour-an-unsung-hero-hoskuld-cg/** Accessed February 11, 2019.

Helm, Karl. *Altgermanische Religionsgeschichte*. 2 vols. Heidelberg: Carl Winters Universitätsbuchhandlung, 1937.

Herder, Johann Gottfried (Michael N. Forster, transl.) *Philosophical Writings*. Cambridge: Cambridge University Press, 2002.

Hermand, Jost (Paul Levesque, transl.). *Old Dreams of a New Reich: Volkisch Utopias and National Socialism*. Bloomington, Ind.: Indiana University Press, 1992.

Herva, Vesa-Pekka, and Antti Lahelma. *Northern Archaeology and Cosmology: A Relational View*. London: Routledge, 2020.

Heschel, Susannah. *The Aryan Jesus: Christian Theologians and the Bible in Nazi Germany*. Princeton, N.J.: Princeton University Press, 2008.

Hitler, Adolf (Ralph Manheim, transl.) *Mein Kampf*. Boston: Houghton Mifflin, 1947.

—. (Hugh R. Trevor-Roper, ed.) *Hitler's Secret Conversations, 1941-44*. New York: Farrar, Straus and Young, 1953.

—. (Max Domarus, ed., Mary Fran Gilvert, transl.) *Hitler: Speeches and Procla-mations, 1932–1945. The Chronicle of a Dictatorship*. 4 vols. Wauconda, Ill.: Bolchazy-Carducci Publishers, 1990.

Hollander, Lee (transl.) *The Saga of the Jómsvíkings*. Austin, Tex.: University of Texas Press, 1955.

— (transl.) *The Poetic Edda*. 2nd ed. Austin: University of Texas Press, 1962.

Holst, Mads Kähler, Marianne Rasmussen, Kristian Kristiansen, and Jens-Henrik Bech. "Bronze Age 'Herostrats': Ritual, Political, and Domestic Economies in Early Bronze Age Denmark." *Proceedings of the Prehistoric Society*, vol. 79 (2013), pp. 1-32.

Holzer, Hans. *Witches: True Encounters with Wicca, Wizards, Covens, Cults, and Magick*. New York: Black Dog & Leventhal, 2002.

Homer (A. T. Murray, transl.) *The Iliad*. 2 vols. Loeb Classical Library. Cambridge, Mass.: Harvard University Press, 1965.

Hondius-Crone, Ada. *The Temple of Nehalennia at Domburg*. Amsterdam: J. M. Meulenhoff, 1955.

Hope-Taylor, Brian. *Yeavering: An Anglo-British Centre of Early Northumbria*. Swindon: English Heritage, 1977.

Horard-Herbin, Marie-Pierre, Anne Tresset, and Jean-Denis Vigne. "Domestication and Uses of the Dog in Western Europe from the Paleolithic to the Iron Age." *Animal Frontiers*, vol. 4, no. 3 (2014), pp. 23-31.

Horn, Christian. "Cupmarks." *Adoranten* (2015), pp. 29-43.

—. "'It's a Man's World'? Sex and Gender in Scandinavian Bronze Age Rock Art." Sophie Bergerbrant and Anna Wessman, eds. *New Perspectives on the Bronze Age: Proceedings of the 13th Nordic Bronze Age Symposium*. Oxford: Archaeopress, 2017. Pp. 237-252.

Hublin, Jean-Jacques, and 10 others. "New Fossils from Jebel Irhoud, Morocco and the Pan-African Origin of *Homo sapiens*." *Nature*, vol. 546, no. 7657 (2017), pp. 289-292.

Huld, Martin E. "The Linguistic Typology of the Old European Substrata in North Central Europe." *Journal of Indo-European Studies*, vol. 18 (1990), pp. 389-423.

—. "Magic, Metathesis and Nudity in Indo-European Thought." Dorothy Disterheft, Martin Huld, and John Greppin, eds. *Studies in Honor of Jaan Puhvel. Part One: Ancient Languages and Philology*. Journal of Indo-European Studies, Monograph 20. Washington, DC: Institute for the Study of Man, 1997. Pp. 75-92.

Hultkrantz, Åke. "Rock Drawings as Evidence of Religion: Some Principal Points of View." Gro Steinsland, ed. *Words and Objects: Towards a Dialogue Between Archaeology and History of Religion*. Oslo: Norwegian University Oress, 1986. Pp. 43-66.

Hutton, Ronald. *The Triumph of the Moon: A History of Modern Pagan Witchcraft*. Oxford; Oxford University Press, 1999.

—. *Shamans: Siberian Spirituality and the Western Imagination*. London: Hambledon and London, 2001.

Ilkjær, Jørgen. *Illerup Ådal: Archaeology as a Magic Mirror.* Højbjerg: Moesgård Museum, 2000.

—. "Danish War Booty Sacrifices." Lars Jørgensen, Birger Storgaard, and Lone Gebauer Thomsen, eds. *The Spoils of Victory: The North in the Shadow of the Roman Empire.* Copenhagen: Nationalmuseet, 2003. Pp. 44-65.

Introvigne, Massimo. "Fidus (1868–1940): A German Artist from Theosophy to Nazism." *Aries: Journal for the Study of Western Esotericism*, vol. 17 (2017), pp. 215-242.

IRMIN (Institute of Research on Northern Mythology and Identity). *Interview with a Gothi: Heimgest Speaks.* [Napa, Calif.:] Odinic Rite / Himminbjorg Publishing, 1996.

Iversen, Rune. "Bronze Age Acrobats." *World Archaeology*, vol. 46, no. 2 (2014), pp. 242-255.

Iversen, Rune and Guus Kroonen. "Talking Neolithic: Linguistic and Archaeological Perspectives on How Indo-European Was Implemented in Southern Scandinavia." *American Journal of Archaeology*, vol. 121, no. 4 (2017), pp. 511-525.

Jackson, Peter. "Light from Distant Asterisks: Towards a Description of the Indo-European Religious Heritage." *Numen*, vol. 49 (2002), pp. 61-102.

Jeffries, Matthew. "Lebensreform: A Middle-Class Antidote to Wilhelminism?" Geoff Eley and James Retallack (eds.) *Wilhelminism and its Legacies: German Modernities, Imperialism, and the Meaning of Reform, 1890-1930.* New York: Berghahn, 2003. Pp. 91-106.

Jensen, Jørgen, Elisabeth Munksgaard, and Thorkild Ramskou. *Prehistoric Denmark.* Copenhagen: National Museum, 1978.

Jernigan, Jean. "Latter-Day Norse Folk Plan a Sacrifice Here." *Berkeley Gazette*, March 11, 1977, p. 10.

Jinarājadāsa, C. *First Principles of Theosophy.* Adyar: Theosophical Publishing House, 1921.

Jochim, Michael. "The Mesolithic." Sarunas Milisauskas, ed. *European Prehistory: A Survey.* New York: Kluwer/Plenum, 2002. Pp. 115-141.

Johannesson, Kurt (James Larson, transl.) *The Renaissance of the Goths in Sixteenth-Century Sweden: Johannes and Olaus Magnus as Politicians and Historians.* Berkeley: University of California Press, 1991.

Johnsen, Berit. *The Cosmic Wedding: A New Interpretation of South Scandinavian Rock Carvings, Stonehenge, and Other Manifestations of Bronze Age Religion.* Copenhagen: Frydenlund, 2005.

Jones, William. *The Works of Sir William Jones. With a Life of the Author, by Lord Teignmouth.* London: John Stockdale and John Walker, 1807.

Jordanes (Charles Christopher Mierow, transl.) *The Gothic History of Jordanes.* 2nd ed. Princeton, N.J.: Princeton University Press, 1915.

Jón Hnefill Aðalsteinsson. *Under the Cloak: A Pagan Ritual Turning Point in the Conversion of Iceland.* Reykjavík: Háskólaútgáfan, 1999.

Jón Karl Helgason. "Continuity? The Icelandic Sagas in Post-Mediaeval Times." Rory McTurk, ed. *A Companion to Old Norse–Icelandic Literature and Culture.* Oxford: Blackwell, 2005.

Jónina K. Berg. "Sveinbjörn Beinteinsson: A Personal Reminiscence." *TYR,* vol. 3 (2007-2008), pp. 263-271.

Julius Caesar (H. J. Edwards, transl.) *The Gallic War.* Loeb Classical Library. Cambridge, Mass.: Harvard University Press, 1917.

Junginger, Horst. "Nordic Ideology in the SS and the SS Ahnenerbe." Horst Junginger and Andreas Åkerlund, eds. *Nordic Ideology Between Religion and Scholarship.* Frankfurt: Peter Lang, 2013. Pp. 39-69.

Jørgensen, Lars. "Gudme and Tissø: Two Magnates' Complexes in Denmark from the 3rd to the 11th Century AD." Babette Ludowici, Hauke Jöns, Sunhild Kleingärtner, Jonathan Scheschkewitz, and Matthias Hardt, eds. *Trade and Communication Networks of the First Millennium AD in the Northern Part of Central Europe: Central Places, Beach Markets, Landing Places and Trading Centres. Neue Studien zur Sachsenforschung,* vol. 1. Hannover: Niedersächsisches Landesmuseum, 2010. Pp. 273-286.

Kaliff, Anders. Fire, Water, Heaven and Earth: Ritual Practice and Cosmology in Ancient Scandinavia: An Indo-European Perspective. Stockholm: Riksantikvarieämbetet, 2007.

Kaplan, Jeffrey. "Reconstruction of the Ásatrú and Odinist Traditions." James R. Lewis, ed. *Magical Religion and Modern Witchcraft.* Albany: State University of New York Press, 1996.

—. Radical Religion in America: Millenarian Movements from the Far Right to the Children of Noah. Syracuse, N.Y.: Syracuse University Press, 1997.

Karlsson, Thomas. "Kabbalah in Sweden." Tore Alhbäck, ed. *Western Esotericism.* Åbo: Donner Institute for Research in Religious and Cultural History, 2008. Pp. 88-97.

Karsten, Rafael. *The Religion of the Samek: Ancient Beliefs and Cults of the Scandinavian and Finnish Lapps.* Leiden: E. J. Brill, 1955.

Kastovsky, Dieter. "Semantics and Vocabulary." Richard M. Hogg, ed. *The Cambridge History of the English Language. Volume I: The Beginnings to 1066.* Cambridge: Cambridge University Press, 1992. Pp. 290-408.

Kaul, Flemming. "The Bog—The Gateway to Another World." Lars Jørgensen, Birger Storgaard, and Lone Gebauer Thomsen, eds. *The Spoils of Victory: The North in the Shadow of the Roman Empire.* Copenhagen: Nationalmuseet, 2003. Pp. 18-43.

—. "Bronze Age Tripartite Cosmologies." *Praehistorische Zeitschrift*, vol. 80, no. 2 (2005), pp. 135-148.

—. "The Nordic Razor and the Mycenaean Lifestyle." *Antiquity*, vol. 87 (2015), pp. 461-472.

—. "Left-Right Logic: An Innovation of the Nordic Bronze Age." Bender Jørgensen, Lise, Joanna Sofaer, and Marie Louise Stig Sørensen (eds.). *Creativity in the Bronze Age: Understanding Innovation in Pottery, Textile, and Metalwork Production.* Cambridge: Cambridge University Press, 2018. Pp. 235-246.

Kehoe, Alice Beck. Shamans and Religion: An Anthropological Exploration in Critical Thinking. Prospect Heights, Ill.: Waveland Press, 2000.

—. The Kensington Runestone: Approaching a Research Question Holistically. Prospect Heights, Ill.: Waveland Press, 2005.

Kelley, Donald R. "*Tacitus noster*: The Germania in the Renaissance and Reformation." T. J. Luce and A. J. Woodman, eds. *Tacitus and the Tacitean Tradition.* Princeton, N. J.: Princeton University Press, 1993. Pp. 151-167.

Kennedy, Gordon. Children of the Sun: A Pictorial Anthology from Germany to California, 1883-1949. Ojai, Calif.: Nivaria Press, 1998.

Kershaw, Kris. *The One-Eyed God: Odin and the (Indo-) Germanic Männerbünde. Journal of Indo-European Studies,* Monograph 36. Washington, DC: Institute for the Study of Man, 2000.

King, David. *Finding Atlantis: A True Story of Genius, Madness, and an Extraordinary Quest for a Lost World.* New York: Harmony Books, 2005.

Kirkpatrick, David D. "Massacre Suspect Traveled World, But Lived on Internet." *New York Times*, March 15, 2019, p. A13.

Kitson, Peter J. "Politics." Nicholas Roe, ed. *Romanticism: An Oxford Guide*. Oxford: Oxford University Press, 2005. Pp. 675-685.

Kleingeld, Pauline. "Kant's Second Thoughts on Race." *The Philosophical Quarterly*, vol. 57, no. 229 (2007), pp. 573-592.

Klejn, Leo S. "Gustaf Kossinna," Tim Murray and Christopher Evans, eds. *Histories of Archaeology: A Reader in the History of Archaeology*. Oxford: Oxford University Press, 2008. Pp. 317-327.

Klejn, Leo S., and 9 others. "Discussion: Are The Origins of Indo-European Languages Explained by the Migration of the Yamnaya Culture to the West?" *European Journal of Archaeology*, vol. 21, no. 1 (2018), pp. 3-17.

Klopstock, Friedrich Gottlieb. *Sämmtliche Werke*. Leipzig: Georg Joachim Göschen, 1839.

Knipper, Corina, and 10 others. "Female Exogamy and Gene Pool Diversification at the Transition from the Final Neolithic to the Early Bronze Age in Central Europe." *Proceedings of the National Academy of Sciences of the USA*, vol. 114, no. 38 (2017), pp. 10083-10088.

Krapp, George Philip and Elliott Van Kirk Dobbie. *The Exeter Book. The Anglo-Saxon Poetic Records, Volume III*. New York: Columbia University Press, 1936.

Krebs, Christopher B. *A Most Dangerous Book: Tacitus's Germania from the Roman Empire to the Third Reich*. New York: W. W. Norton, 2011.

Kristiansen, Kristian. "Rock Art and Religion: The Sun Journey in Indo-European Mythology and Bronze Age Rock Art." A. Fredell, Kristian Kristiansen, and F. Criado Boado, eds. *Representations and Communications: Creating an Archaeological Matrix of Late Prehistoric Rock Art*. Oxford: Oxbow Books, 2010. Pp. 93-115.

Kristiansen, Kristian, and 11 others. "Re-theorising Mobility and the Formation of Culture and Language among the Corded Ware Culture in Europe." *Antiquity*, vol. 91, no. 356 (2017), pp. 334-347.

Kristinsson, Axel. "Lords and Literature: The Icelandic Sagas as Political and Social Instruments." *Scandinavian Journal of History*, vol. 28 (2003), pp. 1-17.

Krueger, David M. *Myths of the Rune Stone: Viking Martyrs and the Birthplace of America*. Minneapolis: University of Minnesota Press, 2015.

Kurlander, Eric. "Hitler's Supernatural Sciences: Astrology, Anthroposophy, and World Ice Theory in the Third Reich." Monica Black and Eric Kurlander, eds. *Revisting the "Nazi Occult": Histories, Realities, Legacies.* Rochester, N.Y.: Camden House, 2015. Pp. 132-156.

Kuyper, Jerry. "Runic Society Revives Nordic Beliefs of Teutonic Tribes." *Kenosha News*, June 7, 1976, p. 5.

Kveldúlfr Gundarsson. "Regional Organization of the Troth." *Idunna*, no. 19 (1993), pp. 24-25.

Kvideland, Reimund and Henning K. Sehmsdorf. "Nordic Folklore Studies Today." *Nordic Folklore: Recent Studies.* Bloomington and Indianapolis: Indiana University Press, 1989. Pp. 3-11.

Küßner, Mario and Tim Schüler. "Truppen in Thüringen: Nordöstlichste Römische Militäranlage Entdeckt." *Archäologie in Deutschland*, vol. 3 (2014), p. 6.

Larsson, Lars. "The Mesolithic of Southern Scandinavia." *Journal of World Prehistory*, vol. 4 (1990), pp. 257-309.

—. "The Sun from the Sea: Amber in the Mesolithic and Neolithic of Southern Scandinavia." A. Butrimas, ed. *Baltic Amber. Proceedings of the International Conference on Baltic Amber in Natural Sciences, Archaeology and Applied Arts. Acta Academiae Artium Vilnensis*, vol. 21, pp. 65-75.

—. "The Iron Age Ritual Building at Uppåkra, Southern Sweden." *Antiquity*, vol. 81, no. 311 (2007), pp. 11-25.

Lazaridis, Iosif, and 119 others. "Ancient Human Genomes Suggest Three Ancestral Populations for Present-Day Europeans." *Nature*, vol. 513 (18 September 2014), pp. 409-413.

Lazaridis, Iosif, and 52 others. "Genomic Insights into the Origin of Farming in the Ancient Near East." *Nature*, vol. 536, no. 7617 (2016), pp. 419-424.

Leigh-Hawkins, Amanda. "Frith Forge: Creating an Alliance to Protect and Promote Inclusive Heathenry." *Idunna*, no. 113 (Fall 2017), pp. 15-17.

Lewis, C. S. *Surprised by Joy: The Shape of My Early Life.* New York: Harcourt, Brace & World, 1955.

Lewis, Robert. "Online Rituals." *Idunna*, no. 119 (Summer 2019), pp. 37-39.

Lewis-Williams, David. *The Mind in the Cave: Consciousness and the Origin of Art.* London: Thames and Hudson, 2002.

Lewis-Williams, J. D., and T. A. Dowson. "The Signs of All Times: Entoptic Phenomena in Upper Palaeolithic Art." *Current Anthropology*, vol. 29, no. 2 (1988), pp. 201-245.

Lincoln, Bruce. "The Indo-European Cattle-Raiding Myth." *History of Religions*, vol. 16, no. 1 (1976), pp. 42-65.

—. *Death, War and Sacrifice: Studies in Ideology and Practice*. Chicago: University of Chicago Press, 1991.

—. *Theorizing Myth: Narrative, Ideology, and Scholarship*. Chicago: University of Chicago Press, 1999.

Ling, Johan, Zofia Stos-Gale, Lena Grandin, Kjell Billström, Eva Hjärthner-Holdar, and Per-Olof Persson. "Moving Metals II: Provenancing Scandinavian Bronze Age Artefacts by Lead Isotope and Elemental Analyses." *Journal of Archaeological Science*, vol. 41 (2014), pp. 106-132.

Ling, Johan, and Claes Uhnér. "Rock Art and Metal Trade." *Adoranten* (2014), pp. 23-43.

Link, Fabian, and J. Laurence Hare. "Pseudoscience Reconsidered: SS Research and the Archaeology of Haithabu." Monica Black and Eric Kurlander, eds. *Revisting the "Nazi Occult": Histories, Realities, Legacies*. Rochester, N.Y.: Camden House, 2015. Pp. 105-131.

List, Guido. *Der Unbesiegbare: Ein Grundzug germanischer Weltanschauung*. Vienna: Verlag Cornelius Vetter, 1898.

Littleton, C. Scott. *The New Comparative Mythology*. 3rd ed. Berkeley: University of California Press, 1982.

Lombardo, Paul A. "'The American Breed': Nazi Eugenics and the Origin of the Pioneer Fund." *Albany Law Review*, vol. 65, no. 3 (2002), pp. 743-830.

Longfellow, Henry Wadsworth. *The Poems of Henry Wadsworth Longfellow*. New York: The Modern Library, 1960.

Loveluck, Christopher P., and 11 others. "Alpine Ice-Core Evidence for the Transformation of the European Monetary System, AD 640–670." *Antiquity*, vol. 92, no. 366 (2018), pp. 1571-1585.

Lowell, James Russell. *The Poetical Works of James Russell Lowell*. 5 vols. New York: AMS Press, 1966.

Lucan (Marcus Annaeus Lucanus; J. D. Duff, transl.) *Lucan*. Loeb Classical Library. Cambridge, Mass.: Harvard University Press, 1928.

Lund, Cajsa S. "The Archaeomusicology of Scandinavia." *World Archaeology*, vol. 12, no. 3 (1981), pp. 246-265.

—. *Fornnordiska Klanger: The Sounds of Prehistoric Scandinavia.* CD recording. Musica Sveciae MS101, 1984.

—. "On Animal Calls in Ancient Scandinavia: Theory and Data." Ellen Hickman and David W. Hughes, eds. *The Archaeology of Early Music Cultures: Third International Meeting of the ICTM Study Group on Music Archaeology.* Bonn: Verlag für systematische Musikwissenschaft GmbH, 1988. Pp. 289-303.

—. "Early Ringing Stones in Scandinavia—Finds and Traditions, Questions and Problems." Gisa Jähnichen, ed. *Studia Instrumentorum Musica Popularis I.* Münster: Verlag MV-Wissenschaft, 2009.

Lunde, Paul and Caroline Stone (eds.) *Ibn Fadlan and the Land of Darkness: Arab Travellers in the Far North.* London: Penguin, 2012.

Lundström, Agneta. "Helgö: A Pre-Viking Trading Center." *Archaeology*, vol. 31 no. 4 (1978), pp. 24-31.

Luhrmann, Tanya M. *Persuasions of the Witch's Craft.* Cambridge, Mass.: Harvard University Press, 1989.

Lyke, M. L. "Pagans, Tribes, Scientists Battle over Ancient Bones." *Washington Post*, September 10, 1997.

Lødøen, Trond and Gro Mandt. *The Rock Art of Norway.* Oxford: Windgather Press, 2009.

Löw, Luitgard. "The Great God's Oldest Runes." Horst Junginger and Andreas Åkerlund, eds. *Nordic Ideology Between Religion and Scholarship.* Frankfurt: Peter Lang, 2013. Pp. 107-131.

Löwenborg, Daniel. "An Iron Age Shock Doctrine—Did the AD 536–7 Event Trigger Large-Scale Social Changes in the Mälaren Valley Area?" *Journal of Archaeology and Ancient History*, no. 4 (2012), pp. 1-29.

Lüsch-Schreiwer, Robert. "The Troth 'In-Reach Program', A Preliminary Description." *Idunna*, no. 96 (2013), p. 32.

—. "From the Tiller." *Idunna*, no. 115 (2018), pp. 1-3.

Mabie, Hamilton Wright. *Norse Stories.* Chicago: Rand, McNally & Co., 1902.

Magee, Bryan. *The Tristan Chord: Wagner and Philosophy.* New York: Henry Holt, 2000.

Magnell, Ola and Elisabeth Iregren. "*Veitstú hvé blóta skal?*: The Old Norse *Blót* in the Light of Osteological Remains from Frösö Church, Jämtland, Sweden." *Current Swedish Archaeology*, vol. 18 (2010), pp. 223-250.

Mallory, J. P. *In Search of the Indo-Europeans.* New York: Thames & Hudson, 1989.

Mallory, J. P. and D. Q. Adams. *Encyclopedia of Indo-European Culture.* London: Fitzroy Dearborn, 1997.

—. *The Oxford Introduction to Proto-Indo-European and the Proto-Indo-European World.* Oxford: Oxford University Press, 2006.

Markey, Tom. "A Tale of Two Helmets: The Negau A and B Inscriptions." *Journal of Indo-European Studies*, vol. 29, nos. 1-2 (2001), pp. 69-172.

Marold, Edith (ed.) "Einarr skálaglamm Helgason, *Vellekla.*" Diana Whaley (ed.), *Poetry from the Kings' Sagas 1: From Mythical Times to c. 1035.* Skaldic Poetry of the Scandinavian Middle Ages 1. Turnhout: Brepols, 2012. Pp. 283-323.

Marwick, Ernest W. *The Folklore of Orkney and Shetland.* Totowa, N.J.: Rowman and Littlefield, 1975.

Mathieson, Iain, and 116 others. "The Genomic History of Southeastern Europe." *Nature*, vol. 555 (2018), pp. 197-203.

McGovern, Patrick E., Gretchen R. Hall, and Armen Mirzoian. "A Biomolecular Archaeological Approach to 'Nordic Grog'." *Danish Journal of Archaeology*, vol. 2, no. 2 (2013), pp. 112-131.

McNallen, Stephen A. *What Is Asatru?* Breckenridge, Tx.: Asatru Free Assembly, 1985.

—. *Ásatrú: A Native European Spirituality.* Nevada City, Calif.: Runestone Press, 2015.

McQueen, Gert. *A Short History of Anglo-Saxon Theodism.* 2nd ed. Watertown, N.Y.: Theod, 1994.

—. "Gert Remembers." Gering Theod. **https://web.archive.org/web/20160507225554/http://gamall-steinn.org/Gering/gerthist.html** Accessed March 31, 2019.

Megaw, J. V. S. "Problems and Non-Problems in Palaeo-Organology: A Musical Miscellany." J. M. Coles and D. D. A. Simpson (eds.) *Studies in Ancient Europe: Essays Presented to Stuart Piggott.* New York: Humanities Press, 1968. Pp. 333-358.

Meiklejohn, Chris, Erik Brinch Petersen, and Verner Alexandersen. "The Anthropology and Archaeology of Mesolithic Gender in the Western Baltic." Moira Donald and Linda Hurcombe, eds. *Gender and Material Culture in Archaeological Perspective*. Basingstoke: Macmillan, 2000. Pp. 222-237.

Melheim, L., and 10 others. "Moving Metals III: Possible Origins for Copper in Bronze Age Denmark Based on Lead Isotopes and Geochemistry." *Journal of Archaeological Science*, vol. 96 (2018), pp. 85-105.

Mees, Bernard. *The Science of the Swastika*. Budapest: Central European University Press, 2008.

Michael, George. "David Lane and the Fourteen Words." *Politics, Religion & Ideology*, vol. 10, no. 1 (2009), pp. 43-61.

Micklos, David and Elof Carlson. "Engineering American Society: The Lesson of Eugenics." *Nature Reviews: Genetics*, vol. 1 (2000), pp. 153-158.

Midgard Rising. Podcast. Season 3, Episode 6, "Stephen McNallen Interview." Midgard Rising podcast. November 26, 2019. **https://midgard-rising.zencast. website/episodes/6** Accessed February 16, 2020.

Mikkelsen, Egil. "Religion and Ecology: Motifs and Locations of Hunters' Rock Carvings in Eastern Norway." Gro Steinsland, ed. *Words and Objects: Towards a Dialogue Between Archaeology and History of Religion*. Oslo: Norwegian University Oress, 1986. Pp. 127-141.

Milisauskas, Sarunas and Janusz Kruk. "Middle Neolithic Continuity, Diversity, Innovations, and Greater Complexity, 5500/5000–3500-3000 BC." Sarunas Milisauskas, ed. *European Prehistory: A Survey*. New York: Kluwer/Plenum, 2002. Pp. 193-246.

Mills, Alexander Rud. *The First Guide Book to the Anglecyn Church of Odin, Containing Some of the Chief Rites of the Church, and Some Hymns for the Use of the Church*. Sydney: Self-published, 1936.

—. *The Odinist Religion: Overcoming Jewish Christianity*. Melbourne: Self-published, 1939.

—. *The Call of our Ancient Nordic Religion*. Coventry: Northern World, 1957.

Mitchell P. M. *Vilhelm Grønbech*. Boston: Twayne Publishers, 1978.

Mitchell, Stephen A. *Heroic Sagas and Ballads*. Ithaca, N.Y.: Cornell University Press, 1991.

Morris, William. *The Collected Works of William Morris. Volume XII: The Story of Sigurd the Volsung and the Fall of the Niblungs.* New York: Russell and Russell, 1966.

Mosse, George L. *The Crisis of German Ideology: Intellectual Origins of the Third Reich.* New York: Grosset and Dunlap, 1964.

Motz, Lotte. *The Faces of the Goddess.* Oxford: Oxford University Press, 1997.

Mócsy, András. *Pannonia and Upper Moesia: A History of the Middle Danube Provinces of the Roman Empire.* Abingdon: Routledge, 2014.

Mukherjee, Anna J., Elisa Roßberger, Matthew A. James, Peter Pfälzner, Catherine L. Higgitt, Raymond White, David A. Peggie, and Dany Azar. "The Qatna Lion: Scientific Confirmation of Baltic Amber in Late Bronze Age Syria." *Antiquity*, vol. 82, no. 315 (2008), pp. 49-59.

Murphy, G. Ronald (transl.) *The Heliand: The Saxon Gospel.* New York: Oxford University Press, 1992.

Musset, Lucien (Edward and Columba James, transl.) *The Germanic Invasions.* New York: Barnes and Noble, 1993.

Müller, Johannes and Rick Peterson. "Ceramics and Society in Northern Europe." Chris Fowler, Jan Harding, and Daniela Hofmann, eds. *The Oxford Handbook of Neolithic Europe.* Oxford: Oxford University Press, 2015. Pp. 573-604.

Müller, Max. *Biographies of Words and the Home of the Aryas.* Collected Works, vol. 10. London: Longmans, Green, & Co. 1912.

—. "On the Philosophy of Mythology." John R. Stone, ed. *The Essential Max Müller: On Language Mythology, and Religion.* New York: Palgrave Macmillan, 2002.

Nijdam, Han and Otto S. Knottnerus. "Redbad, the Once and Future King of the Frisians." Simon Halink, ed. *Northern Myths, Modern Identities: The Nationalisation of Northern Mythologies Since 1800.* Leiden: Brill, 2019. Pp. 87-114.

Niles, John D. "Was There A Legend of Lejre?" John D. Niles, Tom Christensen, and Marijane Osborn, eds. *Beowulf and Lejre.* Tempe, Ariz.: Arizona Center for Medieval and Renaissance Studies, 2007. Pp. 255-265.

Nilsson, P. "Reused Rock Art: Iron Age Activities at Bronze Age Rock Art Sites." Joakim Goldhahn, Ingrid Fuglestvedt, and Andrew Jones (eds.) *Changing Pictures: Rock Art Traditions and Visions in Northern Europe.* Oxford: Oxbow Books, 2010. Pp. 155-168.

Noll, Richard. *The Aryan Christ: The Secret Life of Carl Jung.* New York: Random House, 1997.

Nordeide, Sæbjørg Walaker. "Thor's Hammer in Norway: A Symbol of Reaction Against the Christian Cross?" Anders Andrén, Kristina Jennbert, and Catharina Raudvere, eds. *Old Norse Religion in Long-Term Perspectives: Origins, Changes, and Interactions.* Lund: Nordic Academic Press, 2006. Pp. 218-223.

Nordvig, Mathias, and Felix Riede. "Are There Echoes of the AD 46 Event in the Viking Ragnarok Myth? A Critical Appraisal." *Environment and History,* vol. 24, no. 3 (2018), pp. 303-324.

Näsman, Ulf. "The Ethnogenesis of the Danes and the Making of a Danish Kingdom." Tania Dickinson and David Griffiths, eds. *The Making of Kingdoms. Anglo-Saxon Studies in Archaeology and Histo*ry, vol. 10. Oxford: Oxford University Committee for Archaeology, 1999. Pp. 5-12.

Odinist, The. Articles archive, America First Books. **https://www.amfirstbooks.com/IntroPages/ToolBarTopics/Articles/FeaturedAuthors/Christensen,Else/Christensenindex.html** Accessed March 24, 2019.

Odinist, The. Microfilm. *American Religions Collection: Series 1: Nontraditional American Religions: Western Esotericism from Witchcraft to the New Age, 1st Edition. Part 1: Witchcraft, Paganism, and Magick.* American Religions Collection, University of California at Santa Barbara. Primary Source Media, Gale/CENGAGE Learning, 2005.

Odinist Fellowship. "Newark Odinist Temple." **http://odinisttemple.uk/** Accessed February 26, 2019.

O'Donoghue, Heather. *From Asgard to Valhalla: The Remarkable History of the Norse Myths.* London: I. B. Tauris, 2007.

O'Flaherty, Wendy D., transl. *The Rig-Veda: An Anthology.* London: Penguin Books, 1981.

Olmsted, Garrett. "Archaeology, Social Evolution, and the Spread of Indo-European Languages and Cultures." Edgar C. Polomé, ed. *Miscellanea Indo-Europea. Journal of Indo-European Studies,* Monograph 33. Washington, DC: Institute for the Study of Man, 1999. Pp. 75-116.

Oma, Kristen Armstrong. "Long Time—Long House." Frode Iversen and Håkan Petersson, eds. *The Agrarian Life of the North 2000 BC–AD 1000: Studies in Rural Settlement and Farming in Norway.* Oslo: Cappelen Damm Akademisk, 2017.

Orosius (Roy J. Deferrari, transl.) *The Seven Books of History Against the Pagans.* Washington, D.C.: Catholic University of America Press, 1964.

Osred. *Odinism: Present, Past, and Future.* Melbourne: Renewal Publications, 2010.

—. "A Multi-Faceted Life." Stubba [John Yeowell], *This is Odinism, And Other Essays.* Melbourne: Renewal Publications, 2016. Pp. 103-111.

Page, R. I. "Dumézil Revisited". *Saga-Book of the Viking Society*, vol. 20 (1978-81), pp. 49-69.

Parker, John. *Inside the Foreign Legion: The Sensational Story of the World's Toughest Army.* London: Piatkus, 1998.

Paulsson, Bettina Schulz, Christian Isendahl, and Fredrik Frykman Markurth. "Elk Heads at Sea: Maritime Hunters and Long=Distance Boat Journeys in Late Stone Age Fennoscandia." *Oxford Journal of Archaeology*, vol. 38, no. 4 (2019), pp. 398-419.

Paxson, Diana L. *Trance-Portation: Learning to Navigate the Inner World.* Newburyport, Mass.: Weiser, 2008.

—. *Odin: Ecstasy, Runes and Norse Magic.* Newburyport, Mass.: Weiser, 2017.

Pedersen, Anne. "The Jelling Monuments—Ancient Royal Memorial and Modern World Heritage Site." Marie Stokland, Michael Lerche Nielsen, Bente Holmberg, and Gillian Fellows-Jensen, eds. *Runes and their Secrets: Studies in Runology.* Copenhagen: Museum Tusculanum Press, 2006. Pp. 283-314.

Pedersen, Anne, Else Roesdahl, and James Graham-Campbell. "Dress Accessories and Personal Ornaments of Metal. Amulets." Else Roesdahl, Søren M. Sindbæk, Anne Pedersen, and David M. Wilson, eds. *Aggersborg: The Viking-Age Settlement and Fortress.* Aarhus: National Museum of Denmark / Jutland Archaeological Society, 2014. Pp. 279-289.

Peets, Jüri, Raili Allmäe, and Liina Maldre. "Archaeological Investigations of Pre-Viking Age Burial Boat in Salme Village at Saaremaa." *Archaeological Fieldwork in Estonia* (2010), pp. 29-48.

Pentz, Peter. "Viking Art, Snorri Sturluson and Some Recent Metal Detector Finds." *Fornvannen*, vol. 113 (2018), pp. 17-33.

Pentz, Peter, Maria Panum Baastrup, Sabine Karg, and Ulla Mannering. "Kong Haralds Vølve." *Nationalmuseets Arbejdsmark* 2009, pp. 215-232.

Pew Forum. "America's Changing Religious Landscape." http://www.pewforum.org/2015/05/12/americas-changing-religious-landscape/ Accessed March 24, 2019.

Phelps, Reginald H. "'Before Hitler Came': Thule Society and Germanen Orden." *Journal of Modern History*, vol. 35, no. 3 (1963), pp. 245-261.

Pliny the Elder. *Naturalis historia* [Natural History]. 10 vols. Loeb Classical Library. Cambridge, Mass.: Harvard University Press, 1971-1979.

Polomé, Edgar C. "Who are the Germanic People?" Susan Nacev Skomal and Edgar C. Polomé, eds. *Proto-Indo-European: The Archaeology of a Linguistic Problem. Studies in Honor of Marija Gimbutas. Journal of Indo-European Studies*, Monograph 1. Washington, DC: Institute for the Study of Man, 1987. Pp. 216-244.

—. *Essays on Germanic Religion. Journal of Indo-European Studies*, Monograph 6. Washington DC: Institute for the Study of Man, 1989.

Posth, Cosimo, and 34 others. "Pleistocene Mitochondrial Genomes Suggest a Single Major Dispersal of Non-Africans and a Late Glacial Population Turnover in Europe." *Current Biology*, vol. 26, no. 6 (2016), pp. 827-833.

Price, Neil. *The Viking Way: Magic and Mind in Late Iron Age Scandinavia*. 2nd ed. Oxford: Oxbow Books, 2019.

Price, Neil and Paul Mortimer. "An Eye for Odin? Divine Role-Playing in the Age of Sutton Hoo." *European Journal of Archaeology*, vol. 17, no. 3 (2014), pp. 517-538.

Price, T. Douglas. *Europe Before Rome: A Site-By-Site Tour of the Stone, Bronze, and Iron Ages*. New York: Oxford University Press, 2013.

—. *Ancient Scandinavia: An Archaeological History from the First Humans to the Vikings*. Oxford: Oxford Universiy Press, 2015.

Priestland, David. *Merchant, Soldier, Sage: A New History of Power*. London: Penguin, 2014.

Pringle, Heather. *The Master Plan: Himmler's Scholars and the Holocaust*. New York: Hyperion, 2006.

Procopius of Caesarea (H. B. Dewing, transl.). *History of the Wars*. 7 vols. Loeb Classical Library. Cambridge, Mass.: Harvard University Press, 1959.

Puhvel, Jaan. *Comparative Mythology*. Baltimore and London: Johns Hopkins University Press, 1987.

Puschner, Uwe. "'One People, One Reich, One God': The *Völkische Weltanschauung* and Movement." *Bulletin of the German Historical Institute, London*, vol. 24, no. 1 (2002), pp. 5-28.

—. "The Notions *Völkisch* and Nordic: A Conceptual Approximation." Horst Junginger and Andreas Åkerlund, eds. *Nordic Ideology Between Religion and Scholarship.* Frankfurt: Peter Lang, 2013. Pp. 21-38.

Rabinbach, Anson and Sander L. Gilman (eds.) *The Third Reich Sourcebook.* Berkeley: University of California Press, 2013.

Rainio, Riitta and Kristiina Mannermaa. "Tracing the Rattle of Animal Tooth Pendants from the Middle Neolithic Graves of Ajvide, Gotland, Sweden." *World Archaeology*, vol. 46 no. 3 (2014), pp. 332-348.

Rascovan, Nicolás, Karl-Göran Sjögren, Kristian Kristiansen, Rasmus Nielsen, Eske Willerslev, Christelle Desnues, and Simon Rasmussen. "Emergence and Spread of Basal Lineages of *Yersinia pestis* During the Neolithic Decline." *Cell*, vol. 176, no. 1-2 (2019), pp. 295-305.

Rasmussen, Morten, and 18 others. "The Ancestry and Affiliations of Kennewick Man." *Nature*, vol. 523 (2015), pp. 455-458.

Ratke, Sharon. "Guldgubber—a Glimpse into the Vendel Period." *Lund Archaeological Review*, vol. 15 (2009), pp. 149-159.

Richards, Martin. "The Neolithic Invasion of Europe." *Annual Review of Anthropology*, vol. 32 (2003), pp. 135-162.

Rimbert (Charles H. Robinson, transl.) *Anskar: The Apostle of the North, 801-865.* London: Society for the Propagation of the Gospel in Foreign Parts, 1921.

Ringe, Don. *From Proto-Indo-European to Proto-Germanic.* 2nd ed. Oxford: Oxford University Press, 2017.

Roberts, Michael. *Gustavus Adolphus: A History of Sweden, 1611-1632.* London: Longmans, Green & Co., 1953.

Robinson, Orrin W. *Old English and its Closest Relatives: A Survey of the Earliest Germanic Languages.* Palo Alto: Stanford University Press, 1992.

Roesdahl, Else and David M. Wilson (eds.) *From Viking to Crusader.* New York: Rizzoli, 1992.

Roesdahl, Else and Søren M. Sindbæk. "Introduction." Else Roesdahl, Søren M. Sindbæk, Anne Pedersen, and David M. Wilson, eds. *Aggersborg: The Viking-Age Settlement and Fortress.* Aarhus: National Museum of Denmark / Jutland Archaeological Society, 2014. Pp. 11-16.

Romey, Christine. "This 7,000-Year-Old Woman was Among Sweden's Last Hunter-Gatherers." *National Geographic.* November 11, 2019. **https://www.**

nationalgeographic.com/history/2019/11/7000-year-old-woman-recon-struction-sweden-hunter-gatherer/ Accessed February 20, 2020.

Ross, Anne and Don Robins, *The Life and Death of a Druid Prince*. New York: Summit Books, 1989.

Ross, Margaret Clunies. "The Development of Old Norse Textual Worlds: Genealogical Structure as a Principle of Literary Organisation in Early Iceland." *Journal of English and Germanic Philology*, vol. 92, no. 3 (1993), pp. 372-385.

—. *The Cambridge Introduction to the Old Norse–Icelandic Saga*. Cambridge: Cambridge University Press, 2000.

Rossel, Sven H. *Scandinavian Ballads*. WITS II no. 2. Madison: University of Wisconsin Department of Scandinavian Studies, 1982.

Rowe, Elizabeth Ashman. *The Development of* Flateyjarbók: *Iceland and the Norwegian Dynastic Crisis of 1389*. Odense: University Press of Southern Denmark, 2005.

Rawlings, Louis. "The Roman Conquest of Southern Gaul, 125-121 BC." Michael Whitby and Harry Sidebottom, eds. *The Encyclopedia of Ancient Battles*, Vol. 2. Oxford: Wiley Blackwell, 2017. Pp. 858-864.

Runestone, The. Issues 1 (Spring 1972)–60 (January 1987). Microfilm. *American Religions Collection: Series 1: Nontraditional American Religions: Western Esotericism from Witchcraft to the New Age, 1st Edition. Part 1: Witchcraft, Paganism, and Magick. American Religions Collection, University of California at Santa Barbara*. Primary Source Media, Gale/CENGAGE Learning, 2005.

Rydberg, Viktor (Rasmus B. Anderson, transl.) *Teutonic Mythology*. London: Swan Sonnenschein & Co., 1889.

Saddington, D. B. "Roman Soldiers, Local Gods and *Interpretatio Romana* in Roman Germany." *Acta Classica*, vol. 42 (1999), pp. 145-169.

Sadier, Benjamin, Jean-Jacques Delannoy, Lucilla Benedetti, Didier L. Bourlès, Stéphane Jaillet, Jean-Michel Geneste, Anne-Elisabeth Lebatard, and Maurice Arnold. "Further Constraints on the Chauvet Cave Artwork Elaboration." *Proceedings of the National Academy of Sciences of the USA*, vol. 109, no. 21 (2019), pp. 8002-8006.

Sánchez-Quinto, Federico, and Carles Lalueza-Fox. "Almost 20 Years of Neanderthal Palaeogenetics: Adaptation, Admixture, Diversity, Demography and Extinction." *Philosophical Transactions of the Royal Society of London Series B*, vol. 370 (2015): 20130374.

Sánchez-Quinto, Federico, and 17 others. "Megalithic Tombs in Western and Northern Neolithic Europe Were Linked to a Kindred Society." *Proceedings of the National Academy of Sciences of the USA*, vol. 116 (2019), pp. 9469-9474.

Sandars, N. K. *Prehistoric Art in Europe*. New Haven and London: Yale University Press, 1985.

Sannhet, Thor. "An Interview with Else Christensen." *Vor Trú*, no. 49 (1993), pp. 5-30.

Saunders, Robert A. "Of Gods and Men: Uses and Abuses of Neo-Paganism by Nationalist Movements in the 'North'." Simon Halink, ed. *Northern Myths, Modern Identities: The Nationalisation of Northern Mythologies since 1800*. Leiden: Brill, 2019. Pp. 217-230.

Sausverde, Erika. "*Seewörter* and Substratum in Germanic, Baltic, and Baltic Finno-Ugric Languages." Karlene Jones-Bley and Martin E. Huld, eds. *The Indo-Europeanization of Northern Europe. Journal of Indo-European Studies*, Monograph 33. Washington, DC: Institute for the Study of Man, 1999. Pp. 133-147.

Saxo Grammaticus (Peter Fisher, transl.) *The History of the Danes, Books I-IX*. Woodbridge: D. S. Brewer, 1996.

Schaffer, Gavin. ""'Scientific' Racism Again?"': Reginald Gates, the *Mankind Quarterly* and the Question of "Race" in Science after the Second World War." *Journal of American Studies*, vol. 41, no. 2 (2007), pp. 253-278.

Schellinger, Uwe, Andreas Anton, and Michael T. Schetsche. "Pragmatic Occultism in the Military History of the Third Reich." Monica Black and Eric Kurlander, eds. *Revisting the "Nazi Occult": Histories, Realities, Legacies*. Rochester, N.Y.: Camden House, 2015. Pp. 157-180.

Schiffels, Stephan, and 12 others. "Iron Age and Anglo-Saxon Genomes from East England Reveal British Migration History." *Nature Communications* vol. 7 (2016): 10408. doi: 10.1038/ncomms10408

Schlegel, Friedrich (Ernst Behler and Roman Struc, transl.). *Dialogue on Poetry and Literary Aphorisms*. University Park, Penn.: Pennsylvania State University Press, 1968.

Schnurbein, Siegmar von. "Augustus in *Germania* and His New 'Town' at Waldgirmes East of the Rhine." *Journal of Roman Archaeology*, vol. 16 (2003), pp. 93-107.

Schnurbein, Stefanie von. *Norse Revival: Transformations of Germanic Neopaganism*. Chicago: Haymarket Books, 2017.

Schreiwer, Robert L. *The First Book of Urglaawe Myths.* Bristol, Penn.: Deitscherei. com, 2014.

Schrijver, Peter. "Animal, Vegetable and Mineral: Some Western European Substratum Words." A. Lubotsky, ed. *Sound Law and Analogy: Papers in Honor of Robert S. P. Beekes on the Occasion of his 60ᵗʰ Birthday.* Amsterdam: Rodopi, 1997. Pp. 293-316.

— . *Language Contact and the Origins of the Germanic Languages.* New York: Routledge, 2014.

Schutz, Herbert, *The Prehistory of Germanic Europe.* New Haven: Yale University Press, 1983.

Schultz, Katja. "Crossing the Borders: Loki and the Decline of the Nation State." Simon Halink, ed. *Northern Myths, Modern Identities: The Nationalisation of Northern Mythologies since 1800.* Leiden: Brill, 2019. Pp. 217-230.

Scott, Walter. *Rokeby: A Poem in Six Cantos.* London: Longman, Hurst, Rees, Orme, and Brown, 1813.

—. *The Pirate.* 3 vols. Edinburgh: Archibald Constable & Co., 1822.

Séfériadès, Michel Louis. "*Spondylus* and Long-Distance Trade in Prehistoric Europe." David Anthony and Jennifer Y. Chi, eds. *The Lost World of Old Europe: The Danube Valley, 5000-3500 BC.* New York: Institute for the Study of the Ancient World / Princeton, N.J.: Princeton University Press, 2009. Pp. 178-189.

Semple, Sarah. "A Fear of the Past: The Place of the Prehistoric Burial Mound in the Ideology of Middle and Later Anglo-Saxon England." *World Archaeology,* vol. 30, no. 1 (1998), pp. 109-126.

—. "Defining the OE *hearg*: A Preliminary Archaeological and Topographic Examination of *hearg* Place Names and their Hinterlands." *Early Medieval Europe,* vol. 15, no 4 (2007), pp. 364-385.

—. "In the Open Air." Martin Carver, Alexandra Sanmark, and Sarah Semple, eds. *Signals of Belief in Early England: Anglo-Saxon Paganism Revisited.* Oxford: Oxbow Books, 2010. Pp. 21-48.

Serith, Ceisiwr. *Deep Ancestors: Practicing the Religion of the Proto-Indo-Europeans.* Tucson: ADF Publishing, 2009.

Serpico, Margaret and Raymond White. "Resins, Amber and Bitumen." Paul T. Nicholson and Ian Shaw, eds. *Ancient Egyptian Materials and Technology.* Cambridge: Cambridge University Press, 2009. Pp. 430-475.

Shaw, Philip. "The Origins of the Theophoric Week in the Germanic Languages." *Early Medieval Europe*, vol. 15, no. 4 (2007), pp. 386-401.

—. *Pagan Goddesses in the Early Germanic World: Eostre, Hreda and the Cult of Matronae*. London: Bristol Classical Press, 2011.

Shippey, Tom. "Introduction." T. A. Shippey and Andreas Haarder, eds. *Beowulf: The Critical Heritage*. London: Routledge, 1998. Pp. 1-55.

—. "A Revolution Reconsidered: Mythography and Mythology in the Nineteenth Century." *The Shadow-Walkers: Jacob Grimm's Mythology of the Monstrous*. Tempe, Ariz.: Arizona Center for Medieval and Renaissance Studies, 2005. Pp. 1-28.

Shishlina, Natalia. *Reconstruction of the Bronze Age of the Caspian Steppes: Life Styles and Life Ways of Pastoral Nomads*. BAR International Series, no. 1876. Oxford: Archaeopress, 2008.

Sigríður Sunna Ebenesersdóttir, Ásgeir Sigurðsson, Federico Sánchez-Quinto, Carles Lalueza-Fox, Kári Stefánsson, and Agnar Helgason. "A New Subclade of mtDNA Haplogroup C1 Found in Icelanders: Evidence of Pre-Columbian Contact?" *American Journak of Physical Anthropology*, vol.144 (2011), pp. 92-22.

Sigríður Sunna Ebenesersdóttir and 29 others. "Ancient Genomes from Iceland Reveal the Making of a Human Population." *Science*, vol. 360 (2018), pp. 1028-1032.

Simek, Rudolf (Angela Hall, transl.) *Dictionary of Northern Mythology*. Cambridge: D. S. Brewer, 1993.

—. "The Late Roman Iron Age Cult of the *Matronae* and Related Germanic Deities." *Weibliche Eliten in der Frühgeschichte: Female Elites in Protohistoric Europe*. Dieter Quast, ed. Mainz: Verlag des Römisch-Germanischen Zentralmuseums, 2011. Pp. 219-228.

Singer, Graciela Noemi Gestoso. "Amber Exchange in the Late Bronze Age Levant in Cross-Cultural Perspective." *Aula Orientalis*, vol. 34, no. 2 (2016), pp. 251-264.

Sjöstrand, Ylva. "Product or Production: On the Accumulative Aspect of Rock Art at Nämforsen, Northern Sweden." *Current Swedish Archaeology*, vol. 18 (2010), pp. 251-269.

Sognnes, Kalle. "Symbols in a Changing World: Rock-Art and the Transition from Hunting to Farming in Mid Norway." Christopher Chippindale and Paul S. C. Taçon, eds. *The Archaeology of Rock-Art*. Cambridge: Cambridge University Press, 1998. Pp. 146-162.

Spatzier, André and François Bertemes. "The Ring Sanctuary of Pömmelte, Germany: A Monumental Multi-Layered Metaphor of the Late Third Millennium BC." *Antiquity*, vol. 92 (2018), pp. 655-673.

Speer, Albert. *Inside the Third Reich: Memoirs.* New York: Macmillan, 1970.

Spickermann, Wolfgang. "Waluburg." Hubert Cancik and Helmuth Schneider, (eds.) *Brill's New Pauly: Encyclopaedia of the Ancient World.* **http://dx.doi. org/10.1163/1574-9347bnpe12208850** Accessed May 22, 2019.

Spotts, Frederic. *Bayreuth: A History of the Wagner Festival.* New Haven, Conn.: Yale University Press, 1994.

Stanley, Eric Gerald. *Imagining the Anglo-Saxon Past: The Search for Anglo-Saxon Paganism and Anglo-Saxon Trial by Jury.* Cambridge: D. S. Brewer, 2000.

Staudenmaier, Peter. "Esoteric Alternatives in Imperial Germany: Science, Spirit, and the Modern Occult Revival." Monica Black and Eric Kurlander, eds. *Revisting the "Nazi Occult": Histories, Realities, Legacies.* Rochester, N.Y.: Camden House, 2015. Pp. 23-41.

Steigmann-Gall, Richard. *The Holy Reich: Nazi Conceptions of Christianity, 1919-1945.* Cambridge: Cambridge University Press, 2003.

Stephens, George. *The Old-Northern Runic Monuments of Scandinavia and England.* 2 vols. London: John Russell Smith, 1866-7.

Stinar, Greg. "The Odinic Rite Speaks: *Runestone* Interviews Heimgest!" *The Runestone*, no. 15 (Summer 1996), pp. 3-7.

Storgaard, Birger. "Cosmopolitan Aristocrats." Lars Jørgensen, Birger Storgaard, and Lone Gebauer Thomsen, eds. *The Spoils of Victory: The North in the Shadow of the Roman Empire.* Copenhagen: Nationalmuseet, 2003. Pp. 106-125.

Stothers, Richard B. and Michael R. Rampino. "Volcanic Eruptions in the Mediterranean Before AD 630 from Written and Archaeological Sources." *Journal of Geophysical Research: Solid Earth*, vol. 88 (1983), pp. 6357- 6371.

Strmiska, Michael F. and Baldur A. Sigurvinsson. "Asatru: Nordic Paganism in Iceland and America". Michael F. Strmiska, ed. *Modern Paganism in World Cultures.* Santa Barbara, California: ABC-CLIO, 2005. Pp. 127–179.

Stroeven, Arjen P., and 15 others. "Deglaciation of Fennoscandia." *Quaternary Science Reviews*, vol. 147 (2016), pp. 91-121.

Suetonius (J. C. Rolfe, transl.) *Suetonius.* 2 vols. Loeb Classical Library. Cambridge, Mass.: Harvard University Press, 1964.

Sulimirski, T. *The Sarmatians.* New York: Praeger, 1970.

Sussman, Robert Wald. *The Myth of Race: The Troubling Persistence of an Unscientific Idea.* Cambridge, Mass.: Harvard University Press, 2014.

Sutherland, Patricia D. "The Norse and Native North Americans." William W. Fitzhugh and Elizabeth Ward, eds. *Vikings: The North Atlantic Saga.* Washington DC: Smithsonian Institution Press, 2000. Pp. 238-247.

Swanton, Michael. "The Deeds of Hereward." Thomas H. Ohlgren, ed. *Medieval Outlaws: Ten Tales in Modern English Translation.* Rev. ed. West Lafayette, Ind.: Parlor Press, 2005. Pp. 28-99.

— (ed. transl.) *The Anglo-Saxon Chronicle.* New York: Routledge, 1998.

Tacitus, Cornelius (Clifford H. Moore and John Jackson, transl.) *The Histories. The Annals.* 4 vols. Loeb Classical Library. Cambridge, Mass.: Harvard University Press, 1962.

— (M. Hutton and E. H. Warmington, eds.) *Dialogus, Agricola, Germania.* Loeb Classical Library. Cambridge, Mass.: Harvard University Press, 1980.

Talbot, C. H. (transl.) *The Anglo-Saxon Missionaries in Germany.* New York: Sheed and Ward, 1954.

Telegin, D. Ya and J. P. Mallory. *The Anthropomorphic Stelae of the Ukraine: The Early Iconography of the Indo-Europeans. Journal of Indo-European Studies,* Monograph 11. Washington, DC: Institute for the Study of Man, 1994.

"The Occult: A Substitute Faith." *TIME Magazine,* June 19, 1972. Pp. 62-68.

The Troth. "Louisiana Church Burnings: Hate Has No Place Here." Press release. April 11, 2019. **https://www.thetroth.org/news/20190411-162116** Accessed January 25, 2020.

Thedéen, Susanne. "Immortal Maidens: The Visual Significance of the Colour White in Girls' Graves on Viking-Age Gotland." Fredrik Fahlander and Anna Kjellström, eds. *Making Sense of Things: Archaeologies of Sensory Perception.* Stockholm Studies in Archaeology, vol. 53. Stockholm: Postdoctoral Archaeological Group, Stockholm University. pp. 103-120.

Thorpe, Lewis (transl.) *Einhard and Notker the Stammerer: Two Lives of Charlemagne.* London: Penguin, 1969.

Thompson, E. A. *The Visigoths in the Time of Ulfilas.* Oxford: Oxford University Press, 1966.

—. *The Huns.* Revised ed. Oxford: Blackwell, 1996.

Thrasher, Steven. "America's Top Heathen." *Village Voice*, Nov. 3, 2011.

Todd, Malcolm. *The Early Germans*. 2nd ed. Oxford: Blackwell, 2004.

Tolkien, Christopher (transl.) *The Saga of King Heiðrek the Wise*. London: Thomas Nelson and Sons, 1960.

Tolkien, J. R. R. *The Two Towers*. 2nd ed. Boston: Houghton Mifflin, 1966.

—. (Humphrey Carpenter, ed.) *The Letters of J. R. R. Tolkien*. Boston: Houghton Mifflin, 1981.

Toohey, Matthew, Kirston Krüger, Michael Sigl, Frode Stordal and Henrik Svenden. "Climatic and Social Impacts of a Volcanic Double Event at the Dawn of the Middle Ages." *Climatic Change* (April 2016). doi 10.1007/s10584-016-1648-7

Treitel, Corinna. *A Science for the Soul: Occultism and the Genesis of the German Modern*. Baltimore: Johns Hopkins University Press, 2004.

Tringham, Ruth, and Margaret Conkey. "Rethinking Figurines: A Critical View from Archaeology of Gimbutas, the 'Goddess' and Popular Culture." Lucy Goodison and Christine Morris, eds. *Ancient Goddesses: The Myths and the Evidence*. Madison: University of Wisconsin Press, 1998. Pp. 22-45.

Tulinius, Torfi H. (Randi C. Eldevik, transl.) *The Matter of the North: The Rise of Literary Fiction in Thirteenth-Century Iceland*. Odense: Odense University Press, 2002.

Turcan, Robert (Antonia Nevill, transl.). *The Cults of the Roman Empire*. Oxford: Blackwell, 1996.

Turner, William W. *Power on the Right*. Berkeley: Ramparts Press, 1971.

Turville-Petre, Gabriel. *Myth and Religion of the North*. New York: Holt, Rinehart and Winston, 1964.

Twohey, Elizabeth Shee. "A 'Mother Goddess' in North-West Europe c. 4200-2500 BC?" in Lucy Goodison and Christine Morris, eds. *Ancient Goddesses: The Myths and the Evidence*. Madison: University of Wisconsin Press, 1998. Pp. 164-179.

Varberg, Jeanette. "Lady of the Battle and of the Horse: On Anthropomorphic Gods and their Cult in Late Bronze Age Scandinavia." Sophie Bergerbrat and Serena Sabatini, eds. *Counterpoint: Essags in Archaeology and Hertage Studies in Honour of Professor Kristian Kristiansen*. BAR International Series 2508. Oxford: Archaeopress, 2013. Pp. 147-157.

Varberg, Jeannette, Bernard Gratuze, and Flemming Kaul. "Between Egypt, Mesopotamia and Scandinavia: Late Bronze Age Glass Beads Found in Denmark." *Journal of Archaeological Science*, vol. 54 (2015), pp. 168-181.

Varberg, Jeannette, Bernard Gratuze, Flemming Kaul, Anne Haslund Hansen, Mihai Rotea, and Mihai Wittenberger. "Mesopotamian Glass from Late Bronze Age Egypt, Romania, Germany, and Denmark." *Journal of Archaeological Science*, vol. 74 (2016), pp. 184-194.

Vedeler, Marianne. *Silk for the Vikings. Ancient Textiles*, no. 15. Oxford and Philadelphia: Oxbow Books, 2014.

Vega, Tanzina. "10 Years in Prison for Ex-City Councilman." *New York Times*, March 15, 2015, p. A21.

Velleius Paterculus (Frederick W. Shipley, transl.) *Compendium of Roman History*. [Augustus] *Res Gestae Divi Augusti*. Loeb Classical Library. Cambridge, Mass.: Harvard University Press, 1961.

Velliky, Elizabeth C., Martin Porr, and Nicholas J. Conard. "Ochre and Pigment Use at Hohle Fels Cave: Results of the First Systematic Review of Ochre and Ochre-Related Artefacts from the Upper Palaeolithic in Germany." *PLoS ONE*, vol. 13, no. 12 (2018): e0209874.

Vennemann, Theo. "Languages in Prehistoric Europe North of the Alps." Alfred Bammesberger and Theo Vennemann, eds. *Languages in Prehistoric Europe*. 2nd ed. Heidelberg: Universitätsverlag Winter, 2003. Pp. 319-332.

— (Patrizia Noel Aziz Hanna, ed.), *Europa Vasconica—Europa Semitica*. Berlin and New York: Mouton de Gruyter, 2003.

Verein für Germanisches Heidentum. "Geschichte." **https://www.vfgh.de/der-vfgh/geschichte/** Accessed April 30, 2020.

Vries, Jan de. *Altgermanische Religionsgeschichte*, 2 vols. Berlin: de Gruyter, 1956-57.

Waggoner, Ben (transl.) *Sagas of Fridthjof the Bold*. New Haven, Conn.: Troth Publications, 2009.

— (transl.) *Sagas of Imagination: A Medieval Icelandic Reader*. Philadelphia: The Troth, 2018.

Wagner, Richard. *My Life*. 2 vols. New York: Dodd, Mead, & Co., 1911.

Wallace, Birgitta Linderoth. "The Viking Settlement at L'Anse aux Meadows." William W. Fitzhugh and Elizabeth Ward, eds. *Vikings: The North Atlantic Saga*. Washington DC: Smithsonian Institution Press, 2000. Pp. 208-224.

—. "An Archaeologist's Interpretation of the *Vinland Sagas*." William W. Fitzhugh and Elizabeth Ward, eds. *Vikings: The North Atlantic Saga*. Washington DC: Smithsonian Institution Press, 2000. Pp. 225-231.

Wallace, Birgitta Linderoth and William W. Fitzhugh. "Stumbles and Pitfalls in the Search for Viking America." William W. Fitzhugh and Elizabeth Ward, eds. *Vikings: The North Atlantic Saga*. Washington DC: Smithsonian Institution Press, 2000. Pp. 376-384.

Wallace-Hadrill, J.M. *The Barbarian West, 400-1100*. 4th ed. Oxford: Basil Blackwell, 1990.

Wanscher, Ole. *Sella Curulis: The Folding Stool, An Ancient Symbol of Dignity*. Copenhagen: Rosenkilde and Bagger, 1980.

Ward, Robert. "Stephen McNallen: A Founding Father of our Folkish Faith." *Vor Tru* no. 58 (Summer 1998), pp. 18-25.

Watkins, Calvert, ed. *The American Heritage Dictionary of Indo-European Roots*. 2nd ed. Boston and New York: Houghton Mifflin, 2000.

—. *How to Kill a Dragon*. Cambridge, Mass.: Harvard University Press, 2002.

Watts, Donald. *Dictionary of Plant Lore*. Amsterdam: Elsevier, 2007.

Wawn, Andrew. *The Vikings and the Victorians: Inventing the Old North in Nineteenth-Century Britain*. Cambridge: D. S. Brewer, 2000.

Wells, C. J. *German: A Linguistic History to 1945*. Oxford: Clarendon Press, 1987.

Wells, Peter S. *The Battle that Stopped Rome: Emperor Augustus, Arminius, and the Slaughter of the Legions in the Teutoberg Forest*. New York: W. W. Norton, 2003.

West, William. "The Intriguing Account of the Book *Our Troth*, Which is a Most Curious and Somewhat Disturbing Occurrence." *Idunna*, vol. 6, no. 1, #22 (March 1994), pp. 37-38.

"What Stephen McNallen Really Thinks About Race." *National Vanguard*, March 12, 2017. https://nationalvanguard.org/2017/03/what-stephen-mcnallen-really-thinks-about-race/ Accessed March 21, 2019.

Whaley, Diana Edwards. "Snorri Sturluson." Phillip Pulsiano and Kirsten Wolf, eds. *Medieval Scandinavia: An Encyclopedia*. New York: Garland Publishing, 1993.

White, Ethan Doyle. "Northern Gods for Northern Folk: Racial Identity and Right-Wing Ideology Among Britain's Folkish Heathens." *Journal of Religion in Europe*, vol. 10 (2017), pp. 241-273.

Wiell, Stine. "Denmark's Bog Find Pioneer: The Archaeologist Conrad Engelhardt and His Work." Lars Jørgensen, Birger Storgaard, and Lone Gebauer Thomsen, eds. *The Spoils of Victory: The North in the Shadow of the Roman Empire.* Copenhagen: Nationalmuseet, 2003. Pp. 66-83.

Wilde, Sandra, and 10 others. "Direct Evidence for Positive Selection of Skin, Hair, and Eye Pigmentation in Europeans During the Last 5,000 y." *Proceedings of the National Academy of Sciences of the USA*, vol. 111, no. 13 (1 April 2014), pp. 4832-4837.

Willams, Alan. *The Sword and the Crucible: A History of the Metallurgy of European Swords up to the 16th Century.* Leiden: Brill, 2012.

Williamson, George S. *The Longing for Myth in Germany: Religion and Aesthetic Culture from Romanticism to the Nazis.* Chicago: University of Chicago Press, 2004.

Wilson, David M. *Anglo-Saxon Paganism.* London: Routledge, 1992.

Winter, Barbara. *Dreaming of a National Socialist Australia: The Australia-First Movement and The Publicist, 1936-1942.* Brisbane: Glass House Books, 2005.

Winroth, Anders. *The Conversion of Scandinavia: Vikings, Merchants, and Missionaries in the Remaking of Northern Europe.* New Haven, Conn.: Yale University Press, 2012.

Wodening, Swain. *Þéodisc Geléafa, "The Belief of the Tribe": A Handbook on Germanic Heathenry and Theodish Belief.* Little Elm, Tex.: Miercinga Theod, 2007.

—. *Hammer of the Gods: Anglo-Saxon Paganism in Modern Times.* 2nd ed. Huntsville, Mo.: Wednesbury Shire, 2008.

Wolff, Markus. "Ludwig Fahrenkrog and the Germanic Faith Community: Wodan Triumphant." *TYR*, vol. 2 (2003-2004), pp. 221-242.

Wolfram, Herwig. *History of the Goths.* Berkeley and Los Angeles: University of California Press, 1988.

Wolters, Reinhard. "Emergence of the Provinces." Simon James and Stefan Krmnicek, eds. *The Oxford Handbook of the Archaeology of Roman Germany.* Oxford: Oxford University Press, 2020. Pp. 28-52.

Wright, C. E. "Humfrey Wanley: Saxonist and Library-Keeper." *Proceedings of the British Academy.* London: Oxford University Press, 1960.

York, Michael. "Toward a Proto-Indo-European Vocabulary of the Sacred." *Word*, vol. 44, no. 2 (1993), pp. 235-254.

Zernack, Julia. "Old Norse–Icelandic Literature and German Culture." Sumarlidi R. Ísleifson, ed. *Iceland and Images of the North.* Québec: Presses de l'Université du Québec, 2011. Pp. 157-186.

Zerubavel, Eviatar. *The Seven Day Circle: The History and Meaning of the Week.* Chicago: University of Chicago Press, 1989.

Østmo, Einar. "The Indo-European Question in a Norwegian Perspective: A View from the Wrong End of the Stick?" Karlene Jones-Bley and Martin E. Huld, eds. *The Indo-Europeanization of Northern Europe. Journal of Indo-European Studies,* Monograph 33. Washington, DC: Institute for the Study of Man, 1999. Pp. 23-41.

Östergren, Majvor. "The Spillings Hoard." James Graham-Campbell, Søren M. Sindbæk, and Gareth Williams, eds. *Silver Economies: Monetisation and Society in Scandinavia, AD 800-1100.* Aarhus: Aarhus Universitetsforlag, 2011. Pp. 321-336.

Illustration Sources

Avenarius, Ferdinand. *Balladenbuch.* München: Georg D. W. Callwey, 1912.

Bartoli, Pietro Santi and Giovanni Pietro Bellori. *Columna Antoniniana Marci Aurelii Antonini Augusti rebus gestis insignis.* . . Rome, 1672.

Bell, Malcolm. *Sir Edward Burne-Jones: A Record and Review.* London: G. Bell & Sons, 1910.

Bosworth, Joseph. *The Gothic and Anglo-Saxon Gospels in Parallel Columns.* 2nd ed. London: John Russell Smith, 1874.

Fahrenkrog, Ludwig. *Baldur.* Stuttgart: Greiner and Pfeiffer, 1908.

Fahrenkrog, Ludwig. *Das Deutsche Buch.* 3rd ed. Leipzig: Wilhelm Hartung, 1923.

Fidus. *Aus der Germanenbibel.* Woltersdorf: Fidus-Verlag, 1920.

Flom, George T. *The Kensington Rune-Stone: An Address.* Springfield, Ill.: Illinois State Historical Society, 1910.

Grand-Carteret, John. *Richard Wagner en Caricatures.* Paris: Larousse, 1892.

Haigh, Daniel H. "Notes in Illustration of the Runic Monuments of Kent." Archaeologia Cantiana: Transactions of the Kent Archaeological Society, vol. 8 (1872), pp. 164-270.

Hamconius, Martinus. *Frisia; seu, De viris rebusque Frisiae illustribus libri duo.* Franekarae [Franeker /Frjentsjer]: Ioannis Lamrink and Ioannis Starterus, 1620.

Henckell, Karl (Fidus, illust.) *Aus meinen Gedichten.* Zürich: K. Henckell, 1902.

Hickes, George. *Linguarum Vetterum Septentrionalium Thesaurus.* Oxford: E Theatro Sheldoniae, 1705.

Janssen, L. J. F. *De Romeinsche Beelden en Gedenksteenen van Zeeland.* Middelburg: Gebruder Abrahams, 1845.

Johannes Magnus. *Historia de omnibus Gothorum Sueonumque regibus.* Basel: Isingriniana, 1558.

Lechler, Jörg. *Vom Hakenkreuz: Die Geschichte eines Symbols.* 2nd ed. Leipzig: Curt Kabitzsch Verlag, 1934.

List, Guido. *Der Unbesiegbare: Ein Grundzug germanischer Weltanschauung.* Vienna: Verlag Cornelius Vetter, 1898.

Longfellow, Henry Wadsworth. *The Skeleton in Armor.* Boston: James R. Osgood & Co., 1877.

Marby, Friedrich Bernhard. *Die Rosengärten und das Ewige Land der Rasse.* Marby-Runen-Bücherei vol. 7-8. Stuttgart: Marby-Verlag, 1935.

Menestrier, Claude-François (Gentile Bellini, illus.) *Columna Theodosiana, quam vulgo "historiatam" vocant, ab Arcadio imperatore Constantinopoli erecta in honorem imperatoris Theodosii junioris.* Venice: J. Baptista Pasquali, 1765.

Müller, Sigurd. *Nordens Billedkunst.* Copenhagen: Gyldendal, 1905.

Müller, Sophus. *Vor Oldtid: Danmarks forhistoriske archæologi.* Copenhagen: det Nordiske Forlag, 1897.

Nanni, Giovanni. *Berosvs Babilonicvs, De his quae praecesserũt inundatioñe terrarũ. . . Paris, 1511.

Olaus Magnus. *Historia de Gentibus Septentrionalibus.* Rome, 1555.

Pernice, Erich and Franz Winter. *Der Hildesheimer Silberfund.* Berlin: W. Spemann, 1901.

Schefferus, Johannes. *Lapponia; id est, Regionis Lapponum et Gentis Nova et Verissima Descriptio.* Frankfurt: Christian Wolff, 1673.

Schönheit, Die. Zeitschrift für Kunst und Leben. Vol. 16 (Fidus-Heft), 1919/1920.

Shea, John Gilmary. *Pictorial Lives of the Saints, with Reflections for Every Day in the Year.* New York: Benziger Brothers, 1922.

Smythe, E. Louise. *A Primary Reader: Old-time Stories, Fairy Tales and Myths Retold by Children.* Chicago: Werner School Book Company, 1896.

Snorri Sturluson (Gustav Storm, transl.) *Kongesagaer.* Christiana: I. M. Stenersen & Co. Forlag, 1899.

Spohr, Wilhelm. *Fidus.* Minden: J. C. C. Bruns, 1902.

Stauff, Philipp. *Runenhauser.* Berlin: K. G. Th. Scheffer, 1913.

Stephens, George. *The Old-Northern Runic Monuments of Scandinavia and England.* London: John Russell Smith, 1866-1867.

Stucken, Eduard (Fidus, illust.). *Balladen.* Berlin: S. Fischer, 1898.

Ungewitter, Richard. *Die Nacktheit in enwicklungsgeschichtlicher, gesundheitlicher, moralischer und künstlerischer Beleuchtlung.* Stuttgart: Self-Published, 1906.

The Troth emblem, as it appeared in 1994, 2001, and 2006.

Index

A

Action Française (right-wing group) 47, 246
Adam of Bremen 166, 169, 171, 300
Aðils 150
Adrianopolis 123
Adulruna 186, 187
Aedui 105
Aetius 129
Afzelius, A. A. (Swedish folklorist) 197
agriculture 6, 12, 17, 18, 19, 21, 22, 38, 39, 40, 60, 65, 72, 98, 117
Ahnenerbe (research organization in the SS) 240, 242, 243, 245, 246
Ahueccaniae 115
Ajvide 14
Åker 143
Alamanni 117, 119, 123, 137
Alans 95, 123, 125, 126
Alaric 122, 124, 132
Alateiva 115
Alcuin 139
Aldhelm 135
Alfred the Great, King of Wessex 140, 158, 238, 336
Aliso (Roman fort) 107
Altamira (cave painting site) 6
Alta (rock art site) 14
al-Tartushi 166
Alunda 16
amber 18, 19, 22, 27, 28, 29, 68, 69, 72, 78, 86, 94, 95, 161
Amber Road 112
Ambrones 105
Ambrosius Aurelianus 127
American Indian Movement 263, 264
American Vinland Association 284, 290
Amerisyche 269, 270
Amish 191
Anderson, Rasmus B. (American scholar) 215, 217
Angantyr (Ongentheow) 150
Anglecyn Church of Odin 252, 254
Angles 127, 133, 154, 271
Anglo-Saxon Church of Woden 260
Anglo-Saxons 92, 127, 131, 133, 134, 173, 198, 207, 210

B

Hedelisker 100
Hedemünden 106
Heidengraben 91
Heidnische Gemeinschaft 277
heilagra manna sǫgur (saints' lives) 178
Heimdal League 260, 261
Heimgest (Jeffrey Holley) 261
Heimskringla xiii, 166, 169, 172, 178, 181, 210, 214
Helgö 143, 160, 321
Hengist and Horsa 127
Henry VIII, King of England 184
Hensbacka/Fosna culture 11
Hentschel, Willibald (German racialist) 228, 229
Heorot 147
Herder, Johann Gottfried (German clergyman and scholar) 192, 193, 194, 195, 196, 224, 302, 313
Hereward the Wake 173
Hermunduri 102
Heruli 123
Hervarar saga 172
Hess, Rudolf (Nazi leader) 244
Het Rad 278
Heuneburg 90
Hickes, George (British scholar) 207
Hildesheim 112
Hilmar Örn Hilmarsson (Icelandic composer and Ásatrú leader) 274
Himlingøje 113
Himmler, Heinrich (Nazi leader) 240, 241, 246
Hitler, Adolf (Nazi leader) 237, 238, 239, 240, 241, 242, 243, 244, 245, 252, 254, 255, 259
Hjortspring 102
Hlaðir 148
Hoby 113
Hochdorf 91
Hodde 94
Höfler, Otto (German *völkisch* scholar) 246
hoftollr 176
Hohle Fels 5
Hohlenstein 9
Hohlenstein-Stadel 5
Holand, Hjalmar (Norwegian-American advocate) 217
Hollander, Lee (American scholar and translator) 248
Holle (goddess) 191
Homo neanderthalensis 3
Honorius 125, 126

J

K

N

The Troth is an international organization that brings together many paths and traditions within Germanic Heathenry, such as Ásatrú, Theodish Belief, Urglaawe, Forn Sed, and Anglo-Saxon Heathenry. We welcome all who have been called to follow the elder ways of Heathenry, and who have heard the voices of the Gods and Goddesses of Heathenry, our ancestors, the landvættir, and the spirits around us.

To find out more about our organization or to join us, visit **http://www. thetroth.org/**, contact us at **troth-questions@thetroth.org**, or look for us on Facebook at **https://www.facebook.com/groups/TheTroth/**

Our complete line of books and back issues of our journal *Idunna* may be viewed at **https://www.lulu.com/spotlight/thetroth**

For book reviews, interviews, or any other matters connected with our publications, please contact us at **troth-shope@thetroth.org**

Our Troth is projected to consist of four volumes:

Our Troth, Volume 1: Heathen History
Our Troth, Volume 2: Heathen Gods, Heathen World (expected publication date June 2021)
Our Troth, Volume 3: Heathen Rites (expected publication date December 2021)
Our Troth, Volume 4: Heathen Garb and Gear (expected publication date September 2020)